War, Power and the Economy

War, Power and the Economy contains a comparative history of Great Britain, France and Spain, the three rival empires of the 1700s. It explores how the states prepared for war, what kind of economic means they had, what institutional changes they implemented, and how efficient this was. As such, the book presents the first comparative synthesis aiming to understand the outcome of the global confrontation in the eighteenth century.

Faced with the challenge of paying for new and more costly wars, some countries found flexible ways to get more money and better supplies, whereas others did not. The development of freer colonial markets, the increase of consumption and its taxation, the problems of venal administration or the different systems of patronage with contractors, are some of the factors explaining the divergences that were made clear by 1815. This book explores political and economic dimensions of the eighteenth-century European state in order to explain why and how changes in power as an outcome of war depended upon the available means and the way they were obtained and used. The book takes the idea that making war or preparing for it obliged governments to make important changes in their institutions, so that during the eighteenth century the state in many ways formed itself through war efforts. Ultimately, this study aims to show how closely political and military success was entwined with economic interests.

This volume is of great interest to those who study economic history, political economy and European history.

A. González Enciso is Professor of Early Modern History at the Universidad de Navarra, Spain. His research interests have been focused on the economic history of eighteenth-century Spain, namely industrial and financial history, and he is a member of the international Contractor State Group.

Routledge Explorations in Economic History
Edited by Lars Magnusson, Uppsala University, Sweden

War, Power and the Economy

Mercantilism and state formation in 18th-century Europe

A. González Enciso

Routledge
Taylor & Francis Group

LONDON AND NEW YORK

First published 2017
by Routledge

2 Park Square, Milton Park, Abingdon, Oxfordshire OX14 4RN
52 Vanderbilt Avenue, New York, NY 10017

Routledge is an imprint of the Taylor & Francis Group, an informa business

First issued in paperback 2019

British Library Cataloguing in Publication Data
A catalogue record for this book is available from the British Library

Library of Congress Cataloging in Publication Data
Names: González Enciso, Agustín, author.
Title: War, power and the economy : mercantilism and state formation in 18th century Europe / Agustín González Enciso.
Description: 1 Edition. | New York : Routledge, [2017] | Includes bibliographical references and index.
Identifiers: LCCN 2016020602 | ISBN 9781138855694 (hardback) | ISBN 9781315720197 (ebook)
Subjects: LCSH: Europe—Economic conditions—18th century. | Europe—Commercial policy—History—18th century. | Taxation—Europe—History—18th century. | Europe—History, Military—18th century.
Classification: LCC HC240 .G563 2017 | DDC 336.409/033—dc23LC record available at https://lccn.loc.gov/2016020602

ISBN: 978-1-138-85569-4 (hbk)
ISBN: 978-0-367-87245-8 (pbk)

Typeset in Times New Roman
by diacriTech, Chennai

To Mercedes

Contents

Figures

Tables

Preface

In September 2004 the Economic History Seminar of the Universidad de Navarra organised a seminar on the theme "Mobilising resources for war", which set out with a clearly comparative approach. Fruit of this seminar was a book of the same title (Bowen and González Enciso 2006), a collection of essays comparing and contrasting British and Spanish experiences in the long eighteenth century. As P. O'Brian said in the Foreword, "The theme addressed by this volume is an integral and potentially illuminating part of the master narrative of European history concerned with state formation". Our immediate intention afterwards was to seek further comparison-based enlightenment on early modern state formation in Europe, a study approach little investigated hitherto. Although a fair amount of progress had been made in studies of the fiscal-state (Bonney 1995a, 1999b), little had been done to develop the more specific concept of the "fiscal-military state", a term coined by Brewer (1989), and there were practically no new insights, at least in direct relationship with these themes, into the management of this tax revenue and the spending of the lion's share on war, the process that has come to be called the "contractor state".

Since 2004, therefore, our searchlights have focused on the mobilisation of warfare resources in an attempt either to hone and refine our concept of the fiscal-military state (Torres Sánchez 2007), study state expenditure (Conway and Torres Sánchez 2011) or develop the concept and particular circumstances of the contractor state (Harding and Solbes Ferri 2012; Bowen et al. 2013), among other matters. The abovementioned works refer to diverse European countries, while our own work has paid special attention to Spain (González Enciso 2012a; Torres Sánchez 2012a, 2013a and 2015a; Baudot Monroy 2014).

All the abovementioned works, as well as many others by various colleagues from different countries, have helped to shed light on the matter during recent years. All too often, however, their works are hidden away in specialist publications. There was also a notable lack of any synthesis to bring all this research together in an updated, comparative overview. This is what we have tried to do here. Although we have restricted ourselves primarily to the three great eighteenth-century powers, Great Britain, France and Spain, other countries are sometimes brought into the trawl if need be. In any case these three countries illustrate between them the states' main modus operandi in the matter of concern to us here.

Our study taps into the main works published on Great Britain and France; as far as Spain is concerned we work not only from available bibliography but also primary sources. Part of the bibliography used for Spain, moreover, is based on our own research into this matter in recent years.

The result is a comparative history of the development of the fiscal-military state and the contractor state, apparently the first time such a synthesis has been undertaken. Spain looms large in the analysis because one of the book's objectives is precisely to compare Spain's case with its main rivals; I trust, in any case, that this has not obscured the general view of the problems.

Agustín González Enciso
Pamplona, 16 April 2016

Acknowledgements

As might be expected a book is never a single-handed venture. My first thanks here go to all the authors whose shoulders I've stood on to write mine. They feature in the final bibliography. I trust I have not misconstrued their thoughts and insights. Special mention goes to those who have formed part of the research groups I have been involved in, nurtured by a fruitful dialogue in these groups' various activities and publications. I am referring here not only to those I've worked with in the Financial History Group of the Universidad de Navarra, but also the members of the Tobacco Study Group and, above all, the Contractor State Group (www.unav. edu/web/facultad-de-ciencias-economicas-y-empresariales/contractor-state), with all of whom we have so often debated these problems, always in a climate of scholar exigency compatible with complete amiability and friendship.

Many of the studies that have brought us to this point have been financed by research projects under the Spanish Ministry of Education and Science or the Ministry of Economics and Innovation, especially the projects HAR2011-23570 and HAR2015-64165-C2-1-P. I would also like to thank the Universidad de Navarra for its support through its research aid plan (PIUNA), which has defrayed expenses that would otherwise have been difficult to cope with.

My thanks also to Routledge and all its staff, who have so kindly welcomed my proposal and accompanied me so efficiently throughout the editorial process.

A special mention must go to the translator Dave Langlois, who has so expertly rendered these pages in their new language, doing so in record time.

And special thanks too to Professor Rafael Torres Sánchez, who in so short a time has progressed from outstanding disciple to past master. It was he in fact who kicked off this line of research in our university and he has always led the way, setting challenges, driving projects and bringing new scholars into the fold. Without his help, support and friendship this book would have been completely impossible. Thanks, Rafa.

From all of them I've learnt loads. I hope I've also put in my pennyworth and I apologise beforehand for any errors, all of which are down to me alone.

Introduction

International power in eighteenth-century countries was underpinned by war. War, however, calls for a vast raft of varied resources, so it was in turn underpinned by the economy. If we understand mercantilism as the state's way of organising the economy, then warfare, power, state and mercantilism, in view of the above-mentioned sequence, turn out to be synonyms. Eighteenth-century states waged war largely because they needed to. Their resources depended on their economy, which, aside from the time-honoured estates structure, was regulated by the state itself, mainly to be able to meet its needs. Mercantilism is a state economy and ipso facto a war economy, in the two senses of being built up by and for war.

The purpose of this book is not to explain in detail all these aspects, which spin off into many other connotations and implications. It will simply try to bring out a thread that knitted the whole thing together: the mobilisation of warfare resources. Within this overarching theme two aspects will receive special attention. Firstly, what financial resources did the state have and how could it enhance them? This question is bound up with what has come to be called the fiscal-military state. Secondly, which material resources did the state have to spend money on to be able to wage war? This ties in with what we could call the contractor state or the presence and need of military entrepreneurs.

Another particular question that interests us on this occasion is more general, the relation between warfare and the formation of the early modern state. The topic can be presented more explicitly. We are talking in particular about the capacity states developed of amassing the warfare wherewithal they needed; we are hence speaking, at the end of the day, about the mobilisation of warfare resources (Bowen and González Enciso 2006). This presupposes, on the state's part, not only the possibility of rustling up the necessary resources and paying for them but also its capacity of efficiently transforming them into useful battlefield weapons and facilities, since winning any war or building up hegemonic power called for a global approach to resources.

Three powers looking for resources

We are interested in studying theses questions during the long eighteenth century, when the picture of international pre-eminence changed radically: the decline of

Spain, then of Holland, then of France; the emergence, at the same time, of England/ Great Britain. Total confrontations were few, but the bilateral confrontations are meaningful. Spain's decline was provoked by France; Holland's by England, after the three Anglo-Dutch naval wars, then by France; finally, France dropped down the rankings when Great Britain acquired greater power in 1713. But a whole century would have to pass for Great Britain to overcome, in this historical cycle, a Revolution-boosted France that still proved incapable of winning in the end.

A long-term power transformation was therefore underway. Spain entered the century trying to shrug off its slough of despondency after a brilliant past as a hegemonic international power, a memory that lingered on among eighteenth-century governors and writers. It would pull off significant advances in comparison with the end-of-seventeenth-century situation, a factor that justified its politics in the eyes of some governors, written off by some pundits as "optimists" (Stein and Stein 2005: 367–71), but it did not manage to relive past glories. At the end of the period it fell back into decline, proving incapable of responding to the military challenges of the early nineteenth century.

France had risen to international prominence in the seventeenth century, in dispute with Spain and Holland, countries it successively defeated. From Ryswick on, however, and also following Utrecht, its power slipped below Britain's; this situation could be said to be definitive after the defeats of 1759 (Mclynn 2004) but was not actually rubber-stamped until Waterloo. Other authors might think differently, however. Braudel, for example, argues that England's predominance over France was already clear by 1786, with the Eden Treaty (Braudel 1985: 116), when the British commercial model was enforced upon it.

Great Britain's path was just the opposite. England had ended the seventeenth century with burgeoning importance in the international arena. After defeating Holland and matching France in Ryswick, it soon enforced its "preponderance", as P. Muret labelled it (Muret 1937), which it then held onto throughout the following century, now as Great Britain. It knew how to protect its national market and nascent industry, thanks to its victories on land and at sea. All peace treaties, moreover, tended to uphold its mercantile interests, boosting its trading volume, including its exports and above all re-exports of its colonial products (Davies 1954, 1962).

All these ranking classifications, in any case, are largely a matter of historical hindsight. They are also questionable, depending on the approach or timeframe adopted. The uppermost powers at each particular moment, moreover, tended to be fairly blinkered in their outlook; all of them, including the Spanish, looked to the future with short-sighted confidence and were largely unaware of the advantages taken by their rivals coming up on the rails. The Treaties of Versailles in 1783 seemed, at that moment, to have reinstated the situation of exactly 20 years earlier. Certainly no one was aware of what was going to happen only 10 years later, while historical hindsight has shown that subsequent events, if not inevitable, were indeed consistent with the countries' recent economic policies. In the ultimate analysis, after all, soldiers, ships and cannons represented a demand to be met, a cost to be defrayed.

In any case, why do some countries win wars and others lose them? Why do relations of international supremacy change over time? One key to answering these questions lies, precisely, in the states' varying capacities and ways of mustering material resources and turning them into warfare-waging instruments. These differing capacities and the arrangements made to implement them do reflect in the long term on battlefield success, at least over a period of wars, and on the rise to international supremacy at the end of a given historical cycle. This explanation is certainly not sufficient in itself but it is absolutely necessary to understand the capacity to endure a long period of confrontations, even though specific battles may sway one way or the other due to one-off factors.

If the resource-mobilisation capacity lies behind political-military events, how far might said capacity explain power changeovers? Our interest here is to study this question in a comparative way, in an endeavour to weigh the possibilities of each country in a given period of time and also ascertain the reasons lying behind its performance. Our focus falls above all on financial, material and institutional resources. The generation of these resources – money, raw materials, services, etc. – depends on two main factors: the economy and the government, because the resource-identifying process and the subsequent obtaining thereof and conversion into a battlefield instrument (soldier's wage, food, arms, means of transport ...), implies bureaucratic tasks and a political approach. This process therefore impinges in turn on the formation of state structures and organisations.

The approach necessarily has to take into account the long term; a timeframe of more or less a century without forgetting the past baggage. In Vervins, 1598, for example, Philip II ended up giving in to his rivals, largely because he needed a breathing space after a long period of conflicts, which had drained the country of all its material and human resources. Likewise, a century later in Ryswick, 1698, an equally battle-weary France sued for peace not so much because of the battlefield balance of victories and defeats but rather the accumulated exhaustion of the decades of Louis XIV's reign (Yun Casalilla 2004, Lynn 1999: 265). The eighteenth century is in some ways a rather more complex period than the aforementioned ones because there are more factors at stake: the colonial wars of the whole century and then the French Revolution and its aftermath. In any case international confrontations during this historical cycle can also be seen as a continual wear and tear on the states, which, more or less appreciably, find solutions or accumulate structural problems that will turn out in the end to be decisive. The victory of 1815 can be seen as the success of stamina, the country winning that found the best ways of finding resources and the most efficient way of organising them (Knight 2014). The development of public debt, including its ability to pay off this debt, is therefore a crucial factor in Great Britain's final victory over a France that had shown itself to be incompetent in this matter (Dickson 1967: 11). Spain then participated in the British victory but did so after having suffered a grave crisis due partly to its former financial failure. This crisis was triggered partly by the failure to carry through necessary economic and institutional reforms in time.

From this standpoint, military triumph and political preponderance sit on financial bases. These bases have to be built up over years of establishing the right institutions, the right ways of working and reaping the ensuing benefits; they cannot be ad libbed overnight. But the economic resources have to stem from a strong economy and the right fiscal system and these cannot be improvised either. Only then can expenditure be geared towards the most necessary resources and be stepped up without ruining the country. All these questions will be dealt with here: the various states' warfare-waging resources; how and why they mobilised these resources as they did and why they failed to change tack when historical hindsight shows there still time to do so. The decision makers of the time must surely have expected a different outcome and they had good reason to do so. Why did they turn out to be wrong? Which factors did they misinterpret or fail to take into account at all? We would argue that casual factors – negative or positive – might explain a one-off outcome but can never account for any long-term historical process. Success or failure is measured by the proportion of wrong and right decisions in relation to the wrong and right decisions of the adversary. A doggedly maintained losing scheme is very unlikely to lead to success.

One of the most salient traits in Spain, for example, is foot dragging on reforms. All too often the decision makers know what they want, the first steps are taken, but then the rest of the process drags on inordinately. Apart from the obstacles posed by the political structure and vested interests, and also the cost thereof – it would be unfair on our part to underplay the difficulties faced – the slowness of reform was due also to the contemporary outlook. Decision makers of the time were unable to see the wood for the trees; they failed to perceive that an established organisational scheme was becoming obsolete. This difficulty in recognising the outmodedness of traditional ways of working and established structures meant that changes were rarely made until it was too late. Seldom was this obsolescence 100 per cent, that is true; even the oldest structure may still retain a modicum of effectiveness, so decisions were put off in order to deal with day-to-day urgencies and the necessary changes were never undertaken. Spain's eighteenth-century history chimes in with France's in this aspect, albeit with very different settings in both cases.

We seem to have stumbled on a preliminary conclusion here: the British victory stemmed from its financial clout, from the development of institutions that made this position of power possible and its fleet-footedness in adapting to changing circumstances. This is not exactly news, however. The moot point here is not explaining why Great Britain went down this path but why Spain didn't, and also how far the French case, as some historians have suggested, may be a role model of the Spanish case. First and foremost, it needs to be said that Spain was very different from France and that Spain's achievements and miscarriages did not depend on its similarity or otherwise to France; other factors were much more important. Oddly enough, some of the main economic measures taken by Spain in the eighteenth century adhered to the English model rather than the French.

It should be remembered here that forces were fairly evenly matched throughout the eighteenth century. Rivals greatly respected each other and no one was capable of auguring such a brilliant future for Great Britain. Indeed, the British themselves were well aware of their weaknesses; the British victory in 1763, for example, was offset by the defeat of 1783 and Napoleon proved a hard nut to crack. Looking forward, nothing was clear. Looking back from our current standpoint, however, we can see that Great Britain was edging ahead; this progressive advantage explains why it ended up with more warfare-waging capacity than its rivals. This all boiled down to its resource-mobilisation capacity, or even its ability to "invent" resources if they did not previously exist, as in the abovementioned case of state credit.

Spain and its eighteenth-century rivals

But our fundamental benchmark here will be Spain. Eighteenth-century Spain was still a crucial player in the international power game but is not always taken into consideration; neither is there exactly a wealth of books in English on eighteenth-century Spain. In any case, what is most of interest here is how it stands in comparison with the two great powers of that moment, Great Britain and France. Comparisons between these two countries are more frequent but they do not usually stray beyond the range of specialist reviews. Spain, for its part, is usually sidelined, played down as a France-mimicking minor power, which is by no means true. Spain did indeed slip into the second ranking in this century but it remained a fundamentally important power whose history needs to be looked at in some detail.

From the point of view of the history of power the most characteristic trait of the eighteenth century was the shift in the international power rankings with England rising fairly rapidly to the top of the tree from 1713, when the Treaty of Utrecht spelled out a new international order. This power would never cease to grow thereafter. What was the situation of the Spanish monarchy then?

A fundamental trait of the Spanish monarchy was its dominance of immense territories in the Americas. It also held the Philippines, of course, but the Americas was the key. America kept Spain afloat in the second half of the seventeenth century. England conquered Jamaica in 1655 and entered into brisk contraband activities with the Spanish colonies but it assayed no more significant action against Spain's empire; it did not yet feel capable of doing so. The Treaty of Utrecht left Spanish sovereignty over its American colonies untouched, but for some commercial privileges granted to Great Britain. Given the pre-eminence that international trade had acquired by the time, Utrecht decisions announced a fierce confrontation between Spain and Great Britain over commercial and colonial issues. From the global power picture, therefore, the main concern for Great Britain in 1713 was not so much France, whose maritime power was still inchoate, but rather Spain. Picture will change and France will become a bigger concern for Britain as long as it did extend its colonial power during the first half of the eighteenth century.

By 1713 France's outlook was changing due to significant political developments. During this long interregnum with no undisputed global hegemonic power, culminating in the War of the Spanish Succession, Louis XIV, who by now did seem to dominate on the continent, received a gift from the Spanish when they raised his grandson to their throne. In truth this was a bit of a poisoned chalice; in its efforts to defend this new situation, gearing up from its previous merely diplomatic plans, France was defeated in Italy and the Low Countries by England – by now Great Britain – which had been fighting with unexpected vigour since 1689. Holland had been neutralised first by France and then by England, so it came across by 1713 as a second-rank political power. It was still, however, a mighty economic power, now allied with Great Britain against the French territorial threat. Trade and finances were still Britain's strong suits.

The Treaty of Utrecht acknowledged that Philip V won the war in Spain, and as a consequence, Spain lost its provinces in Italy and the Low Countries but not its colonial empire. Both events came as quite a surprise since the word was that Spain had insufficient military force to defend itself without France's aid. This aid was indeed important up to 1709 but not afterwards. From 1709 to 1714 French presence and its influence on Spain dwindled pretty quickly. Louis XIV's defeat deprived Philip V of his aid but he proved capable of carrying on singlehandedly. It could be said that both Great Britain and Holland lost interest in the war in Spain after 1711; in any case Philip held onto his throne.

If we speak of "pyrrhic victories", meaning conquests marred by bad consequences, might we not also speak of "pyrrhic defeats", meaning setbacks largely free of bad consequences? If so, 1713 was such for Spain, i.e., a defeat that was not so damning, at least considering what might have been. Spain came out of Utrecht weakened but less so than might have been expected. Charles II's Spain, furthermore, had not turned out be as decadent as many observers had thought. It certainly did suffer from an almost complete political incapacity due to the weakness of its monarch and his government; but against all the odds – as recent studies have shown – Charles II's Spain did experience a notable social, economic and cultural renaissance. This was the base Philip V worked from to win the peninsular war and then engender a nigh incredible national rebirth, partly driven by the recovery of trade with America and the precious metal flooding in from there since 1665. Utrecht enabled him to hold onto this fountainhead, which then continued to grow.

Spain clearly took the new post-1713 situation onboard. Great Britain rose to the top of the pile and became enemy number one, i.e., the rival power vying for the same prize: America. A clash between them now seemed inevitable and no pact seemed realistically on the cards. France, for its part, Habsburg Spain's traditional enemy, its victor in Westphalia and the Pyrenees, the great conspirator hitherto set on destroying its empire, had now morphed into its ally. That said, it was a self-seeking, commitment-hedging, shakily loyal ally. Neither did France now have the same clout as under Louis XIV, and its support for Spain tended to play second fiddle to its struggles against its new enemy, Great Britain.

Spain played its pieces pretty adroitly in the eighteenth-century power game, if we bear in mind its tradition – i.e., the inherited structures – and its growth possibilities. It deftly ducked and dived among its rivals. In general, Spain was Great Britain's eighteenth-century enemy, but not always; in general, Spain was France's eighteenth-century ally, but not always. It certainly did not kowtow to French interests cravenly; Spain itself was perfectly aware that this alliance might at some moments be vital in the defence against the growing British threat. Spain's leaders were a motley bunch of Anglophiles and Francophiles; during Ferdinand VI's reign the tug-o'-war between both camps produced a lasting peace. This shows that Spain, for a long period of time, knew how to seek its own best interest in a confronted world, remaining a long time at peace. Was this peace positive? The jury is still out on this.

All the above begs the question of what Spain's role was in the global power game. How did it really fare and rate in the political rankings of the eighteenth century? This is what we will try to study from the viewpoint of what has come to be called the fiscal-military state and contractor state. It comes down to this: Did Spain have sufficient fiscal power and economic force to survive in the eighteenth-century power struggle? If it has been widely claimed that Great Britain defeated France in 1815 on the strength of its finances, what could be said of Spain in this regard? How much financial clout did it have? If we assume it had little, since when and why? And, if so, just why did its empire last so long?

The concern over Spain has to be seen in a comparative manner. It tries to pinpoint the reasons for Spain's longevity, during which time Spain not only showed striking resilience but also enjoyed a fully fledged national recovery. In the first half of the eighteenth century Spain recouped a good deal of the power and prestige it had forfeited in Westphalia and partly in Utrecht. To do so, it pursued a fiscal and economic policy that, if not brilliant, was fairly important and above all in keeping with its resources and situation. In these aspects, in any case, Spain followed the English model rather than the French. Although its political and social structures chimed in more with the French, it was, at the same time, a substantially different country. These considerations necessarily guide us towards to a comparative approach. And this is what this book, in short, is about: Spain's eighteenth-century fiscal and economic capacities, and, ipso facto, its political and military capacities in comparison with Great Britain and France. These three countries represent three models that resemble each other, differ from each other and regard each other. They converge in some ideas and often in economic, social and diplomatic relations, but their mettle is weighed, in the last analysis, on the battlefield. The battle had to be won, but with what means?

War and the early modern state

Behind the theme dealt with in this book lurks an idea that by now can be considered to be traditional: states of early modernity were formed in war, through war and because of war. Although there was not always a conflict underway, there was indeed a certain sense of inevitability, not to say need and even desire for war, so war preparations had to be made even in peacetime. As for new territorial organisations since the end of the fifteenth century, early modern states and their monarchs needed in one way or another to mark out the borders of their inherited territories and affirm their sovereignty over them. This inevitably brought them into conflict sooner or later. The fact that confrontations were now fought abroad could be given a positive spin; it meant that the domestic confrontations that had plagued western European realms since the fifteenth century had been overcome. Or maybe it was even reverse aetiology, with the external conflict being used to forge a sense of unity against the foreign threat and bring internal factions together. Internal problems did not completely die out in the sixteenth and seventeenth centuries, but by then the fundamental bases of internal cohesion of the new states had been laid down. From that moment on states would be exporting war.

By the eighteenth century the territories of the new states were well established, in general, barring border skirmishes. It was therefore still necessary to defend this situation from inside out and clear up thousands of dynastic niceties that had remained pending in the process. This does not mean that all internal problems had disappeared or even that the whole country always pulled together. In general, the starting point was a territory recognised as "national". Territorial instability, however, still existed in the eighteenth century.

Be that as it may, warfare, active or passive, looked for or unforeseen, was taken as a given and thus became to this extent a permanent feature. Although some thinkers of the time spoke of the need of permanent peace and deplored the confrontations, the truth is that each state's identity depended on these confrontations, always providing they worked outwards, to secure the territory against foreign forays. Kings who were able to guarantee inner peace understood that this implied, to some extent, war abroad. The early modern state thus became a space of inner peace, established law and order that served as some guarantee for obtaining the resources needed for overseas war in this continually sabre-rattling world. The adage *si vis pacem para bellum* rang true and times of peace were times of armed peace, often only a truce in truth. Furthermore, since peace treaties seldom failed to clear up many messes, only a new conflict could really be expected to ensue from them. The reality of the time was a stop-go process of war and peace.

Is Tilly right when he claims "war made the state, and the state made war"? (Tilly 1975: 42). Not necessarily in absolute terms. The state did not concern itself solely with war; neither did all states have the selfsame experience. In any case, it would seem to be clear that, both to defend its vested interests and to increase its power, the early modern state was, as Reinhard said, a "state at war" (Reinhard 1996: 12), a state that was constructing itself while waging war: this would seem to be clear for the states and periods at issue here, Great Britain, France and Spain in the long eighteenth century.

The early modern state was also a state at war due to the sheer length of the conflicts. Simple number-crunching for France shows that from 1661 to 1815 (154 years), 90 of those years (nearly 60 per cent of the period) were of open war: this comes out as an average of two years of war for one of peace (Lynn 1999: 363). In some stages warfare intensity even rose above this average figure. France, it should not be forgotten, took part in practically all the wars in the abovementioned period. Almost the same could be said of Spain and Great Britain, though eighteenth-century Spain did opt out of some conflicts. For example, it did not participate in the first five years of the Seven Years' War that broke out in 1756. The figures, in any case, do not tell the whole story. As we have already pointed out, peace at this time was gird-loining armed peace so no time was completely free of the shadow of war.

In short, it cannot be denied that "preparing for, and prosecuting war" (Ertman 1994) was a central aspect of early modern European state formation. This came out, as we will see, in what we could call with anachronistic licence the "national budgets", or more specifically in the amount of state expenditure earmarked directly for war, spent on both army and navy structures and specific operations, or the collateral costs such as propaganda, diplomacy, espionage, information, etc.; and above all the taxation arrangements that had to be made to pay off the war debt in peacetime.

All this meant that monarchs needed to reinforce their power and thereby take measures to ensure military action was, firstly, possible and, secondly, effective. It all boiled down to being capable of waging war and winning it. These resources were of very varied ilk: political and military, social and cultural, bureaucratic-administrative and, to a large extent, economic. Our interest here centres on the latter. The states' economic capacity comes across a key factor in being able to wage war with some guarantee of success. I am not referring here so much to the warfare economy in the immediate aftermath of the conflict, i.e., economic life as affected directly by war; neither am I referring to economic activity in general as an activity in its own right, although this underpins everything else. I am referring rather to the economy as moulded by the need to wage war, i.e., a structural question: the basic economic force and authoritativeness allowing governors to perform such actions as collect taxes, supply armies, recruit soldiers, manufacture arms or build ships without crippling the economy or even boosting it. The main remit, in other words, was to assemble warfare resources and defray associated costs, from the twofold perspective of raking in enough tax revenue and then spending it properly on goods and services needed for tackling the conflict.

If the early modern state is a state at war, the economy of this state is largely a war economy in the abovementioned sense; i.e., an economy that had been forged by the need of raising warfare-waging resources, both material and financial, by the need of knowing how to allocate the resources shrewdly to guarantee success on the battlefield. What is the nature of this relation between economy and war? How far did the economy facilitate war and how did the war, in return, impinge on the economy, weakening it or strengthening it? There is a striking historical example in early modern Europe. This is the case of Holland. Its wars of independence, nearly permanent for 80 years, have recently been described as a "profitable" activity, "an early example of successful commercialization of warfare... securing long-lasting profits" ('t Hart 2014: 2). Holland not only mustered, against the odds, the economic resources that enabled it to wage its wars of independence against Spain, initially, and France latterly, but also thereby boosted its own economy. Did the same occur elsewhere? In this confrontation with Holland both France and Spain appeared to suffer grave disorders in their respective economic setups. True it is that these countries were not only fighting Holland at the time; their warfare activity ranged much wider. But in both cases the war debt weighed like a millstone on their economic activities.

In the eighteenth century Great Britain managed to do what Holland had done a century earlier, wage a profitable war, or in other words achieve "power with profit" (O'Brien 1991), but neither France nor Spain pulled it off. The thing is, however, they did not even try; among other reasons because they stuck with their traditional warfaring methods, whereas England overhauled its procedures at the end of the seventeenth century. Despite the reams that have been written on the subject, no firm conclusions can as yet be drawn from an analysis of the relations between war and the economy in Great Britain, as we will see later, but it does seem safe to claim that "Britain was able to commit huge resources to the struggle against France without suffering too many damaging economic consequences in the long term" largely because it fought all these wars outside its own territory (Bowen 1998: 58, 80). This has been summed up in another phrase: Great Britain's success in 1815 was not due to politics and strategy but rather the economic expansion that enabled it to deploy men and ships and "perhaps most of all, the almost unbelievable financial resources which she was able to muster" (O'Gorman 1997: 240).

France also had vast economic resources to tap into. It has even been argued that its economic growth at some moments of the eighteenth century outstripped England's (Crouzet 1966). There did, however, seem to be a growing mismatch between the actual capabilities of the French economy and the financial demands of the government. This can be deduced from the debt-repayment difficulties of the different governments throughout the century, even though this debt was smaller than England's, both absolutely and in relation to the GDP (Bonney 1999b: 148). The War of the Spanish Succession ran up a sizeable debt of about 2.4 billion livres (Harsin 1970: 275) and this was a burdensome inheritance for Louis XV's reign (Félix 2011). The financial problem then lingered on insolubly throughout the whole eighteenth century. It has therefore been put forward as one of the causes of the Revolution, especially in view of the fact that these financial straits forced the government to bring in tax reforms that hit some of France's social classes very hard indeed.

Spain, for its part, relied too heavily on its colonial resources, obtained under a fiscal monopoly, particularly precious metals and tobacco, financing stalwarts up to 1780 (González Enciso 2007). At the same time, it dragged its feet in introducing fiscal and mercantile reforms that would have increased its tax trawl and solidified its financial bases. "Free trade" with the American colonies, in particular, was very fruitful but it was brought in too late (Fisher 1985).

Neither were economic reforms fortified by warfare activity, in general. In the end the state proved unable to meet soaring military costs; by the mid-nineties it was so lumbered that it was unable to increase its armed forces as much as the situation required. Particularly striking is the fall in the navy budget as from 1796 (Alcalá-Zamora 2004: 126–27). The final recourse to national debt turned out to be a pitfall because the ensuing economic slump, just as more money was required, prevented it from being paid off.

It follows from all the above that if the state had to be capable of mobilising the necessary warfare resources and if these resources came at a cost, then the economy had to be productive enough to support all this. National wealth might be used in various ways. It could be used to make the populace rich enough to support a large tax burden (Great Britain, Holland) or to help the state pay off a big public debt (Great Britain), this impinging in turn on the taxation system. Great Britain fits in perfectly with both cases. In any case the scenario was not always the same and although at some moment of the eighteenth century everyone thought they might be able to finance their needs, later on the situation changed. War became increasingly expensive as a whole, a situation exacerbated by sharp price rises in the final decades of the eighteenth century, making it increasingly difficult to meet the complex web of needs woven by all the conflicts.

As the century wore on, as a consequence of all the above, the various states' relative situations changed in terms of their possibilities of winning a war in the long term. The contemporaries' perception of ongoing events was not always very realistic, perhaps because they underestimated the enemy or overrated the permanence of their own resources. Hence the dogged persistence on policies that then turned out to be ineffective. But the historians' hunch is that some countries, with or without knowing it, were indeed sowing well for the future during the eighteenth century and others less so. The reason for this is also that the economic bases evolved differently and not always in line with military needs. At the end of the day, not all taxpayers were able to withstand the burdens these needs foisted on them. In any case the final result, as in sporting events, did not become known until the final straight, in our case in 1815.

Method and timeframe

As Pagden has pointed out with regard to colonial empires, an observation that also comes in handy here, Spain, France and Britain never took their eyes off each other, always weighing up their own possibilities against the others and, more often than might be thought, aping the rival's tactics (Pagden 1995: Introduction). The upshot is a patchy picture of many similarities among the differences and idiosyncrasies. Comparison is crucial here to gain a better grasp of the situation. The comparative approach will show how history is not written down in stone beforehand; the proof is often in the pudding: the best results are known only a posteriori. But it is also true that these methods, i.e., the resource-mobilisation arrangements, depended on which type of resources were most abundant and the historical baggage in each case; comparison therefore also gives us the chance to delve deeper into the differences and understand why one country acted in one way and another in another way. It will also show how given strategies might reasonably have been expected to have certain consequences, so these consequences were to some extent foreseeable. Witness, in fact, the so-called reformist policies throughout the whole century; these in themselves revealed each country's awareness that things were not going well, that its powers were limited and improvements were needed; quite another thing is political will, which determined the possibility of carrying through these reforms at any particular time. They seemed to know what was coming but did not always confront this future with the best solutions or succeed in putting them into practice.

The response to these resource-mobilisation and organisational arrangements has come under the historical limelight in recent decades. I will refer to these studies later at the opportune moment. Suffice it here to point out these studies can be broken down into at least four historiographical fields. First, (a) the resources, their generation and consumption: i.e., the concept of the fiscal-military state, which looks into the relations between warfare's economic needs, the development of the taxation and bureaucratic system, including the financial question and public debt. Second, (b) the concept of the contractor state, which focuses on the suppliers of the armed forces' non-financial goods and services, in other words how the state chose to spend the resources it raised. Among the resource-raising means and the expenditure, consideration must also be given to how these resources were made possible and also how they were managed. This turns our attention to (c) mercantilism, which speaks of the economic wealth of the realms, of the colonial empires and the reforms brought in to increase this wealth, especially as a source of warfare resources. Finally, we come to (d) bureaucracy, whose study looks at the necessary administrative arrangements for exerting power, taking due measures and mobilising resources. These general questions serve as the backdrop to the book and the subjects dealt with though they do not correspond to any specific chapters. We will better deal more deeply with (a) and (b) topics, whereas questions involved in (c) and (d) topics will only be referred to when necessary.

We do not intend to get bogged down in the detail of these themes for each country. We will have to look to the three of them, though, but we will try to be more detailed on the questions directly related to these themes for Spain's case and work from there to look for similarities, differences, possibilities and limitations on action. The themes in question do not always affect the three countries at once, so at times the comparison will be bilateral.

As for the timeframe, we will concentrate on the eighteenth century. Since our main area of concern is Spain, we take as reference a "Spanish" eighteenth century, i.e., the period generally considered for this purpose, running from 1700 to 1808. For Spain this timeframe makes a lot of sense. The first year marks the death of the heirless king, the Habsburg Charles II. The deceased king's testament brought the Bourbon Philip V to the throne, whereupon protests from his rivals unleashed the War of the Spanish Succession. The latter year marks Napoleon's invasion but it is also the final year of Charles IV's reign, the last Spanish monarch of the eighteenth century, dethroned in the course of a few weeks, first by his son Ferdinand after the Aranjuez revolt and then by Napoleon himself in the abdications of Bayonne, while French troops flooded into Spain, ushering in a radically new political and social situation.

This timeframe also fits in with the history of the other two countries at issue here. Louis XIV's acceptance of Charles II's testament in favour of Felipe de Anjou in 1700 was the prelude to the War of the Spanish Succession, a conflict that would be decisive too for France and Great Britain as well as many other countries, due to its knock-on effects on the balance of power. Indeed, the War of the Spanish Succession is, at once, the end of the earlier war cycle and the start of a new international situation in which, for the moment, after 1713, peace would reign on the basis of Utrecht's provisions. For Great Britain this war coincided with the establishment of a modus operandi for conflicts with continental powers, largely in support of its national debt, which had already been successfully premiered in the previous war but would grow more than twofold in this one. During the years of war, the Act of Settlement would settle the future succession to the English throne on the House of Hanover, giving rise in 1707, to Great Britain. At the end of the conflict Great Britain would emerge as top dog, sparking off Anglo-French hostilities and, ipso facto, the subsequent confrontations throughout nearly the whole of the eighteenth century.

In the French case the War of the Spanish Succession represented a huge financial effort, worsening its fiscal problems from that moment on (Rowlands 2012). The conflict also spelled the end of its European supremacy and the start of its rivalry with Great Britain. Very shortly after the war Louis XIV died, after years of clearly declining power as reflected in the Treaty of Ryswick. The year 1700, therefore, or its immediate hinterland, is a decisive moment not only for Spain but also for its rivals, a year in which the long-awaited death of Charles II of Spain led to an unforeseen change brought about by the final and surprising testament of the Spanish monarch (Ribot García 2010). The Spanish monarchy's weakness opened up unprecedented possibilities in international politics.

Much the same goes for our other bookend date of 1808, as a watershed moment not only for Spain but also for the other countries. Although not quite so clearly on this occasion, things had changed since 1805–06. A pivotal event was probably the Battle of Trafalgar in 1805. Great Britain's victory gave it definitive control over the seas, but Napoleon's response, at a culminating moment of the empire, was a continental blockade, which would have significant consequences for everyone. The blockade, indeed, was one of the motives that would trigger Napoleon's invasion of the Iberian Peninsula (Canales 2008: 91). Subsequent events would scale up the war and rack up its costs.

The years 1700 and 1808 can serve as rough bookend dates for a "less long" eighteenth century. This makeshift expression is to be understood in terms of the traditionally used terms in Spanish history of "long" eighteenth century, referring to the period running from 1688 to 1815 and the "short" eighteenth century running from 1713 to 1789. Indeed, to gain a proper grasp of the whole eighteenth century we need to look at what went on before, since at least 1680s, and its aftermath up to 1815. In any case, although we often work within the 1700–1808 timeframe for Spain we will also take into account the other reference period making up the long eighteenth century, precisely with this idea of seeing the genesis and aftermath; sometimes we will look at them explicitly. The eighties of the seventeenth century were decisive both for Great Britain, due to the Glorious Revolution of 1688, and for Spain, to a lesser extent, because there were signs of a certain upturn after the deepest trough of the seventeenth-century slump and an admittedly lukewarm start of the implementation of reformist policies. For France these years are decisive in another aspect, since they mark the peak of Louis XIV's power, although attention will also have to be given not only to the economic upturn but the effect of the Nine Years' War on finances, the army and the government (Rowlands 2002). The 1808–15 period is clearly important for all of them; it is the denouement of the drama but in a different sense for each one. In 1815, after all, as in 1713, a fairly long period of peace began, a sign that the previous cycle had ended.

1 Changing strategies and global power in the long eighteenth century

Every historical situation comes from somewhere. Without going right back to the dawn of time we do need to kick off our study with a reflection on the geostrategic situation of the powers around 1700, their realistic expectations of dominance in view of their immediately preceding experience and the present challenges posed by these future ambitions. Historians too begin from a given point that reflects the current state of their knowledge. The issues at stake have been debated, sometimes to death, by specialists. The public at large might even pitch in with a few details. The idea in this chapter is to gain, firstly, an overview of the strategic situation according to the main international events of the moment and then take in some methodological lines underlying the issues under study.

1.1 The long consequences of Utrecht

If it is our aim here to compare the accomplishments – and limitations – of Spain with those of its main long-term rivals, France and Great Britain, this is because it was these three monarchies throughout the early modern era, and especially in its final century, that best exemplified the three basic categories of global power: winners, losers and emerging countries that became winners. To boil things down to their simplest terms, as history has tended to do, the sixteenth century was Spanish, the seventeenth century was French – also fleetingly Dutch – and the eighteenth century was English, or rather British, at least as far as the Atlantic world was concerned, which is the space of interest to us here. It also has to be borne in mind, in any case, that the Atlantic world was in the vanguard of worldwide political and economic transformations at that time and that Europe's actions would shift overseas at this time, and above all to the Atlantic arena. Europe's colonial empires, indeed, would take in the whole globe and it was precisely in the eighteenth century when they came to a significant state of maturity (Green and Morgan 2009).

After the volatile situation at the end of the Thirty Years' War the geostrategic position of European countries gradually gelled into situations that could be qualified with the abovementioned adjectives. Things were never really quite so cut-and-dried of course, and questions are begged about the real meaning of each of these adjectives, how they should be applied to the various monarchies and the real sense they take on at each particular juncture. They are being used here only to indicate that the ongoing changes modified the power relations from a geostrategic perspective, i.e., changes have occurred in the dominant international political power at a given moment, in terms of the territorial ranking acquired by each country and how it is likely to fare in any conflict. Also at issue here is that country's military and economic capacity, at least as an instrument of deterrence.

At any rate things might eventually pan out in a very different way than expected, even belying the power ratings assigned by historians. J. Lynn, for example, has posed the question "victory or defeat?" in terms of the effects of the War of the Spanish Succession for France: this country lost in some respects and won in others (Lynn 1999: 359); this, of course, without considering questions that could be considered to be negative like the aforementioned crushing debt left by Louis XIV after this war (Harsin 1970: 275), or the personal problems – fatalities, casualties – and moral problems (Levy 1983: 90), which in any case could be applicable to the ostensible winners. Take another example. According to D. Baugh, "Britain was unquestionably the leading naval power in Europe when war broke out in 1739". No objection could be made to this claim; nonetheless, Great Britain's naval power in this war did not sweep all before it. Even a pundit of the time expressed the opinion in 1747 that the ostensible superiority had become a "shadow of what we had forty years ago" (Baugh 1965: 496; Woodfine 1988: 71). It is indeed curious to see what the contemporaries thought from our standpoint today.

Within the geostrategic change around 1700 the series of agreements known generically as the Treaty of Utrecht of 1713 comes across as one of the red-letter events in the history of international relations (Krieger 1970: 39). It represented a fundamental change that rewrote the power relations between the three key players of the time: Spain, who could consider itself the loser, albeit only up to a certain point; France, which slid down the ranking and was left with no choice than to follow in the wake of Great Britain; and Great Britain itself, which could be classed as "emerging" at the start of the conflict and "winner" in the aftermath, but which would nonetheless take some time to enforce its law, at least another 50 years.

Utrecht ushered in a long period that has been dubbed by many authors as the European power system, relying on mutual recognition of sovereignty over small territories and their inhabitants and also a desire for balance, particularly among the major powers (McKay and Scott 1983). Precisely this advent of small territories, recognised above all to ensure a sense of balance, blurs the neat idea of winners and losers in some cases. Austria, for example, can be considered a winner insofar as it acquired the territories of the former Spanish provinces in the Low Countries and Italy, but the appearance on the scene of Prussia as a kingdom cast doubts on its future. Much the same goes for France as "loser" here, since it did benefit from the appearance on the scene of this new rival for its eternal adversary. Nuancing factors such as this became more evident as the eighteenth century wore on. The system would change, especially as from 1763 (Schroeder 1994).

What was the situation like in 1713? From the word go, for reasons that do not need to bother us here, the new European states born from the end-of-fifteenth-century political transformations, i.e., what in general terms has been dubbed by historians as the early modern state (Naef 1973; Guenée 1973), would build up their relations in conflictive and competitive terms, scrapping not only for a given territory but also for overall power. This tended to brew the idea, among other things, of a "universal monarchy" as the desire to dominate the known world by wielding a power that could be seen as the international arbiter. This "known world", logically, extended to colonial conquests (Pagden 1995: Introduction, Chap. 2, II). This idea more or less held up until the eighteenth century, but it tended to be based more and more on economic rather than political postulates.

Once the political and religious division of Europe had been confirmed in Westphalia, growing attention began to be paid to economic resources, relatively ignored hitherto. This occurred precisely because countries had cottoned on to the fact that waging war called for some monetary means that could no longer be so easily obtained from the traditional resources of agricultural wealth and trading exchanges of European products. Even the loan option became increasingly complicated (Neal 1994); this would lead to tax hikes and innovations in the fiscal system. In the United Provinces, for example, it became necessary in the sixties and seventies of the seventeenth century to resort more and more often to extraordinary taxes. This gave rise, in 't Hart's words, to "the population of Holland becoming the most heavily taxed people in Europe" ('t Hart 2014: 158). The Dutch inherited the sad situation already experienced by the Castilians some decades earlier (Gelabert 1997), albeit with very different consequences. What these seventeenth-century examples show is how war was becoming more and more expensive to wage, so the only possible long-term winner would be the power that best solved this problem.

It so happened that this realisation of increasing warfare needs came bang in the middle of an economic slump, one of the salient traits of which was a fall in the amount of precious metal received from by far the most important revenue source at the time, the Spanish Americas (Morineau 1985). This led to the realisation that wealth could be limited, and it was therefore essential to ensure the biggest possible share of this dwindling source. "The money within the realm cannot be increased without at the same time taking the same sum from neighbouring states", said Colbert in 1664 (Clément 1861: 293). Although these ideas were very widespread, and in fact chime in with the traditional notion of mercantilism (Deyon 1969: 22), they were not shared by all economic writers of the time; to cite only two examples among many, the idea of "bullionism" had already come in for some flak by the mid-sixteenth century from Tomás de Mercado in Spain and J. Bodin in France (Rodríguez Casado 1980: 64). It nonetheless did feature in the political mindset of the time; witness the mercantilist policies of excluding the adversary from the respective colonies, an idea that spread in the mid-seventeenth century if it had not already taken off beforehand. The most significant example was Cromwell's Navigation Acts in England; this idea had been bandied about previously but was now honed to perfection by countries such as England while in others like Spain it became corrupted (García Fuentes 1982).

The result of the political and economic changes of the final decades of the seventeenth century, before the commencement of the eighteenth century, was that the fight for power or survival in Europe went through an idiosyncratic stage characterised by the intrinsic disorientation of a change of era and profound political circumstances. The "crisis of European conscience" about which P. Hazard spoke (Hazard 1968) was not limited to the field of thought explored by this author; it went much further. It in fact affected the very conception of the world and its organisation; it impinged on each one of the countries, all of which saw their political fate and international influence change in a short period of time. As Elliott pointed out, "the middle and later decades of the seventeenth century were marked by profound shifts in the International balance of power" (Elliott 2006: 219). These changes had different consequences in each case. They meant that Spain fell out of the top power ranking, even though many of its capacities remained intact and it even managed to cling onto a good part of its power with a partly surprising resilience (Storrs 2013); its American and Asiatic empire, in particular, remained important. But also France itself, which had ruled the roost in the second half of the seventeenth century, saw its superiority coming under threat from England's rapid development of international power, especially after the Glorious Revolution favoured personal union between England and Holland and the ensuing decidedly anti-French policy of William III (O'Gorman 1997: 41). France had hit a ceiling it could break through only by means of running up a debt that turned out to be untenable. Its armies shrank in size and the country was incapable of keeping up the challenge of fighting on several fronts during the War of the Spanish Succession; all this accounted for its final defeat.

Between the keynote dates of 1713, 1718 and 1721 (representing, respectively, Utrecht and peace for the major warring western states; Passarowitz and peace in southern and eastern Europe; Nystadt and peace for the north) a continental system was established that Krieger defined as "a limited Group of superior Powers whose interests spanned the whole continent in a connected set of relations" (Krieger 1970: 54). What really came out of this, in any case, was British supremacy, or in Muret's words *prépondérance anglaise* (Muret 1937). This meant that "standards of national security and thus…the limits of what could lawfully be done" (Krieger 1970: 54) could now be discussed in major international treaties with a common language and similar objectives. Congresses abounded in the eighteenth century, but with a growing evidence of the powerful arbitration of British interests. As the century wore on this would lead to the "*pax britannica*", or at least a prelude thereto in 1805, though some argued that it had already existed since the victory of Trafalgar (O'Brien 2014: 7).

One of the most salient eighteenth-century features in the Atlantic world, as from 1713, even taking into account all the abovementioned events, is that the three countries of interest to us here all confronted the new century from different starting points. How were these situations different? What are their distinctive traits? These questions call for an answer straddling at least three fields: political, economic and strategic.

Great Britain came out of 1713 with a clear idea, if it had not already entertained it beforehand, of its supremacy. Its fundamental goal, however, was economic. Firstly, because its mercantile concern was an inheritance that the English had been perfectly clear about at least since the times of T. Mun and his *England's Treasure by Forraign Trade*, widely considered to be the quintessential mercantile doctrine, which England was already tentatively putting into practice and then with increasing firmness, albeit with varying intensity at some moments. International trade, in particular colonial trade, was the driving force of England's overseas policy at first and then of Great Britain's later. This policy, after all, was geared towards defending and widening its trading base as the source of its national wealth (Hales 1893). This opulent trade, in turn, and the personal wealth it generated, underpinned its fiscal system based on indirect taxes, in particular, as we will see, on the excises. Great Britain strived to maintain balance on the European continent, not only militarily but also with a huge economic and diplomatic effort; nonetheless its army was not the most outstanding one by the European standards of the time (Black 1989: 1). Above all, Great Britain concentrated on conquering markets, not only in Spanish America but also in Africa and Asia. Its politics would therefore be active, even aggressive in some cases.

France shows to some extent the other side of the coin. Forced to try to maintain its position and follow in the wake of a burgeoning Great Britain, France at first had to accept the Utrecht-imposed power balance, but then tried to work for its own political interests, sidling up to Spain as soon as it could to try to offset British power. But France placed more stress on continental conflicts than the development of maritime trade (Lynn 1999: 29). This did not prevent its trade from soaring in this century. Utrecht's boosting of Austria at the expense of Spain's former European provinces forced France to insist on its classic dynastic policy, together with a time-honoured and powerful hereditary framework, which would dominate its politics in the first half of the century. After 1740, however, the predominant trait was the ongoing tussle with a Great Britain intent on ousting it from colonial trade. It practically managed it in 1763. To tackle these challenges France had to fall back on a taxation system burdened by the huge debt left by Louis XIV, thence worsened by each new war. France would choose to squeeze its direct taxes to the utmost, until they accounted for over 50 per cent of its revenue (Durand 1976: 21), perhaps in the confidence that its vast territory and big population could withstand this burden, perhaps too because the French government ran these taxes directly, whereas indirect taxes were in the hands of the *Ferme général*, a syndicate of financiers that was a double-edged sword: essential for its financial balance but perilous in terms of balking any fiscal innovations.

The Spanish case was simpler, although with apparently limited possibilities. Ostensibly the loser from Utrecht, Spain would then carry out a revisionist policy bucking against those agreements, showing an unexpected dynamism and soon bringing it into confrontation with all and sundry. Its new defeat in 1719 forced it to kowtow to the system and try to force its claims within it, partly achieving this aim in the form of two peace treaties, one in 1738 and another in 1748, which confirmed the position of two of its princes in Italian territory even though this territory was not actually brought under the Spanish sovereignty. It was clear that Spain was working for a dependence-free international situation, prompting it to seek alternative alliances with Austria, Great Britain and France in the first half of the century (Bethencourt Massieu 1998). Then it sued for peace, an armed peace under cover of which it was girding its loins for future bellicose adventures.

Spain had one advantage: it did not have to win an empire because it already had one; moreover, this empire seemed to defend itself alone. Its imposing territorial presence seemed to keep it in place with no other input (Stein and Stein 2000). True it is that Spain carried out some reforms to improve the colonies' industry and trade but these were slow in coming, and only in the final decades of the century did they build up some effect. In practice Spain's colonial empire suffered no significant territorial decline in this century, even swelling somewhat with the addition of French Louisiana.

Spain looked for its resources within its empire. Taxpayers at home could not cough up any more money and the inherited debt had to be paid off. Taxation policy in the first half of the century was dominated by the tax-alleviation principle of *alivio de los vasallos*, i.e., the freezing of its main source of income affecting its most deprived subjects, the Castilian *rentas provinciales*, made up above all by the famous sales tax *alcabalas*, which hardly rose for half a century. For this reason, and barring its policy of Italian revisionism, where, in a second phase, it acted with the acquiescence of France and Great Britain, Spain stuck to a low-key, defensive policy for a good part of the century, breaking it only in 1760. Spain's tax system relied on American precious metal plus extraordinary taxes during times of war, then removed during peacetime. Under normal conditions, revenue from American precious metal was enough to bridge the deficit produced by the ordinary taxation system. This American bale-out explains why Spanish governors did not even bother to draw up a debt policy for a good part of the century, written off as not only unnecessary but also hazardous. American metal worked as a fiscal top-up (Torres Sánchez 2007: 448–49) to cover the deficit of ordinary expenditure. In practice, therefore, it carried out a function similar to that of national debt, i.e., compensating for what was missing. It had one big advantage, however: no interest had to be paid. But it also had a drawback, which did not become evident until too late: it was fickle, not always turning up when needed and sometimes not even turning up at all.

It is curious to note that none of the three countries significantly changed tack despite the numerous wars of the time. Differing in their motivations and possibilities, the three countries were alike in sticking to their respective policies, presumably in the belief that these policies would pan out well in the end or because opportunity cost prevented them from acting otherwise. Military and fiscal policies had a social backdrop: their effect on the social classes that paid, or could afford, the taxes. Any change in these policies could have a significant social cost that rulers of the time tried in general to avoid.

1.2 Warfare interests and motives

Did countries seek power through war? Obviously they did. The moot point, however, is how they stood as regards this power and hence what sort of power they sought. Uztáriz said that monarchies and kingdoms should have armies and strengths "that safeguard them and win them respect" (Uztáriz 1968: 2). On this principle, power calls for a certain pre-eminence in international relations, heading off what was called in the nomenclature of those times an "offence", i.e., any attack on national interests. This posture, in any case, had rather a defensive character and we would argue that defence was by no means the only attitude of eighteenth-century powers. They not only expected an attack but also provoked it. Wielding power, in this sense, meant being able to launch an attack when it most suited the attacker, provoking or declaring war when the winds of war blew in the country's favour.

We have already seen that our three powers faced very different situations in the 1700–13 period and what might be expected there from. Any given historical situation stems from a previous one that the countries concerned cannot overlook and from which they have to project their future, at least the immediate future. What I mean is the simple thing that any war at the start of the eighteenth century would certainly not be the first war these countries had fought and this is where each country's muscle memory comes in; neither would it be the last and this is where future prospects come in.

The three main wars of the first half of the eighteenth century were wars of succession (of Spain, Poland and Austria). From this viewpoint it could be claimed that the main spur of war was purely and simply dynastic: in each case it was necessary to come up with an heir and in each case too there was no clearly recognised candidate. This led to conflict; it was also something the powers were used to. Dynastic strife was consubstantial with hereditary monarchies, which had spent centuries eking out their territories by dint of marriages and inheritance. But this apparently simple traditional situation begs the question of which interests or factors lurked behind the election of one or other of the pretenders, especially in the era we are dealing with here. Why, for example, was Charles II of Spain's testament rejected when its legal claim was clear, or why it was written the way it was (Ribot García 2010). It is usually argued that the testament ran counter to the agreements that Louis XIV had made with the Emperor on earlier occasions (Hatton 1976), but this just pushes the same question further back.

Although dynastic issues still played an important part in the eighteenth century, it is clear they did not have the same effect as in the feudal era when dynastic rights were practically the only claims that could be invoked to back up any territorial claim. Even though this assertion may be challengeable, what does seem to be clear is that eighteenth-century dynastic interests were backed by the understanding of a realm as a differentiated state, with fairly well-defined areas of influence both in Europe and in the colonies. This does not hold true for all realms (take Poland as an extreme example), but it is very valid for western realms. Here only minor territorial depredations were tolerated. The case of Spain itself is very telling here. True it is that Philip V had won the Peninsula War but everyone was aware he could not have enforced his will on the other winning powers. Despite this, these powers did respect the unity of Spain and its American colonies, with the "slight" caveats of Gibraltar, Minorca and Oran. The other territories lost by the Spanish monarchy in Utrecht were not strictly Spanish in essence, though the tie was time-honoured and backed up by dynastic bonds. The winning powers were interested in breaking up the Spanish monarchy, a sort of European empire, but not Spain as such.

The dynastic factor there acted largely as a pretext; it was also used to defend other interests that were rather economic or political in kind. In short the over-riding factor now seems to be *raison d'état*. The so-called maritime powers, England and Holland, opposed the Duke of Anjou's claim to the Spanish throne because it would have meant the appearance of a Franco-Spanish superpower that, among other things would have jeopardised England and Holland's maritime trade supremacy in and around 1700. Holland, moreover, had just come out of a recent war, also an independence dispute ('t Hart 2014), against France. The French danger had been quashed in the Nine Years' War but now the phantom of French power was bigger if added to Spain. In the final years of the seventeenth century, moreover, Spanish trade with its American colonies had clearly suffered from contraband activities by merchants of all countries interested in the Atlantic trade (García Fuentes 1982, Malamud 1986). Spain seemed unable to staunch this drain on its resources; its systems also suffered from structural faults and the colonial authorities even connived with the smugglers. This obviously benefited English and Dutch merchants. Would these fault lines continue if France, united with Spain, managed to bring the Spanish system under control?

Back in 1700 obviously no one knew what was going to happen, but everyone assumed that, whoever won, it was going to have privileged access to this market and that the concomitant circumstances could change. It was therefore no easy matter to accept Charles II's testament in the terms it was written in. War seemed inevitable. Furthermore, at the time of signing the treaty it was more than likely that, although Spain would hold onto its colonies, Philip V would be forced to renounce the French throne, in his own name and that of his heirs and Spain would have to suffer legal inroads by British trade in its colonies in the form of the *navío de permiso* and *asiento de negros*. This struggle to break into the Spanish colonies market, so fierce in the final years of the seventeenth century and the early years of the eighteenth (Pérez-Mallaína Bueno 1982), was cleared up in this way simply because it best suited the strongest power at that time. We therefore see that behind the *raison d'état* existed what we might call a *raison d'entreprise*; economic interests were increasingly merging with political interests. The state had become a company – understood in an economic sense – that was increasingly bound to balance its books and the best way of doing so was to boost revenue sources.

The rest of the century saw nothing more than reruns, enlargements and sometimes distillations of this same situation. As we have already pointed out, regardless of what mercantilist pundits might say about scarcity and wealth, or the true source thereof, politicians and merchants thought that this wealth depended on dominating more territory and enforcing customs control in them, i.e., the standard laid down in the Navigation Acts. This way of thinking and acting moderated only in the final decades of the century. Poland's War of Succession was largely continental in character and Great Britain hardly got involved. This allowed Spain to press its traditional claims in Italy. Taking advantage of British neutrality and with the support of France, keen on someone distracting Austria while it operated in Poland, Spain won back Naples and Sardinia. But Patiño's sights were really set on the Americas, where Spanish coastguards were trying to staunch the seepage of its trade to contraband activities, especially British.

The Spanish attitude, which turned out to be effective, worried London merchants, who feared a reduction of their mercantile interests if Spain continued with this policy. They convinced Walpole to go to war. Thus, the Anglo-Spanish War, which began in 1739 – War of Jenkin's Ear – was probably the first of the century spurred openly by economic interests without other spurious pretexts (Rodger 2004: 235). The conflict would then become mixed up with the War of Austrian Succession. The upshot was that bilateral Spanish-British rivalry was exacerbated by another colonial rivalry, hitherto latent, namely the rivalry with France, which would become crucial in the near future. Thus the inheritance of the three major powers of the eighteenth century, after a standoff *interregnum*, was Franco-British rivalry with Spain lurking in the background, dominant above all in the colonial world (although the biggest naval combats were waged in the European Atlantic), and the Austria-Prussia rivalry on the continent (Scott 2006: 39).

From this moment on dynastic issues took second stage. The countries that became known after 1815 as the "great powers" now began to wage an active struggle in which the main issue at stake, especially for Great Britain, was the mastery of world trade, which it had to win against the colonial powers of Spain and France (Scott 2006: 3). The French question had its first denouement in 1763, but France's natural power, boasting as it did a wide-ranging, rich and densely populated territory, gave it force enough to continue acting as a great power and rise again, after the revolutionary upheavals, with the power shown by Napoleon. Spain stood out better against the power of the British, whose triumphs, if they can be rated as such, were minor between 1763 and 1797. It would not be until the nineteenth century and Spain's grave crisis against Napoleon, that Spain's colonial empire would finally rupture. In any case, confrontations between the three powers, after the last throes of the Seven Years' War, were strictly Atlantic in scope. Until 1793 Great Britain would not fight again on the continent. Spain hardly did so either after 1748 – barring the skirmishes of the Portuguese invasion of 1762 and the siege of Gibraltar of 1780 – until it had to defend itself from the Convention in 1794.

1.3 Spain in eighteenth-century international politics

Although we have already looked briefly at the relative situation of the three countries during the long eighteenth century, we now need to zoom in on Spain for a few pages, since the central concern of this book is Spain and its situation in the general context of the eighteenth century. One good reason for paying more attention to Spain, apart from its importance as an international power in that century, is that so many general European history texts tend to relegate Spain to a minor power bereft of its importance of previous centuries. They therefore spend as much time on it as they do on other smaller powers such as Sweden or Italy. Books on the Americas do grant importance to Spanish colonies of course, but they often do so independently of events at home. Judging from the lack of any reference to Spain itself, the true source of these colonies' social, military and political power, these texts seem to understand the "Spanish empire" as the colonial world alone.

The downplaying of Spain in these history books is largely a feedback effect from post-eighteenth-century events: the defeat against Napoleon, the independence of the colonies and the nineteenth-century decline tend to be blamed on mistakes or limitations of the policies carried out beforehand. Nonetheless, although nineteenth-century events must bear some relationship to the achievements or failures of the previous century, these cannot be put forward as the sole explanation for Spain's nineteenth-century relegation to second-division status. Enlightened Spain, indeed, featured in the top ranking of international powers, thanks not only to colonial inputs but also the resources engendered and procured at home. Throughout the whole eighteenth century Spain remained a decisive power in Europe and the world, especially but not solely in the Atlantic world, above all if we factor in its size, diverse character and potentiality (Fernández Armesto 1999: 89). The ostensible decline of this empire became manifest, if at all, only well into the last decade of the century. Until that time Spain was a growing power that greatly worried the British, who kept a close eye on this political and economic threat from many different points of view. It could quite possibly be argued, in truth, that few realised this growth was slower than elsewhere, thus mortgaging the future. But the future was always open. Its rivals, too, were also aware of their own problems and limitations, so enlightened Spain was much more highly regarded and respected by its enemies of the time than, in general, by the historians of the future.

In what sort of condition did Spain enter the eighteenth century? Received opinion still tends to picture it as a country in decline, its territory being greedily carved up in sundry treaties. Westphalia, on this view, had represented not only a military defeat but also forfeiture of Spain's spiritual hegemony. Bereft of its political power and spiritual ideas, Spain was thenceforth but a shadow of itself. "*Todo en el mundo se desespañolizaba. No nos sorprenderá, puesto que los mismos españoles habían comenzado por desespañolizarse*" (Palacio Atard 1987: 106). (The whole world is shedding its Spanishness: small wonder when the Spanish themselves are doing likewise.) The situation worsened from the sixties onwards with the definitive separation of Portugal, the new defeats against Louis XIV's France and a tricky succession process. Although this image is true from the viewpoint of international politics, and probably from the sense of *Spanishness*, as pointed out in the above quote by Palacio Atard, it is no less true that it needs to be fleshed out with other factors pointing to a slow but palpable economic and demographic upturn in the last two decades of the century (Kamen 1980; Yun Casalilla 1999) or even its endurance and stamina in the international arena (Storrs 2013).

Be that as it may, Spain showed some signs, perhaps unexpectedly, of vitality during the War of the Spanish Succession, which Philip Duke of Anjou (Philip-V-to-be) managed to win, doing so without French help from 1709 onwards. The international defeat of 1713 was less dire in its consequences than might have been expected, due to the failure of France (Albareda 2015: 65). Spain kept its colonial empire together, albeit at the high price of granting Great Britain inroads into its trading monopoly with slaves and the Americas, the *asiento de negros* and *navío de permiso*. This spelled the end of Spain's hitherto exclusive trading rights with the colonies. After 1713 Spain was the only colonial empire that countenanced legal traffic with a privilege-protected foreign company, albeit with the caveat that the King of Spain should always take part in the arrangement and grant the permit for each particular voyage.

In Europe, however, Spain did lose its territories in the Low Countries and Italy, and this was indeed a hard blow to take. The trouble is that France, now Spain's ally, also proved incapable of holding onto the territories Louis XIV had fought for. In 1713 France lost the European hegemony it had enjoyed hitherto; from here on it had to bow to British arbitration in the new international order (Bernardo Ares 2008). It also saw itself excluded from trading arrangements with Spain's American colonies, while Great Britain was brought into the fold. The loss for Spain represented, without any doubt the disappearance of the Habsburg inheritance, to which must be added the additional loss of Minorca, Gibraltar and Oran, of little territorial scope but great strategic and spiritual importance. The first two enclaves were crucial stepping stones for Britain's trading expansion throughout the Mediterranean. Nonetheless, the new situation would allow Spain to concentrate on what was rightfully its own without squandering huge efforts as in the past on "European" adventures.

After this inauspicious and worrying start to the century Spain showed signs of an unexpected resilience. If it failed in its initial attempts to take back Sardinia and Sicilia (1717–18), as part of a unilateral endeavour to redraft the Utrecht Treaty, this did not prevent it from showing a surprising resourcefulness, coming good a few years later in a different international context when it won back Oran in 1732 and Naples and Sicilia in 1734–35. Naples and Sicilia would never be brought back under Spain's sovereignty but the military victory was clear, and at least a Spanish *infante* was enthroned there, future Charles III of Spain, giving rise to a new Bourbon dynasty in Europe. Spanish arms, albeit under favourable circumstances, showed they were capable of once again winning territories in Europe if need be.

During the thirties Spain enjoyed a certain leeway of action; Great Britain showed an initial laissez-faire attitude to Spanish actions and even ended up supporting them outright. The good relations between both countries quickly deteriorated thereafter, coming to an abrupt end in 1739 with renewed sabre-rattling and confrontation. It should be noted here that the scales of war initially tipped in Spain's favour. In successive years Spain checked Great Britain's expansion in the Americas (as in the British failed attempt at Cartagena de Indias in 1741), managed to keep Charles on his Neapolitan throne and, finally, succeeded in overthrowing the Utrecht-brokered American trading licences in 1750. By said year, therefore, Spain re-emerged as a strong power, capable of defending its colonial power, boasting an appreciable military potential on land and sea and enjoying strong economic and demographic growth (González Enciso 2012a).

Its contemporaries certainly understood the significance of Spain's recovery, judging from the qualms of London merchants who had sparked off the War of Jenkin's Ear in 1739, or the worries expressed by the British ambassador Keene. France also deemed it fitting to ally itself with Spain under two *Pactes de Famille*, in 1733 and 1743, respectively, in opposition to British interests. France was taking risks by allying itself with Spain. It was ultimately driven to this expedient because it reckoned self-seekingly that the Spanish force, joined to its own, was strong enough to take on Great Britain. In these years Spain did not come across as just one more power among the pack but a strong ally, needed by France to offset Great Britain and at least stymie it in the Atlantic to suit its own trading interests.

Spain might well have been the third-ranking European power of that time, but this was a third place of notable power and great future possibilities, especially on the strength of a navy outmatched only by Great Britain and France. After 1750, moreover, it no longer needed to get embroiled in continental European conflicts but could afford to concentrate fully on its colonial interests. I would argue that historians have never really done full justice to this Spanish recovery, often attributing it to the subsequent reign of Charles III or merely to French aid, which did not in fact exist in these years. The *Pactes de Famille*, moreover, did not in general fulfil Spanish expectations, France often falling down on its promises. In other words, Spain's success in the first half of the eighteenth century really is a success and is solely Spanish in gestation.

Neither should we historians swing too far the other way, however. Spain's recovery on the world stage during the forties only went so far. It did not manage to get France to keep its promises with regard to Gibraltar and Minorca, which remained in the enemy's hands in 1750. Fear of British reprisals and of the growth of Spain itself marked the limits of French support. Spain did not trail in France's wake in the *Pactes de Famille*, as historians have traditionally argued; no, Spain was pursuing its own policy. But the truth is too that Spain was unable to force France further than France was ready to go.

Neither was the second half of the century straightforward. Ferdinand VI's firm pacifist policy excluded Spain from most of the Seven Years' War. His ministers followed a reformist policy that helped to fuel the fiscal and economic recovery. This zeal may have dipped in the last years or the reign, so the situation by 1759 was no longer what it had been five years earlier. In any case any supposed progress came to naught militarily when Charles III, arrived in Spain in 1759, decided to enter the Seven Years' War. Two military routs ushered in the peace treaty of 1763, from which Spain came off better than might have been expected beforehand. After many years of activity Spain had been forced to improvise its war preparations and organisation, with dire results. The new monarch tried to learn his lessons from this, striving to speed up reforms in subsequent years and overhaul the army and navy, without any resounding success.

Esquilache's swingeing reforms aimed, among other things, to bring the country quickly onto a war footing, but the effort produced little more than a serious revolt in 1766, forcing the minister to flee. It was a grave moment of political instability (Andrés-Gallego 2003), above all because it was not at all clear who was behind the revolt. It fizzled out fairly quickly, however, with the advent of new-broom ministers and scapegoat suppression of the Company of Jesus in 1767.

The rest of Charles III's reign was marked by interior tranquillity, political stability, ongoing economic recovery, with a few important measures brought in, and enhanced international importance, rather in terms of ostensible than actual power, as shown by the Algiers fiasco in 1775. Spain's declaration of war against Great Britain as France's ally in 1779 was lukewarm in its commitment. Nonetheless, the war did give Spain some satisfaction, most of it minor if truth be told – barring the recovery of Florida and Minorca – but enough to provide at least a semblance of victory, despite the mishaps on the way. The overall impression was that the country was now capable of measuring itself against Great Britain on equal terms. The Versailles peace treaties of 1783 rubber-stamped both France's and Spain's claims to power. The ensuing euphoria and self-esteem comes across strongly in the *Instrucción Reservada* (government programme) of Floridablanca (1787), Secretary of State at that time.

Charles III's reign has had a better press, historically speaking. The upturn of the first half of the century, albeit stemming from a period of decline and running out of steam after 1680, has been underestimated, as we have already seen. In Charles III's reign, however, the exact opposite occurred, to the extent that both historians and laymen tend to credit it with more than it actually achieved. Charles III is without doubt one of the highest rated monarchs in Spain's history, also largely due to political correctness of our own time. In international politics, however, success was slow in coming, coinciding in time, when it did arrive, with Great Britain's nadir, especially its colonial crisis, spurring the birth of the United States. Spain's success here gave a false idea of true British power, which did not do itself justice in this dispute, in comparison with the feats of 20 years earlier, but its growth had certainly not stalled. It was in fact after 1783 when Great Britain clocked up its fastest growth rates (Deane and Cole 1963: 51).

In any case the merits of the reign, at least from 1778, are clear. To limit ourselves to the field of interest to us here, mention must be made of the important economic reforms of this time, such as the decree of free trade with the American colonies (1778), the issue of public debt with the *vales reales* and the creation of the *Banco de San Carlos* (1780–82) or the reform of the *alcabalas* (sales taxes) in 1785. All these feats augured well for the future and justified the sense of euphoria. In historians' eyes this was borne out by the events immediately following upon this reign. Charles III died in December 1788, shortly after France's Estates General (*états généraux*) had been convened to meet the following year. The ensuing French Revolution changed the scenario completely and tested the mettle not only of the reforms of the moment but also the cumulative effect of past economic and social structures.

Spain's mood back in 1783/87 had been upbeat and even warmongering, in the English style of expecting only good to come from any conflict at this time (Torres Sánchez 2013a). Little did they imagine then that only 10 years later, in 1793/97, the country would lurch into one of the most critical, problem-ridden periods in its history. Spain proved incapable, firstly, of bearing the brunt of the political crisis brought on by the revolution, completely throwing Spanish authorities off the track. Neither could it withstand the military attack of the revolutionary wars. Ostensibly allied with the British, but to so little effect that there were no actual British boots on the ground in Spain, it was defeated by Convention troops. Allied with France (from 1796 onwards), it suffered the full force of British naval power, then coming under growing pressure from Napoleon, who ended up invading Spain.

Particularly serious, as a threshold of economic problems, was the defeat of 1797, more important from a strategic point of view than as a one-off battle. Only a few ships were lost but the defeat showed up Spain's complete inability to control sea routes, quite the contrary to what it had demonstrated back in 1780, even though there were some naval setbacks then too. The upshot was the opening up of Spain's colonial trade to neutral countries. This not only showed Spain's inability to maintain its system but also facilitated inroads by North American trade, among others, in Spain's colonies, a key element in the country's subsequent march towards its independence. This new scenario meant that some of the country's staple tax earners (tobacco, customs and precious metals) began to cough up only sporadically, depending on the vicissitudes of war and trade cut-offs. The dearth, even if only temporary, of tax income, especially in an era of sharply growing needs, forced the country to fall back anew on more expensive overseas loans, the home loan market having collapsed due to lack of liquidity (Merino Navarro 2014: 86 ff).

All this was merely the start of the country's ills. How was this possible? How could such an apparently powerful country be brought to its knees in such a short period of time? What did Spain do, or omit to do, in the final years of the eighteenth century, to fall into such dire financial straits, despite still being able to draw on such vast stores of precious metals from the Americas? These questions would call for an across-the-board, cohesive answer, which is very hard to come up with. On the contrary there are varied answers from diverse perspectives because there are many variables to factor in. Many descriptions have been made of this situation in the past without ever being able to explain why it turned out like it did, why the looming disaster could not be staved off.

Our own answer involves looking at the long-term picture. There was certainly a grave political problem in Charles IV's reign, but resources cannot be conjured out of thin air. With more resources even bad politicians have some success. With fewer resources even good politicians fail. This is by no means to exonerate Spanish governors for the political disorientation shown as from 1790; but it does serve as a reminder of something already hinted at on three occasions: the slowness – and sometimes the shallowness – of many of the reforms carried out in the eighteenth century, including Charles III's reign (González Enciso 1979). Torres Sánchez has recently cast doubt on whether Charles III's state could really be considered a fiscal-military state, concluding that it could, "but little developed as yet. The war showed that the political and economic reforms brought in by the diverse Bourbon governments were not enough to ensure a state capable of mobilising necessary resources with sufficient flexibility and rapidity" (Torres

Sánchez 2013a: 419). If the country was not able to act with the necessary efficacy in victorious wars, like the one of 1779–83 referred to by this author, what chance would it stand in more aggressive, more expensive wars conducted under worse conditions like the Revolutionary Wars!

In any case, whatever the final outcome, things were not clear to anyone at the time until too late. In the Nootka crisis of 1790, for example, the British preferred to accept Spanish apologies rather than pushing things too far (Knight 2014: 13), just in case. In all likeliness Spain's weakness did not become glaringly obvious until the war against the Convention. If our answer rests on the long term, then we need to study over time the correlation between available resources and the measures taken to increase them, trying thus to work out how Spain was building this fiscal-military state, why it did not become more developed, how it took on the challenges of the market that the contractor state demanded.

Hindsight is a wonderful thing. It is easy for any historian to point out the failings of politicians of the past when weighing up their performance. But it is very difficult to assess whether what we ask for today was possible back then. Spain, for better or worse, was the country it was at that time. It had its own particular history; we have already mentioned the previous decline; it had the territory it had, sprawling, poorly communicated, largely infertile; and it had its own particular society too, with its mindset – for which there is always some explanation – and its groups of vested interests, more or less powerful, with a relatively weak mercantile and financial bourgeoisie. All these factors, and without doubt many more, have to be taken on board and assessed judiciously to reach any precise answer to these questions. In any case, we are only seeking here the best answer possible rather than the perfect one.

2   Eighteenth-century realities and historiographical approaches

As we have already seen, dynastic and strategic questions tended to overlap in the eighteenth century to become new motives for confrontation between vying states. To some extent this was nothing new. In this century states also saw war from the twin viewpoint of threat and opportunity. On the one hand there was the threat to its sovereignty, to a beneficial *status quo*, to its political or economic advantages, etc. On the other, there was the opportunity to inflate these domains and advantages, stealing a march on other states. All this meant, as already said, that monarchs needed to reinforce their power and thereby take measures to ensure military action was possible and effective. It all meant the necessity to be successful in achieving sound political, bureaucratic-administrative, military and economic organisations. The way states managed to do so and the results thereof had been a matter of different historiographical approaches and academic debates. Let us now look to some of the topics lying under the general subject of the book.

2.1 Absolutism vs. parliamentarism

A unique political novelty came in the long eighteenth century, unparalleled in early modern times. This was the development of a monarchist state with a parliamentary regime that had been born at the end of the previous century. British parliamentarism was not simply a prolongation of medieval parliamentarism, because the king also had more power than before. The British regime was not like the republican structure where assemblies had decision-taking power, firstly because it was not a republic and secondly because the most prominent eighteenth-century republic, the United Provinces, had a slightly different system. While the Provinces were united they were not unified from the viewpoint of the state's administrative structure. The situation of the nascent United States would be similar during the regime of the Confederation.

British eighteenth-century parliamentarism, therefore, is an original regime, not tried out hitherto by the great European states. Nonetheless, this new system would become by the end of the cycle, in 1815, the overall winner, after having demonstrated a clear economic and military superiority and an enviable capacity for racking up sky-high *per capita* taxation levels without thereby crippling the country.

Quite the contrary, in fact, as Vries pointed out: "notwithstanding this very high level of taxes and public debt [Britain] was to become the first industrial nation" (Vries 2012: 6). Although these achievements involved considerable hardships, criticised internally at the time and still highlighted today, from the comparative point of view Britain's advantage was clear in all aspects.

Since the only centralised monarchic and parliamentarian state, the British, came out on top of absolutist powers in the long eighteenth century, the question about the reasons for this superiority seems to answer itself: it was the parliamentarian regime that enabled the country to win out in the end. This throws up the parliamentarianism/absolutism dichotomy as two political regimes that are appreciably different, with the clear deduction of the advantage of the former over the latter. Parliamentarism would turn out to be the modern option, whereas absolutism was inefficient and obsolete.

These claims might be true by the end of the process. Above all they tally with nineteenth-century events. Things were rather more complicated in the eighteenth century, however, when the battle had not yet been decided. The dominant historical view for a long time was the Whig theory, which identified absolutism with military power, the prime examples being Prussia, Russia and France. Absolutist monarchs, on this view, would find it easy to recruit soldiers and deploy them on the battlefield on the strength of an equally untrammelled capacity of imposing taxes on their subjects through a well-organised bureaucracy. In comparison with those monarchs, the British regime had a leaner administrative structure, smaller armies, kept together only during times of war, and a taxation trawl limited by the influence of an expenditure-controlling parliament.

This "small state" image, in all likelihood beneficial to British subjects, does not marry, however, with the historical outcome of the small state's century-long dominance and final victory, even though it ostensibly had fewer soldiers and lower taxes. How could this be? Well it wasn't so, quite simply. It has now been known for some time that the British state was not really so gentle with its taxpayers (Mitchell and Deane 1962; Merino Navarro 1981b: 18), although this insight did not at first change the received view. It would not be until 1989 when Brewer's book finally overthrew the "small-state" idea of eighteenth-century Britain (Ertman 1999: 30). What comes out of Brewer's study and subsequent studies is a parliamentary state more in keeping with the real British situation, where there was indeed a parliament but also a strong administrative-bureaucratic structure and an equally resilient set of highly-taxed taxpayers. This tripartite structure of parliament, bureaucracy and hardy taxpayers would seem to be unique in Europe, and it was surely this that underpinned the British triumph rather than the parliamentary regime in itself.

Absolutism too has a different press nowadays after a long historical rethink, especially as from the nineties (Wilson 2000: 2). Far from wielding a total and arbitrary power, as has often been claimed, absolute monarchs were hemmed in by the privileges of various social groups and territories. The society of orders in fact had a constitution, whereupon the king was bound to respect the rights deriving from acquired privileges, which were written down in the various privilege-granting documents (cartularies, noble lineages, city charters, etc.). This gave rise to a varied situation in which each privilege holder fared differently vis-à-vis other privilege holders and royal power. Privilege means private law. The state composed of estates and corporate orders implied precisely a slew of private laws giving a different status to various individuals, groups and communities, all therefore impossible to bring together under one overarching law.

This diversity acted as a brake on royal power. To increase their power, i.e., their capacity of action in favour of the community or the whole realm, absolute monarchs tried to iron out all these difficulties, either by derogating what could be derogated or tapping into new social circumstances that fell within the scope of their royal power. It was impossible to overcome all these limitations to royal power, however, and they were still fairly evident by the end of the eighteenth century.

Waging war, for example, meant recruiting soldiers or sailors, collecting taxes to pay their wages, run the war in one way or another. It thus turns out that an absolute monarch, particularly those of Spain and France, the direct rivals of Great Britain, could not carry anyone off to the army only by their sovereign will. This possibility depended on what family they came from or where they had been born. In many cases political negotiation would be called for. Neither could the king impose any tax just as he wished. Even if representative assemblies were not working there were still privileges in force that forestalled certain payments from given persons or groups without the corresponding haggling. Neither did the king always have the power to replace any government official whose policies he might not like. Many of these officials, up to a certain government level, had bought their posts and it thence fell into the gift of the person concerned and his descendants. Much the same went for military posts. Acting in this political minefield was no easy matter, as many thwarted reform attempts found to their cost.

But the curious thing is that, from this viewpoint, neither did the British government have total freedom of action. There too privileges existed, and not very different from the abovementioned ones. In light of all, if both parliamentarism and absolutism suffered from problems of the same ilk, where did the difference reside? Brewer argued that constructing a fiscal-military state would have been easier for a parliamentarian regime due to its cementation on consensus- and cooperation-based negotiation. Parliamentarism, precisely, would have favoured dialogue and hence assignment to the king of more resources when needed, providing this redounded to the parliament-monitored benefit of the whole nation. This might be true, but as Henshall pointed out, it certainly cannot be applied across the board since France did not try to build up a fiscal-military state by absolutist means but rather by consent and cooperation. This may well have been because it had little choice to do otherwise. In Henshall's words these were "the only realistic options available" (Henshall 1992: 4). French rulers could undoubtedly have tried other methods but failed experiences taught them to seek more reasonable options. Witness the fact that, by 1788, the government of the time had no choice but to reconvene the Estates General (*états généraux*). This would not seem to tally with the received view of an all-powerful absolute government, rather a government incapable of enforcing its will. Nonetheless, thinkers and writers still blithely dubbed it as absolute, especially nineteenth-century historians.

The same occurred in Spain where reforms were slow going, not necessarily due to governmental indolence but rather the difficulty of overcoming vested interests created by old and new privileges. This situation affected the reign of Philip V but also of Charles III, often cited as the acme of absolute power in Spain. As Torres Sánchez has shown, Charles III ministers were hard put to raise warfare resources, falling between the two stools of seeking the consensus of certain social groups or devising administrative wiles to circumvent the need for this consensus. These wiles never came good, however; the money raised was never enough and never on time. The system suffered from an obvious lack of fleet-footedness and this served to show the limits of the monarch's supposedly absolute power (Torres Sánchez 2013a).

For all these reasons these factors of cooperation and consensus-seeking, as well as the interests that each group, non-governmental institution, city or territory might have in the war, were all crucial in the government's resource-mobilisation success. The ideas of coercion and centralisation (the latter to be understood in the modern sense of a real control over the levers of power), erstwhile so readily used by historians to define governments, especially absolute ones, do not hold up when considering the government's difficulties in raising warfare resources. In fact, all states, regardless of their political regime, were faced with similar problems of negotiation and cooperation and none resorted to coercion, at least among the major powers. Governments' capacities of action were always limited and all of them had to set up mechanisms to encourage citizen participation in warfare expenditure. It is quite possible, moreover, that the subjects governed by absolute monarchs were prepared to bow to their monarchs' pretensions in war time, when the defence of common interests was at stake, but they were much more loath to keep up this effort during peacetime or even refused to do so outright (Riley 1986: 69). But the fact is that peacetime money needs were just as high since past debts then needed to be paid off. Despite many claims to the contrary, absolute monarchs were in fact unable to force their subjects to pay up whether they liked it or not.

Parliament, as a privileged seat of negotiation, now comes across as less decisive than claimed hitherto. As we will see in more detail later, Great Britain shunned direct taxes in the eighteenth century because this would have entailed political negotiation with the persons and groups affected, and the government tried to avoid this. Neither would parliament's control of expenditure seem to be a key factor. If by "control" we mean forcing the government to spend less, it has to be pointed out firstly that Great Britain spent much more than its rivals on war in general, so representatives did not seem to be too bothered about cutting costs. These questions did raise their heads in France and Spain, however, simply because their governments did not always have the necessary money. There are also some doubts about the actual effectiveness of parliament's expenditure control, which would seem to have been more a matter of political routine than anything else, with a greater concern shown for avoiding fraud than reckoning war funds (Conway 2007: 53).

But there still remains the question of why the British parliament allowed the country's rulers to spend much more on war, while absolute governments, without such opposition, did not dare to do so, or simply couldn't. The answer may lie precisely in the very existence of the parliament. The parliamentary system seems to have guaranteed an identity of interests between the government and the assembly of representatives, who in turn were representatives of economic power. If all were in agreement about the need for the war in question, this would be waged, whatever it cost. The absolute monarch, always with one eye on his subjects but without ever being able to consult their opinion, was wary of injuring them with wars that, at least in Europe, could only really be justified on dynastic grounds.

Merchants' interest in war was variable. In the British case, merchants benefited from each small chunk of Spanish colonial territory won by warfare, increasing their trading scope. Even more so whenever victory brought said territory under their control. Spanish merchants, on the other hand, lost little if this small territory fell into British hands. Spanish merchants were worried only if colonies in general were lost or the fleet system was cut off. The reason for these different attitudes is clear: British merchants always tried to trade on their own account, territory permitting, and were therefore interested in any conflict that opened new doors. Spanish merchants, on the other hand, were hidebound by a rigidly regulated regime, under which any small territorial losses or gains did not directly affect their business. In principle, therefore, they were not keen to finance war. The word "merchant" here is being used to refer to a wide swathe of the social elite, including nobles also involved in international trade. The English elite, in short, was prepared to finance war because they found a direct benefit in doing so; this was not the case of the Spanish elite and, in many cases, neither of the French.

One of the keys to British efficiency thus lay in the way of organising colonial trade rather than the parliament itself. It should be remembered here that free trade with the colonies had been practised in England since the beginning of the sixteenth century among British subjects, well before any parliamentary revolution. These attitudes were retained later. British policy might be subject to changes in parliamentary majorities, but however this majority might turn out they would all have similar interests. Land interests have traditionally been separated off from moneyed interests, but although both camps might seem different as such, they were often personified in the same individual and therefore merged together. Members of parliament in particular, including those who could be properly classed as landowners, were also keen to invest in trade. Whig predominance during most of the century, moreover, meant that the parliament was largely attracted to mercantile interests. This not only favoured trade-defending war but also debt financing thereof, since MPs were representatives of the same group of merchants and financiers who invested in this debt (Stasavage 2003).

This matter of the parliamentarians' real interests turned out to be crucial not only for trade but also for another question that has been brought out by Ertman (Ertman 1999), referring to the nature of the representation. In Great Britain the parliament was made up by members who did not directly represent the interests of the three estates (clergy, nobility, commoners), typical of many continental countries, in particular Spain and France, but rather, at least in the lower house, local and community interests that tended to look out for the real problems affecting them. The parliamentary representatives, therefore, did not represent only a privileged elite out to defend its estates-based privileges but rather a varied clutch of local interests. Moreover, given that the government was presided over in the parliamentary regime by the head of the majority party, there was more likely to be common interests between the government and parliament. One possible conclusion is that the parliament tended to create a certain identity of interests between, on the one hand, local interests and problems and, on the other, the representative assembly and the government. This did not occur in continental regimes, where representational entitlement was bound up more strictly with membership of one of the privileged estates, whose interests, moreover, were usually far removed from the mercantile world. From these points of view, the existence of the parliament and its representational structure did endow British policies with more efficiency than absolute powers lacking this structure. This, however, was due more to the parliament's representative structure than its presence per se. It would follow from this that a greater weight of representative assemblies in Spain or France would not have changed things much unless the representational structure was tweaked too (cf. Ertman 1999).

2.2 The eighteenth-century military revolution

With the advent of the eighteenth century, as we have already seen, the states were much more developed than hitherto and had hence changed character completely. This is reflected in war: in the way of waging it, the means employed, the reasons and motives behind it. It was not only battle tactics and weapons that had evolved; significant changes had also occurred in the number of soldiers involved, the duration of the conflicts, the enlargement of battle fronts over which the war had to be fought. Up to the seventeenth century, the Spanish monarchy was just about the only power still waging war on several fronts at once, tussling on each front with a different enemy that only fought there. Eighteenth-century confrontations would be continental (in the centre and north of Europe simultaneously) and colonial at the same time. The Low Countries, the north of Italy, the west of Germany, for example, are recurrent arenas in eighteenth-century wars involving France and Great Britain while both of them were also waging colonial confrontations in the Americas and India, in both cases on land and sea. Spain, in this century, avoided such widely diversified fronts and other states centred on their own spaces of interest. The key confrontation, therefore, is without doubt France and Great Britain. Long-term efficacy swung back and forth. It represented a supreme effort for both of them, also dragging in Spain in its desire to protect its empire from the British threat.

The engorgement of military needs and the attempt to meet them, with the concomitant increase of resources and investment, has been dubbed the "military revolution" of early modern Europe; it had in fact been some time brewing but it peaked in the eighteenth century. The term has come to stay despite the debate it has provoked. What exactly did this revolution consist of? Was it really a revolution? When did it happen? Thus broached, the question stems substantially from the work of Roberts (Roberts 1967), who appreciated substantial changes in war-waging methods from 1560 to 1660. Attention had already been drawn to the importance of the appearance of gunpowder and firearms, used in the second half of the fifteenth century, but this had not formerly been tagged as a "military revolution". Roberts did so, on the grounds above all of the use of the musket and the tactical switches this implied to achieve better battlefield efficiency. Parker later claimed that the changes had been greater, including arms, fortifications, artillery, number of soldiers, investments. He also opened up the period for the bulk of the change from 1530 to 1710. The same Parker, in a book published in 1988 and titled precisely *The Military Revolution*, set generic limits of 1500 and 1800 (Parker 1988). He thereby affirmed two things. Firstly, that military growth was already underway by the late-fifteenth-century advent of modern states, thus echoing the aforementioned traditional historical view. Secondly that this revolution did not end in the eighteenth century. Nonetheless, and despite the title, the actual contents of the book fit in with a different timeframe. It picks up some information from before 1500 whereas there is almost none after 1700, so the whole eighteenth century is left out of this description of the military revolution.

More light was shed on this matter by J. Black. In 1991 he resurrected the theme of the military revolution with a wider outlook and a different emphasis. Black argued that the eighteenth century should certainly be included in this revolution and it should not be written off, as sometimes hitherto, as an era with no substantial changes. Furthermore, within a wider timeframe, the key period would not be the sixteenth century nor the moments of the war of Flanders, as some previous authors had claimed, but rather the period 1660–1720, which is, according to Black, when the most important changes occurred. Of course growth continued thereafter until another period of significant changes occurred in the revolutionary wars as from 1793.

The period pointed out by Black as the most innovative includes replacement of the pike by the socket bayonet, the introduction of the flintlock rifle and the development of the pre-packaged cartridge. All this would boost the infantry's firepower and manoeuvrability; this entailed in turn a relative decline of the cavalry and the corresponding tactical changes (Black 1994: 7). As in the navy too, the crucial feature, more and more, was the increase in firepower, meaning more men, more arms, more ammunition. In the period identified by Black, armies grew substantially in the number of men and navies in the number of ships and size of the crews. In any case, as Duffy reminds us, the necessary effort behind this growth was not within the reach of every country, so the military revolution, especially in the long eighteenth century, widened the gap between the countries capable of defraying these costs and the smaller powers (Duffy 1980: 6–7). These differences had not been so glaring in earlier times.

Ongoing debate enhanced our knowledge of the wars of different periods and caused the initial thesis to be tweaked as new discoveries were made. But also reflected in this research were the historical interests of the writers involved in each case, whose knowledge centred on the periods they had most studied. Over time, as well as making us reflect on the importance of one or other innovation of a tactical or technical nature, of armaments or fortifications, etc., what this debate seems to show is that there was an evolution rather than revolution. All these authors would be right in a sense, at least partly, on condition that we rethink the idea of revolution here. The change in fact had been so longwinded as to suggest the idea of transition rather than revolution (Black 1991). These differences in nomenclature have been written off as semantic but they are also substantial (Gat 2006: 763). Terminological nuances such as these help us to understand that there were times when the process sped up, others when it slowed down (Rogers 1995). It then becomes difficult to pinpoint the actual moment of a decisive change; innovations pile up and overlap; in moments of peace they fall back. For the same reason the timeframe also has to be reanalysed: this process must have kicked off well before 1500 and dragged on at least until the Revolutionary Wars or later.

To put it another way, it is difficult to claim there was a military revolution between 1550 and 1660, any more than between, say, 1500 and 1550 or 1660 and 1720, just because changes were not so substantial in the latter two periods. If we look at the long term, however, there is certainly a steep change of level from 1400 to 1800. We can also safely say the military revolution occurred differently in each country. Some started early but then fell into decline (Spain, declining in the second half of the seventeenth century, Holland, in the last third of this century and then in the second half of the eighteenth), while others, like Prussia, started very late, not until the mid-eighteenth. Yet again the growth is long term and does not occur the same or within the same timescale in all countries.

Figure 2.1 shows the number of soldiers, measured in thousands, for Spain, France and Prussia. It is obviously difficult to come up with comprehensive and completely trustworthy figures here. Consideration also has to be given to the fact that some of these were soldiers on call and others soldiers on the ground. There were also glaring differences between peacetime and wartime. Small wonder that historians often differ in their calculations. But they nonetheless serve as ballpark figures giving us some idea of the situation at that time.

Allowing for all the above observations and caveats, Figure 2.1 shows a clear increase in the number of soldiers as from the end of the fifteenth century, sharp in Spain, later in France and, of course, much later in Prussia. In France, the most complete series, the peaks came between the Nine Years' War and the War of the Spanish Succession. Some specialists write off this peak of almost 400,000 soldiers as an overstatement (Black 1991: 29); it was certainly never replicated in the future. On the other hand, these figures are not much higher than Spain's end-of-sixteenth century figures. If we look at these figures from the viewpoint of the number of soldiers available, one of the most striking series, especially if we flatten out the French peak a bit, we then find that timeframes can be chosen to suit the author's viewpoint. But there is no doubt about the general growth trend throughout the period, with appreciable figures by as far back as the mid-sixteenth century.

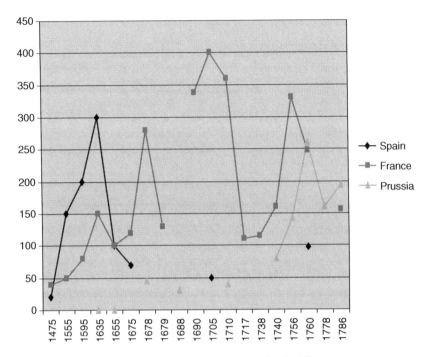

Figure 2.1 Size of some European armies in thousands of soldiers
Source: Black 1991: 6–7.

Some reference to the military-revolution debate was *de rigueur* in our case to see how, in effect, military needs had been growing for some time and that the future called for an even steeper growth rate, if anything. This begs a second question: how much was the increase in military expenditure (including the navy) and in what setting did this increase occur? Here too the debate swung from one side to another. Attention focused at first on the fact that tactical and armament changes called for a growth in infantry. This seems to hold true if applied to the final years of the sixteenth century and the first years of the seventeenth; but then we see that the cavalry also ended up growing, though of course this was no longer the feudal cavalry, which had by now dropped out of the picture completely. Historians then centred on the expenditure increase triggered by firearms, fortifications and ships. Although all these factors called for new inputs, it has been calculated that none of them accounted for a high percentage of the growth of general expenses (Gat 2006: 459).

It would seem to follow from this that the aforementioned outlays were not the main cause of the military revolution. What seems to come out most clearly is that the main cost of war was soldiers' wages and maintenance. As Brewer points out with regard to the navy, one year of ship-of-the-line maintenance cost as much as building it (Brewer 1989: 34), even though ships-of-the-line were one of the biggest outlays. Its annual construction cost would therefore have to include a pro rata calculation of the maintenance cost during its years of service. Much the same could be said of fortifications, arms and other more or less durable resources. The annual cost of personnel, on the other hand, was always the same. Soldiers and sailors making up garrisons and crews ate and spent every day and their wages had to be paid and maintenance defrayed without delay.

Given that the power struggle between Great Britain, Spain and France would be fought out above all at sea, it might be telling to find out whether the "military revolution" was specifically a "naval revolution" and, if so, to what extent.

Table 2.1 shows that the situations differed greatly from country to country. Great Britain and France kicked off with high values at the end of the seventeenth century and both showed smaller figures by the mid-eighteenth century. Great Britain, however, had grown more, albeit with ups and downs, recovering the high levels of 1689 by 1779. France's ship numbers, on the other hand, despite the odd upturn, had halved by 1779. Spain started out with meagre figures in about 1680, totalling about 20 vessels (Merino Navarro 1986), which would have dropped even lower during the War of Succession; it then clocked up sustained growth up to 1790. It therefore outstrips its rivals in terms of percentage growth rates.

What we see here, in any case, is that navies chalked up a higher growth in unit numbers than the army from 1689 to 1789. Great Britain's army recorded similar personnel figures in both dates (70,000 soldiers in 1689 and 100,000 a century later) (Kennedy 1989: 140; Black 1991: 6–7). Although numbers had grown during the Seven Years' War, they fell back afterwards, whereas the navy returned to positive growth before 1790 almost doubling the figure of one century earlier. France's army figures fell during the eighteenth century, with a possible exception too during the Seven Years' War, even if we bring down the 1689 peak. At any rate the navy fell too during the times of La Hogue. Spain's navy, during most of the century, outstripped the army in comparative terms, despite starting from a lower base. Nonetheless, even though the number of ships might grow more than the

Table 2.1 Absolute growth in ship numbers and indexed percentage changes (base 100 = 1689, for each country column)

	England		France		Spain	
1689	100	100	120	100	20	100
1739	124	124	50	41	34	170
1756	105	105	70	58		
1779	90	90	63	52	48	240
1790	195	195	81	67	72	360
1815	214	214	80	66	25	125

Source: Kennedy 1989:141. Spain's 1689 figure in Merino 1986.

number of men in percentage terms, all three countries spent more money on their armies than their navies, including the British (Brewer 1989: 30; O'Brien and Duran 2010: 360). As from the Revolutionary Wars the increase in soldiers was much greater, while navy figures fell in France and above all in Spain.

2.3 The increasing war cost

At the end of day, for whatever reason, whatever the money may have been spent on, armed-forces expenditure was growing. And this is the crux of the matter for now. Waging war cost money, and this cost was rising. This problem had been worsening since the sixteenth century, especially if wars followed on from each other almost without a break, a predicament suffered by Charles V and Philip II. Charles V, for example, negotiated loans for an average yearly value of 400,000 ducats from 1520 to 1532 (Carande 2004). From 1555 to 1556 the average was 2 million a year (Parker 1988: 93). In particular, if the 1547–48 Schmalkaldic War, for example, cost Spain 2 million florins a year, this cost had already doubled by the fifties. In the nineties of the sixteenth century the cost of war in the Low Countries was 9 million florins a year.

Even back in 1630 experts in all countries were saying that the cost of war had increased fivefold since the last century. From 1618 to 1648, according to the calculations of Alberto Marcos, who corrected Parker's figures upwards, Spain spent an average of 3.6 million escudos in Flanders alone (Marcos Martín 2001). Small wonder then that the 2 million escudos spent by Spain on the Messina Revolt from 1674 to 1678 were prudently classified by Ribot as "a not very high sum" (Ribot García 2002: 338), but this was an era of falling military expenditure for Spain and a war it could not fight more vigorously precisely due to a dearth of money.

The increasing costs certainly bore some relationship with the phenomena known as the military revolution (bigger armies, forts and heavier artillery, etc.) but also with the fact that wars tended to be longer, partly due to city sieges (increasing the absolute cost but also the relative cost because more resources had to be mustered for keeping the army longer in the field). The development of heavy artillery used in city sieges forced all combatants to build doughty fortresses, misnamed "Fortifications of Vauban" because they in fact predated the French border forts of the second half of the seventeenth century and were already normal features of the Italian fifteenth-century wars and in the Low Countries in the seventeenth century ('t Hart 2014: 65); whatever their name, these forts also tended to swell war costs.

Longer, more expensive wars inflated the military, political and economic cost. In 1595 Bernardino de Mendoza wrote that "the triumph will be of he who has the last escudo" (Parker 1988: 92). Charles Davenant echoed the same idea 100 years later in 1695: "the whole Art of War is in a manner reduced to Money". And he went on claim that "nowadays that prince who can best find money to feed, clothe, and pay his army, not he that hath the most valiant troops, is surest to success and conquest" (Cobban 1969: 181). In this quote Davenant is also checking the most expensive expenditure items: food, pay and clothes. Curiously enough, this also chimes in with our previous comment that ships, forts and cannons were not the main day-to-day concern of those who had to defray army costs; the really worrying thing was the daily payment on fungibles.

The idea that war cost money was not much discussed in the eighteenth century, it was simply taken for granted. Generals were constantly asking for money for specific campaigns and also stressing the need of prompt and punctual payments. Costs remained high and the toll heavy right up to Waterloo in 1815. It was no coincidence that Great Britain was said to have won because its financial clout enabled it to endure longer. The crux, in any case, is finding out how much each war cost. This is in truth nearly impossible to calculate, although this did not stop many from trying, each according to his own criteria.

The War of the Spanish Succession apparently cost Philip V over 62 million escudos from Spain's coffers (4.1 million per year of war), without counting French input, when it was forthcoming. The brief Spanish foray into Portugal upon the outbreak of the Seven Years' War, involving the mobilisation of 40,000 soldiers over an 11-month period, cost over 7.5 million escudos (González Enciso 2006a: 187). Army expenditure during Charles III's reign rose from 14.7 million escudos in 1760 to 21.6 in 1788, peaking at 26 million in 1782 (Barbier and Klein 1985: 493). Throughout this whole period consideration must also naturally be given to changes in spending power and inflation, which made its presence felt by the eighties. What these figures do make clear is that Charles III spent much more than Charles I and even than Philip IV during the acme of imperial defence.

We do have some more complete eighteenth-century data for Great Britain and France. War costs are always difficult to calculate but we do have some figures to guide us. Table 2.2 shows, on the one hand, total British costs. Given that war years have been chosen (the years of the table show the end of war periods) and that military expenditure, as we know, represented a very high percentage of total costs, the figures may be more indicative of the trend than the actual cost. In the case of France, the table shows the supposed cost of the three wars ending on the indicated dates.

Table 2.2 Wartime expenditure and costs of the war in Great Britain and France (millions of pounds sterling and millions of *livres tournais* respectively)

	Great Britain		France	
1689	49			
1713	93			
1748	95	100	918	100
1763	160		1150	
1783	236	248	1700	185
1815	1657			

Source: Great Britain, Dickson 1967: 10; France, Félix 1999: 34–79.

What springs to the eye here is the much higher war cost in Great Britain than in France. By 1783 the British index had multiplied 2.4 on 1748 and France's by only 1.8. Absolute figures, of course, were also much higher in Great Britain, bearing in mind the *livre tournais*-sterling exchange rate of about 23 livres to the pound (Bonney 2004: 195). In short, the military revolution did bear a relation to increasing armed-forces expenditure; in this aspect too Great Britain forged ahead and was able to spend substantially more than its rivals.

Why did costs grow? Or what comes to the same thing, what is the biggest reason for this increase? I am not referring here so much to specific expenditure items but rather the political decision that lay behind this race of arms, conflicts and expenditure. Any answer here has to be based on increasing needs; that said, where did these needs come from? Why did monarchs feel their military needs had to grow? Foreign policy reflects, time and time again, the ambitions, well-grounded or otherwise, not only of the rulers themselves but also the elites they had to work with in each case, whether aristocratic or mercantile. Behind this ambition lay also the reputation, of both dynasty and the state itself. *Raison d'état* always rears its head in the end, in all likelihood cloaking motives of power and greed (Scott 2006: 141–42).

Arguments brandished, however, were more benign, tailored for public consumption and therefore more likely to be approved. They centred on security of the realm, which in fact cloaked the fear of a destroying enemy. Charles III of Spain, for example, tried to mediate between France and Great Britain in the Seven Years' War while still King of Naples. His efforts came to naught. When he arrived in Spain at the end of 1759 Great Britain had just accomplished its *Annus mirabilis*. The likely situation, he argued, was a serious threat to the Spanish empire. But was this true? Did Great Britain really intend to repeat the attempt of 1741? We don't know. Spain's overhasty entry into the war forced British hands. But Charles III's easy option was to intimidate his subjects and bend them to his will by vaunting the British threat to the Spanish empire. Historians have tended to write off this empire-defending motive as spurious. They centre rather on Charles's rankling resentment of the British ever since an incident 17 years earlier. In 1742 the royal navy squadron commander William Martin had threatened to bombard the city of Naples unless Neapolitan troops fighting in the north of Italy withdrew their support for Spain, giving Charles just half an hour to answer (Rodger 2004: 240). This humiliation to the young king of Naples bit deep. The festering sore of this memory might well have magnified in the Spanish king's mind the threat of the British at this later juncture. Above all, the monarch failed to weigh up Spain's real possibilities at that moment. Spain's entrance in the Seven Years' War was hasty and ended in disaster. It also triggered an all-out confrontation with Great Britain when it had been merely simmering on the back boiler for quite some time.

Whatever the real reasons behind the conflict, once immersed in a serious political power struggle, the countries had to vie against each other in mobilising the biggest possible armed forces. It was supposed that war at that time was still won by amassing more battlefield wherewithal, although we now know that this was not always so. It was still thought too that a big army could be not only an active threat but also a powerful deterrent. In either case, whether actual battlefield prowess or a show of force, it was necessary to flaunt more military power than the adversary. All this formed part of the rulers' "needs". But it also called for a hefty outlay, judiciously spent on the most necessary items. The problem is that these needs were limitless, residing as they did in the ruler's imagination and hunches, whereas the resources to hand were certainly not unlimited. This is why the country that managed to muster most resources would inevitably win in the long term.

This was achieved by striking the right balance between passion and reason. Ferdinand VI's government showed great powers of rational discretion by doggedly remaining neutral for long enough to ensure Spain's economic and military reinforcement. Neutrality, it has been argued, is a luxury (Duffy 1980: 6), this government, in that case, was shrewd enough to allow itself this luxury for strategic purposes. Charles III, on the other hand, was driven much more by passion than reason in 1762, entering the war tardily and badly. What he failed to take into account, among other things, was that resources built up in the previous reign were not enough, at least at this moment, for waging war against an adversary with well-trained troops perfectly honed for the purpose in hand. If Charles III, throughout his whole reign, was capable only of establishing a fiscal-military state as yet little developed (Torres Sánchez 2013a: 419), the situation would have been more premature in 1762 when even the timid reforms of recent years had been shelved. Time for maturity of its system and training of its troops would be needed to ensure battlefield triumph.

From this point of view, the importance of the military revolution, for our purposes here, does not reside so much in monitoring the change of tactics and the increase in the number of soldiers. All this might have happened without great consequences, as had in fact occurred in earlier eras. It turns out to be a necessary but not sufficient condition, serving as some explanation for overall changes in military might but failing to account for continual changes of power without any underlying modernisation or qualitative change in the way of organising states and empires beforehand. This was in fact what happened during millennia, when war-driven political and social change was insubstantial and transformed the countries concerned very little if at all.

The characteristic trait of the early modern era, especially towards its end, the so-called long eighteenth century, is that it occurred at this moment – or rather gelled at this moment because it had been brewing for some time – because there was at this time a significant change not only in the way of waging war, as we are reminded by the theoreticians of the military revolution, but also in the way of governing the country, in social and economic structures and mindsets. And all this was done with war and through war. There is no military revolution unless it is accompanied by a political revolution and such a revolution is what we have come to call, generically, the early modern state. War called for resources; to achieve them the economy was transformed; this forced countries into a social change, which in turn implied a political change. New needs called for more money, but this thread in the picture was mixed up with a whole host of other factors like the fiscal system, the social and political policy of modifying this system, taxpayer possibilities and acquiescence and, of course, the economic base underlying the generation of these resources. European states were increasingly capable of offering their rulers more warfare wherewithal, more people too, willing to change their way of living and being in society. Rulers also changed their modes of governance, at times not very wisely. As Gat reminds us, "it is chiefly on the supply side, Europe's overall resources and the states' ability to tap them, that one should concentrate" (Gat 2006: 471). What were states able to come up with for waging war? This is precisely what we will try to find out through a study of the fiscal-military state.

2.4 Fiscal-military states: the development of a methodological concept

All early modern states, as we have already seen, shared the same experience of defining a new space for political power. This definition turned out to be a source of confrontation, whereby political power led almost inevitably to war. War could only be fought successfully from a position of might. Crucially, however, an essential part of warfaring prowess depends not so much on military factors but rather economic factors: it is the might of money. In any circumstances, and regardless of the triggering motive, war cost money. Human and material battlefield resources came at a price, and a soaring price to boot, at least in nominal terms. If we consider, on the one hand, that war was one of the main occupations and the prime area of competence of early modern states, then it is clear that raising money for war became one of their main concerns. Where could this money be got from? How could it be obtained without rocking the political, constitutional or economic boat? It would follow clearly from the above questions that war was not solely a military activity but also political (interior politics) and economic; it could also be called a constitutional question due to the need of seeking consensus. Its causes, the way of waging it and its aftermath have as many constitutional and economic aspects as strictly military factors.

It is from these mixed problems that the concept of the fiscal-military state arises. The concept as such was coined by J. Brewer, who argued that, as from the Glorious Revolution and throughout the whole eighteenth century, the English – and then the British – state went through an amazing transformation of the following characteristics: the body politic was strengthened and its scope was increased; Great Britain was capable of withstanding an increasingly heavy load of military commitments; this was possible thanks to swinging tax hikes, the development of public debt on an unprecedented scale and a significant growth in administrative structures for organising the state's military and fiscal activities. The upshot was that the state "cut a substantial figure" and became the most important agent of the whole economy (Brewer 1989: xvii).

The concept soon caught on and Brewer's work had a widespread influence. The importance of this approach lay not so much in stressing the relation between war and public finances, or even between public finances and the state, questions that had been dealt with by earlier historians (Bonney 1995a), but rather in having merged the three questions and then tagging on the importance of the economy supporting this whole edifice. It should also be pointed out, as Storrs has noted, that "Brewer's identification of the fiscal-military state addressed the experience of a specific eighteenth-century state and an equally specific interpretation of its success" (Storrs 2009: 3). This therefore ring-fenced a pretty strict timeframe. What then comes across is a new vision of the state, "exceptionally active", which did not tally, as Brewer himself pointed out, with the traditional liberal interpretation. It has therefore been argued that Brewer's book finally put paid to "the tenaciously held belief that late Stuart and Hanoverian England possessed a numerically small, non-bureaucratic and pacific state apparatus" (Ertman 1999: 30).

But we are not going to get involved here in this discussion of whether the state was "small" (as applied by the liberal tradition to Great Britain) or "big" (which would correspond with the continental absolutist model, according to the same traditional historical view), a discussion that Brewer also referred to and largely modified (Stone 1994: 1–21). What interests us here, rather, is the use of the term "fiscal-military state" as a methodological concept, i.e., as an interpretative guide of the fiscal and political-administrative situation at the time. Our specific interest is to gauge how far the concept can be applied to eighteenth-century Spain and make the pertinent comparisons with Great Britain and France, on the assumption that the concept can also be applied to the latter country. We would argue that historiographic concepts coined to explain specific historical problems of a country in particular are effective if we can convert them into methodological concepts applicable to all countries, to facilitate a comparison between them. It sounds simple, but in fact this is no easy matter.

Historiographic concepts always run into problems when their use becomes more widespread (Torres Sánchez 2007: 14). *Habent sua fata...concepti*, we could say, paraphrasing the Latin expression about books and their fate. What use do we make of concepts, we might well ask? The main principal, in most cases, is that historiographic concepts tend to end up being used in a merely descriptive way. Thus, in the case in hand, a fiscal-military state has come to be seen almost solely as the state that hikes its taxes and spends the resulting revenue exclusively on war. In many of today's studies the mere existence of some relation between the taxation system and warfare suffices for this state to be classed as fiscal-military. The concept has hence been spread so thin that it has lost much of its original substance and is now blithely applied to what would previously have been called simply fiscal states. On many occasions, therefore, the study boils down to a more or less detailed examination of the taxation system while the concept's many other component factors, including military action itself (Storrs 2009: 5–7), are ignored. Of course there are also many thoroughgoing studies that look seriously into the nature of the concept and its real implications (Torres Sánchez 2007; Storrs 2009).

The growing fuzziness of this concept can be gauged from the fact that some authors now see the term as a "prevailing paradigm" whereas others call for a more precise definition of the term (Davies 2012). We might well ask ourselves how a concept could become "prevailing" without having been first well defined.

Dunning adds, for his part, that "a comprehensive definition of fiscal-military state is still in the process of formation" (Dunning 2014: 191, 192), although he then describes the concept with a phrase that might well be taken as a definition: "the acceleration of expenditures, coercive taxation, and the build–up of powerful bureaucracy, logistical infrastructure, and military forces in light of the gunpowder revolution". We would argue, however, that the definition given by Brewer is clear and no more detail is needed when speaking in general; what is needed, however, is greater precision in particular cases, both to calibrate the true scope of an ostensible fiscal-military state and to make the pertinent comparisons.

If our term implies giving a new sense to well-established concepts, does this mean it overrides existing ones? The question arises from Hoppit's arguments in his review of Brewer's book. Hoppit stresses first of all the importance given by Brewer to excise, to its organisation, modus operandi and fruitfulness for the state. From this he then goes on to argue that after Brewer's book historians will have to rethink their explanations of eighteenth-century governments. Terms like "mercantilism" or "*ancien régime*", he claimed, "will not do any longer" (Hoppit 1990: 248–49). Along similar lines, though in less forthright terms, different authors have argued that the term *fiscal-military state* might well have to replace *absolutism* in studies of early modern Europe (Dunning and Smith 2006: 44). Torres Sánchez refers to the concept as "a handy and useful term" (2007: 21), making it eligible for replacing earlier terms.

Interesting here is the thesis of Henshall who, in explaining France and Great Britain's disparate ways of mobilising warfare resources, criticises both Brewer and the traditional concept of absolutism. Brewer's thesis, argues Henshall, implies that it was much easier to achieve a fiscal-military state under a parliamentary system than an absolutist system. This might not be true, in Henshall's opinion, because France in fact did not try to create a fiscal-military state by absolutist means; it used the same methods as Great Britain, namely consent and cooperation, which was in fact the only way of going about it (Henshall 1992: 4). Although he also criticises Brewer's conclusions on other counts too, this argument does point to another way forward: Brewer showed that Great Britain was not a small state, like continental powers; Henshell, following his arguments, criticised the absolutist facet but brought out other more positive aspects. We may be homing in on the truth, i.e., the idea that has come to be called "shared mercantilism" (Torres Sánchez 2013b: 178); this goes hand in hand with the concomitant notion that supposedly absolutist powers were in fact hemmed in by far more limitations than had hitherto been supposed (Swann 2003: 295).

I would argue that concepts applied to one area of historical reality are unlikely to replace concepts applied to other areas. Absolutism, mercantilism and fiscal-military state are interrelated terms, without doubt, but they do not refer to the same thing and neither can they be applied alike to different countries. Pre-1689 England, for example, can realistically be analysed from an absolutism viewpoint and as a fiscal-military state after this date, given that absolutism technically disappeared with the Glorious Revolution. This same argument, however, would not hold true for continental countries, barring Holland. When referring to state formation in England, Braddick enumerates the possible different types of state development between 1500 and 1700. He judges that "the essential point is not… the usefulness of…particular terms (patriarchal, fiscal-military, confessional and dynastic), but a *methodological claim* about how to analyse the development of the state" (Braddick 2000: 431[my italics]). In other words, there are various ways of analysing the state, just as there are different ways of analysing the economy.

A concept is a handy instrument for scrutinising a given historical situation but the questions will always be made from a particular analytical viewpoint. The analytical viewpoint of the fiscal-military state might well give us new insights for interpreting absolutism, downplaying the kings' ostensible authoritarianism in light of their proven difficulties in raising their tax revenue, for example. Improving an analytical approach, however, does not necessarily mean replacing it, among other reasons because the concepts already coined, and now with a long historical track record, include other aspects that are not taken in by the new concepts. For example, an analysis from the perspective of the fiscal-military state does not take into account absolutist political thought; neither does it refer to the social change that absolutism implies, etc. The truth is that the concepts that Hoppit assumed would die out are in fact still being used because they take in specific aspects.

In any case the concept of the fiscal-military state, as a methodological approach, offers the possibility of relating questions that had not been directly related hitherto, thus shedding new light on the practice of absolutism or on some aspects of mercantilism that had been largely overlooked beforehand, such as the production of arms and their markets, or the important business activities – finance, trade, transportation – behind army and navy supplies.

It should also be pointed out here that, although the term had been very well defined by Brewer, it is no less true that this definition is highly dependent on the English case described by the author (Torres Sánchez 2007: 15; Storrs 2009: 1–2; Dunning 2014: 191). This is a common problem when historiographic concepts are dragged out of their original comfort zone, such as the specific case in question here: how far can a given concept be applied to other cases, different in time and space and also existing in different environments? This problem has constantly been broached by historians. Sometimes they have come up with pretty odd solutions. A classic case, albeit far removed from our own, is the Renaissance. When this concept was developed it was applied to mid-fifteenth-century Italy. Comparisons soon showed that other situations were different, so the conclusion drawn was that only fifteenth-century Italy had a Renaissance, with merely feeble copycat attempts elsewhere.

Much the same goes for the English industrial revolution. Some even argued that wherever the selfsame British conditions were not replicated there was no real revolution and not even any industry, merely a "pre-industrial" situation that nobody ever defined more nicely or even explained more precisely. Even the very existence of industry came in for its own controversy. The term "proto-industry" saved the situation somewhat, since it claimed to call attention to the specific circumstances of industrial development. The question now was not only to ascertain whether the mechanical transformation had occurred, but also to analyse some pertinent aspects of industrial development of the early modern era such as its organisation, product quality, exportation capacity, the presence of commercial capital, etc. (Mendels 1972). What then emerged was a different picture of industrial regions of greater or lesser importance in their time and with a greater or lesser capacity of carrying out a transformation to modern mechanised industry (Ogilvie 1996). This helped to place each case in its context and make realistic comparisons.

All this, however, brought up another problem: generalisation. If the use of methodological concepts exclusively for a single case tended to die out, it is no less true that there was a parallel tendency to generalise these concepts without proper consideration of the questions they enshrined. Any description of pre-1800 industry thus came to be called "proto-industrialisation", with the result that the former term "pre-industrial" had merely between switched to the in-vogue "proto-industry", and the content of these concepts had been ditched. Eschewing the exclusivity of any term is to some extent a good thing but only if proper attention is paid to the intrinsic differences of each case; only then can the use of said term be really insightful. In the case of the industrial revolution this became pretty clear when everyone recognised that England led the way and others followed on. Telltale terms like "latecomers" or "closing the gap" cropped up and it then became said that the revolution came to a given country in one specific era or another.

The term we are dealing with here, *fiscal-military state*, is now undergoing the same fate as the aforementioned terms when they became generalised without due distinction of the differences. As in the case of the term "proto-industry", overuse can lead to some exaggerations and facile description. At these moments all eighteenth-century states are classed as fiscal-military states because war drove taxes higher in all of them. This certainly occurred, but are they really all fiscal-military states? C. Storrs has forthrightly claimed that "not all the states of eighteenth-century Europe were fiscal-military states" (Storrs 2009: 11), although the "leading powers" were. This then begs the question of which were the "leading powers". But it is quite obvious in any case that the fiscal-military state concept cannot just be generalised across the board on a one-size-fits-all basis.

The need for a judicious, properly considered use of this concept comes out clearly in an important study of Torres Sánchez about the reign of Charles III of Spain. The author concludes that Charles III's Spain was indeed a fiscal-military state, "but still little developed" (Torres Sánchez 2013a: 419). As I have already pointed out elsewhere, Spain was a fiscal-military state in the long eighteenth century only up to a certain point. I argued that eighteenth-century Spain was not capable of developing its whole potential to meet its defence needs, but neither is it clear that it really wanted to, at least not in all moments of the century (González Enciso 2009a).

If we are to make meaningful comparisons, if some states might be fiscal-military and others are not, or if some are only so to a certain degree, then it seems to be clear that we need some sort of yardstick against which to bring out the relative differences. Implicitly we are using the English case defined by Brewer. But if we stick to it 100 per cent we will certainly run into problems, not because England is different but because the other cases are. The question of British "exceptionalism" is not simply that Great Britain was different but how it was different (Prados de la Escosura 2004). None of the characteristics defining possible British exceptionalism are in themselves exclusive of this country; all other countries have their own. We therefore need to look at these "exceptionalities", or rather the particular characteristics of the fiscal, economic structure, etc., of each country, accounting as a whole for its particular capacity of solving its problems by dint of its taxation system. On the one hand, all countries hold characteristics in common and this is what makes comparison possible, but the countries are also different, so we also need to pinpoint specific characteristics. It is within this dichotomy of similarity and difference that comparative concepts have to be handled, without necessarily hallowing some cases or scorning others.

In the case of the fiscal-military state the important thing, I would argue, is the concept's capacity for bringing out the multiple relationship between war, finances, the economy and institutional change; i.e., a) that military needs goaded the taxation system into producing more revenue; b) that this was done according to the objectives set in each case, and according to institutional patterns and the ruling economic force, and c) that despite the set patterns, institutional and fiscal changes had to be brought in. All countries had military needs and all countries hiked taxes or boosted their financial resources. But questions that might be asked here are which economic resources were turned to, which taxes were raised and why, by how much and for how long, which institutional channel was used. We also need to look at the impact on economic life to see whether current incomes could field these tax hikes or whether the country needed to run up a debt and, if so, how much, what kind of debt, involving which type of loans and how resources were raised to pay off this debt and when, if this was actually done, etc., etc.

We also need to find out whether or not this activity brought in institutional changes that forced new changes as a knock-on effect. We will then see that the problems are similar but the way of solving them depended on the particular situation, resources and traditions in each case. Countries that brought in the innovations and changes more quickly and efficiently gained a competitive edge over the rest. As O'Brien pointed out (2006a), in a mercantilist era the winner was the country that best applied mercantilism. But due consideration also has to be given to why these changes were made. The best performer here seems to have been Great Britain, but we also need to take into account that it started from a new-broom situation in 1689 and this enabled it to tackle some expenditure that was comparatively more costly for other countries at that time. It also boasted a mercantile tradition that had not arisen solely by dint of its skills but also due to the need to survive in a world that had previously been dominated, according to the particular part in question, by Spain or Holland.

Elliott argued that historic changes sometimes occur when the current situation is being defended, with serendipitous spinoff modifications that then turn out to be forward-looking advances (Elliott 1969). This is to some extent what happened to England in the early modern age. This explains why other countries did not follow suit at first, simply because no one was sure about which was the right road to go down. From this standpoint the English model should not be considered as conceptually "necessary", as often supposed, simply because other methods might well have won out at the time besides the one actually taken. In the political terrain the dominant system in seventeenth-century Europe was absolutism. The victory of parliamentarianism was inconceivable a century before it happened. In the economic terrain the great transformation arising from the industrial revolution was not only an English achievement. It was really the result of a long transformation process involving the whole of western Europe since the late middle age. Braudel has mapped it out as such: Venice, Bruges, Antwerp, London, New York (Braudel 1985: ch. III). Each country had its model, therefore; each chipped in at its given moment. Historians cannot expect anyone to follow at any given moment a model whose advantages only became known *a posteriori*; even less realistic is to expect the people of that time to have asked it of their rulers. Conceptual models should therefore remain as methodological models. They come in very handy as benchmarks to study particular historical circumstances but less so if used to classify or play down these circumstances.

All the above observations impinge on the concept of fiscal-military state, which refers fundamentally to the way states go about raising warfare resources. But there is also the other side of the coin, how the money, once raised, was spent. Here we could ask a series of similar questions about the expenditure, its object and mechanisms. All these analytical approaches fit within the concept of contractor state, a necessary corollary of the fiscal-military state, which until now had been largely overlooked in studies of mercantilism. Even the financial efforts were usually relegated to a technical study of the finances, as if this bore no relationship with the other economic problems. As we will see, use of the contractor-state concept will naturally lead to a more thoroughgoing assessment of figures like *asentistas*, contractors or *munitionaires*, for example, who doubled up as merchants and financiers, some even adding a revenue-farmer arrow to their bow. Curiosity about these aspects is a way of showing our realisation that these methodological concepts broach different questions and bring to light economic and social relations that would not otherwise have appeared.

New concepts, therefore, are relevant and necessary but do not override former concepts. Indeed, concepts like absolutism and mercantilism still live on and do not seem likely to disappear from historians' lexicon in the short term. The question is not whether a given term is better than another, in general terms, but rather ascertaining how it might be useful to us, in a more specific way. P. O'Brien has stressed the fact that despite the ongoing interest of philosophers, political scientists and historians in constitutional forms and modes of governance since the Enlightenment, such questions, he argues, "have never been clearly correlated with the security of kingdoms and republics from external aggression… functional fiscal systems, social welfare, property rights and other institutions conducive for economic growth" (O'Brien 2006b: 11). In other words, if we want to speak of the questions mentioned by O'Brien, the concept of the fiscal-military state, like that of the contractor state, becomes necessary. But not, I would argue, if we wish to speak of forms of government and political constitutions, including their theoretical aspects, which bear no direct relationship with warfare itself and other concomitant aspects like tactics and morale, etc. Then the concept of absolutism, for example, will still be valid, albeit restricted to certain questions and excluding others.

The usefulness of new concepts is that they act as signposts to new fields of study or aspects and connections between different phenomena that had hitherto gone largely unnoticed. They are new analytical approaches to try to capture more of a reality that always spills beyond historians' grasp. The truth is that all states, particularly in the early modern age, show different forms through which they might be analysed, all of them complementary and none exclusive. A good example is the quote of Braddick, who has explained England in the early modern era as a "patriarchal, fiscal-military, confessional and dynastic" state (Braddick 2000). According to this idea, each concept can help us to grasp different aspects of the social picture of England. If some concepts turn out to be more insightful than others this is often because more work has been done with them; the important point is that no methodological approach overrides another because each one responds to different circumstances throughout a given time period.

As always, a problem that lurks on the ambush here is anachronism. Precisely the term "absolutism", together with "centralism", has suffered from this ill. Twentieth-century historians have all too often tended to look back on the past with present-day hindsight: well-nigh perfectly centralised national states and the totalitarian trend as opposed to the freedom of democracies. Democracies too, on this view, would triumph on the strength of powerful, well-organised bureaucracies (in the Weberian sense). It is curious how absolutist realms of the European continent have always been contrasted with Britain's exceptional parliamentarian status, the latter being presented, it goes without saying, as the final victor. This is probably imbued with an economistic view. We would also need to look hard at the claim that Great Britain was the winner (when? how? for how long?). The aforementioned conclusion that Great Britain's advantage resided in its being a "small" state is a classic example of an anachronism-driven error. In this case the fiscal-military approach has helped to belie to this error.

But historians are also interested in examining in the past questions that concern us today. History – scientific history, historiography – is not a mere telling of past events; this would be a simple chronicle. As Croce might say, all history is contemporary history: "in reality reference is always made to the needs and the situation of the present, in which [past events] propagate their vibrations" (Croce 1938: 5). Does the same occur with our fiscal-military state? To a certain extent it does, because there is still a strong economic concern and a revived interest in war, due to its economic aspects and its influence on empires. Quite apart from specific political regimes, we are interested in the interaction between war and economy and the need of this combination by powerful countries trying strategically to hang onto this predominance. This is also a strand of current historical thought (Kennedy 1989: Introduction), and as such a handy method to help us understand aspects that are familiar to us today but whose details in the past are murkier. A study through the prism of the fiscal-military state brings us pell-mell into the concerns of the historical moment we are interested in here, the eighteenth century, while also responding to today's questions, because the questions that the method evokes for the historian, and which chime in with the concerns of the people of that time, are also some of today's set of concerns.

In short the new method fends off the perils of anachronism without eschewing a search for knowledge that is of interest to us today. This is no panacea, in any case, and we are always likely to need to switch from one method to another to ensure a proper grasp of the circumstances under study, fitting in with both said circumstances and our contemporary requirements as well as taking onboard advances in historiographic knowledge. Hence the importance of new concepts that try to explain new facets of things that are ostensibly already known.

In the case in hand we are going to adopt the fiscal-military-state concept only from some points of view, to bring out aspects of each one of these fields. On the one hand we are interested in revenue and expenditure. In the first case we will be speaking about the amount and dominant types of taxes (revenue sources) in the countries we wish to compare and their *raisons d'êtres*; i.e., using Bonney's terms, the fiscal state lying behind the fiscal-military state. The other complementary aspect, that of expenditure, ushers in the study of the contractor state, a concept from which we will build up an explanation of numerous facets of the states' ways of spending their money, the presence and type of middlemen (contractors), the resource-mobilisation methods and their knock-on effects on the economy. Mixed in with this picture will be the resource sources that underlie said revenue and expenditure (the economy, mercantilism), and also the managerial bureaucracies.

3 Administering the fiscal-military state

Ordinary revenues – trusting in a consumer's world

Spain, like Great Britain and France, was a fiscal-military state, albeit each with a different structure and degree of development. The three of them sought to boost their revenue in order to be able to take on wars as the government's normal task, almost an obligation, with some guarantee of success; all of them adjusted their administrative structures in different ways pushed by the inevitability of war and the need of sustaining it. First and foremost, therefore, the three sought to increase their revenue. That said, the problems they encountered on the way were different and the overall managerial results too. Why was this?

The reasons for the disparate management and also the different financial and military results are very varied in nature. Quite possibly the final explanation boils down to a well-known fact: in 1815 Great Britain came across as the only fiscal state that managed to develop its systems to an advanced phase enabling it to beat its rivals. It must first of all be acknowledged, however, that this triumph became clearly evident only in 1815, not beforehand, and second that other states' taxation systems also had features of a fiscal state geared mainly towards military expenditure, although less developed perhaps (Bonney 1999b: 14). These are the aspects we will try to bring out to make the due comparisons. We will study first the increase in the ordinary tax trawl before moving on to the increasing needs and the ways and forms of confronting them by means of extraordinary income, government borrowing or improving managerial procedures, as we will see in different chapters.

3.1 The increase in the tax trawl

What was the ordinary tax revenue and how much did it add up to? We will leave for later extraordinary warfare-financing taxation (sometimes temporary) and debt, although due consideration does have to be given to the fact that the sums raised as extraordinary revenue were sometimes retained during ensuing peace-time. In practice ordinary revenue was swelled by new ordinary inputs and by these extraordinary wartime inputs that were then kept on afterwards. The displacement hypothesis holds true in all cases: post-war taxes are lower than war taxes but higher than pre-war taxes. For this reason, the very concept of ordinary revenue is partly an artifice. What was considered to be ordinary in a given moment might have been non-existent or regarded as extraordinary at an earlier moment. What comes across clearly, in any case, is that a snapshot picture of ordinary revenue can be given at any particular time and this is what we will be referring to in this section. What we reflect here as ordinary taxes are what the corresponding sources considered in each case to be ordinary receipts, or ordinary budget, or in the Spanish case, for example, *rentas en actualidad*.

The first comparison to be made is the amount of revenue collected. Table 3.1 shows the nominal values of net tax revenue in annual means for the chosen time periods. The period was chosen according to available information in each case, so the elected years coincide as much as possible in the interests of realistic comparisons. The intention here is not to draw up a complete annual series; instead we have chosen certain periods. This might well cloak watershed moments but right now we are not interested in annual precision but rather comparing the revenue figures of the three states during the eighteenth century and establishing period trends[1].

What these figures show us, along very general lines, is that sum totals rose in all cases, more in the second half of the century than in the first, and more in the final decades than beforehand. If we factor in inflation, particularly in the last third of the century, the growth then comes out lower in constant values; but we are interested here in the actual sums received and paid in. The indexed percentage growth figures give us a better idea of the turning points, always in an upwards direction. The first jumps come in the fifties for Spain and the sixties for France and Great Britain. Later on revenue picks up again for all three countries in the eighties, this increase continuing in the nineties and thereafter.

Table 3.1 Total net tax income, and indexed percentage changes (1715–30 = 100) (expressed in millions of *reales de vellón*, *livres tournais* and pounds sterling, respectively)

Years	E	E index	F	F index	GB	GB index
	Spain		*France*		*G. Britain*	
1715–30	253	100	183	100	5.9	100
1735–45	338	133	227	124	6	101
1750–55	457	180	230	125	7.2	122
1765–75	454	179	333	181	10.3	174
1780–85	667	263	421	230	13.5	228
1790–91	815	322	500	273	17.5	296
1800–04	1.042	411	570	311	31	525

Sources: Torres Sánchez 2015; Mathias and O'Brien 1976; O'Brien 1988; Morineau 1980.

This trend fits in with the progressive increase in the number and expensive of wars. Debt-engendered items, as debt progressively grew at this time, might also have been included as ordinary revenue. Be that as it may, the needs increased as from 1789, thus impinging on fiscal policies, a theme we will be coming back to later.

Other noteworthy aspects are, for example, that the biggest taxation growth rate in the first half of the century seemed to be Spain's. This might be because it started out from a very low level, given the tax-alleviation policies of the late seventeenth century (Sánchez Belén 1996; González Enciso 2007). Another reading, however, might stress Spain's fiscal reinforcement capacity during Philip V's reign. Nonetheless, barring the sixties in France, Spain's advantage was maintained up to and including the nineties. Only in the first years of the nineteenth century did Great Britain outgrow Spain and France. The result shows Spain's recovery capacity in the eighteenth century to take up a position just behind the two major powers.

The taxation growth of each country, each from its own base, does not tally, however, with the absolute values. If ordinary taxation grew more in Spain, total Spanish values are much lower than those of its rivals. The gap between France and Great Britain, on the one hand, and the laggard Spain can be seen in Table 3.2.

Table 3.2 is fairly rough-and-ready but it suffices for our purposes here: it has been built up by converting the currencies of France and Great Britain into the Spanish currency of *reales de vellón*. To do so we have assumed in general that the *livre tournais* was worth 4 *reales de vellón* while the pound sterling was worth 90 *reales de vellón*. These equivalences are pretty approximate for the second half of the century, somewhat less trustworthy for the first half. The resulting information is only approximate but it does tally with what we know of the countries' fiscal trends and comes in useful for making a simple comparison of the tax revenue they were able to raise in each case.

Table 3.2 Net income expressed in millions of *reales de vellón*

Years	Spain A	France B	% B/A	G.Britain C	% C/A
1715–30	253	732	289	531	209
1735–45	338	908	268	540	159
1750–55	457	920	201	648	141
1765–75	454	1332	293	927	204
1780–85	667	1684	252	1215	182
1790–91	815	2000	245	1575	193
1800–04	1042	2280	218	2790	267

Source: See Table 3.1.

The clearest deduction in absolute terms is that Spain's total tax revenue always lagged well behind the other two. This gap was variable, however. In the first third of the century Great Britain doubled Spain's tax revenue. Curiously enough, however, this percentage gap closed during most of the central decades of the century, coinciding with two other factors we know: first, Great Britain's relative tax stagnation in these decades (O'Brien 1988: 3), and, second, an increase in Spain's tax revenue due to the introduction of direct administration (González Enciso 2012a: 112). These trends would switch in about 1760. Great Britain once more almost came to double Spain by the end of the century, showing Spain's difficulties in broadening its tax base despite some mercantile reforms, and the gap widened even further in the first decade of the nineteenth.

As for France, the difference with Spain was always greater than with Great Britain, albeit dipping somewhat as from 1800. France's nominal revenue, for its part, was always greater than Britain's up to the end of the century. It would not be until 1799 when Great Britain's total fiscal revenue overtook France's (Kennedy 1989: Chapter 3) thanks, above all, to Pitt's income tax in 1799. In comparative terms Spain's situation picked up somewhat in the forties and fifties, closing the gap on its rivals in terms of its ordinary taxation capacity. It does come across as rather paradoxical that Spain's response to its 1739 bankruptcy was a successful increase in its tax revenue thereafter.

France and Great Britain would again edge ahead in the sixties. Spain pulled things back a bit in the eighties and part of the nineties, but then showed insuperable weakness from 1800 onwards. In truth Spain's really serious financial straits did not come along until 1794 (War against the Convention) and above all in 1797, when the defeat of San Vicente cut off Spain's normal lines of communication with its colonies and deprived it of overseas resources. The situation was of course vacillating up to 1808; Spain also showed a well-nigh inconceivable recuperation capacity back to normal levels after the Treaty of Amiens in 1802 (Cuenca Esteban 2009), but war then showed no truce and Spain could not keep up.

One notable factor here is that Spain diversified its income and expenditure sources in several separate treasuries kept not only in Spain itself but also in its American colonies. The economic resources reflected there would meet a good part of the Spanish empire's army and navy needs, but it should not be forgotten that part of the fiscal resources, especially revenue from precious metals, was spent directly in the colonies. This was the *situado*, money from the king's part of precious metals that was not sent home to Spain but distributed throughout the colonial territories to defray administration and defence costs. Mexico's silver mines, especially in the second half of the century, provided a growing sum spent directly in the Americas (Marichal 2007) and not recorded by the central Madrid treasury. In any case, even factoring in the *situado*, Spain's resources would continue to lag well behind its rivals.

The fiscal figures alone give pause for thought about each country's capacity to meet its military needs from its natural resources converted into tax revenue. In this sense the figures show the weakness of Spain's fiscal capacity, despite the inputs of American metal, while, from the strictly fiscal point of view, France managed to match Great Britain during the century, in all likelihood on the strength of its population, much bigger than Britain's or Spain's. Its almost 30 million inhabitants at the end of the century, 20 at the start (Livi-Bacci 1999: Table 1.1) served as a guarantee for a Treasury that had chosen to rely mainly on direct taxes and its grassroots bases. The population was much smaller in Spain and Great Britain, similar in both countries, although bigger in Great Britain if we tag on Ireland. The figures obviously depend on accounting records. In the case of Spain there is a fair consensus about the figure of 7 million in 1700 and 11 million in 1800, after combining the ancient crowns of Castile and Aragon (Torres Sánchez 2015a: 194). Great Britain's figures vary; some authors restrict themselves to England and Wales alone, others add on Scotland and sometimes Ireland too. Taking all the figures into account, we get 9.3 million inhabitants for Great Britain in 1700 (5.8 for England, 1 for Scotland and 2.5 for Ireland), and 16 million inhabitants in 1800 (9.2 for England, 1.6 for Scotland and 5.2 for Ireland) (Wilson and Parker 1977: 116).

Logically, the problem is not only the size of the population but its spending power. J. de Vries, for example, has referred to the growth of pocket-watch purchases by part of the working population in countries like Holland, England and France. Although the author acknowledges that these purchases would be made only when extraordinary income was to hand, given that the watch would serve mainly as a status symbol, the truth is that, even in the worst cases, this income did exist and people not exactly awash in financial resources were still prepared to splash out on a pocket watch. It thus seems that there was "an increase in *per capita* income in northwest Europe and a concomitant refinement of material life" (De Vries 2009: Chapter 1). This occurred in the century before the industrial revolution, 1680–1780, approximately and in Great Britain's case could be considered as one of the driving forces behind this process as much as the availability of new consumer goods gave people the desire to earn income and work hard (Allen 2009: 12).

This image of wellbeing is reinforced if we consider the proportion of the urban population as a percentage of the total. It is urban dwellers, after all, that are the biggest consumers and therefore need most money to defray these purchases, since they cannot fall back on their own agrarian production. We then find that the English urban population rose from 17 per cent of the total in 1700 to 28 per cent by 1800. In France the proportion in this same period rose from 10 to 11 per cent and in Spain it rose, approximately, from 20 to 23 per cent (Yun Casalilla 2004: 171). Great Britain, in any case, was not the country with the biggest urban-population proportion; this was Holland, whose inhabitants also withstood the highest *per capita* taxation rate ('t Hart 2014). We should also mention the fact that not all cities were equally rich or, above all, productive. If ordinary tax revenue was based, above all, on urban consumers, as we will see later, then the development of a high-consuming urban society was paramount. London here enjoyed a great advantage over Madrid, a less industrial city dominated by the privileged rich and their domestic service (Ringrose 1983).

3.2 The fiscal structure: direct or indirect taxes

All the above observations could provide an answer to how low-population Great Britain managed to build up such fiscal prowess, largely because of a higher spending capacity in general terms and an abundant urban middle class, more developed than in other countries. But from where did Great Britain draw its strength to set up such a broad tax base? Before answering this question, we have to look at each country's tax revenue structure, where we find glaring differences between each one of our three countries. The new Great Britain, as we will see, having suffered from the intrinsic limitations of the traditional direct-tax structure that still dominated in seventeenth-century England, decided to tap into its urban population's consumer demand by means of indirect taxes. This urban population grew in number and became richer throughout the whole century so this tactic greatly boosted the government's eighteenth-century tax revenue.

The fiscal structures of Great Britain, France and Spain were already different by the last third of the seventeenth century. One of historians' ongoing concerns here has been to distinguish between direct and indirect taxes. The burden of the former falls on people, their properties and revenue: *taille*, capitation, poll tax, hearth tax, income tax, *servicios, catastros*, etc., are some of the names given to these direct taxes in the various countries. They do not always mean the same; the peasantry bore the brunt of those that fall on people, while the burden is more variable for taxes that are levied on agricultural property or money income; in particular, this incidence depended on both avoidance and evasion rates, sometimes very high (Riley 1986: 41–42).

In general, direct taxes are based on the era's most abundant source of wealth, agrarian wealth, from which both rich and poor drew their income. For this reason, direct taxes have been historically identified with an ancient economic system, the "domain state", based on agrarian income and feudal relations, with a limited development of markets, more characteristic of the medieval economy. Importance of indirect taxes will grow with the expansion of trade and consumption. It is true that the nineteenth century went back to direct taxes, after the resounding success of the income tax established in Great Britain since 1799. This was done at a time of extreme need, due to the vicissitudes of the conflict with France, and could be carried through because the industrial revolution was favouring a change in the structure of revenue and income sources. But before this moment came the states' attempts to raise their income levels had been geared towards indirect taxes.

As from the thirteenth to fifteenth centuries the development of consumer-product markets and international markets helped to end the dominance of direct taxes within Europe, facilitating a change to indirect taxes based on customs duties and consumer demand. These were necessary and relatively new sources of income for the bigger realms, the nascent states (Naef 1973) that needed to meet their growing military needs. This marked a slow evolution towards the fiscal state, which did not exclude direct taxes but began to grant more importance to indirect taxes, which came from market-based income (Bonney 1999b: 2). It would be in the first centuries of early modernity when indirect taxes experienced their real boom, particularly in some cases like that of sixteenth-century Castile (Yun Casalilla 2004: 341), and would grow across the board during the eighteenth century.

Direct taxes had hung onto some of their importance in seventeenth-century England; in the eighteenth century, however, indirect taxes came into their own as the fiscal base of British military power. This fact has turned eighteenth-century indirect taxes into the cynosure of all historians interested in investigating the long eighteenth century on a comparative basis: indirect taxes were important in this century in practically all countries; they certainly were in Spain and France at that time. Where did the British difference reside? The problem in the eighteenth century did not lie so much in the proportion of these taxes within the state's total income figure but rather their varying growth capacity in each case.

Nonetheless, finding out the relative importance of indirect taxes in total revenue of the various taxation systems is still telling as an indication of each country's fiscal preferences (possibilities, strategies). The results for eighteenth-century France and Great Britain are shown in Table 3.3, with a direct-indirect tax breakdown as annual means within the same periods established for former comparisons.

The relative importance of indirect taxes in Great Britain from 1715 to 1800 is striking (c. 74 per cent, on average, of the total; the figure varies somewhat according to the chosen partial periods). The main indirect taxes were the excise tax (inland tax on the sale of certain goods) and customs duties on importations. Direct taxes had still been important during the War of the Spanish Succession – by now pooled into a single land tax – but would not recoup this importance until Pitt's upward reform of the land tax in 1799, turning it rather into a sort of income tax (Mathias and O'Brien 1976: 613–614; Brewer 1989: 96–97).

Table 3.3 Direct and indirect taxes as percentage of total revenue in Great Britain and France

Years	% dir. GB	% ind. GB	% dir. F	% ind. F
1715–30	24	71.7	52	42
1735–45	25	73	54	41
1750–55	24.5	75	46	45
1765–75	19	76	51	43
1780–85	19.5	74.5	46.5	48
1790–91	17	75	38	51
1800–04	28	63	49	46

Source: Mathias and O'Brien 1976; O'Brien 1988.

France's situation was a bit different, calling for a previous comment on the sources of the figures given. The figures of Table 3.3, from Mathias and O'Brien, are different from those of Durand (1976) and those published a few years later by Morineau (1980). The first pair have the advantage of working from more complete annual information; the latter pair's advantage is that their figures are probably more accurate. If we choose the first two authors, as in Table 3.3, then the difference with Great Britain, barring the period 1780–1800, is that the direct taxes (*taille, capitation, vingtièmes*, according to the particular time considered) were more important than the indirect taxes, though the difference was very small: 50 per cent in times of peace, 50–60 per cent in times of war in favour of direct taxes (Mathias and O'Brien 1976: 625).

According to the figures of Durand and Morineau, shown in Table 3.4, the differences are also small but in this case tip in favour of indirect taxes which would outweigh direct taxes at all times, at least until the revolution.

French taxation sources are extremely complex, among other reasons because many documents have been lost (Riley 1987; Félix 1999), so it is very difficult to reach any consensus about which items are being tallied by the source used at each moment. Neither is this our remit here. In any case the general size and trend, which are of interest to us here, is clear. France's pre-revolution indirect tax revenue varied from 40 to 50 per cent of total income; 50 per cent was not topped until 1790. France's indirect taxes therefore account for 25 percentage points less of the total than Great Britain's, where they always represented over 74 per cent of the total.

If in the abovementioned cases the difference resides in the greater or lesser percentage attributable to indirect taxes, in the Spanish case the situation is slightly

Table 3.4 Direct and indirect taxes as percentages of ordinary revenue in France, according to Morineau and Durand

	% dir Morineau	% ind. Morineau	% ind. Durand
1726	44	49	
1739			47.3
1751	42	45	
1756			44.4
1768			45.3
1773			41.7
1775	40	49	
1788	34.6	46.5	50

Source: Morineau 1980: 314; Durand 1976: 21.

more complex because there is a large amount of minor income, relatively small each one but adding up between them to a significant total. In the British case the taxes, direct or indirect, that we have taken into consideration accounted for 90 per cent of total tax revenue. In Spain, however, the most important taxes that we are going to consider represented only 72 per cent of total revenue. The remaining 28 per cent corresponded to a clutch of small, varied taxes that never impinged on fiscal policy, or derive from an idiosyncrasy in the accounting procedure, since the main source used (Merino Navarro 1987), does not break down each year's carry-over in the totals, thus giving an inflated idea of the real income.

For our purposes here we have chosen in Spain the most significant revenue groups from the fiscal policy point of view, those on which the government most heavily relied and those taken into account when it came to making any reform: these are the group of taxes called *rentas provinciales* (provincial revenue of Castile), customs duties, *rentas de Indias*, monopolies, *rentas eclesiásticas* and *Catastro* of the Crown of Aragon[2]. The first four could be considered to be indirect taxes – although the first not entirely, including as it does the so-called *servicios* (Angulo Teja 2002) – and the last two as indirect taxes. Between them all they accounted for about 72 per cent of total tax revenue, on average, throughout the whole century, a lower percentage than in the previous two cases but still sizeable.

Table 3.5 shows how indirect taxes were substantially more important than direct taxes in eighteenth-century Spain.

The table shows, in any case, that indirect taxes in Spain grew in relative importance throughout the eighteenth century, at least until 1780. From this standpoint Spain followed the British example of largely shunning direct taxes, although, as we will see, it had made some attempts to increase them at the start of the century. But the interesting point here is not only the confirmation that indirect taxes were also important in Spain, but finding out their composition. In Great Britain, in particular, and also in France, indirect taxation was identified with overseas

Table 3.5 Direct taxes and indirect taxes as percentages of total revenue in Spain

Years	Dir. (A)	Ind. (B)	A+B
1715–30	15.5	54.5	70
1735–45	13.4	51.6	65
1750–55	10.6	62.6	73.2
1765–75	13.2	73.1	86.3
1780–85	9	61.6	70.6
1790–91	7.7	62.2	69.9
1800–04	–	48.9	–

Source: Taken from figures of Torres Sánchez 2015: Table A8.1. Total Spanish revenue is the figure shown in Table 3.1.

trade and domestic consumption. In Spain, however, we also need to factor in the notable importance of the monopolies, especially three state monopolies that were very different from each other: precious metal, tobacco and salt. Although they are indirect taxes per se, their character is changed by the fact that they were marketed under a state monopoly. Rather than taxes, therefore, they should by rights be called fiscal monopolies.

Monopolies did not exist in Great Britain but they did in France, logically excluding the case of precious metals. One other difference with France was the proportional importance of tobacco in Spain, where it had been set up as a separate, perfectly organised revenue source, pumping in up to 20 per cent of Spain's total net revenue from 1760 to 1780 (Torres Sánchez 2006: 223). The importance of French tobacco is not so easy to gauge because it was not recorded as a separate revenue as in Spain, but it was certainly very important in France too, accounting in 1788 for 12.2 per cent of indirect revenue, i.e. 7.3 per cent of total revenue (Bonney 1995b: 497). This is obviously a tidy sum. In Great Britain its proportional value was lower, although the absolute sums were much higher.

Table 3.6 shows a breakdown of Spain's various indirect revenue sources: *rentas provinciales* (trade and domestic consumption, only the Crown of Castile in this case), customs (also called *rentas generales*), the state monopolies (pooling tobacco, salt and minor sundries like the lottery, stamped document tax, liquors, etc.). Within the group of monopolies tobacco represented 70 per cent of the total and salt 20 per cent. Finally, there was the revenue streaming in from the American colonies, known under the umbrellas term of *rentas de Indias*, basically a tax on mining, which can be classed among the indirect taxes.

All these taxes increased in absolute terms though their relative importance varied. Inland-trade taxes (*provinciales*) tended over the period to win ground on foreign-trade taxes (customs). This trend would change only in the nineties,

Table 3.6 Main indirect taxes in Spain: amount and percentage of total revenue (in millions of *reales de vellón*)

Years	Total rev	Prov	% A	Customs	% B	% A+B	Mon	% C	Ind	% D
1715–30	253	60	23.7	22	8.6	32.3	41	16.2	10	4
1735–45	338	58	17.1	22	6.5	23.6	61	18	34	10
1750–55	457	61	13.3	41	8.9	22.2	77	16.8	108	23.6
1765–75	454	67	14.7	49	10.7	25.4	111	24.4	106	23.3
1780–85	667	100	14.9	66	9.8	24.7	127	19	120	17.9
1790–91	815	108	13.2	143	17.5	30.7	113	13.8	145	17.7
1800–04	1.042	120	11.5	108	10.3	21.8	152	14.5	132	12.6

Source: See Table 3.1.

the best economic decade of the century, when the effect of the free trade decree with the Americas, eliminating the erstwhile monopoly of the port of Cadiz, really came into its own. Although the decree was passed in 1778, its effects were delayed until after 1783 because of the war. The colonial-trade boom under the new regime (Fisher 1985) ended in 1797. From then on there would be an ad hoc system of trading licences with neutral countries.

Commercial tax revenue (A + B in Table 3.7) represented on average c. 26 per cent of total revenue throughout the whole century. Monopoly revenue, for its part (C + D), outweighed the former as from 1730, continuing to grow until at least 1780 (González Enciso 2009b). The falling trend in this tax revenue thereafter could have two explanations. First, the aforementioned growth in American trade, which was Spain's quickest growing revenue source by about 1790, albeit of brief duration. Second, the fall in tobacco revenue some years as from 1780. The sharp price hike in manufactured tobacco, brought in that year, produced a substantial fall in official consumption figures and a knock-on drop in tax revenue. Meanwhile the *rentas de Indias* remained a stalwart until the continual American trade cut-offs most years after 1797.

This varied composition of indirect taxes had a particularly big effect because the government had to take in a whole raft of variables when contemplating any fiscal policy reforms. Great Britain could change total results by adjusting a single tax like excise; Spain did not have this luxury and had to modify several of them. On the other hand, direct taxes were greatly outweighed in importance by indirect taxes and monopolies. The two sources of direct income are also very different. Church taxes had a long track record, but any modification of them would call for church-state agreements. The church's ordinary contribution tended to grow in absolute terms (Barrio Gozalo 2010), until its revenue was hit by the slump after 1800. Any realistic assessment of the church's fiscal support would also have to take into account the church's extraordinary contributions, which are not considered here.

Table 3.7 Indirect taxes as a percentage of total revenue in Spain

Years	% A+B	% C+D	% total
1715–30	32.3	22.2	54.5
1735–45	23.6	28	51.6
1750–55	22.2	40.4	62.6
1765–75	25.4	47.7	73.1
1780–85	24.7	36.9	61.6
1790–91	30.7	31.5	62.2
1800–04	21.8	27.1	48.9

Source: See Table 3.6.

Table 3.8 Direct taxes: church and Crown of Aragon cadastre, and percentage of total revenue

Years	Church	% A	Cadastre	% B	% A+B
1715–30	11.8	4.6	27.7	10.9	15.5
1735–45	17.3	5.1	28.2	8.3	13.4
1750–55	20.2	4.4	28.5	6.2	10.6
1765–75	33.9	7.4	26.7	5.8	13.2
1780–85	31	4.6	29.5	4.4	9
1790–91	34.9	4.2	28.9	3.5	7.7
1800–04	18.8	0.01	–	–	–

Source: See Table 3.5.

This is not the case of the taxes of the Crown of Aragon. They stemmed from the fiscal reform of 1707, brought in after Philip V's conquest of the territories of the ancient Crown of Aragon, rebels against his cause in the War of Succession. It was then decided that these territories' input to the monarchy's coffers, formerly meagre, should be brought up to the level of Castilian territories. A means-testing cadastre system was set up. The trouble was that the resultant fixed sum soon fell behind the times (Artola 1982: 226). The Crown of Aragon paid more than before, it is true, but still less than Castile. Moreover, it then continued to pay the same over time even though its wealth almost certainty increased most quickly in the whole of Spain in the eighteenth century. At the start of the century Aragon's input was proportionately higher than the church's; as the century wore on, as shown in Table 3.8, this relationship reversed.

Spain's direct taxes tended to provide a falling percentage of the total, above all due to the lower relative value of Aragón's taxes as from the thirties.

3.3 Divergent paths: the trend of the fiscal structure in the long eighteenth century

If the eighteenth-century fiscal structure was as shown above, this then poses the question of whether it had been the same beforehand or if it had varied with the advent of the eighteenth century; in either case we might then ponder the meaning of this structure. This is an important point, above all because this change occurred most notably in Great Britain, which then led the fiscal changeover from that moment on. Its fiscal structures therefore merit our special attention. We would be particularly interested here to ascertain whether or not something similar happened in Spain and then make the comparison with France. To do so we will divide the long eighteenth century into three parts: a lingering *fin de siècle*, the central decades of the short eighteenth century, and the final stage as from 1789.

3.3.1 The long fin de siècle, c. 1670–1720

We will start in this case with England/Great Britain, given that it was the country that underwent the most eye-catching change of all those shown in Figure 3.1. We see there a substantial change between the seventeenth century and the eighteenth. In the seventeenth century, at least up to 1665, direct taxes held sway, whereas in the eighteenth, as from 1720, indirect taxes closed the gap and forged ahead, especially the excise tax. The situation reached by 1720 marked a trend that would then be retained until the end of the century.

Figure 3.1 shows that there is a period between about 1690 and 1715 when the previously scattered trends tended to converge. The structural change was then brought in, its effects becoming clear as from 1720. The change underway at the end of the seventeenth century was a response to the needs created by the new wars with France, waged by the regime of the Glorious Revolution as from 1689. Remember we are speaking here only about fiscal revenue. We know that a wider-ranging response to the revenue-boosting problem was the creation of public debt; but as far as ordinary taxes are concerned what comes out in these years of the seventeenth century is the importance of the excise tax. The land tax, as the traditional grew at first, reversing its percentage downward trend since 1670, but soon began to fall due to the increase in excise tax. The medium-term consequence was a fall in land tax and a progressive increase in consumer taxes, while customs duties held onto their mean late-seventeenth-century levels, albeit with a more regular trend.

In around 1700 a sort of zero point was achieved with all revenue sources recording similar percentage values (Beckett 1985), then plateauing throughout the War of the Spanish Succession. During this conflict the land tax, hiked to

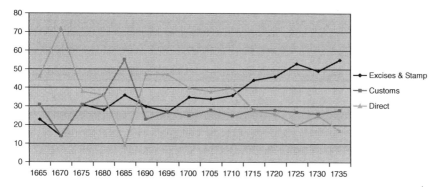

Figure 3.1 Total-revenue percentage of indirect taxes (excises and stamp duty), customs and direct taxes in Great Britain

Source: O'Brien 1988: 9.

defray the conflict, remained the most important tax, although now outweighed by the sum of indirect taxes. As from 1715 the land tax declined with the advent of peace, recording a low percentage value until the end of the eighteenth century (O'Brien 1988: 10; Brewer 1989: 95–96). The main input from 1720 onwards came from indirect taxes, but not all of them, with the excise tax to the fore, while customs wallowed in low percentage values akin to the land tax. The growth in the excise tax was so sharp that it outstripped customs duties in relative terms, recording similar values as the land tax, even though customs duties grew in absolute terms, more than doubling the mid-century value by the 1780s (O'Brien 1988: 9; Brewer 1989: 98–99).

In any case the change in the fiscal structure did not consist solely of a choice between one tax or another. It was also based on important political and administrative changes. As Figure 3.1 shows, the Restoration ushered in a sharp fall in direct taxes, then comprising mainly the hearth tax, introduced in 1662 and scrapped in 1689. The wars with Holland boosted old taxes, like the assessment, or other new ones like the special aids, which in turn gave birth in 1677 to what would come to be called the land tax (Wilson 1965: 211–12). There is therefore a notable trend away from direct taxes, which came in for varied social flak, and a reliance instead on customs duties, whose value grew after the end of the wars with Holland. The Glorious Revolution regime did not change anything at first, but new wars, now against France, forced the government to fall back anew on the land tax. The reaction, in any case, was instant. The social forces emerging with the revolution were also dead set against direct taxes, barring cases of strict urgency, and soon gave their support to debt financing, thanks to the creation of the Bank of England in 1694. This helped to cement the change of fiscal structure, as the government soon realised that the best way of paying off the debt interest was by way of the excise tax, on the strength of increased consumer spending driven by the mercantile upturn of the time.

Apart from political questions and social interests, which defined a particular strategy, England's public finances benefited at this time from three important reforms. The first was unification of revenue; the second was centralisation of management procedures and the third was direct collection. In comparison with Spain's and France's, England's fiscal structure comes across as strikingly simple even as early as the end of the seventeenth century. One key move was to bring all excise-tax procedures together in a single office; this tax would then turn out to be the most important revenue source (Brewer 1989). Other taxes were also revamped, the situation being whittled down in the end to three main taxes: excise, customs duties and land tax. Efforts were also made in England to create a strong treasurer general who could control the whole situation, a trend that had been building up since the times of George Downing in 1667–68.

The third reform was the abolition of tax farming arrangements during the Restoration. The needs created by the wars against Holland called for greater fiscal control, which would put paid in the end to the farming out of the main taxes. The farming out of customs duties ended in 1671, of excise in 1683 and of the hearth tax in 1684, before being abolished after the 1688 revolution. The new land tax was not taken into direct administration but was reserved for local powers; as we have already seen, however, its importance was dwindling in the general scheme of things.

In any case these seventeenth-century reforms are only one side of the coin. One watershed change was the replacement of a venal bureaucracy by a professional civil service, ostensibly efficient and honourable in general terms and very different from any other system on the continent at that time (Ertman 1997: 207). This put paid to the sway of private business within the public finance system, as in France (Bosher 1970), giving way to a much state-controlled bureaucracy. Lines were thus drawn in the sand for private business, whose interests were thus transferred into the parliamentary arena, a situation very different from any other on the continent. The particular constitution of the parliament in Great Britain thus comes across as another key factor in these changes. In the parliament sat people who were looking out for their own economic interests and were not going to let governments run public affairs just as they wished (Brewer 1989: 139). It could thus be argued here that if the restoration favoured administrative and managerial changes, the Glorious Revolution regime would facilitate institutionalisation of both politics (parliament) and the economy (Bank of England).

This then closed the circle of political-fiscal organisation that would underpin British predominance thereafter. The change, it has by now become obvious, did not stem from the Glorious Revolution regime as is usually assumed; it was rather an accretion of measures taken in the authoritarian regime, since this trend existed in Cromwell's times, then afterwards in a regime of absolute monarchy and finally within the incipient parliamentarian system. It could therefore be claimed that it is not so much the regime that matters as the particular vested interests underlying all regimes, which then find the best way at each moment to refine the system for fending off their internal or external rivals. In short, the period 1670–1720 represented a crucial change in the fiscal structure of England/ Great Britain. In those years, traditional ways of working were ditched in favour of a new system. The predominance of indirect taxes over any other source of ordinary tax revenue together with the concentration of these taxes on consumer demand and the prior reforms that support these changes are characteristic traits that had been enshrined by 1720 and were kept as such unchanged throughout the whole century.

What about in France and Spain? Were there similar fiscal changes? Starting with France we see an evolution without any apparent structural change of importance but rather ongoing growth on the basis of pretty much the same tax mix. Indirect taxes, notwithstanding, did win some ground within the whole set of taxes, at least in the first decades of the seventeenth century, but not to the same extent as in Great Britain.

Indirect taxes in France loomed large in the revenue picture until the mid-seventeenth century. The whole set of taxes (*gabelle* on salt, *aides* or taxes on consumer goods and inland customs), could add up to two thirds of total revenue, although it is impossible to establish the real yield of all these farmed-out taxes in the seventeenth century. This yield, moreover, was severely trimmed by the charges levied on them and poor management (Harsin 1970: 267–68). In about 1660 indirect taxes grew in importance and this trend strengthened with Colbert's reforms (Harsin 1970: 269, Durand 1976: 21). Colbert strived to improve expenditure procedures, cut the debt and endow the treasury with the wherewithal for military demands. He did manage to balance the books by means of a sharp hike of the *aides*, a moderate increase of the *gabelle* and a certain reduction of the *taille*, thereby reducing the importance of direct taxes.

He also reduced tax farmers' profits and sought other methods for meeting warfare costs. In short, Colbert tidied things up, reduced corruption and improved collection procedures. In these aspects his policies chime in with those carried out at that time in Spain and England, but no sweeping reforms to match England's were carried out. France chose instead to concentrate on changing administrative procedures, coinciding in part here with Spain's approach. Not only was the general structure of the taxation system left intact but Colbert's reforms lost steam after the man himself left the stage (1683), a phenomenon that did not occur in England or Spain. As a consequence, disorder reappeared and wars needs ended up ruining the financial edifice, an edifice that balked "attempts to solve problems caused by a military policy at loggerheads with the ambitions of a national economic development plan" (Harsin 1970: 268–69).

Here appears a notable difference between France and England, precisely in dealing with the same problem: needs fuelled by a war that brought these two countries into confrontation as from 1689. The English made a virtue of necessity and overhauled the whole system to meet the new money needs; France, on the other hand, pressed on further down the same *cul-de-sac*, repeating the selfsame errors. Maybe the main reason for this is political and resides in the very fact that the French regime was *ancien*. Its monarch, Louis XIV, now had a long track record of military confrontations and an established financial way of dealing with them. Inertia weighed equally heavily on the corresponding elites and administrative arrangements: tradition prevented them from acting differently and the whole government showed itself to be path-dependent on its past inheritance. In England, on the other hand, the regime was a new broom; not only that, it had replaced a regime, the restoration, that in itself had been fairly new. In an era of notable political changes the English had been overhauling their systems to adapt as well as possible to new needs. This was possible partly because the political changes had either modified the relative power of the elites or forced these same elites to adapt to the new situation. In the England of that time, therefore a large part of its society were either unconcerned by the change or even advocated it and were always prepared to accept change if it was consensus based. This is the picture that seems to emerge from debates about changes in public finances.

All this was a question of predominance of the political; not so much wars making the state as politics making the state (Pincus and Robinson 2013), while war itself remained a great opportunity. This opportunity could strengthen the state, by means of new structures, as happened in England (Brewer 1989: 138), but it could also lead to the dissolution of the state by boosting private power and vested interests in the shape of military entrepreneurs or tax farmers, as would seem to be the French case. The English state's reaction to a tricky situation, such as the one that cropped up in 1689, could be tied in with what Ertman dubbed "newcomer states" (Ertman 1994: 42): recently formed states tend to be much more fleet-footed and innovation-friendly that long-standing states encumbered with unwieldy bureaucracy. England of 1689 was, from many points of view, a new state, ready to take the most convenient path at each moment. In comparison with France, moreover, it had not yet run up a heavy debt.

The upshot was that in the period 1670–1720 France showed no signs of any change in its fiscal structure. Figure 3.2 contrasts this with the opposite situation of England.

As Figure 3.2 shows, from about 1660 France's indirect taxes hovered around 50 per cent of total revenue. Barring the moment of the War of the Spanish Succession, this percentage held steady, dropping slightly as from 1720, contrasting markedly with the English trend; the divergence is clear and it means that France hanged onto its existing fiscal structure.

If, as we have already seen, we look at Morineau's figures rather than Durand's, France's indirect taxes are also seen to grow somewhat, thanks to a greater effort demanded from the *fermiers généreaux*; this trend was slight, however, and the swing towards indirect taxes was not enough to change the country's taxation structure. Table 3.9 shows us that, although indirect taxes grew more according to Morineau's figures, they still strike a balanced proportion with direct taxes in terms of the increase of total revenue.

France, moreover, failed to bring in any of the thoroughgoing reforms that we have already looked at in seventeenth-century England, neither the pooling of revenue nor, of course, direct administration. France maintained a system that

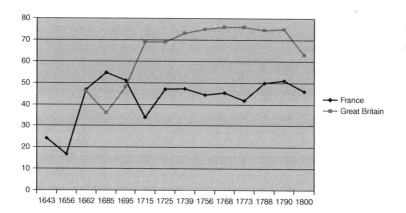

Figure 3.2 Indirect taxes as a percentage of the total in France and Great Britain

Sources: For France, Durand 1976: 21; Mathias and O'Brien 1976: 622; for Great Britain, O'Brien 1988: 10.

Table 3.9 Direct taxes and indirect taxes, according to Morineau, in selected years in
France (in millions of *livres tournais*)

Years	Direct taxes	Indirect taxes	Total revenue
1726	79.9	88.6	181
1751	109	116.6	258.5
1775	150.7	183.9	372.2
1788	163	219.3	471.6

Source: Morineau, 1980, p. 314 (see Table 3.4).

not only had a host of different taxes but also depended on an equally motley
set of regional taxation laws (Riley 1986: 40). These laws had to be carefully
enforced by a high number of officials, most of them venal (Bonney 1995b: 438).
Instead of bringing taxes together under a single heading, under the control of a
central office, as in England, France ploughed on with policy of farming them
out to officials who were then paid a wage, and later on could buy the post. In
1665 in France there were about 46,000 office–holders whose posts were worth
about 419.6 million *livres tournais*. France's ordinary budget at this time was
90 million *livres tournais* (Bonney 1995b: 443, 449); it is therefore clear that it
was impossible for the French government to pay off this debt and "live of its
own", as the English managed from this time on. The French king, on the contrary, had no opportunity but to continue selling off posts (Doyle 1996: 26) as the
only way of rustling up instant cash to pay off costs, especially in the 1630s and
1690s. Colbert, like other ministers before and after, chafed against this yoke but
never managed to shrug it off completely (Bonney 1999a: 133).

One of the possible reasons why France was unable to bring in these reforms
was the maintenance of heavy expenditure during the reign of Louis XIV, in particular after 1689. Comparisons with Spain are telling here. The Conde-Duque de
Olivares complained during one moment of particular urgency that "he had no
time" to bring in some reforms that he saw as necessary (Elliott 1990: 492). What
he was really saying here was that any modification might jeopardise the next
year's revenue, which was absolutely necessary for waging war; he would have
needed more years of peace but this was a pipe dream. Louis XIV's ministers,
especially Colbert, experienced a similar situation (Meyer 1983: 49). They soon
grasped that their reforms had a ceiling, marked out by this same prudent concern
not to rock the boat of next year's revenue by bringing in a drastic change just
when needs were soaring.

This increase affected first and foremost ordinary revenue and was clearest in
the final decades of the seventeenth century, and highest in England, the rival of
that moment. Figure 3.3 shows the ordinary revenue growth rates of France and
England in the brief period we are dealing with here.

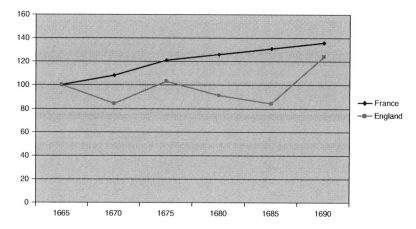

Figure 3.3 Ordinary revenue growth rate in France and England, 1665–90.
Base 100 = 1665

Sources: England, O'Brien 1988: 3; France, Bonney 1995: 449. France's figures are approximate.

The first thing we see is that the French budget was much higher than the English, rising from about 950 million *livres tournais* in 1665 to about 1.3 billion by 1690. The English budget figure comes out lower: 1.65 and 2.05 million pounds sterling in each year, respectively. Furthermore, the French budget did not cease to grow between these two dates, while England's was more up and down. This seems to tell us that the English finance system was much more fleet-footed, with a greater capacity of changing than the French, weighed down by the baggage of the past. This situation would allow England to come up with a new response to fiscal demands as from 1690.

In Spain, for its part, indirect taxes are also seen to grow more now than earlier in the eighteenth century, therefore resembling more the British situation than the French, even though this process did not really kick in until after 1720. Spain presents a different picture from the previous countries. The historical importance of indirect taxes dates back further in Spain than in the other two countries. By the seventeenth century their percentage of total revenue was already over 50 per cent. The eighteenth-century picture falls midway between that of Great Britain and France, with higher percentages than France and similar to Britain's, but with more ups and downs than the British, as shown in Figure 3.4 comparing the three countries.

At the start of the eighteenth century Spain's percentage values were similar to the French, rising thereafter towards British values before dropping back down towards French levels at the end of the period. The long-term differences between Spain and Great Britain may stem from the fact that the latter constantly tended to raise the excise tax rather than customs duties, whereas Spain's situation is more varied because the indirect tax structure was more varied too. On general lines, however Spain's structure resembled Great Britain's rather than France's.

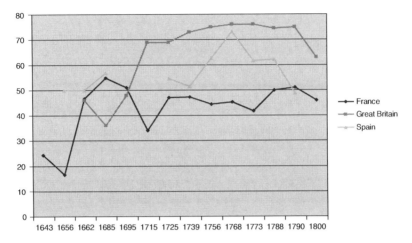

Figure 3.4 Indirect-tax percentage of total ordinary revenue in Great Britain,
          France and Spain

Sources for Spain: Andrés Ucendo and Lanza García 2008: 176, Kamen 1974,
Merino Navarro 1987.

If we zoom in on the initial period, 1670–1720, there was no change of the
fiscal structure in Spain: by 1670 indirect taxes were already important. Great
Britain's eighteenth-century indirect-tax percentages were much higher than back
in 1695. Spain's values, on the contrary, were similar before and after the turn of
the century: the importance of indirect taxes, with all their ups and downs, came
from further back. This was to some extent downplayed in 1720 due to the effects
as from 1707 of the cadastres of the Crown of Aragon, whose proportion, as we
have already seen, tended later to fall away.

There are several reasons for this maintenance of the existing tax structure, with a greater importance of indirect taxes. Prime among them is the
inherited structure and the fiscal policy carried out during Charles II's reign
and the first years of Philip V's. The overriding concern in the former reign
was to reduce the tax burden of Castilian taxpayers, the so called *alivio de los
vasallos*. This was done by lowering direct taxes and some indirect taxes. In the
latter reign this was in coincidence with raising the tax burden of the taxpayers
of the Crown of Aragon. In both cases the government also tried to improve the
yield both of customs duties and of the monopolies, the tobacco monopoly to
the fore (Rodríguez Gordillo 1984).

Charles II's reign, as from 1665, inherited a very old public-finance structure,
forged way back at the very origins of the early-modern centralised Spanish state
of the Catholic Monarchs (Ladero Quesada 1973). Subsequent additions did not
substantially affect the structure other than occasionally bringing in new taxes.
The system established in the Crown of Castile would serve as the core of Spain's
public finance system. Indirect taxes such as the *alcabala* (sales tax), customs
duties and royal monopolies (Artola 1982: 16), had been gaining ground on

the *patrimonio real* (king's domains) since as far back as the fifteenth century. During the sixteenth and seventeenth centuries customs duties were fortified – including the special wool-export tax – and monopolies also came into their own, especially the monopoly on precious American metals. In 1590 the *millones*, an excise type tax on certain consumer goods, were added. In the seventeenth century three important monopolies were implemented on: tobacco, salt and *papel sellado* (tax on official stamped documents).

During Charles II's reign, after defeat against France and Portugal and now facing fewer military obligations, the governments initiated a policy of lightening the tax burden (*alivio fiscal*) for Castile. This policy was brought in in 1669 and then kept in place for the rest of the century (Sánchez Belén 1996). The *alivio* policy bit deep. Total revenue fell from a century high of 18.3 million ducats in 1666 to 11.8 million ducats by 1688, both figures being trustworthy. This means a 6.5 million ducat reduction or a 35.5 per cent fall in revenue. If we reduce these figures to percentages, it was direct taxes that fell most (revenue from crown property fell by 45.6 per cent; personal *servicios* down by 64.3 per cent), while some indirect taxes fell by less (*alcabalas* and others down by 46.5 per cent; customs duties down by 30.9 per cent). Bucking the trend of these reductions there is an eye-catching rise of the tobacco tax (up by 37.4 per cent) and, to a lesser degree, direct church taxes (Andrés Ucendo and Lanza García 2008: 176).

The fiscal policy pursued at this time was recognition of the overriding need to reduce the tax burden on Castilian taxpayers, considered to be close to breaking point. The tax burden of each Castilian taxpayer in the first half of the seventeenth century has been calculated as "a sum tantamount to another tithe, in circumstances of extreme hardship" (Gelabert 1997: 327). These circumstances no longer obtained by 1669, so a start could be made on the tax reduction policy.

The drastic reduction of revenue did not lead to a change in the fiscal structure; it merely strengthened the hand of indirect taxes, which fell less than direct taxes. The lowering of some indirect taxes, moreover, spurred consumer demand, previously at a low ebb due to the heavy taxing of some staples. This heightened demand offset the tax reduction to some extent (Gelabert 1999: 227). There were also some indirect taxes, especially tobacco, that increased in both absolute and percentage terms (Rodríguez Gordillo 1984). Adding all together we find that direct taxes fell by an overall average of 54.9 per cent, while the indirect taxes that did fall, did so by only 38.7 per cent. This fall was offset by the increase of tobacco (plus 37.4 per cent). In 1688 the tobacco tax weighed in with 14.6 per cent of total revenue.

This then set the tone for the whole eighteenth century: the maintenance of some indirect taxes, and the increase of revenue from fiscal monopolies. But before this situation really gelled, other important events occurred. In the early years of the next century the new dynasty tried to continue along these taxation lines but the War of Succession was a long and serious obstacle to this endeavour. The needs engendered by this conflict were met mainly by means of extraordinary measures (Artola 1982: 224; Castro 2004: 199), including ecclesiastical taxes, confiscations, universal taxes and others (Kamen 1974: 245). Ordinary revenue, for its part, was kept at the same level, the value of the tobacco lease continued to increase and finally new taxes were agreed for the Crown of Aragon, the only substantial exception to the rule. This would also be the tonic for the rest of the century: financing wars with extraordinary revenue. The new cadastre for the Crown of Aragon, organised in keeping with the ideas of the time (Bonney 1995b: 439, 480), enforced in the various territories as from 1707, as they fell under control of Philip V's troops, were only of certain percentage importance at the very end of the conflict.

Apart from tinkering with taxes the Spanish finance system underwent a substantial modification in Charles II's reign; these changes were nowhere near as far-reaching as England's, but they were significant enough to introduce a new administrative mindset ahead of the eighteenth century. The French ministers of Philip V, especially Orry, and later the Spanish ministers of the first Bourbon king, would all try to tap into this new mindset.

One of the most important changes involved the attempt to reorganise the *Tesorería General* (General Exchequer). This exchequer had been set up in the sixteenth century with the aim of centralising all royal revenue and expenditure procedures (Ulloa 1977). It fell under the jurisdiction of the *Consejo Supremo de Hacienda* (Exchequer Council). The problems of the sixteenth and seventeenth centuries, however, warped its original purpose of control and centralisation, and it ended up as just another crown-financing facility: offering loans to the king and negotiating financial *asientos* to defray military costs (Carlos Morales 1996: 215). As financing sources snowballed, moreover, new control bodies cropped up, producing a decentralisation trend, with the *Tesorería* largely sidelined (Gelabert 1997). Under Charles II's watch serious attempts were made to regain some sort of centralised control. For example, provincial exchequers were set up to collect ordinary revenue and a *Superintendencia General de la Real Hacienda* (Royal Exchequer General Superintendence) was set up (Sánchez Belén 1996). Some control was indeed regained but many fiscal aspects fell outside the remit of the *Superintendencia*, while the powers of the *Tesorería General* remained stunted (Torres Sánchez 2012a: 23).

During the War of Succession, Orry, rather than reform the former system, created a new institution, a warfare treasury called the *Tesorería Mayor de Guerra* (1703), dependent on the *Secretario de Guerra* (War Minister), which enabled the government to defray warfare costs and partly replaced the *Tesorería General*. The *Tesorería Mayor* was not part of the earlier unification drive; the aim behind setting it up was more to ensure arrival and control of financial resources (Dubet 2008). It was only partly successful in this endeavour and also posed overlapping competence problems with the former *Tesorería General* and the *Consejo de Hacienda* (Castro 2004, Sanz Ayán 2006). In 1718 some serious pruning began to clear things up a bit. The *Tesorería General* was reformed and the *Tesorería Mayor de Guerra* was abolished, its competences passing across to the *General*. The administrative information previously contained by the *Tesorería Mayor* was used for the reform of the *Tesorería General*, showing that its control and centralisation work had not fallen on fallow ground. The fiscal centralisation pathway was now much clearer, but the *Tesorería General* would still have to undergo new changes in the eighteenth century.

Charles II's ministers had more success in other areas than with the *Tesorería*. Witness the attempts to pool various revenue sources in a single one in the interests of unified administration. The aforementioned provincial revenue exchequers and the *Superintendencia General* itself worked along these lines. The greatest feat was perhaps to bring the old taxes of *alcabalas, servicios, millones* and a clutch of other minor ones under one single heading: *rentas provinciales* this umbrella name alluding to the provinces of the Crown of Castile where these taxes were paid, in contrast to the *rentas generales*, the customs, which were paid in all provinces of the realm. It was no easy task in practice to bring in these *rentas provinciales* because it produced an inevitable power clash between the new *intendentes* (intendants) and the former figure of *corregidores* (administrators of cities and districts with both administrative and judicial powers). The idea behind the formation of the *intendentes* was to emulate Colbert's system for controlling local finances, a system not fully brought in until the eighteenth century. The long-standing system of *corregidores*, controlling these resources hitherto, had been closely tied in with the local elites (Gelabert 1999: 228).

Within these processes it is no easy matter to disentangle the strands and ascertain what was actually done and what was left undone, especially in the 1690s, a decade in which there were significant changes of government (Ribot García 1993). What is in any case quite clear is that the finance-system reform due to triumph much later was in fact already underway by 1700. But it would not be until the end of the War of Succession and even later that the king's control over his fiscal system became notably and progressively greater (Torres Sánchez 2015a: 32).

3.3.2 *Maintenance of the fiscal structures during the short eighteenth century, c. 1720–89*

During the 1720–89 period the various fiscal structures that we have seen come to birth were maintained in all three countries under study. If the change of century represented, to some extent, a restructuring process, this would be followed by a period of continuity wherein the ordinary taxation system was kept within the same parameters. This maintenance of ordinary fiscal structures reflects on two parallel questions: ordinary fiscal policy and economic growth. The tax yield could be used to drive the economy or, conversely, could draw on the economy. The impression is that the second idea was more widespread in the eighteenth century (Daniel 2012) and the taxation system served above all to raise warfare resources. The revenue raised fell short of needs so extraordinary arrangements had to be made. At the time these arrangements were said to be temporary but in fact lingered on into times of peace and many extraordinary items ended up being grafted onto the ordinary taxation system. Ordinary taxation therefore grew, impinging increasingly on economic life and its stakeholders.

Governors tended to turn a blind eye to the problems that taxation could pose for the economy but they were certainly mindful of the fact that without national wealth there was no way of wringing more funds out of taxpayers. By 1700 the governors had built up enough experience on the matter: if national wealth was not up to it, no conflicts could be kept up for long and the country's bargaining position in peace treaties would be weakened. For all these reasons fiscal arrangements needed to keep a closer eye on economic possibilities in each case. It came down to this: whence could more money be raised without harming economic production, without hobbling taxpayers and, if possible, without causing any political-constitutional problems.

All these factors led to completely different fiscal policies in the three cases, reflecting not only their economic possibilities but also the respective monarch's political position vis-à-vis the most powerful elites.

The classic case is without doubt the British. Its main taxes boiled down to three: excise, customs and land tax. The reduction to three main taxes, fruit of the administrative reforms carried out in the last third of the seventeenth century, enabled the English government to control revenue sources and to organise later the national debt system. The most notable feature of the ordinary taxation system was the relative simplicity of the fiscal policy. Once the government caught on to the fact that the system worked, a fact that became obvious after successfully negotiating the first two major mettle-testing conflicts, namely the Nine Years' War and the War of the Spanish Succession, there were more than enough reasons for relying on the system and benefiting from its apparent simplicity. In reality there were only three issues that fiscal policy could address: the land tax, overseas trade and certain consumer goods of national manufacture.

The land tax posed long-standing problems of privileges, consent, etc., and could harm influential personages in society and politics who found in the land their main means of support. It should be considered, however, that the governments' wriggle room was very small here (O'Brien 1988: 18). Indeed, all political groups in parliament stood out against any reform of the land tax for over a century. The only thing governments achieved was to raise the rate in war time, bringing it down again when peace returned. Collection of the land tax remained in the hands of an amateur administration under the control of landowners. This had its upside for the government: the land tax was cheap to get in because there was no outlay on its own bureaucracy and few opportunities for patronage (O'Brien 1988: 19). Furthermore, all those who benefited from the tax's lightsome burden were opposed to any reform. Not only the aristocracy and gentry but also merchants and industrialists affected in their landowner facet resisted any hike of the land tax as well as the introduction of any income tax, which did not arrive until 1799.

This stance shows the importance of the *longue durée* (Braudel 1958) and of the weight of the social, economic and political structure. In this case the *status quo* brought in after the Glorious Revolution was maintained; this meant that the tax's absolute value remained almost unaltered in the long term: the land tax yield was practically the same in 1715, at 1.5 million pounds, as in 1775 at 1.9 million pounds. Although the rate might be temporarily hiked in wartime, peace brought it down again; its long-term percentage values of course fell throughout the century.

It comes across as paradoxical that a country where money-based interests, i.e., those of trade and finances, were assumed to outgun landed interests should prove unable to raise the land tax. This shows that there was more coincidence between these two interest groups than is commonly thought. Even more paradoxical is that a mercantile country's customs tax should follow the same trend as the land tax, with low absolute values and falling percentage values throughout the century. The flatlining percentage of both taxes has a different reading in each case: on the one hand there were strong landed interests: on the other, the low customs level would drive exports. Like the land, moreover, the fiscal input of overseas trade was meagre in Great Britain. Customs duties were used as a lever to achieve a protectionist policy. The trouble was that exports of manufactured goods – the country's strong suit – were duty free so duties left little rake-off for the royal coffers. Is this consistent with our ideas of what constitutes mercantilism? If so, it is an idiosyncratic mercantilism with many features that are hard to account for on classic terms.

The recorded figures of overseas trade, especially imports, the most fruitful, took some time to take off. Table 3.10 shows this did not occur until 1750.

The only explanation for this trend, according to Wilson, was a similar and concomitant increase in contraband as customs duties rose. Nonetheless, although this was an important factor that did affect tax revenue (Cheung and Mui 1975), there were other structural factors that were conducive to low growth of customs duties in general. As O'Brien reminds us, customs duties were not only a tax-related money-raising arrangement; they were also a lever of politics in general and economic politics in particular. They reflect a variety of situations involving not only Great Britain's economic needs but also its relations with more or less friendly countries. Importation of manufactured goods, for example, was penalised, while importation of raw materials not produced in Great Britain was favoured. But the latter were cheap so there was less customs yield. Along similar lines, the policies designed to encourage exports of British manufactured goods

Table 3.10 British overseas trade in millions of pounds sterling

Years	Imports	Exports	Total
1700	6.0	6.5	12.5
1710	4.0	6.3	10.3
1720	6.1	6.9	13
1730	7.8	8.5	16.3
1740	6.7	8.2	14.9
1750	7.8	12.7	20.5
1760	9.8	14.7	24.5
1763	11.2	14.7	25.9

Source: Wilson 1965: 264.

and boost shipbuilding ruled out the possibility of taking full tax advantage of these exports or the transport services. Moreover, the regulation of imperial trade and bilateral treaties with friendly countries also greatly restricted the country's leeway in raising customs duties on certain products (O'Brien 1988: 23–24).

This whole situation produced a swarm of regulations that were difficult to remove; it also created a whole web of vested interests that then stood out strongly against any modification of the imperial trading system. It is also quite possible that many financiers lending to the government through the public-debt system reaped their profits from hefty investments in overseas trade, so rocking this boat could be perilous. The overall result was more trade but fewer trading taxes, since the government considered that increasing duties *ad valorem* could be counterproductive, since it would whip up political opposition and encourage contraband and tax evasion. The final result was the aforementioned paradox of customs duties echoing the same curve as land tax, with only the small difference that in times of war the trends switched, land tax rising and customs falling.

In view of these problems in one area and another, the most malleable tax was excise. British governments therefore based their fiscal policy, mainly, on hiking consumer-good taxes and broadening the excise trawl. It is true that, although brought together in a single office, the number of excise-paying products was high. It is no less true, however, that some were more important than others. It has even been argued that "the yield of the malt and beer taxes was by 1763 the main pillar of the national tax system" (Wilson 1965: 320). The reason is that the tax on these products generated nearly half the excise trawl, which in turn represented half of all ordinary fiscal income. But this was all to the good; if a small clutch of products accounted for a high percentage of excise income, this favoured collection procedures and made the whole system much simpler. Another factor that made this tax so convenient was that most of the products involved were manufactured at home and were therefore easy to control.

The downside was that tax hikes might on occasion fuel price increases that affected the public at large and stirred up unrest. Witness the excise crisis of 1733–34, which was almost certainly inspired more by politics than economics, the opposition trying to harness this popular dissent to bring down Walpole (O'Gorman 1997: 81). Be that as it may, the rulers of the time were sensitive to popular needs. They made sure staples were kept free of excise, with the tax's burden falling mainly on items considered to be superfluous, so rates were highest on products that were less necessary. Legislation on the excise tax "was, it seems, framed in order to minimize incidence on the poor" (O'Brien 1988: 27), apparently with some success. It should also be pointed out here that the new products emerging from the nascent industrial revolution (cotton, wool, porcelain, iron, for example) were excise-exempt to encourage their manufacture and consumption; keeping their price low also helped to counter wage demands.

Small wonder, in these circumstances, that the government paid so much attention to the excise scheme. This was reflected above all in the care showed in its collection. The government set up a special administration office that was honed to perfection by the standards of the times. This Excise Office had thousands of employees and about 100,000 supervision sites (Brewer 1989: 101). Broadening the British fiscal base in the central decades of the eighteenth century was therefore based fundamentally on mass consumption products, the burden falling above all on those who could afford to buy the highest-taxed products. This "peoples' wealth", as we might dub it, was based, however, on the general relative wealth of the country, with some spending power filtering down to the lowest classes. This involved the development of rich farming practices, widespread industry and wide-ranging trading networks, producing higher spending power within a "mercantile society" as Adam Smith would put it. In general terms this society was richer than in any continental country, or it might be more accurate to say that this wealth depended more on mercantile activities, freeing up the circulation of money. This is why the British government could afford to tax consumer spending so highly and also why these taxpayers could afford to pay more tax than their counterparts across the channel.

Unlike Great Britain, France kept its inherited system in place during the eighteenth century, including the taxes created in 1695 and 1710, *capitation* and *dixième*, respectively, which were added on to ordinary direct taxation raked in by the government, primarily the traditional *taille*. The *dixième* was really an extraordinary war tax, albeit with a growing tendency to maintain it in peacetime. This occurred above all after 1749, even though only half of the tax was kept on, i.e., a *vingtième*. This would then be maintained as an ordinary tax in practice, during different periods (Riley 1986: 51). All this boosted the ongoing importance of direct taxes. New direct taxes were created or old ones were extended. This obviated the impossibility of upping the *taille* due to the opposition this would have produced. Creating a new tax in times of war was acceptable for French taxpayers; keeping on this tax in peacetime was also a more or less feasible option because its temporary nature meant there was always a hope of its being removed in the near future. But no one would have happily accepted a hike of the *taille*.

The system rested heavily on local institutions and ipso facto their elites, in charge of collecting the taxes in each region. This was especially important in the so-called *pays d'états* where these *états* continued to exist in institutional terms. In any case regional disparity was also great and increased further as the century wore on, with some regions becoming richer than others. From these regions the king also received loans, which were managed by the local assemblies themselves through their own fiscal administration. It would seem that the Crown did not draw on these regions as heavily as it might have done: money raised in the *pays d'états* was also spent locally so less of it filtered through to the treasury. In the *pays d'élections*, on the other hand, the money was sent to Paris where the treasury could record it. For this very reason France based its direct taxation system on the latter territories, not only because they took in a wider swathe of the country but also because the fiscal pressure had been proven to be higher there (Bonney 1999a: 161).

Among direct taxes those paid by the clergy were also important, with a donation every five years. This came from a profit tax administered by the ecclesiastical institutions themselves with their own financial organisation, fairly modern in its managerial procedures (Chaline 2004: 252). These ecclesiastical institutions defended their right to manage the tax themselves, fending off with particular strength a 1725 attempt to levy a *cinquantième* and the *vingtième* attempt of 1749. The church also pitched in with important extraordinary contributions in wartime.

French direct taxes ran headlong into the problem of privilege. This might be said to occur elsewhere but the French case is somewhat special due to the sheer number and prestige of the privilege holders and the direct relation of local elites with the regional *parlements*, including the almighty *parlement* of Paris. As judicial institutions the *parlements* naturally became fierce defenders of privilege and they are known to have caused numerous political problems during Louis XV's reign, precisely due to fiscal questions. Privilege, moreover, was essential for French society as the only realistic source of upward mobility. Land, it should not be forgotten, was still an immensely important factor in such a rich and extensive country. For all these reasons the privilege system could not be tampered with; this stymied any systematic attempt to raise direct taxes, which rose in quantitative terms only by dint of a large population increase (Riley 1986: 49). The only way of increasing direct taxation was therefore to create new taxes and tap into the population growth. In any case, if taxes grew in quantitative terms they trod water in real terms, showing that this was not the cause of any increase in fiscal pressure.

The French government had a better chance of increasing its revenue by means of indirect taxes. Therein lay a rub too, however; these taxes were farmed out to the *ferme général*. Raising the lease was tricky, but in the end this is what was done, even though a large part of this rise worked to the benefit of the *fermiers*, who maintained their position by bribing courtiers (Riley 1986: 61–62). All this ate away at the king's receipts, so the king obtained less benefit than expected from tax rises. Leases, in any case, did tend to rise throughout the century, as shown in Table 3.11. The table works with Marion's list, complete for the six-year rental terms as from 1726, and also Durand's figures, selective and not always tallying with the other author but adding in the value of some loans offered to the king by *fermiers*, involving sums to be paid back in a few months with interest rates varying from 5 to 10 per cent.

Proportional indirect-tax lease increases follow a similar trend to the one already seen for the total value of these farmed-out taxes. These increases could be achieved quite easily in view of the ongoing rise not only of the population but also trade and consumer demand in the France of that time, especially after 1763. Increases in current terms are one thing, however, and increases in real terms quite another, due to inflation, especially in the last third of the century. From this point of view, the fiscal burden of French taxpayers did not seem to vary on this score either in the central decades of the century. This situation changed, apparently, after 1770 (Riley 1987: 236–37). This appreciation, we should remember, refers only to ordinary taxes; if we also factor in extraordinary war-time taxation, the tax burden would be higher (Félix 1999: Chapter 2). In general, however, French taxpayers seem to have suffered a lower tax burden than the British, despite the increasing value of indirect taxes.

Table 3.11 Total value of the indirect tax leasing contract and *ferme général* loans (in millions of *livres tournais*)

Years	Leases Marion	Leases Durand	Loans
1726	80	80	
1732	84		
1738	83	91	
1741			25
1744	91/92		
1750	101		
1755		110	60
1756	110		
1762	118/124		
1768	132		72
1774	152	152	52
1780	123/126		
1786	144/150		

Source: Marion 1979: 234; Durand 1976: 21–22. When there are two figures the higher refers to the lease in times of peace and the lower to times of war.

With direct taxes growing and diversifying and indirect taxes also on the rise, the fiscal structure was left unchanged. The main fiscal policy of the governments, indeed, was to draw on revenue proceeding from the inherited taxation structure, boosted by the general growth in wealth and population. The same factors allowed the *dixième* and *vingtième* taxes, approved to meet warfare urgencies, to be retained in times of peace. In short, the increase in France's ordinary revenue during the short eighteenth century did not centre on a single tax, as in Great Britain. It was shared out among all existing taxes plus some new ones, both direct and indirect. In both cases the reasoning for this decision was based more on political-social than economic considerations.

In France, therefore, there was no real change on the seventeenth-century taxation system. Even though the old scheme had come in for some flak in earlier decades and John Law had made some attempt to modify it, after 1726 it was strengthened by the triumph of the *finances* (financiers) and a renewed *ferme général* under which practically all indirect taxes were farmed out (Durand 1976: 16; Félix 2011: 132). In the French system direct and indirect taxes were fairly evenly balanced in the overall revenue picture, both in terms of value and collection problems; furthermore, a significant chunk of France's financial resources was in private hands under the revenue-farming system or officials who acted as private agents, offering short-term loans, so the king could not change his tax base just as he wished. French governments therefore chose to boost revenue by means of new direct taxes and rate hikes of indirect taxes. The underlying basis was always the richness of the land and the country's demographic potential.

Spain presents a very different picture from both France and Great Britain, though its financial structure bears more resemblance to Great Britain's insofar as the increase in ordinary revenue was fuelled by a clutch of indirect taxes, while direct taxes were held steady for quite some time. Spain's traditional direct tax was the *servicios*, a kind of capitation, ordinary and extraordinary in origin, which turned in practice into an ordinary personal tax. In the eighteenth century it was of little importance (Martínez Ruiz 2007: 342). Within the Crown of Castile, for example, it was included as a minor part of the revenue set called *rentas provinciales*.

Spain, at least until Lerena's 1785 reform, had nothing resembling a land tax, so the most important direct taxes were those paid by the clergy under agreements between the king and the Holy See, sometimes dating back to the fifteenth century. Under this arrangement the church, as an institution, paid three categories of tax: *tercias reales, excusado* and *subsidio*. The first two entitled the king to a share in the ecclesiastical tithes (*diezmos*) paid by the population; this share of the *diezmos* was therefore managed by the diocese but paid to the king. The *subsidio* was an ancient crusade tax that also stemmed from the church's agrarian wealth. Hiking these taxes, given their origin, was difficult, since the agreements had been sanctioned by concordats of great legal and political complexity. The church also offered numerous donations and loans as extraordinary contributions, but the ordinary taxes varied little throughout the century.

Neither was there any variation in revenue based on the aforementioned *Nueva Planta* taxation decrees in the Crown of Aragon after the War of Succession. Their value did not really keep up with the growth of wealth throughout the century, so their real input tended to fall after 1730. This all meant that Spain's most important direct taxes grew very little during the century, although the church's contribution grew more in the second half.

If the direct-tax base could not be broadened, the government had to look to indirect taxes. As we have already seen Spain's indirect taxes made up a motley bunch, all managed together under the umbrella of *rentas provinciales*, Other indirect-tax items were the *rentas generales*, or customs duties, and the monopolies: tobacco, salt and tax on precious-metal mining in the Americas, which, with few exceptions, was just about the only tax revenue arriving from the Americas since colonial taxes were spent *in situ*.

The *rentas provinciales* were collected by means of lump-sum *encabezamiento* agreements and subsequent per capita distribution of the sum agreed, *repartimiento*. These procedures worked roughly as follows: a general calculation was made of the total hypothetical value of all these taxes for a given population; an agreement on the assessed sum was then reached between the king and the council of said population, ending with the subsequent distribution of this agreed sum among all affected taxpayers, depending on the type of product and the class of taxpayer. This means that, in practice, the value of the *rentas provinciales* bore no relationship to the consumer demand or mercantile situation of any given population but rather to the particular lump-sum agreement reached with the king. Throughout the eighteenth century, moreover, these agreements tended to perpetuate themselves, barring a few exceptions, until Lerena's aforementioned 1785 reform. In practice this part of the indirect taxes was heavily influenced by the overarching *alivio de los vasallos* policy, which, as we have already seen, bedded in over time with no variation and without reflecting any increases in the economic growth rate.

The objective of the tax-alleviation policy was therefore maintained, namely, freeing Castilian taxpayers from the heavy burden suffered in the seventeenth century and driving consumer demand and industrial output. The latter benefited from a policy of tax exemptions – especially from the *alcabalas* – which was extended to various industrial sectors as the century wore on. The result, as might be expected, was that the net value of *rentas provinciales* did not budge until the 1760s. After this decade there were certain changes but a real reform was not brought in until 1785. Despite all, it should be noted, *rentas provinciales* where the Crown's biggest revenue source until c. 1770. The tax-alleviation policy was therefore risky, tending as it did to freeze the biggest source of income.

Another component was customs duties but their yield was subject to the ups and downs of war. Customs were also affected by an idiosyncratic policy from the mercantilist protectionism point of view. As a result of the trading treaties signed since the last third of the seventeenth century, Spain had granted various trading benefits to its rivals, so most of its European trade system was not only structurally loss-making – export of raw materials and import of manufactured goods – but also low on customs duties. The value of customs duties rose only in the central decades of the century, thanks to the pacifist policy, but its base was still small until the trading reforms of the eighties. For similar reasons, although of a different contextual meaning, customs yield percentage was just as little in Spain as in Great Britain.

If revenue from consumer demand and trade stagnated due to internal policy and customs did likewise due to international policy, the only real option left for the Spanish government was to manage shrewdly the monopolies, and it tried to, concentrating on American precious metal, tobacco and salt, with other minor monopolies chipping in too. But before looking at this in some detail, we will take a quick glance at the relative importance of these various indirect taxes in comparison with each other, as shown in Table 3.12.

As this table shows, the first revenue source to grow, as from 1730, was precisely the monopolies. Trade – customs – began to grow only after 1750, probably benefiting from the years of peace but also from the change to direct administration. The *rentas provinciales* did not really take off until after 1785. At any rate, if we restrict our attention to the short eighteenth century, i.e., before 1789, which

Table 3.12 Main Spanish indirect taxes (in millions of *reales de vellón*) and their indexed growth rates. Base 100 = 1715–30

Years	Rentas Provinciales	Ind.	Customs	Ind.	Monopolies	Ind.	Indies	Ind.
1715–30	60	100	22	100	41	100	10	100
1735–45	58	96	22	100	61	148	34	340
1750–55	61	101	41	186	77	187	108	1080
1765–75	67	111	49	222	111	270	106	1060
1780–85	100	166	66	300	127	309	120	1200
1790–91	108	180	143	650	113	275	145	1450
1800–04	120	200	108	490	152	370	132	1320

Source: See Table 3.5.

for Spain would be c. 1780 (since the main economic reforms came afterwards), we then find that the only tax-revenue sources to grow substantially in this period were the tobacco and American-metal monopolies, so we will now look at them in more detail.

3.4 Tobacco and metals, the pearls of the Empire

Monopolies were managed in such a way as to try to increase revenue without upping taxes that impinged on taxpayers' daily life. This would be achieved if more money flooded in from the Americas and if tobacco yielded more. Both things happened. In the case of precious metal, little needed to be done, since the yield depended on mining work, but the fiscal yield from the tobacco monopoly could be controlled by means of the right pricing policy, since the raw material supply was assured.

Uztáriz wrote that "tobacco revenue is your Majesty's surest and most useful income, and will become increasingly opulent if your administration gives it the care and attention it deserves" (Uztáriz, 1742: 367). The phrase "most useful" probably means that it had the highest yield with the lowest cost and risk; it was the "surest" because it was the least prone to value swings and also produced the quickest returns; furthermore, it was easy to make it more "opulent" because a simple improvement in management procedures would produce a sharp growth.

Uztáriz knew what he was talking about because he had past experience in both absolute and relative terms with revenue administration, dating back to the last third of the seventeenth century (Rodríguez Gordillo, 2002: 59).

Rodríguez Gordillo has compiled the known values for the tobacco yield in the seventeenth century. We note down some of them in Table 3.13.

This increase in the value of the tobacco revenue was occurring in the aforementioned context of tax alleviation, with *rentas provinciales* in decline. There were also other measures of tax reform. Artola has referred, for example, to the measures taken in 1688. He comments that, rather than increasing income, these measures tended to free up existing income and make it more readily available to the exchequer, doing so on the basis of organisational reforms. In fact, he says "the only item that recorded a significant increase was tobacco revenue" (Artola 1982: 221).

The situation would be similar in the eighteenth century, tending to follow the policy lines laid down by Uztáriz and swelling the tobacco component of the king's income. Tobacco revenue was the first to be brought into direct administration in 1730 (Rodríguez Gordillo 2006: 71). Moreover, this administrative change went hand in hand with a sharp hike in prices throughout the whole of the thirties. These price-rises punctured demand and no doubt spurred a concomitant increase in contraband consumption but the king raked in more: the higher price more than made up for the fall in official sales. In all, tobacco revenue rose from 28.9 million *reales* in 1726 to 44.6 million *reales* by 1736 (Pulido Bueno 1998: 306; Rodríguez Gordillo 2000: 53–103). Changed into eighteenth-century money, the 304.5 million *maravedís* of 1698 (Table 3.13) would convert into about 8.9 million *reales*, giving a good idea of the quantum leap given by this revenue in the first decades of the eighteenth century.

Figure 3.5 compares the growth rates of Spain's most important revenue sources (apart from precious metals), *provinciales, generales* and tobacco.

Figure 3.5 suffers from the drawback, albeit not overly important, of coming from different sources. In terms of the main purpose of establishing the mutual relationship of the various revenue sources, however, Figure 3.5 is clear and telling. It shows what we might call the fiscal success of tobacco, especially from 1680 to 1780. It also clearly shows the stagnation of *rentas provinciales*, the fluctuations of *rentas generales*, caused by mercantile problems, and the clearly upward trend of tobacco revenue in comparison with the other two. The rises in

Table 3.13 Value of the tobacco lease in Spain (in millions of *maravedís*)

Year	Value
1671	114.8
1691	170.7
1694	201.5
1698	304.5

Source: Rodríguez Gordillo 1984: 16.

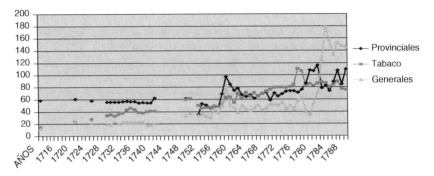

Figure 3.5 Net value trend of the revenue from tobacco, *rentas provinciales* and *rentas generales* (in millions of *reales de vellón*)

Source: Kamen 1974, Fernández Albaladejo 1977, Pieper 1992, Merino 1987.

the three revenues from about 1740 to 1743 were largely due to the introduction of direct administration, but with clearly superior results for tobacco revenue already under direct administration since 1730.

For quite some time, therefore, tobacco revenue was the main leverage for raising total income. Furthermore, the sheer success of this revenue suggested that the old ways, based on state monopolies, were still efficient means of increasing revenue, so it did not seem to be essential to make any thoroughgoing overhaul of the taxation structure (González Enciso, 2006b). Physiocracy pundits claimed that commerce should be the mainstay for increasing economic activity and hence state income, but this was no easy task. The real world called for quicker returns. Experience had shown that the revenue most likely to grow in the first half of the century, and perhaps even afterwards, was tobacco, on the back of price increases. There were drawbacks to this, however. Tobacco revenue could be raised by increasing the price of manufactured tobacco but with the obvious risk of turning consumers away from the king's tobacco. This is why a different tactic was pursued after the price hike of 1741, consisting in freezing the price and improving the organisation of the whole revenue and product-distribution process. This policy was maintained and bore fruit up to 1779, when there was no other choice but to raise the retail price. The immediate consequences were disastrous.

The role of tobacco in the economy lends itself to revealing comparisons between Spain and France, where a monopoly had also been established. The Spanish monopoly covered manufacture and sale; it was set up in 1636 for the Crown of Castile (Rodríguez Gordillo 2002). Other regions were phased into the Castilian monopoly later until building up to a nationwide monopoly by the beginning of the eighteenth century. The raw tobacco was bought in Cuba, to be milled up for snuff, or in Portugal, where coarser Brazilian leaves were procured for smoking tobacco. All processing work, cursory or elaborate depending on the product in each case, was carried out in the Seville factory, which had been expanding in size enormously since the mid-eighteenth century (Rodríguez Gordillo 2005). The official sales outlets, called *estancos*, were spread throughout the whole of Spain.

The tax rake-off depended on the sales price. From 1636 to 1730 this operation was farmed out to financiers who managed the whole process and paid the government the stipulated leasing rental (Rodríguez Gordillo 1984, 2006). In 1730 the revenue was brought into direct administration and the tax farmers disappeared from the picture. Under this new arrangement, although the state took on managerial costs, the net tax revenue increased considerably. From here on the tobacco policy would depend above all on establishing the right sales price for the finished products. It goes without saying that this official trade had to fight against a widespread black market. Quasi-military resources were set up against this contraband trade, including a troop called the *resguardo del tabaco* (tobacco police), which was confidently expected to produce fruitful results.

The situation in France was similar in some respects. In 1674 a monopoly had been set up on the sale only. In 1721 this monopoly was extended to tobacco-manufacture and growing, the latter banned hitherto as in Spain. The indirect tax was brought within the *ferme générale* arrangement in 1730, oddly enough just at the time it was taken into direct administration in Spain. As in Spain, price increases and squabbles about quality spurred a thriving contraband trade. The results of both countries are shown in Figure 3.6. Although figures for France are thin on the ground, they are enough for sketching a comparison. They represent the values reached in each indicated year, the lease rental. Up to 1730 the Spanish figures reflect the lease paid by the tax farmers and then the net revenue thereafter.

Figure 3.6 shows the different results in each country. Spain's tobacco-monopoly yield was higher than France's in the first half of the century, even forging further ahead after the introduction of direct administration in 1730. *Ferme general* management, on the other hand, did not increase the yield until 1750, when the rise was probably fuelled by the war needs of the time. From 1750 to 1780 both systems showed an upward trend. Spanish figures might be inflated by the fact that

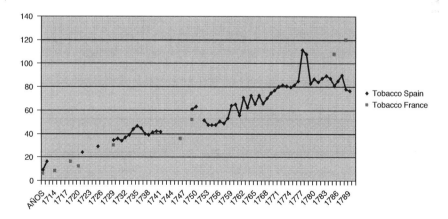

Figure 3.6 Tobacco revenue in Spain and France (both figures in millions of *reales de vellón*)

Sources: Spain, see Figure 3.5; France, Marion 1979: 524–25.

American tobacco sales accounts switched to Madrid at that time (Torres Sánchez 2006: 217) whereas these profits should rightfully be attributed to Spain's imperial tobacco system (Luxán Meléndez et al. 2012: 35; Luxán Meléndez 2014). A watershed moment came in 1780. France's figures soared, mainly due to increased consumption but also thanks to some price rises (Marion 1979: 525). In Spain, on the contrary, the pricing policy threatened to undermine the monopoly's credibility. In comparative terms, however, the monopoly had certainly stood Spain in good stead up to that moment.

Turning to precious metals from the Americas, we find that they flooded into Europe in increasing amounts during the short eighteenth century, as shown by Morineau (Morineau 1985). But it should be borne firmly in mind here that all the Spanish American output did not get to the king of Spain or even to Spain itself. The only part that filtered into the king's coffers was what could strictly be called the tax, i.e., a fifth of the output. This is what counted in taxation terms; the rest belonged to the mercantile world, to private individuals, as pointed out by Hamilton. One characteristic feature of the eighteenth century is that the share of private individuals, fruit of the mercantile activity, grew more than *hacienda*'s share (García-Baquero González 1976: I, 347), although the latter sum also grew. In any case the trade upturn also produced a positive knock-on effect for the government in the form of increased customs duties. The amounts of precious metal arriving in Spain, according to the well-researched figures recently produced by García-Baquero González (García-Baquero González 2003: 55–56), are shown in Table 3.14.

Of these sums the *hacienda* received about 14 per cent on average (García-Baquero González 1976: I, 345), meaning that not all the tax yield was sent to Spain. In some years this was tantamount to almost half the total net value of

Table 3.14 Precious metals arriving in Spain. Five-year means

Years	Millions of pesos
1717–22	6.33
1723–27	10.2
1728–32	10.4
1734–38	10.6
1739–43	4.7
1744–48	6.7
1749–53	23.1
1754–58	17.1

Source: García-Baquero 2003.

ordinary revenue. This shows the importance of American precious metal and the premium that governments placed on its arrival, to help offset the deficits being run up elsewhere. For reasons of security or convenience precious metal did not reach Spain every year and this deficit-repairing event was then eagerly awaited. It was in fact possible to balance the books precisely because of this monetary input from the Americas (Torres Sánchez, 2006).

Although corrected in the interests of greater accuracy, the sums indicated by García-Baquero González (Table 3.14) echo the same trend as Morineau's figures (Morineau 1985). As can be seen, the trend was clearly upwards. From the initial fairly low position (1717–22) imports rose steeply in the second five-year period and then held steady for a long, 15-year period during which arrivals were more substantial than before. These figures may cloak fairly wild year-to-year swings but, year after year, the metal would arrive in the end and fulfil its function. The warfare period running from 1739 to 1748 cut down the flow, although a significant amount continued to arrive. After the war there was an upturn, accounting for the high values recorded in the five-year period 1749–53; in any case the level of activity also rose, because the following five-year period, the last of our series, also chalked up high figures. The best years were still to come.

One conclusion can probably be drawn from these figures. They show that the governors' aim of balancing the books was possible precisely due to a source of natural wealth in the form of precious metals and the *regalía* (exclusive right to tax) that the king held over this trade. This has to be taken into account as an important factor when pondering why Spain did not embark on a public-debt policy in those years. If this natural boon was accompanied by an improvement of trade and a better defence of shipping, the picture would be even brighter; but this would have to be achieved by other methods.

3.5 Possibilities and flexibility of fiscal policies

As we have just seen, during the short eighteenth century, once the political and economic situation had been stabilised in the twenties, the three countries maintained the ordinary revenue structures inherited from the long *fin de siècle*. This does not mean they did not try to swell their revenue stream. Needs grew in part because of the very nature of political management and above all because the wars of the time produced a sharp increase in expenditure. This was catered for largely by means of public debt, the interest of which then had to be paid from ordinary revenue. The problem was permanent in Great Britain and France, less important or tardier in Spain. In any case all three countries sought to increase their ordinary revenue, falling back in each case on very different methods according to the nature of their societies and economies. No preconceived long-term plans seemed to be in place. In general, politicians turned a deaf ear to economic pundits who recommended different methods, some quite fanciful, such as an insistence by some on reducing all revenue to a single contribution or an all-embracing income tax. A pragmatic mindset held sway instead. Urgencies of the time and vested interests prompted governments to fall back on known structures.

In Great Britain, where the most thoroughgoing fiscal overhaul had been brought in, direct management and predominance of a single tax, the excise, the forthright decision was taken to base its ordinary revenue system on consumer demand, a demand driven by growing taxpayer wealth, enabling them to withstand higher tax pressure than their counterparts on the continent. In France there was no real change on the seventeenth-century situation; French governments continued to increase their revenue with new taxes and upping the rates on indirect taxes. It was all still underpinned by the wealth of the land and the kingdom's demographic potential.

Spain's case was completely different. It reined back consumer taxation and made no real attempt to levy a land tax. Witness the failure of the single tax scheme in Ensenada's cadastre (Angulo Teja 2002). The lukewarm success of the Aragon cadastre, introduced after the War of Succession, did not exactly predispose politicians to embark on another similar project. Spain, in any case, boasted a good system of monopolies, especially the American precious-metals monopoly, which made up for any debt left by the ordinary budget. To this was added tobacco, made and sold on the king's account, which in some moments proved to be a very efficient source of revenue. In short, consumer demand, land/population and monopolies are the three mainstays of ordinary revenue in the countries considered, three different sources although related to others in each case, which depend on the idiosyncrasies of countries that also differed in their geography, natural resources and population, history and institutions. Although there are many similarities there are also big differences and each country played its part with the structure it had.

Although the fiscal structures referred to above lasted throughout practically the whole eighteenth century, barring partial modifications in the eighties, only the British solution was flexible enough to be able to enlarge the tax base. It would seem, therefore, that they corresponded not only to political possibilities in each case or simple pragmatism but also a way of thinking. These fiscal attitudes, deeply rooted in the socio-political structure, pose the problem of the capacity of increasing these resources, i.e., to make them yield more. Subsequent historical experience showed that definitive fiscal-growth capacity in the eighteenth century lay in consumer demand, which in turn depended on commercial and agrarian wealth; only on the strength of consumer demand could the tax base be reliably broadened. Even the population increase had a fiscal limit unless this population could be made richer. In France the population grew strongly but by the end of the century Great Britain outstripped France's ordinary revenue with only half its population.

What we are talking about here is an institutional question. Favouring the development of useful citizens, whose wealth not only makes them happy but capable of paying taxes to the king, had been a shibboleth of the Enlightenment since the very start of the century. This called for institutions to channel this social usefulness. Only a more mercantile society could pull this off and Great Britain took the lead in this sense. Only Great Britain plumped decisively for a demand-driven system to increase its ordinary tax revenue. It also encouraged trade, not to cream off more customs duties, we repeat, as some pundits of the time were advocating and other countries were trying, but simply because trade created wealth among all participants therein and ipso facto increased their taxpaying ability. Probably the British government really had no other option, since land was scarce, and trying to screw too much out of customs duties might have jeopardised its overseas trade. If we look at this from the fiscal standpoint, domestic trade comes across as one of the mainstays of British wealth, albeit in connection with overseas markets. Economic historians remind us, after all, that England built up Europe's biggest domestic market, free of the slew of fiscal or institutional barriers that hindered the development of a unified market in Spain or France. Both countries undertook important reforms on this matter (Pérez Sarrión 2012), but Great Britain led the way.

Were each country's fiscal attitudes new or not? Great Britain's principal reliance on consumer demand could certainly be claimed to be new, but not so much the importance of trade in general as the source of wealth both for government and governed. In 1739 M. Decker, one of the writers on these matters at that time, reiterated the long-standing claim that nations with no gold and silver mines could obtain their resources only from overseas trade, building on arguments that T. Mun and others had been trundling out since the sixteenth century (Decker 1756: 1–2; Viner 1965: Chapter IV). England's strategy since the sixteenth century had been very pragmatic, harnessing its only realistic possibilities. Its only way of besieging Spain's towering castle, propped up by its precious-metal monopoly, and the system of *flotas* for the American trade, was with "mercantile guerrilla warfare", based on private trade. Over time this enforced option turned out to be surprisingly and unexpectedly fruitful: the English were rich and their consumer demand could be taxed forcefully. Domestic demand and trading markets, in short, enabled Great Britain to build up a simple and fruitful taxation system without any constitutional complications.

France would seem to be the most conservative state for our purposes here. This comes across with the ongoing importance not only of the *ferme general*, revived in 1726, but also direct taxes. Consumer demand grew, as did trade in general (Léon 1970: 503), but the search for new fiscal resources continued to rely above all on reiterated *vingtièmes* and other similar income taxes, which served only to reproduce the former system. French conservatism stemmed from the rigidity of its inherited structures; these were its only guarantee of being able to pay off at least part of its heavy debt. The efforts made during Louis XIV's reign backfired. Some reforms were brought in at the end of the reign but came to little. Hence the restoration of the old system in 1726.

In spite of Spain's end-of-dynasty situation in 1700, the dominant traits of its eighteenth-century taxation policy came from a long way back. The American precious-metal option, for example, had been a stalwart since the sixteenth century (Yun Casalilla 2004) and the fact that this precious metal began to flow in more strongly from the end of the seventeenth century and continued to do so throughout the whole eighteenth century was good news. Other long-standing features were *alivio de los vasallos* and debt chariness, plus some administrative reforms we have already mentioned. The new dynasty did not therefore really come up with anything new; reformism also had a long tradition behind it (Elliott 1990: 104). Nonetheless, the dynastic change, with the constant reshuffling of the elites close to government, favoured not only intensification of traditional trends – such as the ongoing attempts to reform American trade – but also the trying out of some new reforms, of sketchy success, such as the cadastres, or some more successful ventures like direct administration of tax revenue. From this perspective, Spanish governments were much more innovative and reform-minded than the French in terms of their fiscal traditions. Even before 1726 Spain's reforms had managed to centralise most of the money in the hands of the *Secretario de Hacienda* (Dubet 2015b: 589), and many more reforms were to be brought in in the future.

If trade and mercantile policy offered different fiscal possibilities in each country, what about the land? This question is bound up with an aspect more political than economic, namely privilege. In fiscal terms it balked the levying of taxes on property and also on income from the land. Given that any commercial or consumer-based activity affected the privileged and plebeians alike, in legal terms, the difference between both lay mainly in the land, the symbol par excellence of prestige in the still estates-based society of the eighteenth century. That said, privileges existed everywhere; it was also difficult everywhere to establish taxes on land ownership or income. Where such taxes were paid, they were meagre. Theories blaming fiscal weakness on the fiscal exemption of the privileged do not therefore sit very well with the real situation of the eighteenth century.

In any case there were some differences. Great Britain and France managed to make landed interests pay something, albeit much less than they could rightfully afford, either due to defence of their privileges, evasion (Riley 1986: 52), or from government fear that the tax might rise quicker than the taxpayer's wealth, as occurred in France with the *taille*. The overriding concern was to head off resentment of the tax, a sort of tax-alleviation policy at the end of the day. Land taxes in Spain, in particular, were limited to the clergy and the little that could be milked from Aragon cadastres. In view of the meagre amount that land paid elsewhere, it can hardly be regarded as the main problem of Spain's fiscal system. It should also be pointed out that in times of war landed interests coughed up something in all countries, including Spain, though these special taxes or rate hikes of ordinary taxes were removed afterwards.

Spain's fiscal policy suffered from many restrictions, real or imagined. Political will prevented consumer demand from being taxed more heavily; neither could much be done with customs duties, governed as they were by international agreements. The single-tax attempt also failed. Other restrictions stemmed from the need of fomenting both national industry and domestic trade, so these activities benefited from tax reductions, exemptions and sundry privileges. Spain's taxation system, however, benefited from its control over American precious metals and its tobacco monopoly. To a lesser extent it also drew on its salt monopoly but without pushing things in this case.

3.6 Changes in the fiscal structure as from the eighties and the breakdown of some systems

The American Revolutionary War represented an unprecedented military effort for all contending states. This hit each country's fiscal system hard. Each one reacted differently, however, in due accordance with its former policies and present possibilities. In some cases, especially in Spain, the impact of this war led to a partial change of the country's fiscal policy. In the other two cases the consequences were also different.

Great Britain's debt almost doubled from 1776 to 1786. Something similar had occurred during the Seven Years' War, but the effect was greater this time. The debt burden was now heavier than it had been back in 1763 and the proportion of debt-defrayed expenditure was also higher (Wilson and Parker 1977: 131–32). But what is of interest to us here is that the increase of the debt and its burden, the normal way of paying for wars in Great Britain, represented a 47 per cent cost increase in the period 1776–83 in comparison to the period 1756–63. In line with the country's usual practice, this increase in costs and, in the end, the burden of the debt, was shared out between different taxes. Some were held back specifically for paying off the interest on the new debt (Brewer 1989: 116), while excise bore the brunt, its yield again growing notably as from 1783. The American War brought Great Britain's financing possibilities to the brink but produced no change in its ordinary revenue structure, since indirect taxes, especially excise, proved capable of coping with this new load.

Great Britain's increase of consumer taxes was supported by the mercantile and financial development of the years following 1783, despite the loss of its colonies. The customs yield, indeed, doubled after 1790 (O'Brien 1988: 9). The ensuing series of conflicts, however, triggered by the French Revolution, took a heavy toll on this system, forcing the debt and its burden even higher. It was then, in 1799, that Pitt established an income tax, which proved to be a crucial supplement for successfully financing these conflicts. Until then Great Britain had not had any institutional instrument for tapping into the wealth of the highest-income classes (Mathias and O'Brien 1976: 626). This tax enabled the British fiscal state to overcome some of its former limitations (O'Brien 2009); at this moment direct taxes weighed in with a serious contribution to the country's tax needs. By 1810 excise, customs and direct taxes accounted for a similar proportion of total revenue, standing at 36, 30 and 34 per cent, respectively. This represented a significant change in the fiscal structure. Total revenue, of course, was rising after 1790; hence the importance of income tax's input at a moment when revenue needs were soaring.

In France too the American war had a swingeing impact on royal finances. This war cost France 1.3 billion *livres tournais*, 100 million more than the cost of the Seven Years' War. This cost was financed above all by credit, which was not difficult to raise at the time, including abroad (Félix and Tallet 2009: 161–62). Up to there the situation is similar to Great Britain's. The problem came afterwards. Contrary to Great Britain, France seemed to have problems in increasing taxes after the war to pay off the debt interest. The problem resided not so much in increasing taxes as in the political fallout of doing so. The tax increase, combined with the policies of Necker and Calonne, prompted elites to demand some say in financial management procedures. All this ended up unleashing the Revolution. We will not get involved here in the discussion about the "financial origins" of the French Revolution (Legay, Félix and White 2009), but the political and economic significance of the 1787 fiscal crisis is clear. For the time being the situation impinged little on basic fiscal structures, even though taxpayers did feel the pinch. The *vingtième* was doubled from 1782 and indirect taxes were also raised (Félix 2005), but the fiscal structure was tipped more heavily towards indirect taxes, giving the impression that the elites were inputting less than other taxpayers.

The influence of these changes on the Revolution is more a question of politics and perception, which falls beyond our remit here, but what is clear is the influence of the Revolution on the new tax changes. Abolition of the privileges meant the whole fiscal system had to be overhauled. Tax farming was ended and the debt was channelled through the new *assignats*, paper money representing the value of confiscated church property, declared to be *biens nationaux*. In general, the Revolution relied more on debt – until the bankruptcy of 1797 – and on pillage favoured by its military victories, especially in the Low Countries (deposits of the Bank of Amsterdam) and in Italy (Félix and Tallet 2009: 165). A more coherent fiscal system was eventually restored by Napoleon, including a return to indirect taxes, plus other measures. Napoleon, in any case, also got the war to finance itself, procuring men, money and goods of all types from the conquered countries (Branda 2005a, 2005b), a system harking back to methods of ancient empires. This hit the conquered countries hard, especially Spain, but it was good for France and helped to stave off a fiscal crisis after the system fell in 1815.

In Spain too the eighties brought important changes in fiscal policies and structures. These changes had been to some extent foreshadowed by the 1778 decree of free trade with the Americas. This decree spelled the end of Cadiz's dominance of the state monopoly of trade with the American colonies, with more Spanish ports now entitled to enter American trade. This measure would boost trade and therewith customs revenue only after 1783, because, for now, the outbreak of war with England, after the independence of the United States, brought trade to a standstill.

Apart from mercantile policy, which predates the war, the 1779 conflict triggered several changes in the fiscal policy, affecting the state monopolies, debt and the *rentas provinciales*, each in a different manner. The final result would be a reshuffling of indirect taxes during the eighties and nineties: increased importance of the customs duties, an upwards reassessment of the *rentas provinciales*, albeit with lower values than customs, and a fall in tobacco. All this within the context of a growing importance of American precious metals, recording all-time highs in these decades.

The first war-related ordinary-revenue measure affected tobacco. A 25 per cent price rise was decreed in 1779: manufactured tobacco thus rose from 32 to 40 *reales de vellón* per Castilian *libra*. This price rise sparked off a sharp fall in demand and a wholesale switch to the contraband trade, with a knock-on fall this time in tobacco tax revenue: the revenue nosedived after 1780, the fall lasting until 1793.

A new, gentler price rise in 1794 turned the revenue trend upwards again. In all likelihood the contraband trade was also sluggish at this time, given the situation of the global conflict and, above all, due to the Pyrenean war. After another dip, revenue bucked up again in 1797, then recording values, in nominal terms, similar to the sixties; this represented a stiff revenue loss in times of strong inflation. At a moment when more might be expected of a revenue source once so fruitful, it suffered from the authorities' over-optimistic opinion of demand inelasticity.

Growing war needs forced the Spanish government, finally, to set up a public debt system based on *vales reales* (paper money), in 1780. We will look at this development later on. Our immediate interest here is its direct relationship with an important reform that affected ordinary revenue: the reform of the *alcabalas* by Lerena, in 1785. In justification of this measure the minister referred to the need of increasing taxes to defray the costs "of the past war" and in particular to meet the growing debt obligations. We are therefore dealing here with an arrangement that resembles the British: defraying the war by running up a debt and then paying it off afterwards with peacetime tax hikes; on the understanding that it was only this tax rise that was going to make the debt payment possible.

Nothing was said about the fall in tobacco revenue to justify the *alcabalas* reform but the government must have been mindful of it at the time, even though they were confident of recouping some of the lost revenue on the strength of firm anti-contraband measures underway at the time (Escobedo Romero 2000). The government must also have been aware at this time of the increase in customs revenue. The peace of 1783 not only freed up the war-blocked trade but also began to make good the hopes deposited in "free trade". Despite the expected recovery of tobacco revenue and the growth of customs revenue, plus the arrival of more precious metal, the government decided to go ahead with the *alcabalas* reform, thus breaking a century-long policy of alleviation in this important revenue source.

All the abovementioned circumstances explain the economic and political importance of Lerena's reform, which has been classed as "the chief fiscal innovation of the whole century" (Artola 1982: 338). Its value can also be gauged from its ongoing mould-breaking influence in subsequent decades (Moral Ruiz 1990: 37). It was a realistic response to the growing spending power of the taxpayers of the Crown of Castile, downgrading the previous watchword of general alleviation, introducing a more progressive system whereby the poor would pay proportionately less than the rich. To do so, the rate applied to various consumer goods was lowered. Here we see another reflection of the British excise model.

One fundamental aspect of the measure was to modify the contracts agreed up to then between the king and the towns, i.e., changing the *encabezamiento* regime for another in which the sums to be paid by each locality were reviewed. Not only that, but this review would be conducted not by the interested parties, but by royal officials; furthermore, the tax would be levied on goods in city doors rather than at the sales outlet, thereby saving administrative expenses. Another fundamental aspect of the reform is that it was decided to implement protectionist duties against foreign goods, in keeping with the customs measures included in the free-trade decree with the Americas in 1782. Above all, it introduced a land tax that, although small as yet, broke the landowners' longstanding resistance to contribute towards the nation's revenue.

What were the results? Table 3.15 records the gross yield of *rentas provinciales* in some selected years before and after 1785. Gross values are used here because they tally with the collection procedures of the time.

As this table shows its values rose from 102 million *reales* in 1779, before any war-caused measures had begun to bite, to 155 million by 1791, before Lerena died in January 1792. We mention this fact to show that the minister, while still alive and in the breech, could see how his reform had fuelled an almost 55 per cent revenue spike. Although the measure was wide-ranging the biggest revenue earner was higher trade duties, especially on foreign goods. In some cases, trade taxes in ports accounted for more than 57 per cent of the revenue increase (González Enciso 2008a). The reform showed, as its defenders claimed, that both the population increase and the rise in economic activity vindicated the insistence on indirect taxes and in particular the controversial *rentas provinciales*. This reform vouched for the validity of the traditional system, once suitably improved.

As we have already seen, a substantial part of the increase stemmed from new trade taxes, which in turn depended on a certain level of spending power among the population. The reform's future, therefore called for this demand and ipso facto this trade to be kept up in the future. This begs the question of how far trade would in fact grow to continue underpinning the tax system. We have already pointed out that both *rentas provinciales* and customs grew in Spain in 1783–85, thanks to trade with America. We have also seen that tobacco revenue fell, while more precious metal arrived from the Americas. In other words, despite Lerena's reform, and even though this reform did introduce the odd direct tax, the over-arching fiscal structure remained basically the same but with a new bias towards indirect taxes, now above all tapping into booming American trade and precious metals. The overall result of all these factors was that Spain's fiscal structure had swung towards a greater dependence on the Americas during the period 1783–85.

Table 3.15 Gross value of *rentas provinciales*, 1779–91 (in millions of reales de vellón)

1779	102
1781	116
1783	121
1785	125
1787	132
1789	136
1791	155

Source: Artola 1982: 349.

How much did it do so and what consequences did it have? Working from the series of net values of Spain's main tax-revenue items drawn up by Merino and selecting key years from the period running from 1778, before the war with Great Britain, up to 1801, we see Spain's new fiscal structure quite clearly (Figure 3.7a) and can consider its financial effect in the international circumstances of the times.

There are two striking features in Figure 3.7a: the regularity of some series and the haphazardness of others. *Rentas provinciales* and tobacco, indeed, hold pretty steady throughout the period. In comparison with the past, the increase in *rentas provinciales* helped to offset the fall in tobacco. In other words, the two revenue items that had been the mainstays up to 1778 held their own. Taken together, the twosome seems to have withstood the difficulties of the times without falling in real terms. Nonetheless, the fall in tobacco revenue practically wiped out the rise in *rentas provinciales*, since the sum of the two together held steady throughout the period, as Figure 3.7a clearly shows.

The most fickle revenue items were *rentas generales* and *rentas de Indias* (including precious metals). The latter had always been important, if highly variable, but after 1788 the Indies revenue soared to an all-time high (Morineau 1985). Customs had always been low but lurched upwards after 1783. Customs and Indies made up Spain's two most important revenue items, the other two lagging way behind in the period 1783–96. Pairing up the four revenue items (*Provinciales* with tobacco and customs with *Indias* as in Figure 3.7b) brings out the heavy dependence of Spain's finances on the Americas. Tobacco also came from the Americas but not all from Spain's colonies. Sold tobacco included a growing proportion of Brazilian tobacco as smoking took over from snuff (Rodríguez Gordillo and Gárate Ojanguren 2007). The dependence of this revenue on Spain's own colonies was therefore declining.

In summary we could say that fiscal growth up to 1796 was based above all on the most American twosome of the time, customs and precious metals. Their

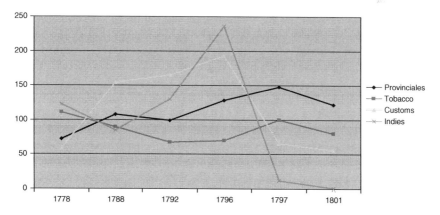

Figure 3.7a The breakdown of Spain's trading system at the end of the eighteenth century (Values in millions of *reales de vellón*)

Source: Merino 1987.

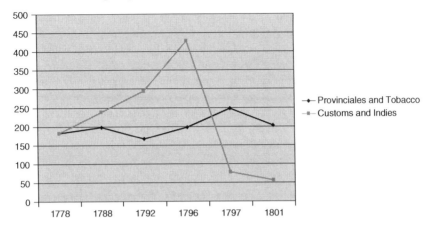

Figure 3.7b The breakdown of Spain's trading system at the end of the eighteenth
century (Values in millions of *reales de vellón*)

Source: Merino 1987.

proportion was by now much higher than before when customs revenue was low
and precious metal arrived at a slower rate. Both revenues together grew much
quicker than the other twosome of *rentas provinciales* and tobacco until 1796 and
then fell off a cliff.

In this context the breakdown of Spain's trading system with the Americas
was one of the main causes of the fiscal crisis. The alliance with France and
the ensuing confrontation with Great Britain led to defeat at the Battle of Cape
St. Vincent (1797), which cut off sea trade between Spain and its American
colonies. By and large, Spanish trade with the Americas was dependent on the
ups and downs of international warfare (García-Baquero González 1972). There
were only few moments of recovery, for example after the Treaty of Amiens
(1802). Despite an empire-wide permission for neutral trade as from 1797, no
money actually got to Spain many years, so the financial system proved incapable
of paying off the debts of an increasingly expensive war. Lerena's reform had
probably fallen short; Spain's fiscal structure should in all likelihood have phased
in a higher proportion of direct taxes, as Great Britain did in 1799. At least until
1797, in any case, the system held up pretty well.

Like France and Great Britain, Spain met rising needs by turning to the debt
option. There lay the key for being able to defray warfare costs. The trouble was
the ordinary revenue system needed to cater for the increasing debt burden and
to do so needed to grow more; in general, it failed to do so. In comparative terms
British ordinary revenue did manage to pay off the debt and could do so because
the country was able to increase domestic and foreign trade and thus boost taxpayers' spending power. France fell back more on the land but failed to pay off its
debt despite its large population, due to the high evasion rates. The fiscal failure
was closely bound up with the Revolution, but when war broke out, the demise of
privileges unearthed fiscal resources that had previously been hidden.

Spain placed its trust in the Americas. The idea was not a bad one and was certainly being advocated by most pundits of the time. But the liberalisation of the trade, which had boosted general wealth, came too late and by 1797 the fiscal system was bereft of necessary resources for coping with the situation. In France a glut of privileges limited its fiscal capacity – above all with direct taxes – and led to the Revolution. But French land was still under the governance of the new regime, which was able once more to procure the necessary wherewithal. In Spain a surfeit of monopolies rigidified the tax system and limited recourse to other revenue options. The trouble was that America was much further off for Spain than French land for France. Harnessing the resources of the Americas called for controlling the Atlantic and this is something Spain never managed to pull off.

Notes

1 The figures for Spain and Great Britain are net, as indicated by the sources used. Those of France are net for direct taxes only, not farmed out, which accounted for 55 per cent of total revenue during most of the eighteenth century (Durand 1976: 21). In the French case, therefore, allowance will have to be made, for comparison purposes, for a slight reduction due to the management of direct revenue. In the case of France, we have chosen the figures of Mathias and O'Brien rather than those of Riley (Riley 1987), merely to give more uniformity to the France-Great Britain comparison, already made by the first two authors. Riley's figures, for their part, give a better picture of extraordinary revenue.

2 The *rentas provinciales* (provincial revenue) were paid in the provinces (hence their name) of the Crown of Castile. They were a group of traditional taxes pooled under this heading since the late seventeenth century (Gelabert 1999). They comprised the *alcabalas* (sales tax), the *millones* (consumer tax), the *servicios* (an indirect poll tax) plus many sundries. The ones mentioned, especially the first two, accounted for the bulk of the *rentas provinciales* (Angulo Teja, 2002); they can therefore, as a set, be considered as a direct tax on trade and consumers. The brunt of the burden fell on the cities.

The *rentas de Indias* were taxes levied on silver mining in the Americas (one-fifth was a rake-off for the king), plus the value of some *derechos reales* (rights in rem) which were sent home to Spain instead of being spent in the colonies like most of the other taxes raised there.

The *rentas eclesiásticas* were a varied group of taxes, in general levied on products of the land, paid by the church to the king. The *catastro* of the Crown of Aragon is the generic name of the new taxes levied in the Crown of Aragon as part of the reform brought in by the centralising decrees called *Decretos de Nueva Planta* after the War of Succession. Although they took in some traditional taxes, their most important feature was a means-tested income tax according to the wealth recorded in the *catastro* (cadastral survey).

4 Increasing revenue through administration change
Direct administration of taxes

In the previous chapter we looked at the fiscal structure and saw how governors made attempts to increase ordinary revenue, a task fraught with serious difficulties. It is true that in some cases a tax might yield more without intrinsic changes due to growth of concomitant factors such as population or economic activity. During wars, moreover, new taxes were brought in, existing taxes were hiked and debt arrangements were made. In some cases, these increases were kept on in peacetime, as was the usual practice with the French *vingtièmes*. Then there was the British system of raising the rates of ordinary taxes in peacetime to pay off the debt run up during the war without, in general, creating new taxes. Was it possible to avoid all these new taxes? The question, in this case, would be to increase the income while charging the same, i.e., without increasing the burden on taxpayers. Regarding this matter, governors could act implementing organisational changes and improving collection procedures. These measures were political and administrative in type rather than fiscal per se.

Possible changes in that direction were debated for a long time, since they enshrined larger questions like theoretical approaches to the best fiscal strategy and the existing web of vested interests in each country. Any changes were obviously likely to alter the existing situation. The ideas most often mulled over were the single-tax and direct administration options. The former was called in Spain *única contribución* and was never actually brought in anywhere. The latter was called *universal administración*, i.e., state administration of all its revenue. This system had been phased in in England from 1671 to 1684 at least for the two biggest revenue items; in Spain it was implemented in two stages, tobacco in 1730 and all other revenue in 1741–49; in France it would not be established in general until after the Revolution although France did run direct taxes *en régie*.

4.1 Direct administration vs. tax farming. Why were taxes farmed out?

The revenue-farming system, like its direct-collection alternative, was known in Europe in the middle ages. The general tendency was to farm out indirect taxes, less important back then and more difficult to collect due to their scattered nature, and to run direct taxes directly (Bonney 1995b: 439–40). Fiscal systems then gave progressively more importance to tax farming, producing a very patchy tax-collection picture, in keeping with the nature of most taxes in those times and the decentralised nature of society in general. In Spain too there were well-organised farming arrangements since at least as far back as the fifteenth century (Ladero Quesada 1981: 48).

Why were tax-collection procedures farmed out? Although tax farming has been sometimes written off as a shirking of the government's rightful duties, it did have its raison d'être. Some saw it as the best option for any government that did not have the capacity for collecting its taxes itself over a scattered national territory. The government would thereby save the cost of setting up its own corps of functionaries and officials and ensure that taxes arrived on time (Clay 1978: 93). Others argued that it was the most efficient method, on the grounds that private, profit-seeking individuals worked better than indolent government officials. Bosher points out that French ministers, until well into the eighteenth century, defended the tax-farming system with all its consequences on the grounds that those working in their own interests were more "energetic, efficient and economic that wage-earning officials" (Bosher 1970: 174–75). For quite some time, therefore, kings preferred their mercantile affairs to be run by expert businessmen rather than government officials.

Another factor was the tax-farmers' ability to double up as financiers offering short-term loans to the king. In France, for example, given that the tax-collection procedure was long-winded, the *fermiers* agreed to pay the king part of the final sum upfront in monthly sums, ensuring the king sure and fixed income while the collection procedures rumbled on (Matthews 1958: 217). As well as collateral money loans, the revenue-farming procedure itself was a form of loan and the king's dodgy creditworthiness would not have got lenders queuing up to provide him with funds otherwise. Tax farmers, if correctly chosen, were regarded as much more creditworthy. J. Félix has reminded us of Le Peletier's 1726 comments upon bringing back the *ferme générale* system in all its force, opining that the king's main financial problems at the time stemmed from his difficulty in obtaining credit, precisely because lenders trusted the traditional *fermiers* much more than some functionaries (Félix 2011: 148). The situation remained much the same in the eighties, judging from Joly de Fleury's opinion that the king's short-term credit necessarily depended on the personal creditworthiness of those who were running these resources. This personal creditworthiness was much higher among financiers than functionaries (Bosher 1970: 175). Tax farming, therefore, boosted the sovereign's creditworthiness, since it was not now based on his own shaky solvency but the solider solvency of the financiers (Dent 1973: 63).

But tax farming, especially for historians, was a double-edged sword. On the one hand it was necessary insofar as it fulfilled three basic functions: obtaining the tax revenue without the king having to set up administration arrangements, ensuring punctual yearly payment of these taxes, with the tax farmer doubling up as short-term lender. Despite these advantages, however, the system still came in for some flak. Opposition had managed to remove the system in England by the end of the seventeenth century. As in Spain the main charges against the system were excessive earnings by the farmers and shackling of the government's freedom to run its own taxes. Tax farming therefore always had its detractors and defenders and involved a complex web of vested interests. Both arguments, pro and con, rumbled on throughout the seventeenth century and also in the eighteenth, where the system was still in force (Durand 1971: 432–37).

In England's case criticism led to attempts to improve the system, trimming the revenue-farming term to short periods, but the farmers continued to earn appreciable sums of money, even allowing them to sublease. Many were calling for the end of tax farming by 1640, but the government was not yet ready to take over collection procedures. The Long Parliament tried unsuccessfully to abolish tax farming completely. Criticism fell away with the start of the Restoration, as from 1661, when tax farming's virtues came to the fore: short-term advanced payments by farmers and even supplementary loans. But tax farming soon came to be wielded as a reward for services loyally rendered (Wilson 1965: 212), a privilege, in short, so parallels were once more drawn with arbitrariness. Fewer private lenders also came to the plate as confidence in royal finances fell.

All in all, the main downside of tax farming was fiscal subordination of the government to private interests. The king was considered to have less leeway in managing his fiscal resources; he could not raise rates as he liked, to harness all price-rising possibilities in full. Above all, farmers were suspected of creaming off huge profits that should rightfully have gone to the king (Kindleberger 1984: third part). The king could try to play off different groups of financiers against each other to bargain up the revenue-farming terms in his favour but he would in the end benefit little from any tax hikes since a percentage would continue to remain in the farmers' hands.

Tax farming therefore set up a well-nigh unwinnable tug-of-war between two opposed fiscal needs: on the one hand ensuring that the taxes came in, something that tax farming achieved; on the other, controlling revenue sources, something it balked. As borrower the state was more comfortable with the revenue-farming option but from the collection point of view direct administration would improve fiscal control (Brewer 1989: 93). Tax farming suffered from other drawbacks too. Taxpayers often came out losing because the tax farmers' enforcement procedures were sometimes heavy handed. The government, to this extent, was in a no-win situation. Any demands it might make of the farmers were simply passed on to the taxpayers. But the taxpayers' anger was directed not at the farmers but at the king as the person ultimately responsible for the whole system.

It was no easy task to solve this question, above all due to the sheer number of interests at stake. The more complex the financial system was, the harder it was to change. The prime example here is France. Constant emergencies, the burden of inherited debt, the clout of the *fermiers* and intermeddling too by finance functionaries themselves all made it very difficult to negotiate a solution. Spain's case became less complex in the last third of the seventeenth century largely because its finance system was downsized and also because the level of military confrontation dropped too. At this time direct administration itself was not brought in, but measures were taken that indicated a government desire in that direction (Sánchez

Belén 1996). The selfsame factors perhaps made it easier for England to take the plunge: a smaller and less indebted finance system. Furthermore, the Restoration favoured a reshuffling of protégés.

For that reason, when England brought in direct administration before 1680, the same did not occur elsewhere. France had to wait for tax farming to be swept away along with many *ancien régime* facets by the Revolution. In comparative terms Spain's mid-eighteenth-century establishment of direct administration was an idiosyncratic feature of its short-eighteenth-century fiscal policy that sets it apart from the rest. Apart from fine details, this switch from tax farming to direct administration was complete by 1749.

The Europeans of the time, witnessing Britain's eighteenth-century growth, credited direct administration with giving more power to the sovereign's elbow. Many thought that what Dickson would come to call the "financial revolution" was based on efficient management, increasing investors' confidence in public debt. Tax farming, on the contrary, was maintained on the continent for the whole first half of the eighteenth century. It would only be from shortly before the middle of the century that direct administration was partly established (Durand 1971: 51–52), at least for the most important taxes; this was the case of Spain[1]. In Holland the social disquiet of the forties (1747–48) triggered a change in the collection system for some taxes, direct and indirect, which fell under the control of collectors expressly appointed for that purpose ('t Hart 1999: 320; Fritschy, 't Hart and Horlings 2012: 45–46), thus establishing a system very close to direct administration, although in Holland the collection procedure was still controlled at province level rather than central-government level. Other countries that joined the direct-administration camp later were Prussia (Beloff 1966: 113), Austria (Pieper 2012: 178–79), Bohemia and Sweden. In all cases the introduction of direct administration was attributed with an increase of the country's tax revenue.

4.2 England takes the lead

During the Restoration, England began to control the problem by inclining towards greater fiscal control, an increasingly urgent need in light of the military pressure the country was experiencing with the second war against Holland. The reforms undertaken at this time paved the way for a new financial overhaul, including the scrapping of tax farming, at least for the main taxes.

Apart from political questions and social interests, which defined a specific strategy, England's public finances benefited from two far-reaching reforms in the final decades of the seventeenth century. First, concentration of administration procedures and, second, direct collection. That produced a surprisingly simple fiscal structure in which most taxes were brought together in the same office and managed jointly, as was the case of the excise raised on a vast raft of products. Apart from the fact that some of these products were much more important than others, the key aspect was their single management, which also turned out to be good, as Brewer has just shown. As we have already seen, some of England's most important financial changes predated the Glorious Revolution.

The triumph of direct administration was from then on equated with modernity, though not by everyone. Nonetheless, the state's ability to take on its rightful powers in tax matters was considered to be a litmus test of its clout, as well as a sign that the economy itself was now strong enough to take on indirect taxes. The king, therefore, was now able to address public-private relationships from a position of supremacy, riding the mercantile wave of the time. Taxpayer wealth gave more power to the sovereign; richer taxpayers could afford to pay more. Some intermediate powers also swung behind the idea of fiscal concerns being brought under sole state administration.

Towards the end of the seventeenth century, sovereignty arrogated to itself the idea of the unity of political power and began to claim jurisdiction over all public business (Krieger 1970: 4–5). These developments have been understood as a sign of the modernity that allowed England to forge ahead both in the economic and political arena. Direct administration was certainly better understood in a country soon to be able to control the whole of public expenditure through parliament and the Bank of England, which channelled the interests of merchants and financiers. These were not sidelined by direct administration, as happened in Spain and as it was feared would happen in France too if direct administration were adopted.

Another important factor was that England had already changed the nature of its society, with more of a mercantile structure, thus expediting a change in fiscal management. Witness the case of excise, a tax on consumer goods paid by manufacturers or distributors, whose cost could be passed on to consumers thanks to strong demand (De Vries 2009: 199–200). By 1660 the influence of the nobility close to the king or of the financiers dominating revenue-farming arrangements had raised the profile of the land tax within the country's taxation system. In the eighteenth century, on the contrary, all social classes paid and collaborated in the fiscal system differently from before, through domestic trade, on the strength of thriving trade activity and its profits. In the first decades of the eighteenth century, moreover, prices were fairly stable (Wilson 1965: 238); this favoured an increase of indirect taxes and helped to finance the government's direct administration itself.

Direct administration, in any case, is only one aspect of England's administrative changes in the final decades of the seventeenth century. Another crucial change was the replacement of a jobbery-ridden bureaucracy by a professional civil service, ostensibly efficient and upright, in general terms, and hence very different from any other government system elsewhere in Europe (Ertman 1997: 207). The picture that is emerging here is an English system of public-private relationships that differed from the French and also partly from the Spanish. In England this "shared mercantilism" in which the king's and his subjects' interests coincided in the benefit of the state (Torres Sánchez 2013a: 178), was hosted in the representative assembly rather than grafted onto government structures, corrupting them as we might say. In France, insofar as tax farming was retained and in default of a representative assembly, financiers, although private, exerted some influence on government arrangements, as in pre-1749 Spain. Ertman has stressed the end of the proprietary office-holding system as a crucial difference between English bureaucracy and the continent in general. This "depatrimonialisation" was carried out at the end of the seventeenth century and maintained thereafter (Ertman 1999: 49). England's representative structure also had other features setting it apart from continental countries but Ertman stresses the fact that offices were no longer bought and sold, making the whole bureaucracy more professional and giving governments much more control over the bureaucracy in general and fiscal management in particular. Direct administration is more efficient when working with such a bureaucracy. In France direct administration was impossible; in Spain it was brought in but, pending future confirmation, we suspect that management was always hobbled by ongoing jobbery and patrimonialism.

4.3 The impossible reform of the French system

The fact that direct administration was not established in France until the Revolution is bound up with both technical and political factors. The sheer complexity of French finances in the times of Louis XIV and the accumulated debt made it difficult to change a system that posed many problems for the king but also involved him in many obligations. Many politicians and public officials therefore considered it essential to keep the tax farming system in force. It was a political stance, without doubt, insofar as it defended a mindset and some vested interests, but it was also a technical question because any change would have been tricky. The view was no doubt held that tax farmers and other private agents enriched themselves at the government's cost but the state had little choice but to cave in or at best sit on the fence (Bruguière 1991). Without a shadow of a doubt the financiers were driven by profit-seeking motives but the government had to turn a blind eye to this, pressed as it was by urgent needs and unable to turn to any other viable alternative better suited to the objectives and duration of the conflicts to be fought (Félix 2011).

Colbert himself had fallen back on the *finances*. His system introduced administrative reforms but no radical change. Around 1660 indirect taxes grew in importance and this trend strengthened with Colbert's reforms (Harsin 1970: 269; Durand 1976: 21). Colbert tried to balance the books, trim expenditure, cut down the debt and provide the *trésorier* with the resources to meet military obligations. He also trimmed the farmers' profits, and though he made no attempt to abolish them, he did tend to create *fermes générales*, i.e., to pool as many farmed-out taxes as possible in one place and avoid excessive dispersion (Marion 1979: 232). Then, when war broke out, he had to seek new revenue. He found it first of all by generalisation of the *timbre* (stamp tax) and creating the tobacco tax monopoly, which turned out to be bountiful, but above all with the *Caisse des emprunts*, 1674, which drew in many floating savers. Success was patchy but at least the worst-case scenario was staved off. In short, Colbert tidied things up, reduced corruption and improved the collection procedure; he also reorganised the leases, whose contracted rentals would continue to increase in the years following his watch.

The trend towards tighter control by the Treasurer and administrative concentration of tax management is similar to the procedure followed by England at the time. Measures of this type were also taken in Spain. All three countries in this sense resemble each other due to the problems experienced in the seventeenth century. Although this experience was different in each case the conclusion drawn was the same: the need for tighter government control over fiscal arrangements and the attempt to bring more money into the nation's coffers with the same effort. The results were different, however. In England tax farming was wiped out; this did not occur for the moment in Spain and neither in France. In the latter country Colbert's reforms did not go so far as modifying the general taxation structure or the system. To make matters even worse, after him (1683) things went back to how they were before. Nonetheless, the tax integration process that had begun in 1664 continued, culminating with the Fauconnet lease of 1680. This marked the start of the *fermes générales* with the pooling of the taxes that would later make up "the corps" of the *ferme général* (Durand 1976: 16).

Time, meanwhile, pressed on, with problems ganging up and solutions dragging their heels. During the War of the Spanish Succession farming profits fell and some taxes even had to be taken into direct administration when no farmers came forward. Even so, the situation was still not changed, although tax farming was no longer such a regular practice (Marion 1979: 233). On the death of Louis XIV the debt in the form of sundry bills and papers was sizeable and there was a good deal of confusion about how best to try to reduce the financiers' profits (Félix 1994). The Regency assayed important changes but without any success. The *frères* Paris created a common *caisse* for the *receveurs généraux* and brought in a new accounting system, but it failed. Everything then became embroiled in the fiasco of Law's system. By 1723, ten years after the peace treaty, the Paris brothers themselves considered the situation to be worse than in 1713. After all this the ministerial change of 1726, with the appointment of Le Peletier des Forts, and the return to the *finances* system, was not only a volte face to Colbert's method but it also marked the definitive triumph, for nearly the whole century, of the indirect-tax farming system, an inseparable companion of the *finances* system (Félix 2011: 126, 135).

4.4 Spain facing the modernity of direct administration

Spain comes across as a continental trailblazer in terms of following the English lead here. The abolition of tax farming could be seen as a perfect corollary to the tax-alleviation policy: lost earnings on one side would be offset by gains on the other (González Enciso 2007, 2015). The idea was clear: increase state revenue without raising the tax burden. Rake in more while charging the same. This idea would work insofar as state management could capture the profits of the farmers, which were assumed to be huge, thus compensating for higher management costs.

Tax farming in Spain differed from the French system in that Spain had no general company to unify the interests of one and all; instead each tax was farmed out to one or several financiers. This situation probably gave the farmers less clout and made it easier for the Spanish government to abolish the system when this decision was finally taken. But the functions carried out by Spain's tax farmers were the same as those of France or any other country. The advantages of the system, apart from the management of tax collection, included the built-in, short-term loan system and this undoubtedly worked to the benefit of the king, who obtained liquidity quickly and easily. Above all this arrangement ensured the king receipt of his tax revenue. There was a downside. The farmer's profits were assumed to be high, eating into the king's revenue. Furthermore, the very existence of the tax-farming arrangement hobbled the government's fiscal policy, since any attempted modification would have to take the tax farmers into account.

Canga Argüelles described Spanish tax farmers as people who "take on responsibility under a competitive bid for collecting tax revenue and paying the stipulated sum thereof into the state's coffers, retaining as reward for their efforts the difference between the amount collected from taxpayers and the amount actually paid in" (Canga Argüelles 1968: I, 95). This definition takes in the three fundamental facets of tax farming: (a) the function: "collecting the tax revenue and paying it into the state's coffers"; (b) the procedure by which the lease is won: "under a competitive bid"; and (c) its profit: "retaining as reward [...]". In this third aspect the definition centres on the system's main problem: the difference between what was "collected from taxpayers" and what was paid in. Everyone considered this rake-off to be too big. It is by no means easy to confirm or rebut this general appreciation with hard facts. In reference to seventeenth-century England, Kindleberger described the tax farmer as the person who buys the right to collect the tax for a stipulated amount, kept what he extracted above that and had use of the money between its collection and payment to the Lords of the Treasury (Kindleberger 1984: Chapter 9). There is a striking similarity between the definition of Canga Argüelles (written in 1833) and that of Kindleberger, two totally disparate authors speaking of different countries and different times; this just shows how general and long-lasting this arrangement was.

Spanish historians have stressed the modernity of the abolition of tax farming in 1749. Carrera Pujal, for example, cites it as one of Ensenada's outstanding measures "for the modernisation of Spanish politics" (Carrera Pujal 1945: III, 323). This modernity claim rested above all on the supposed efficiency of the subsequent direct administration. The idea, in any case, feeds into the general interpretation of the success of England's changes. To this must be added the current echo of the complaints of the writers and ministers of the time against the tax farmers, both in Spain, where the flak was thick (Moya Torres y Velasco 1992: 141, 304), and elsewhere. The French, in particular, wrote reams against the *fermiers généraux* (Durand 1971: 424), and the Dutch staged fiscal revolts on this score in 1747–48.

The censure went even further back than the eighteenth century. Nonetheless, it should also be remembered that, in Spain and elsewhere, the tax farmers also had their defenders. The matter was debated in its time, coinciding with the dismantling "of a whole series of direct state administrative activities" between the end of the sixteenth century and the first decades of the seventeenth (Thompson 1976: 283). For followers of Thompson's views, this means above all the failure of Spain's Habsburg state. Nonetheless this factor does not necessarily need to have a solely negative meaning (Torres Sánchez 2013a: 160–64); indeed, in the times of Philip IV things were not so clear and there were many who upheld the tax-farming system (Elliott and de la Peña 1981: II, 120–23). In the next reign, especially in the final decades, tax farming arrangements seemed to be more fruitful simply because a wider trawl of bidding financiers tended to force up the price paid to the state (Sánchez Belén 2002: 61–63). In the nineties, in particular, the government received more revenue from many outsourced taxes thanks to this financial rivalry (Storrs 2013: 206).

The debate of that time over tax farming or direct administration was bound up, above all, with the government's desire, backed up by thinkers, to boost its revenue. This revenue was necessary, above all, to meet military expenditure. The medium used, as long as it was reliable, was not considered to be the most important factor. The overriding concern at that time was that the king could be sure of obtaining the economic resources it needed, that taxes should reach its coffers in time. In this case it was not a question so much of modernity as pragmatism, and perhaps of the ruling concept of sovereignty. In Spain, from that moment on, it began to be thought that direct administration was the surest, most efficient and most sovereign-empowering method. This idea would be fleshed out during the reign of Philip V. Although not in linear fashion, this option won out over others, establishing "two fundamental mainstays of the Exchequer's immediate future: the need of ousting the tax farmers in order to increase tax revenue without increasing tax bases" and the single tax (Artola 1982: 260).

The fiscal question here merged with economic activity, adding to the ongoing debate about fiscal management. It was thought that economic activation was a sine qua non of obtaining more revenue. As in the English case a population made richer by the increase of industry and trade could in theory afford to pay more taxes. The other side of the same coin was the general admission at this time that economic growth could be obtained and maintained only by reducing tax loads; this led to an ongoing policy of tax exemptions, both in Spain and elsewhere, on various economic activities, especially domestic trade and industry. It is quite clear that these two factors, boosting the economy to engender more taxes while also reducing the tax burden on given economic activities, were to some extent contradictory unless policies were very shrewdly chosen in each case.

For the moment the tax-exemption policy won out (González Enciso 1980: 235). Better revenue-boosting solutions were found but Spain, at the start of the forties, came up with the real answer to this conundrum, which was precisely the establishment of direct administration; this would pull off the miracle of increasing total revenue without having to raise taxes and, at the same time, guaranteeing exemptions for diverse industrial activities. The government officials of that time highlighted this fact: revenue had increased whilst also maintaining both the tax-alleviation policy, checking the growth of *rentas provinciales*, and the industry tax-exemption policy.

The picture was clear by 1749, although it might have been appreciable beforehand in some cases, and this situation lasted throughout the fifties as the new method was phased in. The pacifist policy of Ferdinand VI's government as from 1748 favoured this implementation without running the risk of disruption and complication by sudden war emergencies. Paradoxically, the definitive progress towards implementation of direct administration was made in order to finance war, in 1741; nonetheless, the development of the system was only possible thanks to peace, which offered the necessary tranquillity for revamping all the administrative mechanisms.

In this same year of 1749, direct-administration tax revenue topped the all-time tax-farming high by over 12 million *reales*[2]. An official statement of the fifties recorded a 50 million *reales* revenue increase in 1750 as compared with 1742, within a total revenue figure (without counting Indies revenue) of less than 300 million *reales de vellón*. It is clear there had been a significant increase in revenue, as borne out by many documents of the time that compare current revenue with "the times of tax farming".

4.5 Administering to implement a new system

How was this situation arrived at and what was the process towards "universal administration"? Did the arrival of the new reign and a growing centralist mentality change the mindset of the time? Should some taxes continue to be farmed out? There is no uniform, across-the-board answer to these questions (Dubet 2008: 19, 34). To start with, a bureaucratic apparatus had to be built up, capable of reaching all corners of the realm. Apparently it did not exist at the beginning.

Apart from some ad hoc, need-driven, one-off expedients, such as the direct administration of tobacco revenue in 1684 (Escobedo Romero 2007: 31), and despite international examples of the success of this system, as in England, or the criticisms of tax farming in France (Durand 1971: 401–04), direct administration was not seriously mooted in Spain until much later. Since the second half of the seventeenth century there had indeed been an underlying desire of greater government control of its revenue (Torres Sánchez 2015a: 67); nonetheless, although some did speak of a direct relation between state and taxpayer, the idea that, for the moment, won out over the rest was unification of revenue. This could be seen as one more of the eighteenth century's many unification schemes (Bonney 1995b: 438) but, at least in Spain, it dated back further, thanks to the reforms at the end of Charles II's reign (Gelabert 1999: 227).

At the start of the eighteenth century more systematic efforts were made in this direction. Orry's revenue-centralising plan had been on the table since 1703; in all likelihood it was shelved due to the war needs, at first, and then Orry's departure to France in 1706. The plan was structured around four points: set up a new fiscal system, recover alienated property rights, shake off the hold of the *juristas* (holders of *juros*) and ensure an increase in revenue (Kamen, 1974: 252–54). Orry, evidently, did not advocate direct administration but rather concentration of the tax collection business in fewer hands. When Orry returned to Spain he was able to try to put the new revenue leasing scheme of 1713, *Nueva planta*, into practice, under which there would be a head revenue farmer in each province with responsibility for all taxes in that province. A bit more progress was made with tobacco revenue.

Since 1701 there had been a general administrator who fulfilled the functions of a tax farmer for the tobacco revenue in all provinces; although this administrator was a private financier, it was a post designated by the king. The system maintained similar features to the former regime and further modification was put off until more centralisation had been achieved (Escobedo Romero 2007: 38–41).

As from 1713 some attempts were made to shrug off the yoke of tax farmers in other taxes or at least reduce their number and bring them under closer control (Dubet 2013: 25–49). Witness the arrangements made for customs and wool revenue, which would become a single tax as from 1715 controlled by a board chaired by Orry. This board also comprised some high-ups from the administration plus some well-known financiers, such as Flon and Sartine. The plan failed in general terms, due to the destitution of Orry in early 1715, but there was at least one legacy: customs and wool revenue remained in administration for some time, in the former case from 1714 to 1725. It is revealing to investigate the reasons both for bringing these two taxes into direct administration and the subsequent return to tax farming. The 1714 Decree speaks of establishing "formal, yield-boosting administration in all customs". The lack of any real profit was a good pretext, for returning to tax farming in 1725 (Artola 1982: 284–85). Wool revenue, for its part, was run by direct administration from 1714 to 1730, whereupon it was newly farmed out until late 1748 (Aquerreta 2001b: 117).

The fact that wool revenue was farmed out again in 1730, precisely when firm moves were being made for bringing tobacco into direct administration, shows that the change of system was no easy task; there was considerable resistance and inconsistency; some people even held opposite opinions on different taxes. The marquise of Campoflorido, for example, thought the important dichotomy for customs was not tax farming or direct administration but collegiate or individual governance (in fact he was influential in getting the board of directors of 1714 replaced by a superintendent in 1716). He also expressed the opinion that direct administration of *rentas provinciales* enabled the powerful to cover up all sorts of abuses against taxpayers and therefore preferred tax farming in this case (Dubet 2012: 20–52). Other high-ups like Vega argued that all taxes did not have the same nature and should therefore not necessarily all be brought under the same collection procedure.

Patiño, in his 1726 *Memoria*, calculated that customs were losing value and to head off further losses he proposed a new higher-revenue administration method based on tax-farming assignment negotiated with the commercial world. In other words, according to Patiño's opinion at this moment, a reform project could include implementation of one formula or the other, as need be (Solbes Ferri 2016). The important point seemed to be to achieve control by dint of some centralisation method; Uztáriz, for example, rejoiced to see the farming arrangements of some taxes so subject to immediate subordination to the Superintendent General of the same tax as to be able to protect the tax, avoid abuses by the farmer and punish the fraudulent. In this way, he concluded, this tax achieves all the advantages of an authorised administration (Uztáriz 1968: 247). The crux of the matter was the result – control – rather than the means, about which different opinions might well be held.

Small wonder, then, that progress was so patchy, judging from the partial results of each measure. It is telling, for example, that farming out of *rentas provinciales*, one of Castile's most important taxes, was practically constant during Philip V's reign until 1741. Only provinces for which no farmer came forward were brought under administration (Artola 1982: 258). In these cases, the practice followed dated back to the eighties of the seventeenth century with tobacco revenue, i.e., occasional or ad hoc farming out as need be. This same stop-go procedure was also implemented with other taxes on several occasions at the start of the eighteenth century (Castro 2004: 70, 81; Carrera Pujal 1945: 179–80).

The first firm step forward with no backsliding afterwards was taken with tobacco, one of the surest and quickest-growing revenue sources at this time (González Enciso 2007, 2009a). In 1730 the revenue was brought into direct administration definitively and would not be farmed out again for the whole eighteenth century. The reasons for tobacco's trailblazing role here are not only its importance and flexibility but also the fact that this revenue source was not heavily earmarked, i.e., its yield was not destined beforehand to specific expenditure, so none of this expenditure was jeopardised. Whatever the reason, Patiño was particularly keen to bring this tax revenue into direct administration.

The consequences were soon felt and at first they were not so positive. The implementation of direct administration was accompanied by a spike in prices (Rodríguez Gordillo 2000, 2006). The government took advantage of the change to introduce a new pricing policy, whereupon retail prices soared. The immediate result was a huge fall in demand for the government's product (Rodríguez Gordillo and Gárate Ojanguren 2007). Despite this, revenue did grow considerably, as the tax farmers' past profits were now received directly by the state. Crucially, too, contraband trade was still low key. Everything seemed to vouch for the efficiency of the direct administration system, not only in terms of the increasing revenue flow for the king, but also because it had been proven that the revenue could be freely managed by the government in this way, successfully setting the sales price of the manufactured product.

There is not much news of the rest of the direct-administration implementation process up to 1741. Barring the aforementioned cases, the question fell into abeyance until that year. The minister who reopened the debate was Campillo, though not forthrightly. In 1741, for example, it was ordered that the eau-de-vie tax be established in Catalonia as in Castile, "whether farmed out or run by direct administration"; the tax-farming arrangement was finally formalised in 1742 (Carrera Pujal 1945: III, 185). This shows once more that direct administration was not the only aim in sight.

In the same year of 1741, however, a sort of direct-administration pilot trial was introduced for *rentas provinciales*, taking advantage of the fact that some provinces had failed to find a farmer. Thought was then given to the possibility of generalising the procedure. The provinces concerned were Seville, Toledo, Córdoba, La Mancha and Palencia (Artola 1982: 260). In 1746 and 1748 other provinces were tagged on (Ibáñez Molina 1994: 52). The calculation made of the value of directly administered *rentas provinciales* in 1746 and 1748 shows an increase from 32.3 to 37 million *reales*[3]. This increase, at a moment of flatlining tax revenue, can be explained only by the increase of provinces under direct administration. This shows there was a first phase, before the 1749 decreeing of across-the-board direct administration for all *rentas provinciales*.

Nearly all the other taxes were brought into direct administration by 1749, with confident hopes of an ensuing increase in total revenue, not only demand driven but also due to the capture of the profits previously creamed off by the tax farmers. The general problem, and Campillo's stance, comes across clearly in the following quote:

> "Wool revenue" says Campillo, "is leased out on atrocious terms …, for it is worth over eleven million *reales*, and has been farmed out to Miguel de Arizcun for a fixed price of five and a half million. He himself has acknowledged the outrageous situation, voluntarily offering three million more at the last leasing arrangement … This should have opened the eyes of the minister he was dealing with and the *Consejo* if one and the other were not falling asleep on the job". (Ibáñez Molina 1994: 56–57)

The quote, as we can see, also criticises the infighting between different factions and institutions, which were responsible for deciding whether or not the reforms would go ahead. Campillo turned out to be right; not in terms of the increase offered by the revenue farmer, which seemed to be less than quoted, but certainly in terms of the overall result, for in 1749, once brought into direct administration, revenue yielded 11.6 million *reales*, and even more in the following years. The 1749 measure thus seemed to produce a good result.

The 1749 measure, however, did not mean the king's entire revenue had been brought into direct administration. Minor tax revenue and other special taxes escaped the net. One important example is the *rentas provinciales* of Madrid, leased out to the *Cinco Gremios Mayores* (Torres Sánchez 2013a: 195). Sundry revenue of an ecclesiastical origin – *subsidio, excusado* – was also farmed out at some moments of the second half of the century (Artola 1982: 294). Technically, in fact, this church revenue had not exactly been farmed out. It was run in each case by the corresponding ecclesiastical entities, which handed over the assigned sums to the government. The system changed in 1751 when it was ordered that this revenue be run directly by the *Real Hacienda*, but the attempt was defeated by the opposition of diocese high-ups. To head off conflict the king set up a third-party farming system to be renewed as from 1761 (Iturrioz Magaña 1987: Chapters VI and VII). It could nonetheless be claimed that the immense majority of tax revenue, and certainly the most important taxes, came into direct administration in 1749, although the process would not be completed until a few years later.

4.6 A political agenda against tax farmers?

We might ask how far the government was working with an agenda and enforced it on the tax farmers. Or to put it another way: were there preconceived plans of financial reform targeting direct administration? No clear answer can be given. The evidence to hand suggests it was not a very well-defined process, and it was also weighed down by doubts, difficulties and sundry interests. If there was a clear idea of achieving more centralisation and control, it was certainly already in place by the 1680s. At that time some steps were taken in this direction, which, as they prospered, suggested that direct administration might be a realistic possibility. Bringing tobacco into direct administration in 1684 was need-driven, but by the eighteenth century, especially in 1714, it was established in some cases as a temporary, makeshift measure when no suitable farmer came forward; it was also always made conditional on good results, which in fact did not occur. It is clear that the idea of enforcing direct administration as the best form of fiscal management had already crossed the mind of some but we have no clear idea who they were or how far they might be convinced of the viability of the measure.

A specific case that could shed light on this situation is that of Patiño. The minister mistrusted the private agents working for the government, whether as tax farmers or contractors (*asentistas*) (Pulido Bueno 1998: 307); he also left a written record of his complaints about the corrupt practices of the tax farmers, from which it would follow that he was in favour of scrapping the system. He did in fact try to bring in direct administration of *rentas provinciales* in some provinces but was thwarted by emergency situations and staunch opposition. As Carrera Pujal points out, "tax farming was revived because there was no way of procuring the money quickly at moments of pressing urgency" (Carrera Pujal 1945: III, 182, 186). This phrase also brings out the short-term-loan facet of the tax-farming function and the importance this might have at times of military emergencies during the 1730s, as when Patiño's hand was forced by the wars in Italy.

It thus turned out that any direct-administration ideas or projects were scuppered by military emergencies and the opposition of doubters. Patiño brought it in only for tobacco. The following finance ministers, Campillo and then Ensenada, took their cue from him. Campillo initiated the decisive move towards direct administration in 1741 and Ensenada culminated it in 1749. Both had worked for years under the orders of Patiño. Both introduced a radical change of direction, phasing out quite briskly the previous policy of tax farming arrangements until it practically disappeared.

It is therefore clear that the direct-administration idea was entertained at the time but it is hard to ascertain whether or not these ideas involved real plans of action. There was certainly no consensus on this matter and the actual situation was a matter of fierce defence for several decades. This defence was more widespread and unanimous in the case of *rentas provinciales* than with the other taxes, where stances were more varied, pro and contra. This different attitude can be seen in authors as important as Uztáriz (Uztáriz 1968: XLVI–XLVII). True it is too that even within this tax-farming bastion of *rentas provinciales* there had been a trend towards a single tax farmer per province or even one farmer responsible for several provinces, thus whittling down the number of private participants to deal with.

There would therefore also seem to be a clear desire of limiting the role of private agents in fiscal management. In 1724, for example, according to tax-farming arrangements agreed two years earlier, the *rentas provinciales* of 22 Castilian provinces were dealt with by only 16 tax farmers, some of whom were responsible for two or three provinces (Uztáriz 1968: 390–91). In the case of customs, Uztáriz himself boasted that control over the tax farmer was so absolute that it was tantamount to direct administration. The zeitgeist idea, therefore, seemed to be that many taxes, other than *rentas provinciales*, could be brought into direct administration but this would not be necessary if the government already exerted strong control. The overriding concern was to avoid fraud. The increasing yield of these revenue items was also bound up with this possibility. In practice there would seem to be just as many arguments in favour of one situation or the other with a constant switching back and forth in the first half of the century between administration and tax farming without any clear, overarching criterion.

In accordance with all that, until 1741 the policy is not uniform. Apart from the possible inheritance from the seventeenth century, and the 1701 tobacco measures, which signposted the way towards direct administration, there were no more forthright moves in this direction. In 1714 two taxes were brought into direct administration, but in 1725 and 1730 both were farmed out again. Even so, in this same year of 1730 the tobacco revenue direct administration decree was passed. The *rentas provinciales* had always been farmed out, despite which they would be the first to be taken into direct administration as from 1741. It was not until 1741 that there was a forthright movement towards direct administration applicable to all taxes. It was then when there was a real sea change in the policies followed hitherto by Torrenueva and Iturralde (Zafra Oteiza 1991: 93; Delgado Barrado 2007: 202–03). It is nonetheless telling that when Campillo finally brought *rentas provinciales* into direct administration, war needs were pressing. The 1739 bankruptcy situation also still had to be overcome, a situation itself brought on by the high military costs of the preceding period. It was therefore not until these years that, after tackling the complicated phase of the War of Succession, Spain's rulers were once again faced with an urgent need of money to defray warfare. From this point of view, it could safely be claimed that the ultimate reason from the definitive move to direct administration was war.

Be that as it may, and despite the urgent needs, when it was considered that the moment had come to switch some tax revenue to direct administration the decisions were not taken hastily. In all revenue for which we have data, direct administration was brought in when no suitable tax farmer was found or when current leases expired. The overall impression is that the most timely moment was awaited in each case. This forestalled any confrontation with financial interests. No one was despoiled of their acquired rights and the authorities observed ongoing commitments. It is true that any tax farmer would always have expected his lease to be renewed, so this must have come as some disappointment. But no one could complain of any injustice. Many of these former tax farmers were in fact fobbed off with the functionary job for the same tax management, thus tapping into their expertise and detailed knowledge of the tasks involved.

4.7 Consequences and stocktaking

At any rate, although the shift to direct administration did not involve any breach of ongoing commitments with the private financiers, the government did take the upper hand in public management after the reform. It ended up enforcing its model, which was reckoned to be the best option in the forties. According to the idea of "shared mercantilism" the private agents would have participated in fiscal management by means of their tax-collection activities. But they did so only for as long as the tax-farming arrangements lasted; then, with the advent of direct administration, the model changed and private participation was slashed. Although the former farmers were sometimes taken on as managers, indicating a blurred limit between public administration and private business (Torres Sánchez 2013a: 189), the truth is that the tax farmer, as a private financier, dropped out of the picture. In other words, the private tax-farming function disappeared. Direct administration thus wiped out an important part of the business world, and private agents, henceforth relegated to onlookers of these reforms, played second fiddle to political exigencies.

All this shows that politics was in fact the top-priority concern: when it came to the crunch, governors knew what they wanted and applied it in benefit of their policy. In this field, therefore, a new picture begins to emerge with a much clearer distinction between public affairs, run by the government, and private affairs, for now sidelined. The state won itself a position of pre-eminence, which is what it was after: control revenue collection and receive more at the expense of the profits formerly creamed off by private agents. It was without any doubt a more modern vision of the state, wherein the government is technically capable of controlling all its resources and managing them more flexibly. The state was morphing into an entrepreneur-state, which began to grow on the basis of an increasing centralisation of resources. In the fiscal field it was the English model that had worked in Spain since the end of the seventeenth century and Spanish ministers were very proud of having achieved this. France by now was moving in the opposite direction.

What were the consequences of such a political-administrative feat? Direct administration was brought in for one fundamental reason: increasing the king's revenue. This was achieved in two ways. First, the government took on greater control over management; although it had to assume direct responsibility for this management it was now free to lay down rules and pricing policies as it saw fit. Second, the excessive profits previously raked off by the tax farmers now flowed straight into the royal coffers. The downside is that it also had to take on the cost but the overall result was positive. From all these facets we will be looking here at the fundamental one, the increase in ordinary tax revenue. If we calculate Spain's tax revenue before and after completion of the process, the figures show a constant increase in the state's net income during these years. Table 4.1 shows the results of "current revenue", i.e., the set of principal taxes in direct administration rather than total revenue, to bring out the difference made by reforms in this particular revenue set. Thus the net values of all the "current revenue" are shown in Table 4.1 (figures in millions of *reales de vellón*).

Apart from the dip of 1750–51, which may have been due to difficulties in adjusting to the new system or accounting problems, the increase was already appreciable by 1746 – according to this first phase we mentioned above – and definitive as from 1752. The process seems to have been well established by now.

Table 4.1 Net direct-administration revenue of the Spanish state, 1747–52 (in millions of *reales de vellón*)

1747	214.6
1748	292.2
1749	292.2
1750	280.6
1751	280.6
1752	376.6

Source: Merino Navarro 1987: 33–35.

As can be seen from the table, the increase in this revenue was about 43 per cent, a staggering rise. Was this all due to profit won back by direct administration? Probably not. Consideration also have to be given to the fact that all indicators were on an upward trend in these years: population, trade (with the arrival of peace), industrial activity, and although some of this profit would be lost to the public-finance system due to exemptions, another decent chunk would be paid into the king's coffers. Nonetheless the increase attributable to direct administration was in all likelihood sizeable. We should not forget that, in Campillo's abovementioned quote about wool revenue lease, the tax farmer's rake-off was almost 50 per cent of the king's portion.

If we now look at Spain's total revenue figures, the increase is crystal clear. Witness Table 4.2.

In this case the increase in the chosen period comes down to 36 per cent. In a period of about 10 years ordinary revenue rose substantially. The difference from the 43 per cent rise of "current revenue" in the former table tells us that said revenue was the state's prime source of income. This seems to vouch for the importance of the direct-administration measure, even though the exact value cannot now be calculated. Probably the aforementioned figure of 43 per cent is a slight overstatement, due to the reasons given, but it is unlikely to be far from the truth.

Although the measure managed to boost revenue considerably, the trouble is that it was unrepeatable. This is its built-in limitation. The increase, however much it might have been, was one-off, for good and all. Abolition of the tax leases channelled towards the exchequer the profits formerly pocketed by the tax farmers, but once achieved there were no more possibilities of growth on this score. It was a measure that grafted no flexibility onto the system looking forward. Nevertheless, direct administration increased the confidence of Spain's rulers in the country's ordinary tax base. The measure's short-term efficacy also had a lot to do with Spain's international role in the forties and the luxury of being able to remain neutral in Ferdinand VI's reign while maintaining the Castile tax-alleviation policy for a long time.

Table 4.2 Net total revenue, Spain, 1747–56 (in millions of
reales de vellón)

1747	338.9
1748	338.9
1749	401.3
1750	401.3
1751	480.8
1752	480.8
1753	560.8
1754	515.1
1755	506.4
1756	529.9

Source: Merino 1987.

Driven by the growth of wealth in general, ordinary revenue would continue to rise in the following years, allowing the government the unusual luxury of saving tax surpluses and storing up a good deal of the incoming precious metal. During these years, indeed, the country was able to build up a literal "treasure trove", replete with coins and bars of precious metal of notable value (Barbier 1980). Once the period of peace ended, this store would defray Spain's invasion of Portugal during its short stint in the Seven Years' War (González Enciso 2006a: 187), as well as other extraordinary expenses.

One aspect more effective in the long term is that the government managed to wrest back more control over the management of its own revenue. This control had already been shown in the case of tobacco revenue, in which the authorities were able to fix prices as they saw fit, not only in the thirties, as we have already seen, but in another crucial moment, for example, in 1741, while Campillo forged onwards towards direct administration of *rentas provinciales*. Direct administration also expedited other aspects of fiscal management, such as modifying customs duties in the government's favour or benefiting from industry by lowering certain payments of *alcabalas* and *millones*. The reform would also facilitate, when the time came, the subsequent modification of the *alcabalas*, a reform that would in all likelihood have been more difficult if tax farming had been retained.

It is difficult to assess if all these small or grand measures, which were taken above all in the second half of the century, would have been possible if the tax-farming system had been maintained; it would at least have called for a complicated negotiation with the tax farmers in possession at the time. To this extent it can be claimed that direct administration empowered the government to run its own revenue sources. From this point of view this reform strengthened state management and stole a march on other countries. Quite another thing is the meaning and consequences this state reinforcement might have in the long term.

As such this measure, at the moment it was taken and within the scope it had, should be seen as clearly Spanish. It might have drawn on the English example and the theoretical discussions of this issue during this century in England, France, in Spain itself and elsewhere, but at the end of the day the problem solved was purely Spanish. In France, moreover, the tax-farming system was retained and in other countries any measures to this end were taken later. The Spanish reform was therefore Spanish in nature and took its cue from Spain's financial problems of the forties.

4.8 The tax farmers' profit

Nonetheless there is a big problem, ostensibly negative, that has been little looked at as yet: the harm done to Spain's finance system by wiping out without any trade-off an important private business that also doubled up as short-term lender to the government. How far did the establishment of direct administration weaken Spain's finance system? It is not easy to weigh up the effect of the loss of private financiers because there is still too little to go on, but we do have an indirect indication of the growth of state revenue after the abolition of tax farming and the quote involving the case of the wool revenue farmer. Can these figures be generalised? As we will see, not always at the same level. The wool farmer, Arizcun, belonged to a generation and family of financiers who had won themselves a pre-eminent position at court and without any doubt would have had privileged connections to obtain a very favourable tax-farming arrangement (Aquerreta 2001b); quite possibly, other leaseholders of revenue of similar importance would have earned a lower profit as a percentage of the leased.

But this is all guesswork. Table 4.3 gives us some guideline information; how accurate it is depends on the trust we place in calculations made at the end of 1759 by finance high-ups. The table shows the figures of a document that set out expressly to explain the nature and value of each one of the taxes during the years 1752–57. The figures are the mean values for those years[4]. In practice, what is being done is to compare, on the one hand, the gross and net value of some taxes in the indicated years with, on the other, the value of these same taxes at the moment of the last tax-farming arrangement, which the document sets at 1740, presumably for convenience. The end of 1759 is an important date for Spain's finance system because it was the moment when Esquilache took over as finance minister at the start of Charles III's reign. As other cases have shown, the new minister asked for a host of reports to bring him up to speed on the finance system (Andrés-Gallego 2003: 133). The figures are therefore pretty trustworthy, not only due to their origin and the precision being asked for by Esquilache but also because they tally with other figures to hand.

The table shows the gross value of some taxes in each year of the indicated period (A), their net value, after discounting management costs, *juro* charges and

Table 4.3 Possible earnings of tax farmers in some taxes (in millions of *reales de vellón*)

Tax	A gross 1752/57	B net 1752/57	C before 1740	D difference B–C	E % D/A	F % D/B
Rentas Provinciales	88.5	63.2	52.3	10.9	12.3	17.2
Rentas Generales	45.4	35.8	25.8	10	22	27.9
Salt	23.5	18.5	12.5	6	25.5	32.4
Wool	13.7	11.3	8 (5.5)	3 (6.8)	21.8 (49.6)	26.5 (60)
Eau-de-vie	3.7	1.4	1.2	0.2	5.4	14.2
Gunpowder	2.7	1.2	0.5	0.7	25.9	58.3

Source: See Note 4 at the end of the chapter.

other similar costs (B), and the value clocked up by these taxes in 1740, when they were still farmed out (C). Judging from the document's procedure elsewhere, this latter figure is presumably a net figure of state income after discounting *juro* charges and other similar charges. We are especially interested here in column D, which shows the difference between the net value of the 1750s and the 1740 figure. This is presumably the sum previously pocketed by the tax farmers, but we would have to factor in their own management costs, not indicated here: in other words, they are not net figures indicating real earnings but they at least give us a working idea of the sums involved.

The difference (D) logically varies according to the value of the tax: about 10 million *reales* for the biggest taxes and less for those of lower value. The telling figure here, however, is the percentage of this difference against the state's paid-in revenue, which also varies. This figure is significantly lower for *rentas provinciales* than for the other taxes (barring eau-de-vie, of little importance overall); this reflects the government's particular concern about this tax as the one with the biggest effect on the taxpayers' pocket. Other cases were different. The high percentage in the case of gunpowder is striking. This would no doubt have been because of the *asentista*'s bargaining power in a product of such strategic value but of little economic importance.

An interesting difference comes out depending on whether we compare the tax farmers' percentage gains against the taxes' net or gross value. If we look at the tax farmer's earnings against the net revenue value (F), which is what the government officials recorded, at the end of the day, because it was the money actually paid in to the king, we then find figures hovering around 30 per cent or slightly lower. These figures must obviously have weighed heavily on the mood of anyone observing the government's financial straits in the forties, above all if these straits were long-lasting. People of that time who knew these figures, with the tax farmer pocketing 30 per cent or more of the net value paid in to the king, would logically have seen this system as unjustifiable.

Under direct administration, however, the king did not receive the gross value either; he had to discount costs and charges. The tax farmer's gain, therefore, should rightfully be contrasted against the net revenue received in the fifties. In this case the percentages are much lower (E), hovering around 25 per cent or less. The tax farmers would also have had their own expenses, and this must also be deducted from the indicated gain.

Had this situation always been so? We do not know for certain, but it would seem that the government's circumstances improved somewhat as compared with earlier times. Another document, this time dated 1716, signed by J. Rodrigo, *Fiscal* (procurator) of the Court of Zaragoza, later Marqués de la Compuesta (Kamen 1974: 287, 377), put the tax farmers' gains, albeit *grosso modo*, at about 30 per cent[5]. The tax farmer, according to this author, was entitled to collect all the taxes and if he collected, say, 100,000 *reales*, paid a lease of 30,000. This is only a rough idea but the author was familiar with financial affairs of the time. These figures seem to show, therefore, that the tax farmers' percentage gain against the gross revenue fell from 30 to 25 per cent or less between 1716 and 1740.

But it was not necessarily always so. The case of wool revenue is revealing. As we said above, Arizcun had leased it for 5.5 million *reales* (shown in brackets in the table) before 1740, when it was supposed to be worth more than 11 million, as confirmed at the end of the tax-farming arrangement. Arizcun himself raised the government payment to 8 million. After the change, the percentage gains from woollen revenue fell into line with that of salt. But had the lease been kept at 5.5 million, then the percentage received by Arizcun would have been more than 49 per cent of the gross value and 60 per cent of the net value. This was a scandalously high profit, which, moreover, corresponded to a sizeable absolute sum, about seven million *reales*, for a tax revenue that was fairly straightforward to manage: once in direct administration, the management costs of this revenue amounted to 0.7 million *reales*, 5 per cent of the gross value according to the abovementioned document.

What is clear, in any case, is that whether we consider the percentage gain against the gross value or net value, the tax farmer would pocket a tidy sum. Whether this represented a small or big net profit is difficult to ascertain. Some idea is given by collection costs after the revenue had been brought into direct administration, also indicated in the document we are using here. These are shown in Table 4.4.

According to Table 4.4 we can break down revenue into high value (*provinciales* and *generales*), medium value (wool and salt) and low value (eau-de-vie and gunpowder). Administration costs within high-value revenue were more than 10 per cent of gross value. Within low-value revenue the percentages were very high, over 55 per cent; in medium-value revenue the percentage was about 5 per cent. If administration expense percentages vary inversely with gross value, this means that the unit administration cost was higher in smaller revenues.

Working from the assumption that administration expense percentages were similar under direct administration and tax farming, we can now apply these expense percentages to the tax farmers' gains shown in Table 4.3. Table 4.5 then shows a reduction of possible profit by the indicated percentages.

Table 4.4 Administration expenses as percentage of tax gross value. Chosen tax revenues (in millions of *reales de vellón*)

Tax	A Gross value	B Expenses	C % B/A
Rentas Provinciales	88.5	9.4	10.6
Rentas Generales	45.4	6.3	13
Salt	23.5	1.1	4.6
Wool	13.7	0.7	5
Aguardiente	3.7	2.2	59
Gunpowder	2.7	1.5	55.5

Source: See Note 4 at the end of the chapter.

Table 4.5 Net profit of tax farmers in some taxes (in millions of *reales de vellón*)

Tax	1 Gross earnings (mill. rs.)	2 Expense %	3 Value of 2 (mill. rs.)	4 Profit (1 − 3) (mill. rs.)
Rentas Provinciales	10.9	10.6	1.1	9.8
Rentas Generales	10	13	1.3	8.7
Salt	6	4.6	0.2	5.8
Wool	3 (6.8)	5	0.1 (0.3)	2.9 (6.5)
Eau-de-vie	0.2	59	0.1	0.1
Gunpowder	0.7	55.5	0.3	0.4

Source: See Note 4 at the end of the chapter.

Table 4.5 shows (1) tax farmers' gross earnings (according to Table 4.3, D). To this figure we then apply (2) administration expense percentages (according to Table 4.4, C). Column 4 shows the difference between the earnings (1) and the value of the applied expense percentages (3), which is tantamount to the approximate profit of the tax farmers. We then see that profit remains fairly high in the higher-value revenue (*provinciales* and *generales*), while it falls appreciably in the smaller revenue. This would seem to account for the high percentage gains in small revenue, otherwise the high administration costs would have left very little profit margin for the tax farmer. The net result is that tax-farming contracts seem to be of higher percentage value in low-yield revenue, while the tax farmer's profit falls in the bigger revenue items.

On these figures, was the opposition to tax farmers justified or not? From the purely quantitative point of view, it would seem it was. An alleged profit of about 9 million *reales* a year for the leaseholders of *rentas provinciales* or *rentas generales* was a huge sum. Equally important are the sums that would have been earned by salt and wool tax farmers, especially the latter if he had not voluntary relinquished 3 million *reales*, as we have seen. Another factor is what these sums might have represented within these financiers' total business and the risks they had to take, all very difficult to quantify. A more detailed analysis might well show that the tax farmers were often not individuals but companies who employed a considerable staff and hence incurred considerable transaction costs.

The sums involved were large, but, taking into account the problem as a whole, it could be argued they were not exaggerated. Rather than the profit per se what possibly rankled the opponents more was rampant fraud and strong-arming of tax-payers. What does come across quite clearly is that, after abolition of the leases, financiers lost a significant and bountiful business outlet. Furthermore, money ceased to circulate freely through a financial market, restricted as it might have been, to be locked up instead in the salaries of government officials. The government, for its part, won out in terms of greater control over its own fiscal policies and a significant percentage increase in revenue, but it did not broaden its tax base. This therefore represented an organisational improvement but not a fiscal change.

4.9 Looking to the future of finance possibilities

If we look at direct administration from the standpoint of the king's needs, we see that the change came at a timely moment, with many years of peace ahead for consolidating the new system and then reaping the profits. Except for the brief, one-and-a-half-year episode of war from 1761 to 1763, Spain enjoyed continuous peace with no large scale conflicts from 1749 to 1779, though it could be considered to be on a war footing after 1774, both due to Ceballos's expedition and the invasion of Algiers in 1775. During these years of peace, as we have already seen, the country could afford to save, first of all, and then channel towards the exchequer the fruits of the increasing growth rate. In this context the fact that the government could now freely run its tax and finance affairs, planning more or less ambitious reforms in American trade and its *rentas provinciales*, even bringing some to fruition, created the impression that direct administration had been a brilliant reform underpinning all this splendour, an idea that has been handed down in historical studies since.

The years after Algiers, however, showed the trap the government had fallen into by doing things by halves. This comes out from a simple comparison with Great Britain and France. The first country had brought the reform in early, but England at that time boasted two institutions that Spain lacked, the parliament and the Bank of England. Both institutions helped to guarantee the flow of huge loans needed by the British government as far back as 1689 and then throughout the whole eighteenth century. It could also be quite plausibly argued that the abolition of tax farming posed no great problem for English financiers, for they could continue to invest in state loans with great confidence; the state itself also wanted this situation to continue. It seems unlikely that direct administration could have been maintained in late-seventeenth-century England without the government-spending control built up by parliament; the Bank of England was set up for the same reasons of control. It should also be remembered here that this system was based on transatlantic trade, free within the limits of British interests. The benefits of this burgeoning trade buoyed up the creditworthiness of the Bank of England and backed the interests represented in parliament.

In Spain there was no such representative institution on which both investors and the government itself could rely. Neither did the government wish it, because its overriding principle was to balance the books rather than run up a debt. Spain's trading system with the Americas, moreover, did not benefit very much Spanish private commercial interests: state privileges and international participation reduced Spanish merchants' share, and the country had no central bank, since there was not much to broker when no loans were required; neither was there much mercantile capital in circulation. After 1780 things changed in Spain, due to the force of circumstances, but up to that time the situation was as sketched out above, so financial business declined during these years in Spain. When the watershed moment of 1780 arrived, Spain found it difficult to come up with the necessary capital.

France's case was completely different. Tax farming was retained there, especially after the crushing failure of Law's system. It is true that farmed-out taxes represented only 50 per cent of state revenue by the middle of the century, and that these taxes – all indirect – grew more in the second half of the century than those run directly by the government. As an example of the ensuing situation, after the reinforcement of the *ferme général* in 1726 with the triumph of Fleury, witness the words of the financier and *munitionnaire* Jacques Marquet de Bourgade in 1769. For this author, staunch defender of the *fermiers*, there was no other corps like this in the whole of Europe. They catered for the king's need of quickly delivered tax revenue by filling the gap between approval of the tax and actual collection, as well as pitching in with other short-term loans. Bourgade reiterated Fleury's arguments of 1726, presenting the *fermiers* as mainstays of the state (Félix 2011: 125–28). Although the tax farmers did come in for their share of criticism, there was less argument about their efficacy and timeliness.

Historians have generally agreed (Riley 1986: 63–65) that the *fermiers* were absolutely essential in France up to 1789. France's situation was certainly very different from Spain's. France had inherited a hefty debt from Louis XIV's reign, a debt that was barely reduced during the Regency. To make matters worse, the cost of the central wars of the eighteenth century, Austria's War of Succession and, above all, the Seven Years' War, racked up financial needs to a level that would have been impossible to tackle without a reliable system. And this system was, precisely, the *ferme* and all it entailed. If the *ferme* had been abolished, it would have been very difficult for the king to find financiers ready to invest large sums in his support, at least in peacetime. The twin examples of the Regency and Louis XIV's final decades both weighed heavily in France's short-term memory: a better bet was to reinforce the old tax-farming system. The system certainly did not come up with the whole answer to France's financial problem or prevent it from becoming one of the causes of the Revolution; but in the meantime it had allowed France to keep up an enviable international level. Although the Seven Years' War was a resounding failure, France did recover its reputation in 1783 (Félix and Tallet 2009: 160). Spain, France's ally, also triumphed in 1783, but it did not have to carry France's baggage of an inherited debt; Spain's debt at this moment was new and small.

If the French tax farmers kept their king's creditworthiness at otherwise untenable levels, this was because they were sure of the soundness of the business involved. Tax farming was a good business for them but also for the king. The rising public-borrowing requirement could not be blamed on the farmers but rather on military needs of the time. Any assessment of whether or not France's eighteenth-century system was viable would have to factor in France's borrowing requirement as far back as Louis XIV. As we have already seen, England's ability to set up a successful system at the end of the seventeenth century depended on its lack of debt at that time. France was forced to shoulder this baggage up to 1789 and afterwards, largely because it started out at such a high level. What was the real effect of the lack of tax farming on Spain's financial system? Quite simply, the king's freedom from debt. But this was a voluntary question. Spain had opted to shun debt and for this reason tax farmers ceased to be necessary. England got rid of the tax farmers but created a public-debt system that not only provided the government with the necessary money but also boosted private business. France chose not to get rid of tax farmers; its growing debt bankrupted the state but the tax farmers, among others, sustained a private financial system that kept up the country's richness even as times changed. Spain ousted the farmers and shunned public debt, thereby stymieing the public and private finance system.

Up to 1779 Spain had no debt problems, but when this crucial moment came it had to improvise one and rush through reforms of all types, otherwise it could not have fought in the American War. Until that time, however, the downside of its policies was to fall behind as a military power, because the absence of loans, above all in peacetime, pre-empted proper growth of its armed forces. It is not that Spain's army, and above all its navy, did not grow at this time; neither did it cease to be a feared rival or desired ally; rather was it a case of Spain developing a much lower-profile military expenditure than Great Britain or France (Torres Sánchez 2015a: 200–03), with knock-on effects for the future.

The consequences of the tax-farming abolition in Spain are clear in terms of the ensuing increase in state control and revenue received but it seems to have a negative effect on the finance system in the long run. There was certainly a more centralised way of running fiscal policy afterwards, side-lining previously involved sectors of private participation. The downside is that his tended to reinforce the monopolistic trend in this area of administration. This did not bode well for the future of a monopoly enshrouded finance system; the problems this created would come home to roost when greater needs had to be tackled at the end of the century.

Notes

1 In the case of Spain Durand refers to Charles III's reign, apparently overlooking the fact that direct administration had already been established back in 1749.

2 *"Razon del valor liquido que produjeron las Rentas Generales de Customs del Reyno en el año de 1748, el que ha tenido en el de 1749 y differencia que resulta"*. Archivo General de Simancas, Dirección General de Rentas, 2ª remesa, legajo 10. The direct administration figures come mainly from this document, plus *legajo* 2354 of the *Secretaría and Superintendencia de Hacienda*, also kept in Simancas.

3 The source document is the same one cited in the previous footnote.

4 Report signed by Luis de Ibarra y Larrea of the Contaduría Mayor de Cuentas, and by Conde de Valparaíso (outgoing minister), 15 October 1759. Ms. 10695, fols. 301–59, Biblioteca Nacional, Madrid.

5 Rodrigo, J., *"Instrucción presentada a S. M. ... por D. José Rodrigo, marqués de la Compuesta, en el año de 1716"*. Ms. 18055, fols. 186–94, *Biblioteca Nacional*, Madrid.

5   Growing needs

The cost of war and extraordinary revenue

5.1 The management of extraordinary expenditure

In previous chapters we have seen how a fiscal-state was built up, i.e., a state that set up an ordinary fiscal system to produce regular income to meet its ordinary needs. This revenue no longer came from the king's seigneurial income or family wealth but rather from his subjects and their own economic activity. Although in some cases direct taxes held on to their past importance, albeit no longer so directly related to feudal domains, it was indirect taxes that little by little built up to become the lion's share of the state's ordinary revenue. Economic activity, therefore, became the bedrock of the fiscal system and the necessary condition of any increase in tax revenue. To increase this base, governments brought in the suitable reforms to enable the country to tap into this economic improvement. Population growth was obviously crucial here, a population that was increasingly urban and consumerist, and with a dwindling proportion of privileged classes.

As we have seen, ordinary revenue thus organised kept up nonstop growth throughout the whole century. To this must be added ostensibly wartime additions that were then permanently grafted onto the revenue base when peace came along. Despite these developments, ordinary revenue still served only to meet ordinary expenditure, a term referring to states' peacetime operational expenses. When war broke out no ordinary budget was able to withstand a single year of conflict.

This brings up the problem of managing the added expense since the war-caused extraordinary expenditure. This enables us to analyse all extraordinary-revenue aspects as management of extraordinary expenditure: faced with likely costs much higher than normal, states had to come up with an extraordinary-revenue policy that would cater for those costs. Management of extraordinary expenditure hence includes the previous attention paid to extraordinary revenue. In the following paragraphs, therefore, we will look at both fiscal and non-fiscal extraordinary revenue, before addressing the debt in the next chapter.

Table 5.1 shows a possible two-part scheme of this expenditure management. These two parts, 1 and 2, are in turn divided into two stages: the fiscal-military state and the contractor state. In the first place war provokes an immediate need that tends to raise extraordinary revenue by means of taxes, non-tax revenue and debt. This is the fiscal-military-state stage, i.e., the state that is driven by war needs to boost its revenue. Consecutively, or concurrently if the war drags on, this revenue

Table 5.1 Management of likely war expenses over and above peacetime expenses

	1.- Immediate expenditure	*2.- Future expenditure*
New revenue	A Fiscal-military state	
	Extraordinary taxes	More ordinary taxes
	Non-extraordinary tax resources	
	Debt	Debt service
New military expenditure	B Contractor state	
	Payments	Armed forces in peacetime
	Transport	
	Means (ships, weapons)	
	Supplies	

has to be spent on war-waging supplies and wherewithal. The state has to rely on contractors for ensuring, in one way or other, that all these goods and services get to the armed forces to make sure they are ready to fight. This is the contractor state. All this means an instant expense in wartime, with the debts and payment backlogs then being carried over into peacetime, whereby there is a future, war-caused expense over and above ordinary expenditure. This expense will have to be tackled in peacetime, thereby extending both the fiscal-military state and the contractor state. In short, extraordinary revenue, debt management, war cost and contractor state are all questions that can be addressed through the prism of the management of war-caused expenditure. Apart from administrative reforms, as with the direct administration, the common decision was turning to extraordinary revenue.

What exactly was extraordinary revenue? The prevailing eighteenth-century trend, at least in France, followed the recommendations of Forbonnais, who proposed a warfare-financing model that drew on the theories of the Englishman Davenant. The clearest recipe was simple: increasing taxes, albeit complemented with a nicely calculated system of loans, which, according to the French financial theorist, would preferably be short term (Le Goff 1999: 379). The French put Forbonnais's tenets fairly faithfully into practice, at least during the central wars of the century, without sticking to them religiously, while the British strayed away from this method in favour of defraying warfare by directly increasing the debt. Be that as it may, extraordinary wartime taxation was also an important line of action in Great Britain, although progressively losing out, percentage-wise, to instant debt financing.

Although extraordinary taxation is sometimes spoken of, it would strictly be more accurate to speak of extraordinary resources, insofar as they did not exist in peacetime and were thus ostensibly temporary during the years of war. This umbrella term would then embrace extraordinary taxation per se, i.e., hikes of existing taxes or the creation of new ones. But extraordinary revenue ranges well beyond taxes, taking in a whole range of other resources such as donations, lotteries, jobbery, etc. Short-term debt was another component, designed to be paid off in a relatively brief period of time.

As for extraordinary taxation, the increments from tax hikes or new taxes should in theory have been discontinued at the end of the war or shortly afterwards. In practice, however, it was not always so. It often turned out that the main difficulty was not so much defraying the war as paying the pending debts and expenses in the following years of peace, with a carryover of backlogs and compound delays. For that very reason many extraordinary taxes lingered on for years or even remained for good. This had been well-nigh standard practice in the seventeenth century, especially in Spain, which discontinued this procedure, however, in the following century. New taxes were sometimes created even in peacetime to pay off the outstanding war debts. Witness the 1749 *vingtième* in France as one of the classic examples, including also different objectives of fiscal policy (Le Goff 1999: 392). Various fiscal reforms of the eighties in Spain and Great Britain also followed along these lines. What happened in the end is that ordinary taxes were racked up in stages and were then grafted onto the ordinary tax system. As a result, ordinary taxation levels always rose after periods of war. As pointed out by Morineau, one of the characteristic traits of France's eighteenth-century taxation was phased-in, peacetime, ordinary-tax hikes (Morineau 1980).

This was also done systematically and continually in Great Britain, with a debt-smoothing effect, i.e., a gentle but steady upward trend of ordinary taxes, resulting in a "widening but slowly expanding tax base" (O'Brien 1988: 7). This made gradual debt payment possible, the servicing of which also represented a steadily growing burden.

5.2 Two different and similar models: Great Britain and France

The British case is idiosyncratic. It is usually said that British governors decided to defray eighteenth-century wars with debt and then hike taxes in the ensuing periods of peace, barring the case of direct taxes. This is basically true but does not tell the whole story. It might be more accurate to say the British governors, faced with the necessary choice between loans or taxes, "opted to finance *most* of the incremental costs, imposed by augmented levels of military expenditure" (O'Brien 1988: 2 [my italics]). It turns out, according to the figures to hand, that although debt grew a lot in absolute terms, its percentage share of total expenditure did not grow correlatively during most of the century, since expenditure and income also grew substantially.

Table 5.2 shows loans' percentage share of total expenditure (col. 3), and also tax receipts as the percentage of the extra revenue raised to finance wars (col. 4).

Table 5.2 Percentage of loans and taxes in war costs in Britain (millions of pounds sterling)

Years	1.- Total expenditure	2.- Amount raised by loans	3.- Col. 2 as % of col. 1	4.- Tax receipts as % of extra revenue
1688–97	49.3	16.5	33.6	49
1702–13	93.6	29.4	31.4	26
1739–48	95.6	29.7	31.1	21
1756–63	160.5	60	37.4	20
1776–83	236.4	94.5	39.9	19
1793–1815	1657.8	440.2	26.6	58

Sources: cols. 1–3, Dickson 1968: 10; O'Brien 1988: 4.

As column 3 shows, the loan percentage of war costs was always slightly over 30 per cent, increasing only during the Seven Years' War and the American Revolutionary War. Taxes also loomed large in this extra revenue, though somewhat less in the two aforementioned conflicts. During the revolutionary wars added taxes were more important than at any other moment of the period under study.

Taxes also grew during the wars, therefore, i.e., the extraordinary taxation formed, normally, by hikes of existing taxes, indirect (excise) as well as direct (land tax). According to the figures of O'Brien and Brewer (1988 and 1989), the excise rate and the number of articles on which it was levied did not stop growing throughout the century, even during war years. This tax began to increase in absolute terms and steadily as from 1713, dropping somewhat during the Austrian War of Succession but increasing thereafter, more sharply during the Seven Years' War, especially after 1759. This pattern would be repeated in the American War, without this growth falling away in the interregnum of peace. This growth accounts for the high excise yield and was also reflected in the increase in staff numbers, multiplying fourfold in the 100 years following 1690 (Brewer 1989: 104–05). Excise offices grew quicker than any other government body.

The revenue source that did grow during all the wars was land tax. Government demands on landowners increased during the wars, normally up to a rate of 20 per cent, dropping back to only 5 per cent in peacetime. The long-term trend after 1730, in any case, was steady growth in nominal terms (O'Brien and Hunt 1999: 76–77, 87). Nonetheless, as agrarian revenue grew substantially too, the end result may well have been favourable for landowners in real terms until Pitt's reform at the end of the century (O'Brien 1988: 16).

The taxation percentage of Britain's war defrayment is well vouched for by the calculations of several different authors. Additional tax revenue collected during the war years is deemed to be the contribution made by taxes towards the cost of war, although the debt built up during the war would also chip in too. In the Nine Years' War taxes represented 49 per cent of the extra revenue raised to finance the war; this percentage would later fall as debt's percentage rose. Until the American War taxes accounted for only about 20 per cent of the extra revenue (O'Brien 1988: 4). This trend changed afterwards and the tax share of extra revenue rose to 58 per cent during the Napoleonic wars. In these wars 542 million pounds was raised by taxes, shared out as follows: 298 million from tax hikes, 197 million from new taxes or innovations to the tax base and 47 million from changes in the quantity or value of the commodities taxed (O'Brien 1988: 4, 7). Not everything was new debt, therefore, even during conflicts.

France's tactics followed Forbonnais's theories more closely, thus differing slightly from Great Britain's. Both countries resembled each other in their growing resort to debt; they differed from each other, however, in the way this debt was obtained and managed, above all because in France a good deal of the debt corresponded to sums invested in the buying and selling of offices, even though this extraordinary war-financing option was in decline after 1749 (Le Goff 1999: 386–87). Neither did France manage to raise such a high proportion of war-financing loans as Great Britain, although it did edge up very close to British percentages during the Seven Years' War (Bonney 2004: 203). On this reading, taxes would have played a greater war-defrayment role in France than in Great Britain though in all likelihood the difference was slight.

We certainly know that France raised ordinary direct and indirect taxes during the wars, but we also know that debt was hard-wired into the French system; both finance officials and *fermiers* granted short-term loans and advanced payments to the government when necessary. New extraordinary-revenue sources were also sought, such as the sale of offices, forced loans, church donations, provincial-state donations and currency devaluation (Félix and Tallett 2009: 156). New direct taxes strictly speaking were not created, lest they whip up fierce opposition from various privileged groups. The only exception to this rule was the *capitation* of 1695. The prevailing tactic was rather to hike existing taxes such as the *dixième* and *vingtième*.

The *dixième* was established in 1710 to offset the overspend of the War of the Spanish Succession. Although it was a war tax, it lasted until 1717. It was re-established in 1733, at the start of the War of the Polish Succession. In this case it lasted until 1737, just before the war ended. This tax cropped up again in 1741 to help pay for the War of the Austrian Succession, lingering on until 1749. At this moment, however, rather than being scrapped completely it was halved, becoming a *vingtième* (Marion 1979: 181). The differential trait of this first *vingtième* is that it was established in peacetime; to this extent it could be considered as ordinary rather than extraordinary. A second *vingtième* came along in 1756 (Seven Years' War), effectively regrading it back to a *dixième* although the other name was retained. Another three came between 1760 and 1763 and again from 1782 to 1786, the latter threesome also in peacetime. Each one of these taxes was maintained for a few years, meaning that what was ostensibly a war-financing extraordinary supplement led to a real increase of ordinary taxes. Even so, the nominal tax increase might not necessarily have meant a real increase in the tax burden of the French during the years of peace running from 1725 to 1785 (Bonney 2004: 196). Or at least the charge would have been temporary and variable according to the tax under consideration, for some charges not normally recorded for accounts purposes would have upped the tax pressure for all the French, at least for the period 1735–63 (Félix 1999; Félix and Tallett 2009: 161).

Some historians have argued that the *vingtièmes* were the "most correct and least objectionable" French taxes on the grounds that the tax was levied on the income of every person (Marion 1979: 556), representing a serious attempt to increase the landowners' fiscal contribution (Le Goff 1999: 388–89). Although the actual levy did not always live up to its name and there were always collection problems, it is also true that these taxes were divided by classes and tried to punish trade and industry as little as possible, for example. Along the same lines some authors have stressed that the new taxes, taken together with existing ones, guaranteed, for all their faults, that even "the privileged elements were brought increasingly into the tax net" (Félix and Tallett 2009: 161). The privileged were also being asked to pay diverse types of indirect taxes, leading to the oxymoron term of "privileged taxpayer" (Kwass 1999: 375–76). This certainly did not change the situation and the privileged few continued to pay less than if they had belonged to the commoner class, but it could no longer be claimed that they were entirely exempt (Félix 1999: 44).

As well as the abovementioned extraordinary taxes, wars, as we have already mentioned, had to be defrayed also with extraordinary revenue that was not strictly speaking fiscal. This begs the question of which part was played by one and the other of these resources in paying for each war. Calculating the exact proportions is difficult. The sine qua non of doing so is some initial idea of the total cost of the wars, which is no easy task to start with. Educated guesses can be made, however, about the amount of added tax or extraordinary revenue each war called for.

Let us centre on the best-known conflicts, the War of the Austrian Succession and the Seven Years' War. In the former case it has been calculated that added taxes in the war years added 667 million *livres tournais* to the taxes that would have been paid if peace had been maintained. Each of the eight war years between 1741 and 1748 thus cost 83.4 million livres more than if there had been no war (Morineau 1980; Le Goff 1999: 383).

Morineau, for his part, calculated that total war costs would have topped normal peacetime expenditure by 919 million livres. Since taxes represented 667 million there would have been a 252 million deficit to be plugged with non-tax revenue. Le Goff has increased this last sum substantially. He not only took into account items that Morineau was not aware of but also factored in the war-debt to be paid off in peacetime, extending the period up to 1740–54. Le Goff's estimate of non-tax resources soars to 707 million livres (Le Goff 1999: 383–87).

If we add together the two sums, additional taxes and non-tax revenue, we then get a total of 1.374 billion *livres tournais*, which would give us a rough idea of the total cost of the War of the Austrian Succession over and above normal peacetime expenditure. New taxes would have defrayed 48 per cent of this cost.

Félix, using other budgetary documents, has nonetheless come up with similar percentages: fiscal supplements during the War of the Austrian Succession would have represented between 25 and 28 per cent of peacetime taxation and would have defrayed nearly half of the war expenses (Félix 1999: 46). This proportion more than doubles the British percentage for this same war. The rest, just over half, would correspond to non-tax revenue, the breakdown of which we will see later.

Calculations of the Seven Years' War cost are more difficult because there is no consensus among the various authors. Following the same procedure as before, Morineau calculated that additional taxes in wartime would have added up to 543 million *livres tournais*; i.e., 77.6 million livres on average more than if peace had obtained for each one of the seven war years.

Morineau's calculation of a total war cost (above peacetime costs) of 1.150 billion livres means that the 543 million input of new taxes would have left a black hole of 607 million to be filled with non-tax revenue. In this case Riley ups Morineau's figures: on his calculations the total war-added cost comes out as 1.325 billion and the input of non-tax revenue as 939 million, although he lowers the input of new taxes to 386 million (Riley 1986: 140). Le Goff's figures are higher, taking into account too the post-war debts. He points out that the total value of non-tax revenue for the period 1755–69 would have amounted to 1.015 billion livres. The total war cost, therefore (additional taxes plus non-tax revenue) would have added up to 1.558 billion livres (Le Goff 1999: 387). According to Le Goff's figures, the new taxes would be about 29 per cent higher than the yearly average in peacetime and would have weighed in with 34.8 per cent of war costs.

According to the three cited authors the new-tax financing of the Seven Years' War would have been lower than in the earlier conflict. In the War of the Austrian Succession taxes defrayed nearly half the costs; in the Seven Years' War this input would have been 35 per cent at most. Félix puts the new-tax input even lower. This author modifies the calculations made from Riley's figures and calculates the new taxes actually spent on war costs and also deducts other costs, coming up with a figure of about 300 million livres, which would not have financed more than 26 per cent of the estimated war cost. Félix, for his part, estimates an "immediate delivery" loan input of 850 million livres. Treasury expenses during the war years, according to Félix, would have been 1.475 billion livres (Félix 1999: 50, 53). This would be close to the total war cost, excluding ordinary taxes. Adding all together, the total war cost would come out as 4 billion (Félix 1999: 42; Bonney 2004: 198).

During this war, therefore, the government had to fall back on loans more than before. This does not mean that extraordinary taxation was not resorted to as well, above all in the form of new *vingtièmes*. But this war was more expensive than the former one and the increased cost was met more with debt than taxes, although taxes did rise too in absolute terms; to this must be added other extraordinary revenue that fed from such sources as church donations, sales of stipends and offices plus loans from *fermiers*. Despite all these expedients the yield of the *vingtièmes* had to be spent on this war, diverting them from their initial remit of paying off the debts of the previous war. Only a third *vingtième*, brought in in 1760, put the government on a reasonable keel. But the financial breach had been opened, so there was no other option than to tap into the *caisse des amortissements*, a new bankruptcy in effect that would complicate the future even more (Félix 1999: 51).

In short, the central wars of the eighteenth century obliged France to fall back increasingly on loans to defray conflicts. As Table 5.3 shows, the loan input to extraordinary revenue was on an upward trend, not only during the wars themselves but also in the ensuing periods when the war debt had to be paid off.

The quickest growing components were term loans and, above all, life annuities and *tontines*. On the other hand, the extraordinary-revenue input of donations in general, which had still been sizeable in 1740 (46.8 per cent), fell away thereafter.

During the American War the situation would become even trickier, with increasing loan takeup. The reason for this was increasing costs. The total cost of this war, shorter than the Seven Years' War, is usually put at about 1.3 billion *livres tournais* above ordinary peacetime costs (Félix and Tallett 2009: 160); this sum could be even higher if we made the same ancillary calculations as for the former conflicts. Credit now played a much bigger part than beforehand. Credit takeup was certainly nothing new, nor even rare; the new feature now was that the credit was dearer (because Necker turned above all to life annuities) and also the relative extraordinary-revenue input of loans, thus reducing the proportional participation of taxes in financing this war. This was due to the king's reluctance to raise taxes. Necker also had to resort to negotiable state debt. He could no longer rely on the collaboration of traditional financiers, in particular the *fermiers*, since he himself had amputated the system by bringing *aides* and *domaines* into direct administration (Durand 1976: 16) in an attempt to abolish tax farming. He therefore had to turn to the normal credit market. Life annuities now weighed in with 230 million, nearly half the total extraordinary revenue of 530 million (Félix 2006: 259); total loans added up to 900 million livres.

France was not much different from Great Britain in its form of paying for eighteenth-century wars. Debt played an increasing role in both countries, as shown by Table 5.4.

In the interests of consistency, we have chosen Morineau's figures here, even though they differ slightly from those shown in Table 5.3 and are considered to be less accurate. British figures are also different from those shown in Table 5.2, since here they refer only to the percentage of war-caused extraordinary costs.

Table 5.3 Percentage loan input to extraordinary revenue in France

	1740–48	*1740–54*	*1755–62*	*1755–69*
Loans	32.8	44.6	56.5	60.2

Source: Le Goff 1999: 387.

Table 5.4 Proportion of extraordinary war expenditure covered by loans in France and Great Britain

	France	Great Britain
War of Austrian Succession	28	85
Seven Years	65	81
American War	91	100, *119*

Source: Morineau 1980: 326. For the figure in italics, see the discussion in the text.

For the American War two figures have been given. First of all, Morineau's round figure of 100 per cent is dubious, since there were also extraordinary taxes in this war; the other figure has been italicised to differentiate it. This is the figure given by Crouzet, who has raised the percentage to 119, including loans taken up to pay the ordinary debt-service expense. Quite apart from the total accuracy of these figures, which we continue to regard as rough and ready, the table does give us a point of comparison. France's choice to pay for war with more debt and fewer taxes, in proportional terms, almost chimed in with Great Britain. This was particularly true during the Seven Years' War and the American War. Things would change, however, in the post-Revolution conflicts and with Napoleon. In these wars the two countries had to turn to taxes more than before simply because loans fell short of needs. In any case Great Britain spent much more on its military activities than France, both in absolute terms and when it came to mobilising debt (Bonney 2004: 195, 201).

5.3   Spain: from the extraordinary single tax to the need of debt

Spain pursued a variable war-defrayment model in the eighteenth century, depending on the particular moment, the possibilities in hand and the needs to be met. Spain's situation, indeed, at the start of the century was very different, not only in comparison with its rivals but also with its own situation beforehand. It was working from a period of crisis and had not yet shaken off the effects. By about 1700 Spain's state revenue was very low and there were still hefty debts to be paid off. Later on, however, revenue grew and economic activity picked up, making it more feasible to finance warfare. With time, however, Spain had no choice but to set up a public-debt system to raise the necessary warfare revenue. Spain, in effect, would follow a very similar path to France and Great Britain. In general, it resembled more the French experience, in terms of the progressive importance of debt in extraordinary war expenditure, building up to a lion's share in the late-century revolutionary conflicts.

5.3.1 The War of Succession

Financing of the War of the Spanish Succession was a challenge for Philip V. The war cost more than Philip V could muster and part of it had to be financed with the aid of France, which sent troops and weapons. Here, of course, we refer only to the expenses defrayed with Spanish resources because, quite apart from French aid, Spain had to make a notable effort itself. This is what interests us here. In any case French aid was significant only up to 1709, practically disappearing thereafter.

Spain obtained the necessary resources above all by dint of an efficient administration that managed to boost both ordinary revenue (by 20 per cent) and extraordinary revenue (by 350 per cent) during the war. Spain's ordinary revenue rose from 96 million *reales* in 1702 to 136 million by 1713, while total revenue, including extraordinary items, rose from 120 to 229 million *reales* (Kamen 1974: 237). These sums more or less matched Spain's total expenditure at home, which has been calculated as follows, as an annual average: 131 million *reales* in 1704–08; 171 million in 1709–13 and 231 million in 1714–18 (Torres Sánchez 2015b: 59). To this must be added the Indies revenue, rather meagre at that time. War hindered normal traffic with the Americas and the king of Spain had to settle for the remnant rescued from the fleet burned in Vigo by the English in 1702; the ships at the time were lost but most of the money had already been unloaded (Rodríguez-Villasante 1984: 98; Tourón Yebra 1995). It was a tidy sum, about 104 million *reales*; only part of this money, however (14.9 million) was paid into the king's coffers; the rest was rushed off to France to help pay the costs of the French armies on the Italian front. Ironically, the sums sent by France to Spain in the years 1703–04 were offset by the American silver shipped out from Spain. In the end the amount sent by France added up to only 18 per cent of what Spain sent to France (Sanz Ayán 2006: 142–43). In the following years the amount of money arriving from the Americas declined significantly.

Although it is sometimes difficult to work out the timing of events year by year, it does seem that debts must have outweighed tax inputs in the first years of war. In the final throes, however, total revenue, which had grown meanwhile, could cover more of the expenditure, even though outstanding debt still had to be paid off.

Spain's war effort called for growth of all its revenue sources. How did it achieve this? One of the most important innovations was the whole set of organisational improvements, some carried over from the previous reign and partly improved in this one. A red-letter event here was the creation in 1703 of the *Tesorería Mayor de Guerra*, which complemented the existing *Tesorería General* and would in theory take on responsibility for all revenue to be spent on warfare, though this was not always the case in practice (Kamen 1974: 249; Sanz Ayán 2006: 150). As for the taxation system, according to Kamen, few new taxes were tagged on and the administrative efficacy showed up mostly in the increased tax-leasing rental. Although this occurred above all in 1713, it was helpful in paying off the backlog.

It is interesting to note here that some of the new taxes were levied on landowners. In 1705, for example, each *fanega* of cultivated land paid tax of one or two *reales*, depending on the type of crop involved. Attempts were also made to hike existing taxes, most of them indirect, especially the *millones* tax (Angulo Teja 2002: 373). The sums involved were not huge.

Increasing extraordinary revenue would be an easier task. The components thereof were very varied and were harnessed throughout all the war years, especially at the start, then 1707–09, and at the end. We have fairly detailed information on the extraordinary revenue of 1705–07 because it is recorded in the documentation of the *Tesorería Mayor*. This could then be extrapolated for the whole conflict. In the abovementioned two-year period extraordinary revenue accounted for 59.79 per cent of treasury revenue, while the rest (40.21 per cent) consisted of ordinary revenue. The most important extraordinary revenue items are shown in Table 5.5.

As Table 5.5 shows, the biggest chunk of ordinary revenue came from donations, more or less enforced, and the establishment of a tax on offices that had already been sold and on property sold to the crown in earlier years. A complete venal system was also set up, coming into its own in subsequent years. We also have partial information on these and other types of similar extraordinary expedients for the rest of the war years. One of the most fruitful was the tax on sold offices, which added up in 1713 to over 21 million *reales*. The chance was then also taken to suspend *juro* payments and investigate the validity of the certificates, some of which were then no longer honoured, helping to trim the debt further. Also administration-related were the percentage taxes on certain sectors, which

Table 5.5 Principal extraordinary expedients, 1705–07 as percentage of income of the *Tesorería Mayor de Guerra*

Total ordinary taxes			40.21
Principal extraordinary expedients			
	Extraordinary revenue: sales of jurisdictions, donations, etc.	35.23	
	Sales of offices (new)	7.11	
	Ceded debts	6.66	
	Loans from France	3.70	
Total extraordinary revenue			59.79
Total income	215,668,786 *reales de vellón*		100

Source: Sanz Ayán 2006: 153–55.

in practice helped to bring down the salaries of different types of officials. These brought in a total of about 1.7 million *reales* (Kamen 1974: 238–39).

Maybe of more interest were the donations, which were in theory voluntary, such as the 1702 "loyalty" donation and others of that ilk, though there may often have been covert government pressure or even ulterior motives of the donors. In any case participation in this government aid scheme did have a certain grassroots character, which worked much to the benefit of Philip V. Donation schemes took in cities and towns, entire provinces and regions, such as the one offered by the *Reino de Navarra* in 1706. The church also pitched in and at least 20 *grandees*. The total sum of recorded donations added up to 13 million *reales*, but many would have gone unrecorded so the real sum was certainly higher (Kamen 1974: 240–41).

The church was asked for another extraordinary donation of 20 million *reales* in 1707. By the following year slightly more than half had been brought in. But the Crown also benefited from one of its privileges vis-à-vis the clergy, the right to *sede vacante* income. What with the sees that were already vacant and those that then fell vacant during the war, it is calculated that the crown received in 1713 income from about 13 vacant sees, albeit of very uneven value, worth about 2 million *reales* a year between them. This sum was then swelled by new applications made to Castilian households and the country's financiers. In 1712 and 1714 poll tax schemes in Castile and also now in Aragon yielded a total of 14 million *reales*, one of the biggest sums among this extraordinary revenue. Mention must finally be made of property confiscations from traitors: these involved about 120 individuals with total income of nearly 3 million a year (Kamen 1974: 242–43).

Less known until recently is the fact that, due to the war, venal practices of the previous century continued. The period running from 1704 to 1711 saw a particularly intense series of buying and selling of honours and offices under various forms, both in Spain and in the colonies. At this time, indeed, some offices were sold that had never previously been up for sale. The income would have accounted for 7.11 per cent of extraordinary revenue in 1705–07 (about 15 million *reales*). The total sum raked in under this heading would add up to 75 million *reales* (Andújar Castillo 2014: 195–97). Not all of this was spent on war, but it is still one of the most sizeable extraordinary items. This practice broke off temporarily in Spain but continued in the Americas.

The most important new fiscal feature in these years was the fiscal reform in the Crown of Aragon, but its war-financing effects were small, simply because it came when the war was well underway. It has been calculated that between 1708 and 1712 the net yield of royal revenue in these territories already conquered by Philip V was about 5.3 million *reales*, but only 70 per cent came from new taxes (Artola 1982: 230). It would not be until a few years later that the financial reorganisation of the Crown of Aragon bore fruit.

Despite all these reforms and innovations expenses still sometimes exceeded revenue. To make matters worse the tax money always arrived late. The king therefore had to fall back on short-term loans from financiers, tax farmers and army- and navy-*asentistas*, roles that in those moments were often shared by the same persons (González Enciso 2008a; Dedieu 2011). Part of the debt generated by these and other possible loans, understood as short-term reimbursable loans, would end up being converted into *juros* as consolidated debt. The total *juro* sum added up in 1702 to a little over 101 million *reales*, an inherited sum that was unlikely to be paid back in the near future. By 1713 it had risen to 108.7 million *reales*; in Kamen's opinion this meant that war debts had not been paid off; in fact, there were prohibitions on doing so. Indeed, current *juro* payments stood at about the same amount on both dates. Nonetheless, a detailed comparison of Kamen's figures shows that there was not mere continuity in the servicing of this debt. In some revenue, on which *juro* interest was earmarked, *juros* grew and their interest was paid; in others, no. In the end the amount of *juros* being serviced remained the same but the components had shifted. This begs the question of whether there was any political agenda behind this situation – a question we cannot at the moment answer.

5.3.2 The mid-century wars

Spain's financing of the conflicts it took part in was varied and unsystematic, although we do know that in all cases the procedures followed were similar to those already seen for the War of Succession: slight increase of ordinary taxation, almost always phased out when peace came; a varied clutch of extraordinary contributions, also disappearing with peace; more or less voluntary donations from various social groups, with the initial objective of paying war costs; and, finally, short-term debt raised from *asentistas* and tax farmers, with the latter only up to 1749, only partly consolidable in *juros*. This scheme might seem pretty clear but in fact we have no detailed knowledge of details or proportions.

In about 1730, before Spain embarked on a whole series of military ventures, its taxation situation was fairly stable. There was at the same time a twofold debt situation: firstly, the government tried to solve the inherited debt problem by repudiating some *juros* and whittling down the interest; secondly, the debt also grew due to the warfare costs of 1717–19 and new small conflicts such as the 1726–27 siege of Gibraltar and the tensions of an authentic "cold war" (Horn 1967: 290). Spain would soon be taking on new conflicts in Italy and northern Africa before war with Great Britain broke out in 1739, and the fiscal machinery came under stress once more. The *infante* Charles's 1731 expedition to take possession of Naples, the 1732 conquest of Oran and the Italian expeditions sparked off by the War of the Polish Succession as from 1733, including the conquests of Naples in 1734 and Sicily in 1735, detonated Spain's military needs and strained its finance system anew.

Centring only on Italy, we can estimate the cost of operations in light of some items that were paid from Cadiz against the fleets arriving in the years shown in Table 5.6. These are only partial figures but they do give us some idea of the increased expense provoked by the Italian campaigns and also the immediate recourse to Indies funds, crucial in the thirties.

Table 5.6 Indies funds spent on the Italian campaign or payment of *asentistas* (in millions of *reales de vellón*)

	For Italy	To asentistas	Total
1731	4		4
1732	5.8	8.3	14.1
1734	16.1	2	16.3

Source: Pulido 1998: 306–08.

Could the wars of the thirties have been paid with ordinary revenue? If we bear in mind that in 1739, before the war with Great Britain, there was a suspension of payments, the answer has to be no. The suspended payments were worth 100 million *reales*, a tidy sum in view of the country's revenue at that time. A hefty debt was being built up too, despite the fact that ordinary revenue also helped to pay a large part of the wars.

Table 5.7 tells us that ordinary revenue in total grew substantially from 1725 to 1739: an increase of 64.7 million *reales*, which would have doubt-less come in handy for Patiño's Italian policy. Where did this increase come from? Although the table does not show all revenue it does feature the most important items. The most notable fact is that the biggest item of all, provincial revenue, did not grow. The biggest increases came from Indies funds, booming at this time (Morineau 1985; García-Baquero González 2003: 55) and monopolies, especially tobacco, which was brought into direct administration in 1730. This action was accompanied by a rise in the retail price of the finished product (Rodríguez Gordillo 2000), whereby the yield rose from 31.8 million in 1725–29, before the reform, to 42.8 in 1735–39 (Torres Sánchez 2015a: 216). The church's contribution edged upwards while the most detailed examination of customs shows an increase from 19.9 million *reales* in 1731 to 24.1 in 1739 (Fernández Albaladejo 1977: 55, 77).

Debt must have been growing nonetheless. The main concern of the ministers after Patiño was precisely to try and control expenditure. Several measures geared towards this end were taken in 1737, also aiming to speed up collection of outstanding debts (Angulo Teja 2002: 377). The *Junta de Medios* (advisory board on resources) set up this year could come up with no better option than the devil-deep-blue-sea idea of cutting costs or suspending payments (Marina Barba 1993; Delgado Barrado 2015: 20; Dubet 2015a: 15). If ordinary revenue grew by nearly 65 million *reales* and the suspension of payments affected a sum of 100 million, which was not even the total debt figure, it follows that debt played a much bigger part in debt financing than ordinary revenue.

Shortly after the suspension of payments of 1739 came war with Great Britain, linking straight in with a new war in Italy in 1740. From then on the situation changed. In the first years of the forties costs grew substantially more.

Table 5.7 Spain's ordinary revenue in 1725–39, annual mean
(in millions of *reales de vellón*)

	Total revenue	Provinciales	Monopolies	Church	Customs	Indies
1725–29	254.5	59.4	46.3	13.7	22.7	10.7
1730–34	257	57.2	48.9	17.1	22.1	69.5
1735–39	319.2	57.1	56.6	17.5	23.8	54.2

Source: Torres Sánchez 2015a: Appendix.

Navy consignments began to grow after 1740. Merino's figures bear this out: increase in the thirties (90 per cent on average more than in the twenties) and then a sharp increase in 1740, with an average threefold increase on earlier years (Merino Navarro 1981a: 155). This shows that the War of Jenkin's Ear had been prepared beforehand, with previous defence expenditure on ships and fortifications, and that the declaration of 1739 served as justification for new expenditure. But it was above all war in Italy, not only in the Americas, that really caused expenditure to soar.

But by now ordinary revenue was no longer growing as much as in the previous decade. The Atlantic war hindered trade with the Americas, slashing the yield of both customs and precious metal for a good few years. The only significant growth was recorded by tobacco, on the back of a retail price hike in 1740. But this increased yield took some time to kick in because the price rise, a seat-of-the-pants response to immediate war needs, produced a whole-sale demand switch from the official product to the contraband product. Even so, net tobacco revenue did grow from 41 million *reales* in 1742 to 63 million in 1743 and would continue to grow thereafter (Rodríguez Gordillo and Gárate Ojanguren 2007; González Enciso 2006b).

The financial difficulties necessarily led to the taking of extraordinary measures. The first one was organisational in character, although benefits were confidently expected to ensue therefrom. This was the bringing of all tax revenue into direct administration, which began precisely in 1741, as we have already seen. The decision was not an easy one: carrying the whole process through would take years, posing a risk in times of war. A good example of these difficulties is the *Junta de Medios*'s apparently counterintuitive proposal in 1740 that tax farmers who wished to continue the lease should be allowed to do so at the same price, albeit upfronting six monthly payments. This would seem to fly in the face of the government's intention. Witness also the fact that tobacco revenue was again farmed out and the general revenue lease was awarded to Girardeli, a former tax farmer (Canga Argüelles 1968: II, 23). Although the *Junta de Medios* might be reflecting the tax farmers' interests here, this is also a sign that the emergency situation was balking the overall change. In the end the board's advice fell on deaf ears and Campillo's government pressed on with the change.

The reform boosted revenue as the profits previously creamed off by the tax farmers now flowed into royal coffers under the direct administration scheme, but the process took some time to complete and it was therefore unreasonable to expect a rapid increase in ordinary revenue. In the short term it was necessary to look for more extraordinary revenue. The first measure taken to this end involved venality. Patiño, to increase his resources, had continued with venal practices in the Americas upon becoming minster in 1726, but it was in 1739 when venality in the Americas really took off, then lasting until 1750. After 1740 some offices were also once more sold in Spain (Andújar Castillo 2014: 197–99).

There were also temporary extraordinary taxation measures. In 1739 Madrid's *alcabalas* were hiked by 4 per cent, plus a 13 *reales* surcharge on each *fanega* of salt when war spread to Italy. The *servicio de millones* was also extended in time (Angulo Teja 2002: 378). More radical measures were called for, however. A 10 per cent *valimiento* was therefore decreed, i.e., a royal "availment" of each subject's liquid income from any possession (house, land, mills, etc.). Attempts were also made to collect it from all landowners. Furthermore, in 1741 the king pocketed half of the *arbitrios* (local land revenue) and *sisas* (excise tax) which were conceded to all towns and villages of the realm (Artola 1982: 252–53; Marina Barba 1993: 281).

The measures taken, however, were not easy to enforce. Artola points out that the "spectacular decision" of the *valimiento* came across as a threat of direct taxation but it proved impossible to enforce due to lack of knowledge about the taxable material. A lump sum per province was calculated, at the discretion of local judges, then to be shared out among local residents on the basis of their wealth. The *Consejo de Castilla* expressed its difficulties in enforcing the 10 per cent *valimiento*; it stood out against it and decided on a series of measures such as demanding one third of the revenue from sold-off offices, a contribution from ministers, royal household employees, grandees and title holders, a forced donation from *asentistas* and tax farmers, a contribution from commerce guilds, among other expedients (Canga Argüelles 1968: II, 23–24; Marina Barba 1993: 283), measures that recall some of those taken during the War of Succession.

In fact, we know about these measures only from the enabling legislation and do not know which ones were actually brought in and which not, since the news we have is only partial. The most important was the *décima*, stemming from the 10 per cent *valimiento*, but modified according to subsequent instructions and adapted to each case. Each town, village or city paid the required sum as it saw fit, on the basis of consumer demand or property ownership. Some places came up with the sum promptly; others took longer. It would seem that no real results were forthcoming until 1743 in any case (Fernández de Pinedo 2009).

The middle class paid tax on most food and manufactured commodities but the nobility also paid something; even though their contribution was still paltry, this does show the government's keenness to bring privileged classes into the direct-tax trawl. Staples were normally kept tax-free, enabling the poorest to escape most of the new tax burden. In the case of Madrid, part of the tax was collected by the *Cinco Gremios Mayores*, who paid the king 2.6 million *reales* upfront.

In 1748, when the accounting operation ended, the *Gremios* asked for 3.1 million *reales* to be paid back. The increase was due to interest payments, administrative costs and some debts that the *Gremios* had to pay. This whittled down the king's share, which ended up at 2.1 million *reales* (Fernández de Pinedo 2009). This sum strikes us as small for Madrid, although there was another 1.2 million not managed by the *Gremios*. The total value of the *décima* added up to 65.9 million *reales*, a large sum but shared out very unevenly: Seville and Catalonia both paid eyecatching sums (26 per cent between them); equally striking was the small amount paid by Madrid, 6 per cent (Marina Barba 1993: 332), possibly other charges had already been introduced there back in 1739.

We also know that the royal availment of *arbitrios*, increasing them by 4 per cent and of *sisas*, increasing them by one half, was collected in the whole of Spain, but we do not know the sum involved[1].

If we pool together such epoch-making features as the bringing of revenue into direct administration, the attempt of levying direct taxes on the nobility plus the direct tax experiment with the *décima*, a term with strong French resonances in this case, then we see that this war was very important from the fiscal point of view, not so much in terms of the sums mustered but the far-reaching changes attempted, some successfully. The *décima* comes across as an interesting experiment: it laid down no fixed collection procedure but left it up to the towns to choose the best taxation arrangement for the sums to be handed over; this opened up a new horizon of extraordinary-taxation possibilities. As long as the sums sought were actually raised, each different locality could act as it saw fit, thus passing the fiscal responsibility on to them and favouring prompt collection (Marina Barba 1993: 285–86).

As for the church's input, judging from the provisions laid down in the Concordat with the Holy See of 1737, the government was keen to bring the clergy into the extraordinary taxation trawl, especially the two arrangements of 1745 and 1746 (Angulo Teja 2002: 380). In the end peace brought some calm; even venal operations seem to have ended in about 1750, according to our current knowledge of events (Andújar Castillo 2014: 199–200).

Now came the time of fiscal recovery. In 1751, with peace now secured, Ensenada's *Representación* preened itself on a spruced-up finance system, with the 1739 bankruptcy now a distant memory. This seemed to bode well for a continuation of current policies, even maintaining tax alleviation in *rentas provinciales*. There is no doubt that most of the growth of ordinary revenue had occurred when war needs were most pressing, in the thirties and the first half of the forties, and that Spain's society had coped fairly straightforwardly with the extraordinary measures. Fiscal mechanisms had been shown to work smoothly and even successfully, bearing in mind that by 1750 Spain had achieved an international situation that would have been inconceivable back in 1713. It had also shaken off Great Britain's shackles on its colonial trade.

But this favourable situation now had to be cemented. The governors therefore opted for peace, even the luxury of neutrality in 1756. This even allowed the country to put something by for later, as shown by Spain's fleeting participation in the

Seven Years' War. This intervention was two-pronged: the invasion of Portugal in 1762 and the maritime combats in the Americas and the Philippines. Preparation for maritime defence must have been minimal, at least not enough, and without any doubt, tardy. After Ensenada's fall in 1754 the Atlantic policy changed; the show of neutrality even went so far as an apparent relaxation of the empire's maritime defences (Baudot Monroy 2012: 438–39). By the time Charles III came to the throne the decision to declare war on Great Britain had already been taken; hence the new king's immediate interest in the number of ships ready for war in late 1759 and those being readied in the first months of 1760 (Barrio Gozalo 1988: 21). This preparation must certainly have increased the expenditure of the maritime departments (Merino Navarro 1981a: 156–57); we do not know for sure where these funds came from but some extraordinary source must surely have been tapped into, probably the short-term loans of naval *asentistas*, because ordinary revenue did not seem to rise at the time. Some debt remained and donations were sought to defray it. There are records, for example, of the Basque provinces being asked for donations in 1779, on the basis of a comparison with their previous donation in 1765 (Torres Sánchez 2013a: 73, 92; García Zúñiga 1993: 312). Given that the war had already ended by this time, these donations could have been justified only on the grounds of paying off the debt backlog and bringing the government's budget back on an even keel.

What is really striking about this war, in any case, is the financing of the 40,000-strong army that invaded Portugal in 1762, most of whom had to be brought across the Peninsula up from the east coast and Andalusia, where they were quartered, to the Portuguese border. In Table 5.8, we will look at the costs of this army, since it is one of the few cases in which we can arrive at a fairly detailed breakdown.

Table 5.8 Costs of the army of Portugal in 1762 (in millions of *reales de vellón*)

			Total
Provisions by *asiento*			35.4
	Transport contractors	21.8	
	Grain contractor	10.9	
	Hospital contractor	2.7	
Wages			27.8
Extraordinary costs			7
Other minor costs			2.6
Army provisions			1.5
TOTAL			74.3

Source: González Enciso 2006: 185.

The interesting point here is that the war funds came from the so-called *depósito*, a room in the Treasury offices containing bullion: the surpluses carried over from one year to another in the years of peace. Every year, in other words, sums of pieces of various types of precious metal – coins, silver plates, jewels – were put aside in the *depósito* against any unforeseen event or extraordinary expenditure of the future (Barbier 1984; Pieper 1992; Andrés-Gallego 2003: 162). By 1761 the sum deposited there added up to 200 million *reales* (Pieper 1992: 164–65), so it was fairly straightforward to siphon off from there the 74 million plus needed by the army invading Portugal. The money was sent in cash to the Portuguese front, most arriving just before hostilities began (González Enciso 2006a: 187).

5.3.3 Conflicts from the eighties on: taxes and, at last, national debt

If the Portugal campaign of 1762 was a fairly idiosyncratic financing case, the ensuing conflicts would represent a significant change in Spain's eighteenth-century war-financing arrangements. Both in the American War, as from 1779, and in the War against the Convention in 1794–95, the war-financing attitude underwent a progressive change. Many of the expedients used hitherto were certainly retained, on a temporary or convenience basis, but the new feature was the increasing role played by new forms of state borrowing, in particular a consolidated national debt that had hitherto been shunned by the government. But the debt question will be dealt with in the following chapter and for now, barring essential allusions, we will be concentrating on other extraordinary resources.

The 1779–83 war against Great Britain forced Spain to find more resources and do so with more urgency than before. The odds, after all, were formidable. If Spain was to fight in the Americas, for example, the Royal Navy could pitch against it over 300 ships in the seventies (Morris 2011: 13–32), deployed in various parts of the world. That meant, among other things, a lot of expensive resources. This war was not going to cost the same as before and the resource need had soared.

Could Charles III increase taxes just as he wished? It is sometimes assumed that an absolute monarch could do so at the drop of a hat. We have already seen that it was not always so straightforward and that not even the French monarch could afford to pursue an arbitrary taxation policy. What we call absolutism also had its rules and limits. Indeed, in other conflicts of the century Spain had hiked taxes only on a limited and temporary basis. At this particular juncture, as already pointed out, tax rises came much later than might have been expected (Torres Sánchez 2013a: 172). In fact, the *Junta de Medios*, meeting up in 1779, came up with a list of traditional remedies: donations, lotteries, life-annuity issues, sales of titles and offices. Only right at the very end of this list came the last-ditch suggestion of increasing some taxes such as *rentas provinciales*, salt and tobacco (Canga Argüelles 1968: II, 24). Charles III, as well as employing other resources, had no option but to accept tax increases in the end, though he did so with caution, systematically communicating his motives and setting his own barriers, such as exceptions to the rule and temporary limitations. In other words, he was concerned above all to ensure that this did not mark the start of uncontrolled fiscal development.

The most important fiscal operation was the four-year, one-third increase in Castile's *rentas provinciales* and the *equivalentes* of the Crown of Aragon. The measure was presented as straightforward and rapid, since it involved only hiking the rate of taxes that were already being collected (Artola 1982: 330). In practice, however, no end of snags cropped up (Torres Sánchez 2013a: 161). Since both taxes, especially the *rentas provinciales*, were a motley set of different revenue sources, this posed the problem of which of them should bear the brunt of the hike to save the poorest from the worst effects. Then came the question of the necessary speed in the collection procedures. As this seemed likely to be slow, thought was given to the possibility of drawing first on funds held by local authorities. This seemed to be reasonable; after all, it was the local councils that also collected the *rentas provinciales*, but it turned out that most councils did not have enough funds available; in other cases, they did not even have enough to cater for the rise; all of this led to numerous delays (Torres Sánchez 2013a: 187).

In the end, albeit tardily, the "extraordinary" contribution was accomplished. The haul from the Crown of Castile was 124.6 million *reales*; from the Crown of Aragon, 35.7 million. To this must be added the salt-tax hike decreed in 1779, which added up to 31 million *reales*. The state's total haul with these measures could be estimated at about 191 million *reales* (Torres Sánchez 2013a: 237). Most of it was raised while war was still raging but not in the first moments, as had been the aim.

The other important tax rise referred to tobacco. The yield of tobacco revenue had been increasing since 1741 even with prices held steady. It was deemed to be a solid and easily taxable commodity, simply by raising the retail price at the state-monopoly outlets called *estancos*. The view was also held that any price hike was socially acceptable since tobacco use was a vice rather than a staple. It was also known, however, that contraband tobacco undercut the state product and it proved to be a difficult nut to crack despite considerable campaigns against it. In the end it was therefore decided to hold the price steady for many years. By 1779 the government had been backed into a corner, so it decreed a 25 per cent price rise.

Back in 1741, the last price rise, the result had been an increase in the contraband trade, but tobacco revenue still rose. The result in this new case was quite otherwise. The consumer response was to turn *en masse* from the official product to the contraband product. The fall in demand for the official product more than offset the price rise; as a result, the yield fell by nearly 10 per cent. The situation then remained the same during the war years. Quite possibly, at the end of the war, more attention could be paid to the fight against contraband, whereupon the revenue turned upwards again towards its previous levels. In any case this measure not only failed to increase necessary warfare resources but even reduced them and also demonstrated the elasticity limits of the complex taxation system.

The war was also financed with the aid of donations and other extraordinary revenue. The donations were numerous and varied, in terms of both the sum donated and the donors. Some of them could be considered to be voluntary, although many donations were presumably driven not by patriotism or loyalty but some sort of ulterior vested interest. Voluntary donations came in from private individuals, who took this chance to flaunt their support for the monarchy, from leading figures of society and from cities and institutions. The donations also took various forms: in cash, in kind, in services – fitting out ships for privateering purposes, raising regiments – in strategically important supplies such as wood or iron, in jewels and similar valuables. The cash amounts varied widely from a few thousand *reales* up to nearly 4 million *reales* (Torres Sánchez 2013a: 29, 42, 50, 57). It is impossible to gauge the total amount of these donations, especially since so many were made in kind or services, as we have already seen.

Other donations were clearly forced, albeit with a trade-off for the donors. For example, the Basque and northern provinces of *Señorío de Vizcaya* and Navarre were always keen to defend their hard-won regional privileges and charters. This gave Madrid a lot of bargaining power in its negotiations with these areas (Rodríguez Garraza 1974, 2003). The three Basque provinces offered a total of 1.5 million *reales* in 1779–80. On its part, Navarre's contribution called for a long drawn-out negotiation with the *cortes* of the realm, since Madrid was calling not only for a generous donation but also tax hikes, especially on tobacco. Finally, the *cortes* were forced to hand over 4.5 million *reales* (Torres Sánchez 2013a: 70, 88, 93). This would have meant a big effort at local level but it was meagre within total war costs. Navarre's donation, for example, was spent on the conquest of Minorca and on wood purchases, also helping in the construction of a 74-gun ship in Pasajes (Guipuzcoa).

The donations also took in the Americas. The viceroy of New Spain, rather than offering a donation, suggested the raising of some taxes, especially tobacco, the yield of which was sent to Cuba to help in imperial defence. About 13 million *reales*, apparently, were obtained from Mexico (Torres Sánchez 2013a: 101; Marichal 2007: 90), a sum that also fell well short of American defence needs, though there are no records of any other contributions.

The biggest donation came from the clergy, though it took various forms: part of the sums offered by bishops and cathedral chapters was really a donation, more or less voluntary, and in other cases a returnable loan, sometimes with interest and sometimes without, similar to France's *don gratuite*. Table 5.9 sums up these items.

Table 5.9 Church donations and loans in Spain, 1780 (millions *reales de vellón*)

Type	Sum	%
Donations	5.6	25.6
Interest-free loan	13.9	63.6
Interest-bearing loan	2.3	10.7
Total	21.9	100

Source: Torres Sánchez 2013a: 125.

In the end the sums do not differ much from the church's offerings during the War of Succession, proving that the arable land upon which church revenue was based was still producing a similar yield (Barrio Gozalo 2010). The total sum of nearly 22 million *reales* represented one of the biggest donation sources, even though part of it came in the form of loans. Other donations, however, also had something of a loan character since the donors expected some sort of kickback in the form of an office, benefice, pension, etc., whereby the government had to effectively reimburse part of the sum "donated". In the case of church loans, this loan aspect was at least upfront and easy to account for.

In the end we cannot gauge how much the war cost. We can measure it in terms of extraordinary financing, i.e., the revenue haul over and above peacetime fiscal resources, but it is by now impossible to come up with any more precise idea since all the donations we have looked at were not recorded for accounts purposes, not even the biggest ones. Working from the biggest figures to hand, adding the increase in ordinary revenue to church donations plus other donations whose amount we know, the final sum comes out at about 250 million *reales*. To this must be added debt issues and the wartime availment of private deposits, which represented no less than 659 million *reales*. All in all, we must be speaking about a total sum of over 910 million *reales*. The debt part would be 565 million (61.9 per cent of the total), of which 114 million would correspond to life annuities and 451 million to *vales reales* (Artola 1982: 417). This, at least, is the known sum obtained from extraordinary resources during the war years and was presumably spent on the war itself. This sum is fairly small in comparison with France but not in terms of Spanish levels, since it doubles the ordinary revenue yield.

These costs and the debts thereby incurred represented a huge budgetary effort, which was covered in following years above all by hiking some ordinary taxes such as the *provinciales* (after the 1785 reforms) and customs, which benefited from the free trade decree with the American colonies, bountiful in times of peace. Nonetheless, the budgetary scenery remained shaky during the years of peace and finally came crashing down with the new war in 1794.

The costs of 1793–96 opened a deficit of 2.767 billion *reales*, exceeding by 140 per cent the total ordinary revenue of the period (Artola 1982: 404, 412); this revenue had failed to keep pace with events and the war also turned off the tap of some important revenue sources like customs and American precious metal. Inflation complicated things even more. War and its problems soon turned the dodgy financial situation into outright crisis (Artola 1982: 403). We will focus here on the first crisis-triggering episode, the War against the Convention and its costs.

To tackle this war, the government turned, as in other cases, to all types of extraordinary resources such as tax hikes, debt call-ins and confiscation of the property of French subjects (Angulo Teja 2002: 447–52); there were also donations, some genuine, i.e., without payback, others of a loan character. It soon became clear that these expedients would not rustle up enough money, so the government turned to voluntary or enforced loans, from people or institutions that could offer more money, such as the church, the *Cinco Gremios Mayores* of

Table 5.10 Spain's extraordinary resources during the war against the Convention, 1792–96 (in millions of *reales de vellón*)

	A	%	B	%
Tax hikes 1792–96	154.1	5.1	154.1	7.1
Donations and loans 1794–96	607	20.2	607	
Money from the Americas, 1792–96	842.3	28	-	28
Debt	1,403.2	46.7	1,403.2	64.8
TOTAL	3,006.7	100	2,164.3	100

Source: Artola 1982: 404–05. A: with America; B: without America.

Madrid or the *Banco de San Carlos* itself, which from this moment began to give large short-term loans to the government and build up a hefty credit. Even so debt takeup was the fundamental factor.

Table 5.10 gives us a rough idea of the war-financing resources. It works from a government *Nota* that presumably sums up the current situation. It is not completely accurate because there is no guarantee that all items are included and it also records some information from 1792. But it is the best idea we have of the extraordinary resources for this war. Tax hikes, as we can see, represented an appreciable sum in comparison with ordinary revenue, already high in its own right. These rises, however, were shared out among various items to spread the burden thinner. More important were the donations and the crucial funds from the Americas. But the main deficit-plugging measure, as might have been expected, was the issue of new *vales reales*. In 1794 and 1795 another three issues were made, worth 964 million *reales*, i.e., more than doubling the first three issues of 1780–83. New loans were also taken up with Holland and there were also new issues of life annuities in Spain, on tobacco and as consulate loans.

Table 5.10 does not record the issues of *vales reales*. Neither does it specify if the "money from the Americas" involved ordinary funds (which is possible because during most of the nineties the annual mean topped 140 million *reales*) or if it was due to extraordinary revenue. If, as seems more likely, it was the former, then it should be excluded from extraordinary-revenue figures. This is why two cases have been considered in Table 5.10: Column A gives the figures of Artola's *Nota*, including the money from America; Column B repeats the same figures without including the American money we consider to be ordinary revenue. The result, in the second case, is that the various debt expedients accounted for nearly 65 per cent of extraordinary war-financing resources, slightly higher than the percentage in the previous war. If we also take into account the fact that part of the tax hikes recorded in the table correspond to a pre-war period, then the debt proportion would be somewhat higher. In short, as the century wore on, and especially from the seventies onwards, Spain's wars were increasingly debt-financed, paralleling the French experience without ever matching it. In any case, if the mechanisms were similar, the debt policy and its management were very different in both cases and, of course, differed even more from the British debt approach.

Note

1   The proceedings pertaining to this tax can be seen in the Archivo General de Simancas, Tribunal Mayor de Cuentas, series 691 and 692.

6 Foreseeing difficulties and administering for the future
The public debt

6.1 The necessary public debt

If states were unable to increase ordinary tax revenue much, neither did they fare a lot better with extraordinary revenue. Several expedients assayed in this regard also had its limits and still fell short of needs in times of war. Wars at this time were becoming more and more expensive and this expense had to be catered for in some way. Debt, therefore, was the only realistic option. Although any debt would have to be paid off eventually, whereby taxes would continue rising in the end, debt was the only solution to the emergency situation; the problem of paying if off could be left for later. In the long eighteenth century, some states sidled into debt almost by inertia, as a simple continuation of their past procedure; others, on the contrary, struck out down this path when they became embroiled in larger wars than they had tackled hitherto. Others, finally, preferred to keep their heads down and avoid incurring bigger financial problems.

The three states we are looking at are classic examples of this tripartite scheme. Spain pursued a tax-alleviation policy, in the interests of which it tried to avoid state borrowing as far as possible. Eighteenth-century Spain was strongly debt averse, in all probability because the excessive expenses and the huge debt run up before 1650 had been credited with dire effects on economic and social life without even achieving the main political ends in view, such as keeping Spain's foothold in the Low Countries and then in Portugal. Spain could be said to have built up a negative path dependency vis-à-vis debt, which prompted it to reject long-term debt for quite some time.

France's case was different. In the last third of the seventeenth century it stood at the peak of its power, achieved on the back of a long borrowing process, which it then maintained, logically, by strict necessity. England, for its part, had just restored a monarchic regime and despite the "relative backwardness" of its economy (Wilson and Parker 1977: 131), it could boast a balanced, debt-free finance system now ready to embark from scratch on a policy of heavy state borrowing that the new military demands called for, first due to the wars with Holland and above all after the Nine Years' War.

These three models are three political and economic cases at once. Political because the decisions to be taken depended not only on the need, similar in all cases although differing in size, but also a will that was in turn based on a given tradition of varying length. But they are also economic standpoints too because the economic power had to respond to the borrowing challenge. The government knew that any debts had to be paid off in one way or another and the ability to do so would depend, in the end, on tax revenue and this depended in turn on taxpayers' spending power. If the taxpayers were up to it, therefore, the debt, or its interest at least, would be paid off; otherwise it would not. The political decision on debt was therefore based also on the government's assessment of its subjects' tax-paying capacity. This assessment was pretty easy to make; it sufficed to look at the takeup rate each time there was any debt issue. England had hardly any problems on this score (Dickson 1967). In France, however, the takeup was lacklustre due to its subjects' mistrust of the government. In Spain there were some takers when debt was issued as from 1780, but not too many. The problem here was to ascertain whether this rejection was due to lack of money or chariness of credit systems and the state's ability to pay.

Great Britain did weigh up its subjects' fiscal and financial capacity and the government was able to step up its borrowing level, racking up taxes, especially in the second half of the century, as need be, until reaching really high taxation levels after 1799. In other countries, however, this taxpayer-capacity assessment was fairly low in general and state borrowing was therefore limited and tax rises kept down to the essential minimum. The subjects' tax burden in all parts was therefore substantially lower than it could have been in theory, judging from the spread of exemptions and the evasion rate, suggesting there was a lot of slack that could be taken up. Lingering memories of seventeenth-century tax problems might well have loomed large in this reluctance to up the tax burden, especially in Spain, but another factor might well have been resistance from privileged groups to see their taxes raised. This was certainly the case in France, posing for governments the problem of raising tax revenue almost exclusively from the third estate. Certainly no attempt was made to touch direct taxes; neither was it at all easy to raise indirect taxes since their brunt was borne above all by the urban world and in most European cities this was at a low ebb until practically the middle of the century (Doyle 1981: 29).

Be that as it may, the upshot was that the per capita tax burden was much higher in Great Britain than in France or in other parts of the German region, as shown in Table 6.1.

Table 6.1 Tax pressure in certain parts of Europe (*livres tournais* per capita)

	1758	*1788*
Great Britain	23.3	33.3
France	9.5	15
Spain	12	14.6
Prussia	7.5	10.8
Austria	7.5	

Source: Hartmann 1979: 336. For Spain, Torres Sánchez 2015a: 220.

The reason why Great Britain's taxpayers could afford a higher tax burden than elsewhere probably lies in the importance of indirect taxes in that country and in particular, consumer demand. Direct taxes and greater reliance on an agrarian economy make it more difficult in any country to increase the tax burden on the back of a rise in output, whereas indirect taxes make it easier for taxes to be brought into line with real consumer demand. This flexibility and the possibilities it offers also made it much simpler to build up a consolidated debt system, as was the case in Great Britain.

If borrowing is fruit of need and if this need is caused by war, affecting all countries at once, this begs the question of whether borrowing did likewise. All three countries, faced with these war needs, considered the debt option but the three of them came up with different answers for different reasons. In all three cases, however, these responses can be broken down, albeit *grosso modo*, into three stages. This rough-and-ready scheme is nonetheless revealing.

The first stage, then, runs from 1689 to the 1720s, in particular the years 1726–27. This period can be considered as a spadework response to the debt problem. Spain confirmed its loathness to run up a long-term debt. France switched towards a new and bigger debt line. For France the period 1688–1714 represented "the first large-scale recourse to borrowing in the form of publicly sold annuities" (Sargent and Velde 1995: 486), and the recourse was kept up afterwards. England, for its part, discovered as from 1689, that borrowing was the way of being able to take on Louis XIV successfully, so it struck off down this path decisively. The solutions taken up in this period ran into a crunch test in the crisis of 1720, which was very severe, especially the failures of Law and the South Sea Company. This juncture also made its presence felt in Spain, to some extent, where 1720 was also a crucial year for its public-finance system (Torres Sánchez 2013a: 46).

After the crisis there was a reconsolidation. For this reason, the date of 1726–27 is significant for all three countries. In Spain Patiño was appointed as finance minister (Pulido Bueno 1998). Patiño not only spruced up the public-finance system, but also ended up imposing a direction that in itself represented a political change (Dubet 2015b: 602); this change also affected the way of paying off current debt and negotiating new short-term debt with the country's set of businessmen. In France 1726 was the triumph of Fleury and of his *contrôleur général*, Le Peletier des Forts. After the fiasco of Law's System and its immediate aftermath, impinging also on private credit (Hoffman et al. 1995), Fleury's system spelled the re-establishment of the traditional *finance* based above all on *fermiers*, (Félix 2011; Legay 2011). Great Britain, for its part, now had to reinforce its debt option systematically, above all by cutting interest payments, a key question to ensure the debt system was not overly expensive for the state. The crisis sparked off by the South Sea Bubble had not exactly been conducive to this end and it was necessary to bring things back into control. A turning point in this process came in 1727 when the government managed to reduce the redeemable annuity interest to 4 per cent (Dickson 1967: 186, 209), thus initiating a South Sea Company debt-reduction process that would later lead to its demise as a trading company.

The next phase represented a consolidation of the chosen systems, which in all cases had started out amidst difficulties and debates about the best solution, rumbling on until 1776–80. This is a long period beginning with the peace treaty, which helped finances to settle down everywhere, thanks to the general monetary stabilisation of 1726 (Vilar 1972: 284). This phase continued with two serious conflicts and finally ushered in another period of peace in 1763. Austria's War of Succession, first, and then the Seven Years' War showed that the system worked across the board. The latter conflict tested its mettle but the ensuing peace treaty brought the situation back into balance. Although each experience was different, confirmation of each one of the systems was a common denominator.

Spain maintained its debt aversion, defraying the 1740s conflict with Great Britain by exceptional taxes. Not only that, by means of direct administration and other procedures, it tried to shrug off all pending debt completely. Although France also turned to new taxes such as the various *vingtièmes* and raising other charges, it had to forge on too with the debt experience. The system would continue growing along the path laid down in 1726. Great Britain continued in its line of trying to pay off part of its debt and reducing interest payments on the remaining chunk. Pelham's reforms were crucial here, culminating in 1752 (Neal 2015) with the whittling down of debt securities to two types, both at low interest. The new situation also put paid to the role played hitherto by the privileged trading companies, the *monied companies*. Although debt grew anew, and sizeably, from 1757, it then dipped slightly as from 1776.

The third phase of the state's borrowing policies began in the eighties, as a result of the American War of Independence. This kick-started a definitive development or transformation of these policies, differing in kind in each case. For Great Britain it was the moment of the system's final takeoff. Although debt had grown significantly during the Seven Years' War, after 1776 the growth was even steeper. This is summed up by Williamson, speaking in real terms and in comparison with national income: "net additions to the war debt were 3.6 per cent of national income as early as the 1760s ... The share had risen to 6.5 per cent by the 1780s, a near doubling. It reached a peak of 11.5 per cent in the 1790s" (Williamson 1984: 696). Two consequences, at least, stemmed from this fact in the British case. First, as from the 1760s the amount of debt paid off was "negligible"; second, that the intention of paying off the debt within a reasonable time was by now untenable due to the sheer amount involved. It was by now a question, therefore, of simply shoring up the public-credit system's creditworthiness and affordability in order to underpin state borrowing for the necessary time. This feat was pulled off on the back of various reforms, especially Pitt's in the 1780s, and tax hikes from the nineties.

For France and Spain things were much trickier in this definitive phase. Instead of the development of a system, in both cases we need to speak rather of an authentic transformation. As from 1780 any risk had to be run in order not to go under. France had to ditch the *finance* system and strike out on two paths little trod beforehand. First, the ousting of tax farming and direct control of collection procedures by the government; second, the new *assignats*-based paper-money borrowing system. Spain changed too. Since the advent of Charles III in late 1759 the new government had addressed the problem of pending debt more decisively than previous ones. But the watershed moment came in 1780 with the creation of paper money – the *vales reales* – and the *Banco de San Carlos*, a state bank theoretically designed to support the government in its financial problems. The new French and Spanish schemes outlasted 1800 but they were beset by appreciably more problems than Britain's system because the trading disorder and inflation provoked by wars as from 1793 hit these two countries much harder than their rival: if war had created the pressing need for a public-debt system, the trading disorders stunted the yield of the new taxes set up to tackle this situation and hindered payment of interest.

France changed its finances due to a revolution that was undoubtedly triggered partially by financial matters (Legay, Félix and White 2009) but was also driven by much deeper motives. Spain did not need such a revolution to goad it into change; it simply needed to weigh up its needs and read the runes of the times. Charles III chose a path that was certainly the right one at the time. Quite another thing is whether or not the government was determined to continue down that path. Neither did Spain need the support of parliament, as Great Britain did, for increasing its taxes, revamping its trading system with the Americas, creating a national bank or embarking on a new and modern system of public debt, paper money included. All this would be successful until war problems worsened after 1794. What we are saying here is that although changes of the political regime were important, they were not so crucial, after all, from an economic point of view. Any system could serve as the basis of the right economic policy on a one-off basis, but its maintenance and ongoing success might call for long-term, if not revolutionary, social and political changes.

6.2 British borrowing: the love of debt

As already mentioned, the British government's go-to war-defrayment option was borrowing; only later would it raise its taxes. Unlike its continental rivals it had no negative debt experience in the past and was also driven by strict necessity, since England's financial resources in 1689 were not great in comparison with France's and even in comparison with its own needs. One of the system's greatest advantages, from the taxpayers' point of view, was that taxes would increase in peacetime, when the economy would be more buoyant. This was conducive to better acceptance not only of the tax but also of war itself, because it had no immediate tax burden. Another aspect favouring acceptance of war in fiscal terms was that many taxpayers would also benefit from government policy as debt purchasers and hence interest earners. Britain's efficient organisation and control of its finances (North and Weingast 1989) was therefore noted and admired not only by its continental rivals, who invested therein (Wilson 1965: 313; Wilson and Parker 1977: 133), but also by British taxpayers themselves.

The most obvious feature of Figure 6.1, reflecting the cumulative debt each year, is the sustained growth of British debt from 1689 up to the end of our period. A close inspection of Figure 6.1 shows up not only war-driven rises (1714, 1739, 1757, 1776, 1793) but also the fact that said rises are increasingly big in nominal terms; this comes out more clearly after 1757, 1776 and 1793.

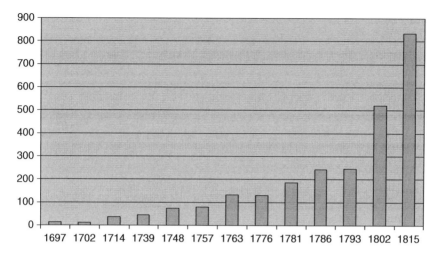

Figure 6.1 British eighteenth-century debt (millions of pound sterling)
Source: Hargreaves 1930: 291.

The increases therefore reflect increasing war costs, especially noticeable after 1757–63. Despite its absolute increase, however, debt's contribution to warfare expenditure held steady throughout the century, as shown in Table 6.2, recording the cumulative debt in each period of war, doing so as the percentage of debt-defrayed military expenditure. The table shows that, in the War of the Spanish Succession, the debt-defrayed expenditure percentage fell slightly as compared with the previous war and then remained at similar levels until 1748. This relative participation in warfare expenditure rose in the two following wars, before Pitt's fiscal reforms, and then dropped again after 1793.

If the debt-defrayed expenditure percentage held steady, while both expenditure and debt were rising in absolute terms, this must mean that other revenue items were also weighing in with their own contribution towards warfare expenditure. Indeed, the rise in total tax revenue, especially after 1776–86, meant that an increasing amount of this could now be spent on war, even though all items rose substantially in absolute terms. In any case the problem was not so much the debt principal itself, which was now reckoned to be impossible to pay off, but rather the interest payments, which could never be shirked. The nominal increase of the burden was also notable and had to be met from tax revenue or new debt. There were at least three stages in the debt-burden tax-revenue relationship. Up to 1757 the revenue growth rate was only just below the burden's. From then on the burden began to outstrip revenue; this was in all likelihood the time when debt came to be seen as a problem. As from the eighties revenue grew but still lagged behind the debt. Small wonder, then, especially in the eighties when neither Spain nor France yet had grave problems, that many should think Great Britain was headed for disaster. In the end its revenue capacity managed to stave off this disaster.

Table 6.2 Debt and its percentage of expenditure in Britain (millions of pound sterling)

War periods	Debt increase in the period	Percentage of total expenditure
1688/97	14	33.6
1702/14	23	31.4
1739/48	30	31.1
1757/63	60	37.4
1776/86	113	40
1793/1802	278.5	
1802/1815	311	26.6*

Source: Hargreaves 1930, Wilson 1965, Dickson 1967. *The figure refers to the 1793–1815 period.

Debt, therefore, was a key feature of Great Britain's military-expenditure payment policy, but it relied on a continued growth of tax revenue that vouched for the state's creditworthiness. It is this revenue, at the end of the day, that was most important. The debt repayment effort, moreover, had a notable effect in times of peace, when the burden falls.

How did Great Britain manage its debt? Without going into a detailed study of its finances, we do need to point out the most important structural aspects of this matter. Before 1692 there was already a body of short-term debt that had to be paid off against taxes. There was also a growing amount of long-term debt, recognised and consolidated and backed up by the king's authority. It was this quality of "*permanence* in the public debt" (Wilson 1965: 314), maintained thereafter, that distinguishes it from the pre-1692 period. But what was this debt like? Four aspects need to be taken into account. First, the type of debt, i.e., whether it was short- or long-term; second, the intermediary, i.e., whether the government dealt with the investor directly or through intermediary companies; third, the amount of interest; and, fourth, whether the government wished to pay off the debt principal and, if so, how.

All these questions would have different answers within each of the above-mentioned three periods. The general trend was to achieve consolidated, long-term debt, repayable at will, according to the government's possibilities at each time, cheap and unencumbered by middlemen. Right from the word go, of course, the government set itself two firm commitments: first and foremost, pay interest upon falling due; second, and with less sense of urgency, paying off only part of the principal. Another factor that weighed against debt redemption, apart from relative government disinterest, was that the debt holders themselves preferred to continue receiving the interest rather than see their credit paid off.

Between 1689 and 1727 the system was set up on a secure basis. Little by little non-redeemable life annuities, whose interest peaked at 8 per cent, were replaced by permanent annuities that could be redeemed by the government at will, whose interest rate slid back to 3 or 4 per cent, according to the type involved. The government's sureness of hand during this period boosted investor confidence. During these years a large part of the debt was channelled through privileged institutions acting as intermediaries: the Bank of England and the two major trading companies, the East India Company and the South Sea Company (Wilson and Parker 1977: 132). These institutions, dubbed "monied companies", loaned money to the state in return for trading or financial privileges. These privileges drew in profit-seeking investors. Indeed, business grew and the companies were able to increase their capital.

The government rode this wave to turn former life-annuity or short-term-debt investors into shareholders of the new companies, especially after the end of the War of the Spanish Succession, because the market's money-transfer methods were much better than the Exchequer's (Dickson 1967: 457). Investors came out winning from the enhanced profit-making prospects, and the state benefited because the interest on the long-term debt now paid to the companies was lower than the interest formerly paid to the short-term debt holders. The state's creditworthiness also benefited from the support of successful companies. This produced a "securitisation" of the system. The long-term result was enhanced creditworthiness of the system and the government itself, enabling it to raise credit on better terms. This shows that rather than the political system (parliament), what really counted in England's debt system was the role of the trading companies (Sussman and Yafeh 2006) and trade's money-making capacity. Without money there were no investors; neither would they have agreed to give long-term, low-interest loans.

Around 1714, however, interest rates were still fairly high, so the government came up with an idea to drive down the interest rate: i.e., buying cheaper equity on the secondary market and then using it to redeem higher-interest debt. One of the main factors that made this transaction possible was public debt's even higher yield at that time than private debt, whose interest has been capped at 5 per cent by the Usury Law of 1714 (Dickson 1967: 39). Taking advantage of this situation, Walpole converted by law a sizeable amount of short-term debt into long-term debt at lower interest than that paid hitherto by the state. He also set up a sinking fund (1717) financed by debt-conversion operations and geared towards redemption of as much debt as possible. The South Sea Company crisis called for the company's capital to be slashed. The chosen arrangement was mainly a swap between the company's equity and Bank of England shares. The transaction also brought interest rates down, just as the aforementioned 1727 transaction had done.

The consolidation phase, as we have chosen to call it, c. 1726–80, was particularly fruitful for Great Britain. Not only did it help to tidy up and settle the system but it also empowered a large increase of debt in the two major mid-century conflicts. The years of peace, however, posed some problems because interest payments still had to be met and the principal paid off; some taxes, moreover, like the land tax, had fallen. Walpole sometimes had to tap into the sinking fund, distorting its founding remit. The government also ran into other problems when it came to the moment of reducing public-debt interest; this proved to be not always possible, as in 1737: the debt holders did not regard the terms as reasonable and managed to block the operation, thereby demonstrating that the vested interests impinging on the debt were very varied. In 1750, on the other hand, Pelham did manage to reduce the interest rate (Dickson 1967: 229; Chamley 2011).

The crux came in 1752 when Pelham pulled off the Great Consolidation. The operation involved whittling down the varied range of debt certificates, all run by different institutions with different interest rates, to only two: the "Reduced Annuities", popularly referred to as 3 per cent reduced annuities, and the "Consolidated Annuities", also known as consols or perpetual bonds. The former were so called because their interest rate had been reduced from 4 to 3 per cent. The others already stood at 3 per cent. At the same time, the funds previously used to pay the interest on the scrapped securities were paid into the sinking fund, which now became a de facto interest-payment rather than debt-redemption instrument. An attempt was made to pass over to a direct-subscription system but this turned out to be harder than thought. The pressing borrowing need in 1758, for example, forced the government to fall back on past practices: Newcastle saw himself obliged to "speak" – as he put it – with the most influential people in the city to drum up an 8-million pound loan subscribed by 20 financiers including prominent personages and trading companies. The remit of the latter, however, had now changed; no longer were they asked to provide government institutions with corporate support but simply "to tap the resources of their Business friends" (Wilson 1965: 321). The British system, in any case, was drawing more and more investors to the plate, including some foreigners, particularly Dutch, who were confident of healthy and secure interest rates.

The situation created in 1763, with the debt burden now outstripping the revenue input led to a partial change of mindset: attention turned from redeeming the debt, though some was still paid off, to financing it. This called for low-interest loans from then on. It was no doubt the state's creditworthiness that in fact managed to keep the interest rate down to about 3 per cent, or only slightly more. Any pre-war sabre-rattling would force rates up but they always remained at a reasonable rate for the government that had to pay them.

As from 1776/1783 the system was greatly developed but it was never easy. First, the debt and its burden had to be increased much more than before, and second, investors upped the stakes upon seeing how desperate the government was. Some previous expedients had to revived, such as the sinking fund and purchases in secondary markets. Especially striking is the creation of a new sinking fund in 1786, financed from a single budgetary item and brought under the supervision of an *ad hoc* committee. Secondary-market purchases were not so easy, among other reasons because consols were expensive right from the word go, so the state lost out from cheap purchases in the secondary market. It has been argued that if consols were not issued at a lower price this was because it was girding its loins for upcoming war with France (O'Brien 2008). Be that as it may, things worked smoothly in peacetime.

When war broke out, debt soared anew. Some have even spoken of a dread of debt (Wilkinson 2004: 211). The idea was still to issue debt at 3 per cent but the government sometimes had to offer up to 5 per cent. Despite concomitant difficulties, the sinking fund was retained, probably for political reasons, because investors knew the debt would be honoured after the war and this inspired market confidence (O'Brien 2008). In this way the state also managed to offset its higher borrowing rates. In any case the system continued to triumph because taxes were also able to rise and cover a substantial part of the expenditure until 1815 (Daunton 2001).

6.3 France, the unmanageable debt

Debt was high in France too and its trend was steadily upward in our period although it is difficult to establish the exact amount. Some idea of its importance, however, can be gained from the sums set aside to pay off the interest. Morineau (1980) gives the following *service de la dette* figures for the indicated years in millions of *livres tournais*: 1726, 61; 1751, 71.8; 1775, 154.4; 1788, 261.1. A revealing comparison can be made at least with Great Britain. The post-1783 French debt was lower than Britain's in absolute terms and much lower as a proportion of GDP. The problem of France's debt resided not so much in its size as the difficulty of paying it off. Furthermore, the burden as a proportion of the debt itself was also higher in France than in Great Britain (Bonney 2004: 194–95). The problem also seemed to be a growing one since; as Figure 6.2 shows, debt interest grew quicker in France than in Great Britain from the middle of the century onwards.

The difference between both trends is also explained by the interest payments, with higher rates too in France (Velde and Weir 1992).

The situation had come to this because, in Marion's words, loans had been "used and abused" during recent centuries (Marion 1979: 201). The problem therefore went back a long way. To start with, it was based on a structural inheritance that dated right back to at least 1522. From that date a permanent debt had

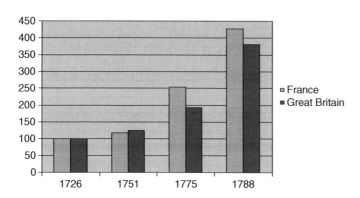

Figure 6.2 Indexed growth rate of the debt burden in France and Great Britain. 1726 = 100

Sources: Morineau, 1980; Hargreaves 1930.

built up in the form of annuities (*rentes sur l'Hôtel de Ville*) of Paris. This whole system was steeped in venality. Attempts were made in the seventeenth century to counter this by creating a regular source of income from office-holding, the *droit annuel*. Although this right fell into abeyance during the 1709 crisis, it was later brought back, in 1722, lasting then until 1771 (Bonney 1999a: 152). The *rentes sur l'Hôtel de Ville*, however, were still considered to be untouchable in 1780.

What exactly did this debt consist of? France's ordinary taxation structure was far from being as simple as Great Britain's and the same went, apparently, for its debt. As Marion points out, all forms of loans (*emprunts*) were used: perpetual bonds; life annuities; redeemable bonds; group annuities in the form of *tontines*; loans with premiums; upfront loans or loans disguised as sale of offices, voluntary or, all too often, enforced. But the problem lay not so much in the glut of possibilities, which also existed elsewhere, as the confused management, involving myriad types of employees, financiers or institutions. A good deal of the debt market was managed by the various agents (whether notaries public, financiers – the *finance*, i.e., officials or tax farmers – or bankers). It was these agents who collected the money from the public at large and loaned it to the king (Hoffman et al. 2000). The problem is that the state was responsible for all this, since debt service was assigned to ordinary revenue. It proved incapable, however, of handling all these reins at the same time. The diversity of French management procedures was an idiosyncrasy that set it apart from the growing centralisation trend underway in both Great Britain and Spain. If France was able to up its expenditure, it was always incapable of controlling its accountancy procedures properly (Legay 2011: 42).

France's revenue structure itself continued to depend on two corporate systems, one informal, one formal; the smooth operation of both served as a sort of debt security. The first was the venal system, informally organised and developed over time on the basis of buying and selling government positions, in particular those dealing with the collection of direct taxes; the other, well organised in this case, was the *ferme général* for collecting indirect taxes. The permanence of these two organic structures was the most important aspect of the whole fiscal structure. They were also the reason, as we have already seen, for the fact that neither direct nor indirect taxes changed structurally; each one only changed proportionally as need be to meet expenditure requirements.

Venality drove the development of a powerful administrative apparatus that was outside the government's control. This posed several problems; for example, salaries had to be paid but the system balked proper reforms. During the eighteenth century the venal system remained firmly in force, albeit amidst a fierce debate. Some there were too who argued that it should be left in place simply because it was difficult to replace (Doyle 1996: 239). This debate had been raging for some time and various reform attempts had been made in the past. All came to naught, either due to their intrinsic difficulty or the opposition of vested interests. Another hindrance in any continuing reform attempt was the short term of office, on average, of each *contrôleur général* (Bayard, Félix and Hamon 2000). The reforms brought in to pay warfare expenditure – especially the successive *dixièmes* – also tended to reinforce the office-selling system because it was the office-holders who were best placed to advance loans on the sums to be collected; this system also helped to keep the venal structure in force.

The history of venality in Louis XV's reign offered few hopes of any substantial change in this state of affairs. Although perhaps less serious than in the previous reign, any reform attempts failed in the final instance, due to urgencies of the time and the growing debt. The strongest crises, as in 1768, could shake the whole system and even partly transform it, but it came back vigorously on a needs-must basis. As Calonne would acknowledge later, venality was fundamental not only for financing wars; properly run, the system was also able to make a sizeable input to state finances in peacetime, too. For this reason, attempts were made in the final years of the Revolution to ensure that this corrupt system, impossible to eradicate, was at least capable of making a more effective fiscal contribution (Doyle 1996: 112, 143).

Differentiating between long- and short-term debt in France is no easy matter. It was also bound up with the type of intermediary, which varied over time. The main long-term debt was the aforementioned *rentes sur l'Hôtel de ville*, which, together with other revenue, was controlled by the notaries of Paris and also involved all revenue stemming from the office buying-and-selling process we have been looking at. A good deal of budgetary increases had been financed by the sale of offices since at least the last third of the seventeenth century, so the practice was still on the rise.

Short-term debt involved a different cast of characters. Some of them, like public officials and *fermiers*, were directly related with the government, even though the tax farmers themselves were private financiers. These personages advanced loans on the taxes they were to collect and thus created a current debt that could be sizeable in some cases. The state then had to honour this debt. These problems cropped up above all in times of war, so interest payments were appreciable if not excessively high; they hovered around 5 per cent, the same interest rate paid by the state on its long-term debt in peacetime.

Officials and tax farmers had always existed and their role in debt matters was growing, even though they did not really come into their own until the eighteenth century. Meanwhile, up to the end of Louis XIV's reign, an important role was played by the *traitants*, who dealt exclusively with "extraordinary business" that cropped up to meet warfare needs. It was this arrangement that provided most of the government credit in the final conflicts of Louis XIV. They were a varied clutch of loan forms including sales of rights and taxes, exemptions from recently created taxes and even the sale of offices under these circumstances. The *traitants* were the intermediaries of these transactions, by means of which private individuals, often under obligation, gave money to the king in return for revenue. The rake-off from this revenue was the *traitants'* business profit. *Traitants* mushroomed during Louis XIV's reign, especially after 1689, and then faded out after 1709 when loan needs fell (Félix 2015). At the same time, above all after 1702, an increasingly important role was played by the treasurer of special war expenditure (*trésorier de l'extraordinaire des guerres*), who ended up as another provider of funds (Legay 2011: 45; Rowlands 2012).

This figure arose due to the pressing needs of the nineties, when all sorts of moneyed persons had to be appealed to. The middlemen were often *traitants*, but another machination to tap into their money was by increasing unnecessary offices, creating enormous disorder. Although Colbert had managed to tidy things up a bit, improving collection procedures and reducing corruption (Harsin 1970: 268), subsequent events meant that extraordinary expenditure escaped this greater control of ordinary revenue procedures, and it was extraordinary expenditure that was the most important (Legay 2011: 24, 39). This dichotomy between greater accounting control over ordinary revenue and chaotic extraordinary procedures would be maintained in the eighteenth century.

During the Regency things changed. Peace meant the work of the *traitants* was no longer necessary, so they tended to die out as such. The need of paying off the heavy debt left by Louis XIV's wars prompted all sorts of experiments, above all John Law's System, which brought into the foreground the state's direct relation with the public for debt purchase purposes and also granted decisive importance to the French *monied companies*, particularly the Mississippi Company or Company of the Indies. We will not go into the detail of the development of Law's system, which is well known. Suffice it here to mention that its failure caused new debt arrangements to be shunned and a tendency to fall back on the old system of treasury officials, who knew how to manage taxes and could upfront the necessary funds, and also the *fermiers généraux*, reinforced and set up on a firmer basis in 1726. From then on, and up to 1789, it was these two figures, officials and tax farmers, who handled the king's finances, both for the management of taxes and for raising debt. The notaries of Paris continued to work on the sidelines.

After overcoming the defaults of 1721 and 1726, which settled things down after Law's system, financial fortune seemed to favour France up to 1740. The years of peace allowed some order to be imposed on the preceding chaos; furthermore, taking advantage of a generalised situation of stability, a debt-interest-reduction policy was carried out, as also occurred in Great Britain and Spain, almost halving the charge on perpetual annuities. Although the government also began to issue life annuities (*rentes viagères*), which were more expensive, the debt burden fell substantially up to 1740 (Riley 1986: 166). Debt principal as a whole was also brought down, apparently, partly as a result of the abovementioned defaults, which wiped out a good deal of the debt.

The Austrian War of Succession would begin to complicate things. When it ended, not only was the *vingtième* enforced, with the idea of paying off part of the debt, both pending and new, but other not overly convincing measures were taken, too. For example, Machault d'Arnouville suggested that perpetual annuities should be changed into life annuities. This was the opposite procedure to the so-called Dutch financing structure and also ran counter to England's current procedures, but it was still done. Riley rated it as a grave defect of his reform, since life annuities charged a higher interest rate than perpetuals (Riley 1986: 170). But this very fact made them more attractive to investors and their value in fact held up on the secondary market (Velde and Weir 1992: 36).

There was some method in this madness, therefore, but the French state thereby racked up its debt burden hugely, while ordinary expenses and state bonds continued to grow (Félix 1999: 19). In fact, it is estimated that by 1753 total debt had risen to 2.2 billion *livres tournais*, which generated interest (debt service) of 70 million or more (Morineau 1980: 315; Riley 1986: 182). This interest represented 30 per cent of ordinary tax revenue. The situation had not been brought under control, therefore, and the Seven Years' War shattered the government's debt-management forecasts. A new default became necessary in 1759 to bring down the borrowing requirement but the war had a notable effect, not so much on the total debt level, which stood at about 2.3 billion *livres tournais*, only slightly more than the figure of 10 years earlier, but rather on interest payments, which were little by little eroding the whole system. Yet another default in 1770 showed the situation was untenable even in years of peace.

The problem, in any case, was the interest payments. As Table 6.3 shows, debt principal held pretty steady at start-of-century levels, although there is a notable leap with the American War of Independence. Debt-service interest payments, on the other hand, soared, easily outstripping ordinary revenue. The comparison with Great Britain is clear: this country could offset its debt effort with a sharp tax increase, especially in the eighties. It is interesting to note here that, in the three major wars from 1740 to 1783, France relied increasingly heavily on debt, while Great Britain depended also on taxes. Crouzet has calculated the percentage of loan-defrayed supplementary war costs (Crouzet 1993: 66). In the Austrian War of Succession this figure was 28 per cent for France and 85 per cent for Great Britain, i.e., 57 percentage points more for Great Britain. In the American War, the percentages were, respectively, 91 and 119, i.e., only 28 percentage points

Table 6.3 Increase of French debt and its interest. In millions of *livres tournais*

Years	Principal	Interest payments	Ordinary Revenue
1715	2600		
1726		61	181
1753	2200	70/72	258
1764	2300	88	
1769		196	
1775		155	377
1782	3315	165	
1788		261	471

Sources: Principal and interest payments, Riley 1986: 177–84; Interest payments and ordinary revenue, Morineau 1980: 314–15. Morineau's figures refer to the years 1726, 1751, 1775 and 1788.

more for Great Britain. Thus, while this figure rose by 63 percentage points in France, the rise was only 34 percentage points for Great Britain. In proportional terms, therefore, in the indicated period, Great Britain was capable of covering a rising share of its military expenditure by taxes as well as loans, while France was incapable of raising its own taxes to the same amount. Something quite similar occurred in Spain. Since taxes failed to rise in line with needs, France became increasingly debt dependent and interest payments turned out to be crippling.

In summary then, France ran up a very heavy debt, which grew much quicker than Britain's debt. The principal was difficult to pay off and the high interest payments meant that the debt was increasingly difficult to service because financing sources failed to keep up in real terms. This situation called for a drastic change in the fiscal structure and this step was not taken until 1789.

One of the most notable aspects of French debt management is the defaults, non-existent in Great Britain, despite its high borrowing requirement. These defaults were necessary to trim down a body of debt whose interest was by now unpayable. What exactly did these defaults consist of? One of the prime causes of the high debt level was the increase in short-term loans made by officials and bankers to enable the king to pay for his supplies or continue redeeming the debt. One way of default, therefore, was to convert these unpayable short-term debts into long-term debt, thus putting of the dreaded moment of paying them. This occurred, for example, in 1759. Payments were then resumed in peacetime. In 1770 a seven-year debt-payment suspension on short-term debt was announced but in fact these payments were never resumed. In 1788 it lasted only two years (Velde and Weir 1992: 8).

Another method, euphemised as "reform", involved lowering interest on loans that had been bought at a rate of over 5 per cent, considered to be the legal maximum. This method affected many loans, since the government had often agreed in the past to pay higher interest to draw in more investors, who would now see their hopes of high earnings dashed. This method also included converting some life annuities and *tontines* into long-term debt at lower interest. This occurred above all in 1793–94, although it was a practice that did not necessarily call for default strictly speaking. A third method was repudiation, which involved reducing original interest below the 5 per cent legal cap. In practice part of the debt was being repudiated, the part that would now no longer be paid after the haircut. Some of Terray's measures in 1770 were of this tenor, so the cuts of 1770 were a bigger threat to capital than the former suspensions of interest payments. More serious would be the 1797 cut, which reduced public debt by two-thirds (Velde and Weir 1992: 9).

These defaults undermined government creditworthiness and frightened off future investors. Turgot and Necker therefore decided not to continue in this direction. But these ministers' economising efforts were sunk by the outbreak of the American War, which called for new loans. Of course, to draw in new investors, high-interest annuities had to be offered anew, worsening the debt situation looking ahead. The best solution here would have been to hike taxes as in Great Britain, but this was difficult in France. Some sort of enabling constitutional measure was necessary. The measure of this sort that was finally taken was to convene the *États Généraux* to vote in new taxes. In 1788 the suspension of payments was set to last only one year in the hope that the new taxes would solve the problem, but what the convening of the *États Généraux* did instead was to spark off the Revolution.

Some authors argue that the financial situation of 1788 could have been solved by new reductions, not much worse than those of 1770; in fact, the high interest rates paid by the state were described by Riley as a "prepaid repudiation" (Riley 1986: 184), on the grounds that any investor receiving such a high interest rate at first should have expected a reduction later. Although high interest rates were again being paid by the eighties; therefore, the future repudiation had been to some extent foreshadowed. Nonetheless, default included, the debt would continue to grow afterwards. What is difficult to ascertain here is how far the French government, in the absence of any political problems, could have withstood such a high debt without changing the fiscal system. Why was there no default strictly speaking in 1788? If it was due to the stance of the bankers (Bonney 2004: 205), then we see that finances had already hit a glass ceiling. Moreover, the suspension of payments of 1788 hit some rentiers really hard; their confidence of one day getting their money back fell even further (Legay 2011: 242–43). If the government was cornered into calling the *États Généraux* it is clear that the political problem had grown as much if not more than the financial problem, both of them intermingling inextricably.

At this point we could begin to enumerate the causes of the Revolution but it would be no easy matter to rank them or even separate one from the other. What does seem to be clear is the progressive negative interrelation between many questions, in particular financial and constitutional questions: the difficulty of constitutional reform forestalled tax increases and forced the government to fall back on debt, and the relation of debt with estates-based interests made this reform even more difficult in a sort of vicious circle. When the political and financial difficulties reached a certain critical mass, the Revolution broke out. But this critical mass was defined by the government itself upon calling the *États Généraux*, demonstrating the crucial, epoch-making importance of political decisions. If the *États Généraux* had not been called, it is by now impossible to know whether the system might have held up. The odd thing here is that *États Généraux* were actually called while peace reigned. The war had been one of the causes of the prevailing financial stress but it was peace that prompted the government to take such a new-broom measure, sweeping in far more change than had been intended.

The Revolution transformed the tax base, whereupon the new governments could get only high-interest loans. The National Assembly tried to come up with a solution by confiscating and selling off the church's property, considered to be *biens nationaux*, to plug the gap and pay off part of the debt. The anticlerical feeling of a good deal of the assembly favoured the taking of this measure against established property rights, without even any guarantee that this confiscated property would be enough to pay off the state debt (Crouzet 1993: 100–07). The financial mechanism revolved around two instruments, the *Caisse de l'extraordinaire* and the *assignats*. The former was designed to complement the *Caisse d'escompte*, which had been up and running since 1776. This would carry on with its remit, albeit more private in nature now, while the new *caisse* would take on responsibility for the *assignats*, new official paper currency. The *assignats* were created to meet treasury needs, especially its debt-repayment obligations (Crouzet 1993: 108); a top-priority use of this currency was also to pay state creditors, who in turn could use this money to buy nationalised property. The *Caisse de l'extraordinaire* came to control this whole process (Bosher 1970: 270–71). The market believed that the state could sort out its problems and by 1791 interest rates were falling, while the system seemed to be working. But the outbreak of war in 1792 worsened the government's situation again (Bosher 1970: 252). New *assignats* were issued to deal with these problems but they soon depreciated: 80 per cent in 1792, 60 per cent in 1793 and bottoming out at 30 per cent in 1794 (White 1995: 235). The main reason is that they were being used not to pay debt but to defray the war and the government's ordinary expenditure (Bosher 1970: 265).

The *assignats* process was accompanied by inflation; this forced the government to hike taxes and take forced war-defraying loans. This did not work and the situation when peace returned was similar to former occasions, since the only way of paying off the debt was by issuing more paper money. This only unleashed hyperinflation and totally discredited the *assignats*, which had to be scrapped in 1796. All this led to the aforementioned crisis of 1797, which reduced the debt by two-thirds and cancelled debt repayment to émigrés and other supposed enemies of the Revolution: by 1799 the debt burden stood at 75 million *livres tournais*.

Revolutionary France, therefore, was able to improve the situation somewhat by ad hoc defaulting on its debts but failed to follow any consistent policy, thereby storing up problems for itself in terms of financing future conflicts (Bordo and White 1991: 310). Hereinafter it would have to fall back primarily on its fiscal capacity. This would occur during the imperial era; Napoleon himself made matters worse by fighting shy of debt and paper money, perhaps in light of past experience. Even so, his coup d'état of 1799 did lead to a series of important reforms in the finance system: direct taxes were improved; indirect taxes – abolished by the Revolution – were reintroduced; a redemption fund was set up; and, finally, the Bank of France was founded in 1800.

The situation seemed to resemble Great Britain's: high taxes and lower interest rates. Renewed investor confidence would have allowed France to rack up its debt anew, although the high tax rates also meant it could afford not to do so. The Empire chose the second route; state borrowing remained low during its watch despite the possibilities now offered by the Bank of France. If taxes were now directly contributing towards war financing in Great Britain, more than in earlier eras and partially relieving debt of this function, in France the tax input was much lower: in 1805 the contribution through the Bank of France added up to less than 10 per cent of expenditure (Bordo and White 1991: 314).

In any case the relations of the Bank of France proved in the end to be little help in the struggle to control activities (Crouzet 1993: 539). The last French crisis during the period we have marked out for this book (1808) was bound up with this problem; curiously enough, it was also related to Spain. The problems of autumn 1805 placed the bank in a dire situation. This crisis stemmed from the transactions of the *Négociants réunis*, state suppliers, and those of the banker Ouvrard, in charge of the monthly subsidies that Spain had been forced to pay to France, against the collateral of Mexican silver. For making this payment, Ouvrard tried to transfer to France a huge amount of *piastres* amassed in Mexico. War broke out in December 1804, whereupon he had to turn to Baring and Hope, an amalgamation of British and Dutch trading houses, obtain the consent of the British government and use North American and even British ships (Buist 1974: 295; Merino Navarro 1989). This whole process led to delays so the bankers involved had to strike deals between themselves and procure massive discounts from the bank, unbeknownst to the Treasury. All this piled up more problems for the bank, which ran out of funds for meeting spiralling war needs.

It was only victory at Austerlitz that saved the bank. The crisis drove many financiers to the wall and prompted the top-down reform law of 1806: more privileges but also more government control for the bank. In 1808 the bank's definitive statute was drawn up, remaining in force until 1937. Nonetheless, the Bank of France inspired much less confidence that the Bank of England; the metallic-reserve/note-circulation ratio was much lower in Paris, suggesting a much lower level of economic development and, in particular, cramped circulation of credit and commercial paper, even lower than before 1789 (Crouzet 1993: 543–45). All this limited the government's financial possibilities. Great Britain, despite all, was still way ahead of the field.

6.4 Spain, debt phobia

Eighteenth-century Spain is an idiosyncratic case, insofar as it refused to set up a systematic national debt system: at the same time, it also obeys a similar historical logic to the other two countries, bearing certain resemblances to France but including some England-style changes too. In France the debt level was very high as early as 1689 and was still high in 1713. After Law, the French preferred to revive the traditional *finance* system. The seventeenth-century inheritance was a heavy millstone round French's neck and the early eighteenth-century experience also had a lasting effect. From here on French governments pursued a traditional debt system. This system, however, was only partly open to the market insofar as state-borrowing depended mainly on loans and advanced payments from *fermiers* and treasury officials themselves, so the market was largely exclusive. The public at large, moreover, was fairly chary about the state's creditworthiness, so it was lured in only by high-interest issues.

Of Spain it could be said there was no debt market until 1780. This claim might sound far-fetched in view of the ongoing *juros* system plus short-term loans made by tax farmers and *asentistas*, but it still holds up because the *juros* were not negotiated between private parties and the system fizzled out anyway during the eighteenth century, while businessmen's loans were ad hoc affairs involving only the minimum negotiations to ensure state transactions could go ahead.

The most characteristic trait of the Spanish system is the onus of the past inheritance, dating right back to the bankruptcies of the sixteenth and seventeenth centuries and the difficulties encountered to pay off that debt. Philip V himself felt lumbered with an inherited debt that neither he nor his successors really took on as their own; it was to some extent written off as an inheritance from the former dynasty that was now difficult to pay off. The serious problems caused by debt in the past had bitten deep into the Spanish mentality, this effect still lingering on throughout the eighteenth century. The upshot was a dread of debt, the desire to balance the books and the idea of defraying expenditure without financing (Torres Sánchez 2008), albeit with ad hoc recourse to short-term loans from the businessmen it did business with (Ibáñez Molina 1986).

The high debt levels run up during the seventeenth century were now a thing of the past, but the debt backlog still needed to be paid off. The total debt interest at the start of the century has been calculated at 100 million *reales*, at a time when ordinary revenue added up to only 90 million *reales*. Quite clearly this could not be paid off at a stroke. The loan debt run up in the sixteenth- and seventeenth-century was still pending in the form of interest on *juros*, interest-bearing state bonds assigned to a given tax revenue. But not all this *juro* debt had been taken up voluntarily; much of it had been imposed on the bearers when the state declared suspension of payments in the seventeenth century. The lack of liquidity prevented Charles II's governments, like those that preceded him, from paying off this debt, so meanwhile it was always running up new debt in the form of its interest payments.

This was not the only debt Philip V had to deal with. Although we have no detailed knowledge of the financial history of his reign, we do know that Charles III inherited a debt dubbed "dynastic", which was in fact the payment defaults of his predecessors, especially Philip V. This debt stemmed mainly from the various wars of that as far as governments had received advanced payments on farmed-out taxes and services of *asentistas*, which were not paid on time; quite simply the pay was delayed, building up a sizeable current-account debt (Torres Sánchez 2013a: 293). The suspension of payments decreed in 1739 wiped out some of the more recent debt but did not affect the longest-standing debt.

One of the reasons why governments before Charles III did not set up a public-debt system was the continual leg-up given to its finances by American precious metal. The government's own phraseology is telling here. Its missives often speak of "ordinary revenue", meaning all tax revenue that did not include "American shipments". In peacetime ordinary revenue covered ordinary expenditure, including *juro* interest. Also in peacetime the American shipments held up over there during the war then served to pay off the war-engendered debts and delays. These were also paid with ad hoc extraordinary resources. This was only a stop-gap solution, certainly, but it enabled the government to muddle on until 1780, with the blip of the 1739 suspension of payments and the larger glitch of the hefty debt left by Philip V, a debt that Charles III would try to pay off. This is one of the reasons why Ferdinand VI opted for peace. The possibilities by about 1750 were clear: on the one hand, the introduction of direct administration increased ordinary revenue, even while eliminating the option of short-term loans from tax farmers, which would not pose a problem in peacetime; on the other, the American shipments, which began to grow sharply in the middle of the century (Brading 1971; Morineau 1985), could balance the books. Under these circumstances peace facilitated saving of the sums that no longer had to be spent on war and a good deal of the debt remained pending as a backlog. At the same time a *Depósito General* was set up, a veritable cash treasury to be dipped into for emergencies.

When Charles III felt the need to pay off the debt backlog and made plans to that end, he soon found that his debt-reduction allowance was siphoned off for other emergencies. The advantage Charles III worked with under these circumstances was precisely American precious metal. On occasion of the war with Great Britain, in 1780, the king said several times through his mouthpiece ministers that the country could not afford the risk of the American metal being lost in battle, so it should remain in America. Debt then became necessary as a makeshift solution to defray war emergencies, but for this purpose only, because once the peace treaty had been signed the renewed flow of precious metal from the Americas would serve "to thrust off this new burden as soon as might be practicably possible" (Torres Sánchez 2013a: 344). This phrase indicates a recurrent political way of thinking. For Charles III, therefore, the American shipments fulfilled the role of bringing back into balance the budget thrown out of kilter by extraordinary warfare expenditure. The conclusion, somewhat naïve but not necessarily unrealistic, is that Spain's governors thought the country did not need to set up a public-debt system because it would always be bailed out by American precious metals. This stance did come up with a makeshift response to needs until 1780, but it was also very short-sighted. It might cope with the needs of the moment or even those expected in the very near future on the basis of past experience, but it took no account of the longer-term future and certainly could not cater for any lasting interruption in precious-metal arrivals. This policy of relying so heavily on the American trading monopoly and using it as the excuse for not setting up a public-debt market was only storing up problems for the future, as experience will show after 1797.

6.4.1 Debt-for-Juros and payment defaults

We will now look at the transformation of existing debt and the appearance of other types that ended up being developed. The consolidated *juro* debt had always been the traditional debt, at last since the reign of the Catholic Monarchs (Ladero Quesada 1973), but it grew substantially during the sixteenth and seventeenth centuries (Marcos Martín 2006). Although the borrowing rate was checked in Charles II's reign, the debt was huge by 1700; witness the aforementioned figure of 100 million *reales* in interest payments. During the War of the Spanish Succession Philip V's *juro* policy was to freeze interest payments. At a time of extraordinary expenditure, the government suspended all payments with the single exception of financiers' debts (Kamen 1974: 245), so the *juro* debt problem was simply put off for the future.

After the end of the war two other telltale measures were taken with this public debt: first, not to pay off the principal; second, whittle down its financial burden. In pursuit of the first aim the government set up the *Pagaduría de Juros*, a payment office that centralised *juro* management, accepted some, rejected others and worked out all the discounts. The *Pagaduría* became a source of funds for the crown, since sums not paid to *juro* holders remained in this office at the king's disposition. The government could thus kid itself that the interest now no longer paid on the *juros* withdrawn from the former holders was a new source of revenue. In the second case, the main measure was to cut the interest rate. This was a long-standing trend since Charles II's reign. These financial-burden-lowering efforts bore fruit. After peaking at 14 per cent in the past, *juro* interest was brought down to only 5 per cent (Toboso Sánchez 1987: 177).

This policy would be kept up throughout the whole eighteenth century, the interest rate finally being wrested down to under 3 per cent. The results of the interest reduction policy and other *juro* measures are shown in Table 6.4.

As this table shows, the total *juro* bill was still huge by the middle of the century, about 2 billion *reales*, a sum that was impossible to pay off; by then, however, the total interest burden had been reduced to about one quarter of what it had been at the start of the century. A great help in this endeavour was a drastic measure taken after the War of Austrian Succession. A *Junta* (board) was then set up with the remit of ascertaining which *juros* were "*de calidad*" (bona fide). Those so rated would continue to be acknowledged by the government, while it refused to honour others. The rejected *juros* were mainly those owned by businessmen, many of them tax farmers who had been fobbed off with *juros* during the bankruptcy of 1739. The policy pursued from 1749 to 1752, including the phasing out of tax farming arrangements, reneged on the agreements made in 1739 and substantially reduced the total value of the *juros* and, ipso facto, their financial burden.

Table 6.4 Fall in the *juro* financial burden (in millions of *reales*)

Year	Total juro value	Annual financial burden
1700		101
1713		108
1740	2000	
1748		26.7
1752	1200	
1758		24.4
1788	1260	20.4
1788		12.9

Source: Kamen 1974: 232, 246; Torres Sánchez 2013a: 289–90.

Other measures were taken too, such as state appropriation of redeemed *juros*, which were not terminated. From here on these certificates, now owned by the Crown, would generate interest for the king. This is the reason why, by 1788, the government's annual *juro* burden interest had fallen to only 12.9 million *reales*, including principal and interest. This sum represented about 2 per cent of yearly ordinary revenue, so by the end of Charles III's reign the financial burden of *juros* payable to third parties was more than affordable (Torres Sánchez 2013a: 291; Merino Navarro 2014: 49). Historians have traditionally tended to construe non-payment of *juros* as a failure of enlightened finances (Artola 1982, Toboso Sánchez 1987), on the premise that debt should always be paid off. In fact, this debt was by now unpayable due to its sheer size. From this viewpoint the option taken since Philip V's reign and maintained up to the end of the century would seem to be, as Torres Sánchez says, a reasonable political decision.

It has to be admitted, moreover, that the decision to reduce the financial burden on the strength of a *juro*- and interest-reduction policy was arbitrary and harmful to the creditors. The cost to the government of this sleight of hand was that the breach of its past promises with the debt holders brought its own reputation into disrepute and weakened the whole financial world. The biggest losers of the policy were business-men so this placed one more obstacle between pubic credit and financial resources. *Juros* had been phased out with no other public-debt arrangement to replace them; tax farmers too had been removed from the picture, with the net result that the Spanish financial market was non-existent by the middle of the century, barring the normal negotiation of bills of exchange, never a very common resource in any case.

Another debt that never seemed to be institutionalised but was nonetheless real arose from non-payment of salaries to public officials and debts to businessmen in general, especially those accruing in the eighteenth century itself (Torres Sánchez 2013a: 293). We know something about them thanks to the effort made to pay them off during Charles III's reign, since it was deemed to be a dynastic debt and one the king wished to honour. It makes sense to call this debt dynastic because, in fact, debt pending from the times of the Hapsburgs was scorned, whereas the need of paying Philip V's debt often came up in discussions (Andrés-Gallego 2003: 159). The debt had been run up above all in this reign rather than the following one of Ferdinand VI; this is logical in view of the fact that ordinary revenue increased on Ferdinand VI's watch and it was also a time of peace. This meant there were no extraordinary expenses, and ordinary expenditure could be paid for as it occurred. We do not know if the previous debt was serviced in Ferdinand VI's time but there are records of its being paid under Charles III. In any case this payment-default debt was a current account debt and was therefore unaffected by the interest rates or deadlines of a proper debt market. It was simply money that had not been paid in its time due to lack of liquidity and was now owed to the putative holders.

In 1754 the debt amounted to 520 million *reales*. This debt had been run up since the War of Succession but over 75 per cent of the outstanding amount now corresponded to post-1731 payment defaults, i.e., the cycle of wars in the last part of Philip V's reign. The bulk of it involved *asentistas'* services and short-term loans and advances made mainly before 1739; during that period warfare emergencies had generated a spiral of debt based on courtly relations. This reflected the influence of the businessmen of that time (Ibáñez Molina 1986), trading outside any debt market and without interest rates or deadlines. Nearly 50 per cent of the outstanding debt in 1754 corresponded to payment backlogs of functionaries and military personnel.

In 1760, already under Charles III, a start was made on paying off this debt at the good rate of 10 per cent for each item. This tells us several things. First, that if dynastic prestige was at stake, it was also necessary to restore financiers' faith in the state's creditworthiness in a sabre-rattling environment. Paying off the backlog of debt would stand the government in good stead with financiers for the upcoming wars. Second, that the state was also keen to pay salary backlogs of public officials at a time when improving bureaucracy was one of the main aims, even if this went hand in hand with other types of reductions for the same public officials as part of a streamlining endeavour (Andrés-Gallego 2003: 133). In this case the payment rate fell away in later years, in line with the lower percentage to be paid off, finally settling at only 4 per cent.

But the situation worsened, despite the peace, so the third thing told us by this debt-repayment effort, in view of the rate at which the payments were made, is that emergencies always overrode any debt-repayment effort when money was scarce. The good intentions of Charles III's government lasted only until 1771. The first years of the seventies could be considered again to be a sabre-rattling time. Some sort of war was underway from 1775 in the Mediterranean (Algiers), and military expenditure rose even further with the looming conflict in North America (Delgado Ribas 2007: 321–22, 361). The most important effect for our purposes here was the falling rate in the repayment of Philip V's debt as from 1771, while more was paid into the *Real Depósito*. This meant the government preferred to save against future warfare emergencies rather than paying off the debt backlog (Torres Sánchez 2013a: 304–05).

6.4.2 Towards a public-debt market. A. – life annuities

All the above paints a general picture of the Spanish government's attitudes and priorities in the sixties. Even after the peace treaty of 1763, needs never ceased to grow due to the swelling backlog. This situation was relatively new in eighteenth-century Spain. Avoiding debt but was no easy matter as expenses soared and public debt came to seem the only way of boosting liquidity, as in other countries. The trouble is that the Bourbon's rather maverick public-debt policy up to that time was not exactly reassuring to potential investors. Payment of the *juros* had been handled in a flagrantly arbitrary way; repayment of Philip V's debt, which had promised so much at the start, soon fell to rock-bottom levels. If a public-debt system was now necessary, and little by little this view was winning out, it was necessary to build up a trustworthy public-debt market run under proper rules and with some guarantee of payment. *Juros* themselves had worked on that basis for two centuries; hence their past success. But the Bourbons put paid to this good-will. Now it was necessary to look for new, equally efficient formulas.

The first option investigated was that of *rentas vitalicias* (life annuities) (Matilla Tascón 1980). Curiously enough, as in France, Spain opted for short-term, high-interest debt over longer-term, lower-interest debt. This was largely because public credit was required on a trouble-shooting basis to solve immediate problems, without incurring a permanent load or increasing historic debt. It was this build-up of debt over time that both France and Spain were keen to avoid; even Great Britain feared an accumulation of debt at that time. The new *fondo de vitalicios* (life-annuity fund) created in 1769, when the *Real Depósito* was running out of steam, was conceived to reduce the historic public debt and maintain budgetary balance even though the finance minister himself, Múzquiz, doubted that its funds would actually end up being used for extraordinary warfare costs, and his guess turned out to be right (Torres Sánchez 2013a: 310, 334).

The fund offered its investors a high interest rate of 9 per cent, fairly generous in the international context of that time, although there was no obligation to return the principal, only pay interest for life. There did not seem to be much magnanimity in the scheme, however, given that total interest to be paid was capped at 4 million *reales*. The guiding idea was to forestall higher debt and ensure the "good health" of Spain's finances, understood as the avoidance of the wild borrowing spiral currently being suffered in France (Luckett 1996). The revenue was earmarked on the funds of the *Pagaduría de Juros* which served as collateral until 1779. By that year the investment cap set at the start had already been reached; shedding this initial prudence, the government decided to increase the capital in view of the war needs of the time. This time the new issue was earmarked against the whole set of royal revenue, through the treasury thereof, since the *juros* now seemed to be insufficient collateral. Up to that time over 19 million *reales* of interest had been paid.

The life annuity called for new administrative arrangements. One of the offices, for physically receiving the money, was housed in the *Cinco Gremios Mayores de Madrid*. Although the hosting of a royal revenue office on a private company was sufficiently explained and accounted for as a necessary expedient at that time, the truth is that this decision, at the end of the day, empowered the company to run public funds. As such it was favourable treatment and betrayed the importance of the *Cinco Gremios* for Charles III's finances (Torres Sánchez 2013a: 314–15, 338). This affair brought out the weakness of Spain's financial system as a knock-on effect of the abolition of tax farming followed by the policy of restricting the pool of *asentistas*, especially after Esquilache. The upshot was not only a cash-strapped finance system but a situation in which there was only one company in Spain that could now provide this liquidity. Relations between the state and the *Cinco Gremios* grew unstoppably thereafter (Capella and Matilla Tascón 1957). The *Gremios* held onto this privilege until 1799.

The second life-annuity issue in 1779 came at a moment when there seemed to be keen investor take-up, driven by a patriotic sense of the government's military needs; even so the issue was made with the same restrictions as in 1769. In any case, as Torres Sánchez points out, the important aspect of these life annuities was that, against the rub, and together with other debt components, they did mark a trend towards a genuine national public debt. This finally occurred in 1782 when a third issue was authorised.

The most important aspect of this issue was its collateral. This was now declared to be not only the whole set of royal revenue, as in 1779, but was even widened further to take in other revenue (the tobacco revenue); furthermore, the issue was declared to be state debt secured against tax revenue. There was therefore a specific declaration that the government was ready to guarantee debt payment with all its revenue. The idea behind this declaration was to engender confidence among potential investors, who were not very used to buying public debt. This situation also brought out what O'Brien stressed in the British case: the important thing is not the debt per se, as Dickson had claimed, but the taxes that empower the king to meet this debt and even, as intended in this case, secure it. Charles III's government was mooting this possibility: that the state, not only of Charles III himself but also his successors, should pay the debt with their own tax revenue; this was now a true national debt. Spain might have no parliament, insinuated the official propaganda of the time, but the king took it upon himself to run finances well and pay his debts. The possibility was also open for foreigners to buy this debt, as in other countries.

The third life-annuity issue, now smack in the middle of the war, had two new features and one surprise. The new features were, first, a slight reduction in the interest rate. Investments could also now be made with two beneficiaries, albeit thereby earning a lower rate of interest. Even for the two-beneficiary option the interest rate was still 7 per cent, much higher than the 4 per cent offered by *vales reales*. Second, there was now no cap on the total fund capital. Military emergencies forced the government to throw caution to the wind and try to raise as much money as possible from the market. This market existed now, investments continued and even spread because there were more takers than before. Torres Sánchez, gainsaying former opinions on this score (Matilla Tascón 1980: 280; Artola 1982: 318), stresses the success of this type of debt and the demand for it that existed in the Spain of the time, despite the war, as shown by the growing rate of invested capital: the total drawn in up to 1784 was 114 million *reales*; this might seem meagre but over 50 per cent of it had been raised in war years. In 1784, now in times of peace, investments peaked.

The surprise feature was that, despite the fact that peacetime seem to spur the market even more, the government closed the issue, thus showing its loathness to multiply its public-debt products (Torres Sánchez 2013a: 321). Even so, the crown would continue to receive funds under this heading up to 1803, although the amounts were modest: 117 million in all, of which 76 were paid in between 1790 and 1803 (Merino Navarro 2014: 51). The success of the life-annuity scheme was in all likelihood a result of the higher interest rate offered to investors than other debt arrangements. This did not seem to impress the government as much as the fact that this debt would have to be paid off in the future, and it seemed to suffer a fit of dizziness at the rising figure. As Torres Sánchez also points out, life annuities were similar to other public-debt instruments in that they had solved the problem of paying current expenses during the war and their interest was payable. The only explanation, therefore, for the decision to scrap them was the overriding desire to ring-fence public borrowing (Torres Sánchez 2013a: 337).

In 1780, before the third issue of life annuities, the government had set up another two forms of national public debt, some extraordinary deposits and the *vales reales*. The deposits were formed by tapping into captive private funds held by their owners to support *Mayorazgos* (primogeniture and entail), pious works and other similar institutions. It had already been ascertained in 1768 that there could be up to about 52 million *reales* held in such private deposits (Torres Sánchez 2013a: 340). In 1780 the state decided to invest this money for its own purposes, converting it into *censos* that would earn their owners an annual interest rate of 3 per cent. The government was hard put to justify this interference in private affairs, bending over itself to stress that this was no form of seizure; according to government propaganda the transfer of these captive funds to public coffers was a private decision by the owners and the capital sum would be returned once the war emergency situation was over. Meanwhile these owners would be benefiting from the annual interest payment; this was a bonus since their money had previously been non-interest-bearing.

Whether this transaction was enforced or voluntary, it certainly had things going for it. First, this capital was put to a more fruitful purpose for the owners; a second advantage was the chosen depositing and interest-collecting site. It was decided that tobacco revenue's provincial offices would take on this task. This made the whole operation much more national, unlike the life annuities that had been almost exclusively a Madrid affair. It was necessary, in any case, to act with caution since any enforced handover of funds might damage trade. For example, the *Cinco Gremios* had some deposited capital proceeding from court orders, which the company had now invested in its business. Handing it over now could threaten its financial stability. Despite all these teething problems the government received a total of 95 million *reales* from 1780 to 1786. The sum was not huge, but it almost doubled the government's 1768 estimate of only 52 million held in these private funds.

Although the decision to authorise investment of these erstwhile captive funds could be considered to be to some extent enforced, in this case it played in the market's favour and increased investor confidence since the state bound itself to carry out the operation and meet all its commitments. Another notable feature of this operation is the way the government went about it (Torres Sánchez 2013a: 359). As an absolute monarchy it did feel authorised to change the legal situation to suit its own needs, but it did so in a considered and judicious way, seeking benefits for investors too instead of launching out into a no-holds-barred hunt for new capital or resorting to seizure, as had sometimes been the practice in the seventeenth century. Moreover, as with the life annuities, the operation was suspended when peace returned, only small sums being admitted up to 1786.

As in France, in Spain too the public-debt system lacked any public accounting procedure and we have no knowledge of the government's detailed management of the debt. There is no way of knowing whether the public-debt input was actually spent on its ostensible purpose or whether it was diverted elsewhere; neither could the public officials involved be held accountable. Nonetheless, we do know that for some time the market responded. It was not a blinkered or ignorant market, as in the France of those years (White 1989); investors could rest assured that their interest would be paid. If the debt mechanism failed to work smoothly or to be developed properly this was as much due to the administrative and managerial obstacles inserted by the government in the issue terms and conditions (Torres Sánchez 2013a: 339). Charles III's reign was able to solve the absence of efficient financial mechanisms, partly because there were long periods of peace after 1783, but the problem reared its head again in the reign of Charles IV: when difficulties piled up and resources dwindled, management of the debt proved almost impossible.

6.4.3 *Towards a public-debt market. B. – vales reales*

This problem would make its presence felt in the following reign, especially with the most important public-debt arrangement, the *vales reales*. This instrument, created in Charles III's reign, was a sort of paper-money *cum* public-debt, both things at once. Although this operation was closely bound up, as is well known, with the machinations of Cabarrús and the influence he managed to build up over the finance minister, Múzquiz, it should also be pointed out that, one year earlier, in 1779, the secretary of state, Floridablanca, had tried to set up Spain's first ever paper-money scheme to offset a possible shortage of ordinary tax revenue (Torres Sánchez 2013a: 361–71). Floridablanca had pinpointed the plight Spain would be in if any conflict should cut off its communications with America and the inflow of precious metals. This risk was certainly growing after 1776. The free-trade decree of 1778 aimed to develop the ongoing policy of improving and broadening trading relations between the two Atlantic shores of the Hispanic world. Trading uncertainty, however, was still great at the time, and trade was indeed cut off when war was declared. Now the last metal-bearing fleet had docked in 1778 and, in current conditions, no more would be arriving in the foreseeable future.

There was no other option than to look for a solution to this likely lack of precious metals for some years. Floridablanca found this solution in paper money. His plan was to issue paper money against the collateral of the Indies fund. The paper would be a makeshift while metal was missing and then the debt could be paid off once it began to flood in again with the return of peace. The paper would be legal tender but with limits, since it could be used only by merchants and financiers. It was simply a case of plugging the absence of metal with state surety. It was considered at the time, however, that even greater security would be needed to encourage public confidence in paper money, an unprecedented venture in Spain. The suggestion was therefore made that a 500-million-*real* national fund should be set up against the security of the state's tax revenue. Against this fund the paper would be discounted at the rate of 3 per cent, the legal price. This was tantamount to the creation of public debt. The Indies Secretary, Gálvez, thought this scheme could be extended to the Americans, mortgaging American revenue in the fund too. This would mean, as Torres Sánchez has pointed out, creating an "empire-wide public debt". Finally, the scheme was honed by bringing in a financial institution to run the operation, a task that fell on the *Cinco Gremios Mayores*. The draft scheme was ready for publication by June 1779.

Although the scheme had been well pondered, things were still not clear. It would call for a far-reaching political decision, choosing between paying for warfare emergencies with ordinary revenue, thereby running the risk of economic shutdown, or shunning this risk but leaving these emergencies unprovided for. The dilemma led to dithering. Meanwhile the second issue of life annuities had been made, a loan had been secured from the *Cinco Gremios*, and some taxes had been hiked, namely tobacco, *rentas provinciales* and the *equivalentes* of Aragon. By the start of 1780, however, it had become clear that none of these expedients would provide instant cash to meet emergencies; it was also reckoned that ordinary revenue would not be capable of guaranteeing the proposed paper money, so the whole project was shelved (Torres Sánchez 2013a: 372).

But needs were ganging up. Things became so desperate that the government was forced to lend an ear to Cabarrús, a French financier with a past history of risky projects, all rejected. What he was putting forward now seemed to some to be the solution. This would be an issue of paper-money public debt: the Crown would receive an upfront sum of 9 million *pesos* in cash and bills of exchange in return for paper money, the *vales reales*, worth 9.9 million *pesos*. Cabarrús managed to raise this sum from a bevy of bankers, most Spanish, who supported him (Tedde de Lorca 1987). The *vales* would bear 4 per cent interest, slightly higher than other forms of debt; they would be negotiable and obligatorily acceptable legal tender by merchants. Circulation in other ambits would be unlikely as their face value was 600 pesos (9000 *reales*).

The plan wasn't bad per se, but it did place the government's whole finance system in the hands of Cabarrús, who could then use this position to wield control over the American silver trade. Many opposed the plan on these grounds. Once more, as we have already seen in France, opposition arose between two factions. On one side was the finance system we could call "old" and the vested interests that represented; on the other, the "new" finance system proposed by emerging people and groups with greater managerial skills, who were therefore capable of offering good solutions but at the cost of receiving a de facto monopoly that earned them a huge profit. The *Cinco Gremios*, the Consulate of Cádiz or Simón de Aragorri, until then the trading house most interested in the silver trade, with representatives in the *Caisse d'escompte* of Paris, would see Cabarrús and his partners ride roughshod all over them (Tedde de Lorca 1988; Kuethe 1999; Torres Sánchez 2013a).

The government itself was also chary about the system on technical, personal and political grounds. Necessity ruled, however, and the *vales* proposal not only went ahead but even spawned a second issue after only six months to oil the wheels of circulation, albeit more limited in scope and at a lower face value (Artola 1982: 321, 380). But the situation was certainly not easy. On the one hand, war had led to the expected cut-off in American metal; on the other, the government had opted for a system of reductions or discounts (*Caja de Reducción*). The advocates of this *Caja* appealed to the examples of France (*Caisse d'escompte*), the Bank of England and other sites like Amsterdam, Hamburg, Genoa or Venice, where similar expedients had been adopted. But this placed the government on the horns of a dilemma: the *Caja de Reducción* might be conducive to public confidence but there was no spare money at that time for setting up such a fund (Torres Sánchez 2013a: 387).

While debate raged, needs soared as war advanced, forcing a third *vales* issue in 1782 (Artola 1982: 383). This was Cabarrús's triumph; he seemed to be the only one capable of lending the government enough money to make up for the current dearth of resources. The third issue raised the amount of *vales* to 147 million pesos and left open the possibility of creating the *Caja de Reducción*. This function was eventually taken on by the *Banco de San Carlos*, a bank born a few months later partly as a result of this operation. This led to a closed situation "which began with the issue of *vales reales* and ended up in a bank" controlled by Cabarrús, who also had a silver-exportation monopoly (Torres Sánchez 2013a: 391).

The new *Banco de San Carlos* was fruit of its time. As Vilar pointed out, the bank responded to a particular need; it did not create prosperity but it was necessary at the time (Vilar 1972: 288). The *Banco* had been set up to meet a specific need but it could not create future prosperity because it did not take in all the functions of other banks, like the Bank of England, for example. In truth the bank was set up to take over the *Cinco Gremios Mayores*'s army-provisioning duties, since the government no longer had the money to pay for this; the bank's main trade-off, after all, was a monopoly over this supply. It also had a monopoly of external payments. Nonetheless, its functions were opened up to discounting *vales reales*, bills of exchange and promissory notes, and this brought it into relation with public debt. But no provision had been made for a reserve fund; it could not receive deposits or carry out other commercial activities. We mention these details to underline the fact that, in the immediate future, the bank would not be an efficient instrument for the Spanish economy. It was conceived only for government convenience and this very restriction meant it was not even efficient for that purpose. Quite on the contrary, its sole responsibility for army provisioning and debt brought it up against the financial limitations of the government, now bereft of regular revenue and American metals. It therefore continually defaulted on its payments and sucked the very life out of the bank, which then proved incapable of paying provisioning *asientos* or coping with arrears in external payments (Artola 1982: 386, 397; Tedde de Lorca 1988).

But before all this happened the years of peace after 1783 came as a soothing balm. All economic indicators turned sharply upwards. Tax reforms, burgeoning American trade and a massive influx of silver (Artola 1982: 396), all helped to pay off the debt, instrumented through the bank but financed by the Crown's now healthier ordinary revenue. There was also a notable redemption of *vales*: by 1788 their interest added up to 21.4 million *reales* (Merino Navarro 2014: 57), a figure that had been pared down to 17.4 million *reales* by 1791, a now affordable sum in comparison with other expenses. This was reflected in the currency's return to par value or better (Artola 1982: 389–90, 395, 416; Jurado Sánchez 2006: 62–64, 94).

These good prices were clocked up not only in Madrid but also in Cádiz and Barcelona (Vázquez de Prada 1969).

This perfectly balanced situation soon tipped desperately out of kilter. For reasons we do not know for certain, the cost of the War against the Convention was sky high. The expenses of 1792–96 opened up a black hole of 2.767 billion *reales*, outgunning total ordinary revenue of the period by 140 per cent (Artola 1982: 404, 412). Inflation played an important part in this cost increase (Hamilton 1988: 85, 190), while revenue fell way behind with particular, war-affected failures of customs and American metal. The interesting thing for our purposes here is that the main measure used to fill the gap, as might have been expected, was the new issue of *vales reales*. In 1794 and 1795 there were three issues to a total value of 964 million *reales*, i.e., more than doubling the first three issues of 1780–83, which had amounted to 451 million (Artola 1982: 417).

The problem was not the scheme itself but the amount issued. At that time Spain's mean ordinary revenue had risen from 668 million *reales* in 1780–83 to 816 million *reales* by 1794–95 (Torres Sánchez 2015a: 215); in other words, the *vales* issues rose from an ordinary-revenue proportion of 67.5 per cent on the first date to 118 per cent by the second. This massive issue would increase the debt burden by a proportion that would have been possible to pay off only with a correlative increase in tax revenue. But this increase did not actually occur. As from these years, ordinary tax revenue stalled (Merino Navarro 2014: 83). The state increased its resources only by resorting to other borrowing methods, but tax revenue itself was practically at a standstill in the last decade of the century, so paying off the debt was increasingly difficult.

As for the *vales reales*, this situation led to a trend of continual depreciation, interrupted only in the brief moments of peace when precious metals from America freed ordinary revenue to take on other spending tasks such as partial *vales* redemption. But the periods of peace were short. The *vales* depreciation was an added hindrance to their convertibility, not only discrediting them more but also generating problems for the *Banco de San Carlos*, which was in theory bound by law to accept the paper at par value and this only increased its deficit (Hamilton 1946).

The reason for such a big issue was because the *Consejo de Estado* had decided to defray the new war only with debt, ruling out the idea of new taxes as untoward. In this case the issues were indeed accompanied by the creation of a *fondo de amortización* (sinking fund) which would enable some *vales* to be extinguished. This was done, however, by tapping into the funds of *propios y arbitrios*. Use of these municipal funds for this purpose would hinder local authorities from meeting their own debts. Rural economies therefore suffered, although other sources were added to this fund in the end. This marked the start of a recurrent trend up to 1808, in which payment of the most important debt ran up new partial debts; on more than one occasion this was done, as in the abovementioned case, by issuing royal decrees ordering holders of alleged resources to hand over cash in return for paper. This dragged the public into the maelstrom of debt and stoked their sense of resentment.

By 1797 *vales* had been redeemed only to a value of 58 million *reales*. The face value of issued *vales* amounted at that time to a little over 1.5 billion *reales* in round numbers. If we deduct from this the 58 million *reales* of redeemed *vales* and then tag on another 400 million *reales* of sundry loans, the total debt in 1797 was about 1.757 billion *reales*. Despite redemption plans, such a glut of issued certificates had an immediate effect on the parallel market, where there a constant downward trend of *vales* as a means of payment; by the end of 1797 this depreciation had reached 18 per cent; only two years later it reached 47 per cent (Artola 1982: 429, 430–32, 435).

The government now became obsessed by redemption, given that the interest rate was so high. As from 1798 debt management changed drastically; the problem was that these changes failed to come up with a solution, because finding any external financing was no easy task. The first attempt was a disentailment of church property (Herr 1971), the government then turning to other mortmain funds. In 1799 the minister Soler took drastic measures: devaluation, forced legal tender of the *vales* and limited exchange in new *Cajas de reducción* scattered in several different localities. New subscriptions were sought to raise funds, thereby creating more paper money. Even so new loans also had to be taken up (Artola 1982: 437). Funds raised were still insufficient so in mid-1800, for the first time, the government ceased to pay interest due on *vales*, which then depreciated by 60 per cent. In 1800 a new institution was created to collect and manage all income assigned for redemption of vales, issuing new decrees to continue covering them. This was called *Comisión gubernativa de consolidación*, controlled by the *Consejo de Castilla*, little involved hitherto in debt management procedures. By 1808, 99 million *reales* had been raised by this new arrangement, while also managing to redeem vales worth 136 million *reales* by 1801 (Artola 1982: 444–45).

But the important aspect here was to obtain tax revenue that could cater not only for ordinary expenditure but also the debt burden. The Treaty of Amiens gave the government a breathing space. The ensuing peace enabled trade with the Americas to be re-established. This freed up the backlog not only of held-up goods and trading instruments but also precious metals, including the king's share (García-Baquero González 1972). This fuelled further redemption, bringing the redeemed total up to 253 million *reales* by 1803. A tidy sum; had this redemption rate been kept up the debt could realistically have been wiped out in 15 years; this means things were not so desperate in times of peace. The trouble was that general war returned, as from mid-1803. To make matters even worse Napoleon called in Spain's backlog payments of its neutrality subsidy as an ally, even though not yet at war itself; this worsened its financial straits (Fugier 1930). Ouvrard's negotiations for making this payment enabled some funds to be paid into the *Caja de Consolidación*, improving its liquidity (Buist 1974; Merino Navarro 2014: 152–54). In the end, however, the bankruptcy of Ouvrard and his partners after the failed transaction of 1804, reopened the problem of the debt with France and cut off redemption options (Merino Navarro 2014: 163).

The situation was complicated even further by a three-way system of Mexican silver trade that had been built up since 1804, involving both enemies and friends (Mexico, United States, Great Britain, Holland), brokered by Ouvrard while he could and excluding Spain. As Merino points out, this accounts for the mismatch between silver mined in Mexico and actually arriving in Spain during these years, especially 1805–07 (Merino Navarro 2014: 129). In any case the *vales* story is not all bad. As well as serving as a valuable complement for several years, they never lost their complete value even in the worst moments. If the government could not push this debt arrangement further, this can be considered a failure, but devaluation never became so rampant as in France or Austria, for example and never triggered a suspension of payments. To this extent, "the struggle to set up national debt was a relative success" (Merino Navarro 2014: 116). Napoleon's invasion of Spain changed the picture completely; for the worse, of course.

6.4.4 Recourse to international debt

During the reigns of Charles III and his son, Spain once more resorted to foreign loans. Charles III did so sparingly, showing his chariness, in Torres Sánchez's opinion, of any type of debt. The case of Charles IV is different, because the situation was more serious by then. We would argue that Charles III fell into a flagrant contradiction by restricting debt issues, when we have already seen there was a stable demand not only in Spain but even abroad, while also turning abroad for money where interest rates were higher. This broke a tradition of prudence dating back more than a century. But he was driven to this by necessity, and the government considered that sufficient funds did not exist at home.

The best place to go was Amsterdam, where capital was abundant, the monetary system was stable and interest rates were affordable ('t Hart 1997). Holland's own keenness to invest in foreign debt merged with the desires of other international investors to use the city's financial facilities. Since the seventeenth century Amsterdam had become the main source of information on exchanges and loans, so it could perform a unique function as an international financial hub (Smith 1984: 987; Neal 1990: 44). All these functions of Amsterdam drew on its past experience in financing its long wars of independence ('t Hart 2014: Chap. 7). At the end of the seventeenth century, once internal emergencies had been dealt with, its capital was looking for other outlets and found an investment opportunity in the national debts of the major powers, England to the fore. Although the United Province's economic importance declined in the eighteenth century, Amsterdam was still playing its role as a financial centre, receiving information from the whole world. Although this role seemed to decline in the thirties (Aalbers 1977; Wilson 1939), Amsterdam bounced back in the following decade and continued to play an important international financial role from then on (Riley 1980: 88–89). Turning to Amsterdam for foreign credit was therefore nothing new or rare. It was the Dutch who bought up French or English debt (Wilson 1966), for example, just as they bought debt from the citizens of those countries.

It was less frequent, however, for states to apply directly for loans to Dutch bankers. The British state never seemed to do so. France, according to Riley, "seldom issued loans on foreign capital markets" and he mentions specifically the loan of a life-annuity commissioned by Terray from Dutch bankers in 1772 (Riley 1980: 174–75). The Dutch did, however, invest in French paper debt, as did other foreigners, especially the Swiss. Other states, that eventually sought loans in the Dutch market were Denmark, Sweden, Russia, Poland and even the United States. They would seem to have been one-off cases, apparently always driven by the same motive: the belief that the internal market was saturated and they would not find takers to meet their urgent financing needs.

This was not exactly Spain's case. It all started with a private initiative, the loans negotiated by the Badín company in Holland for construction of the *Canal Imperial* (Pérez Sarrión 1984). But the company folded in 1778 and passed into state ownership, the state also taking over its debt. Not only that, the debt was renegotiated and enlarged, taking advantage of favourable interest rates of 3.5 per cent; shortly afterwards it negotiated another two loans. In all, the Spanish government took out a loan of 51.2 million *reales* (6.4 million florins), thereby managing to refinance the company's debt at low interest plus 22 million *reales* in cash (Torres Sánchez 2013a: 394).

Although war with Great Britain had begun by then, the chance was not taken to raise more Dutch money at this time. Instead it chose to go down the preferred path in all states at that time, Spain included, i.e., national credit. Witness the third issue of *vales reales* at this time. The next loan with Holland did have definite links with war urgencies. After an administrative and diplomatic mix-up which we do not need to go into here, Charles III's government accepted in late 1782 a 24-million-*real* (3 million florins) loan arrangement negotiated by Cabarrús and Lalanne in Holland (with Hope, Fizeaux and Grand) at 5 per cent (Buist 1974: 279). But the government's intention here was to keep afloat of the emergency and raise cash to back the recent issue of *vales*. Although this loan was secured against public debt for which the state was answerable, it in no way represented the will to pursue a consistent borrowing policy but only to meet urgent needs without hiking taxes. The *Tesorero General*, Francisco Montes, also criticised the loan on the grounds of unduly and unfairly benefiting Cabarrús. Although this was true, as well as a whole series of other conditions favourable to the French banker, the finance minister, Múzquiz, justified the loan on the grounds of Spain's need for cash, which was running dangerously short (Torres Sánchez 2013a: 397–400).

But since the loan was dear, the government tried to pay it off as soon as possible. The Dutch lenders, however, refused to play ball. This refusal has to be taken as a sign that Charles III's government was seen as solvent at that time, otherwise the Dutch bankers would have been glad to get their money back as soon as possible. In fact, they were not worried and Spain was regarded as a safe option in the Amsterdam market. But Charles III was determined not to run up a debt and asked only for limited amounts for ad hoc purposes.

During Charles IV's reign, however, the government once again turned back to the foreign debt option, again with Holland. The first loan, to the value of 48 million *reales* (Merino Navarro 2014: 75), was taken out with Hope in 1792, showing what seemed to be a change of attitude towards overseas borrowing. This option was taken up anew later when more money was needed to back up the recently created *Caja de Amortización* in 1798. In this same year, without yet having paid off the former debt, a new one was raised from Amsterdam's Croese and company. The sum originally asked for was 24 million *reales*, though in the end less than half was raised (Herr 1971: 44; Buist 1974: 283). In 1799 a new 24-million *reales* loan was raised in Amsterdam. As financial problems were ganging up and internal borrowing sources seem to have dried up, the government turned back once more to Holland (Buist 1974: 284; Merino Navarro 2014: 121–24). Between 1801 and 1806 at least three other loans were negotiated to a total value of about 34.5 million florins (c. 276 million *reales*).

In general, Charles III's government had largely eschewed borrowing as a war-financing option. Indeed, loans accounted for only 25 per cent of total revenue. This and other pending debts placed a 7- or 10-per cent burden on its revenue (Torres Sánchez 2013a: 406; Merino Navarro 2014: 58). By way of comparison Great Britain's yearly debt service in 1783 accounted for 62 per cent of its revenue and 56 per cent in France (Bonney 2004: 195). Things changed with Charles IV; in 1799 alone debt service topped 150 million *reales*, i.e., between 25 and 30 per cent of tax revenue (Merino Navarro 2014: 111). From this date state borrowing in all its forms never stopped growing. Table 6.5 gives a rough idea of the situation.

As this table shows, from 1799 to 1807, national-debt revenue grew at about half the rate of tax revenue. But the main problem, in any case, resides not so much in these sums as in the steady reduction of Spain's fiscal capacity as from 1799. By this year ordinary taxes represented about 300 million *reales* a year less than in the nineties. Furthermore, the revenue from the Americas also dried up as tighter international control was exerted over Mexican metal, especially after 1804, earmarked for international payments, including the neutrality subsidy to Napoleon. With falling tax revenue, therefore, maintaining a growing borrowing capacity was literally impossible.

Table 6.5 Spain's net revenue, 1799–1807, in millions of *reales de vellón*

	1799	*1803–07* *(annual mean)*
Taxes	463	476
America	91	132
Extraordinary revenue	674	400

Source: Merino 2014: 135.

6.5 Debt and destiny

O'Brien has argued that taxes were more important than debt in Great Britain, since it was the former that could pay the latter. The government chose to defray warfare costs with debt but this was possible only because of the taxes that could pay off debt interest (O'Brien 1988: 2). It would thus seem that the borrowing capacity and the ability to pay off this debt depended above all on the country's tax-hiking potential. This implied several conditions. The first set of conditions involved the political decision to go down this road, public compliance and a sufficient level of per capital income to ensure taxpayers were not ruined in the process or a shrewd choice of the best taxes to take the brunt. The second set of conditions was a trustworthy administrative system plus an equally dependable financial system. All these circumstances obtained in Great Britain and this enabled it to rack up its borrowing. In France, on the contrary, the pieces missing from this puzzle were the political will, compliance and the reliable administrative and fiscal systems, all beset by disorder or arbitrariness. This is not to say that the French situation was not without its own logic and reasons, but it is clear that the system had its limits and could hold up only in peace. This in turn made it dependent on British interests, because Great Britain showed, throughout the century, its hair-trigger war readiness whenever conflict most suited it.

The difference between France and Great Britain, therefore, lay not so much in the amount drawn in to pay the debt. In absolute terms France raked in more during the eighteenth century than Great Britain. It could perhaps be argued that the French paid little and supported less fiscal pressure than the British; nonetheless, "the population paid more than the central government received" (Riley 1987: 211). Everything suggests, rather, that the failure lay in the organisation of the system, in the administrative-financial mechanism. The British administrative-financial system, on the contrary, held up well. One essential trait of the British system is the distinction between the source of the taxes (the taxpayers, some more than others) and the source of the debt (the Bank of England, which in turn received money from national and foreign investors, especially the Dutch). It was all underpinned basically by trade, not so much trade-engendered taxes (customs duties were never an important tax source in Great Britain), but rather to guarantee the earnings of the people who would then become investors. On top of that, tax-collection management, run by professionals, was also set apart from the debt system. In Great Britain, unlike in France (Legay 2011), there was greater separation between management and control.

In France all the roles overlapped. Managers of the tax-collection procedure, i.e. venal officials, *fermiers*, the clergy insofar as they were involved, also doubled up as lenders. This meant they needed money, which they did not get from trade, necessarily, but from their land revenue or their salary from a venally acquired administrative post or their handling of the king's money, with very little top-down control. Even the *fermiers*, top dogs of the finance world, were related above all to administrative and judicial posts and their wealth came above all from real estate (Durand 1971). What they collected served largely for paying interest on the loans they themselves gave to the king.

In Great Britain the taxes-debt mechanism was linear and geared from two poles towards the government. On the one hand taxes flowed from taxpayer to the government, which paid its expenses or debts. On the other hand, the government also received through the Bank of England the money loaned, which was then distributed by this same government to make the necessary payments, ranging from payment of the creditor to payment of military expenditure. The government therefore stood at the centre of two independent flows of funds from the organic point of view.

The picture in France was different. Here the flow of money was circular since the tax money and loans came from the same sources. It was also the managers themselves, completely involved in the process, who had to cover government expenses, including repayment of their own debts. The only solution for such an arrangement was a radical reform. Like all radical reforms, however, this called for some political upheaval and time. England had both things in the first revolutionary period, and by the time of the restoration things were already well on course, at least from the point of view of organisational reforms in the exchequer, carried out as from the 1660s (O'Brien 2002); France, for its part, would not have this revolution until 1789; only then would things begin to change, albeit weighed down by past baggage.

Spain followed a completely different path, because it eschewed debt in general. Its administrative system improved greatly, albeit swinging towards excessive centralisation as from 1780. Working without tax farmers and boasting a tax administration now set up on a fairly professional basis, Spain was unlikely to suffer from the same threats hovering over the French system, but neither did it benefit from its advantages: quick money when necessary. It also took some time to set up a minimally trustworthy financial system, which did not appear on the scene until 1782 and was not yet fully honed. Spain's administrative-financial system was therefore lame on the financial side. Neither is it clear that Spain could have hiked taxes any higher, because the country's wealth had not risen enough to be able to afford this: when trade did pick up in the eighties, agriculture began to run into problems, worsening shortly afterwards.

The final problem, in any case, is bound up with the exterior situation. France went bust because its situation was corrupt and it had to cope with a revolution. Spain went bust due to external aggression, i.e. the French invasion, overstretching Spain's defence capabilities. In both cases there is a long story behind these situations; no doubt many poor decisions were taken at critical times. But the crucial lack was enough resources to allow the country to take riskier decisions. The curious thing is that Great Britain had no direct role in the sinking of its rivals. Not even Trafalgar could be considered to be a definitive defeat for Spain, had it not been followed by Napoleon's invasion. The pre-1802 situation shows that, with peace, recovery was possible. Neither did Great Britain provoke the French Revolution – which broke out in a time of peace – and it finally triumphed over France only many years later, with inestimable Prussian aid too. The British system turned out to be better because it had undertaken the changes earlier than the other two, which it could then hone on the hoof, and this won it resources that enabled it to hang on until 1815. Its rivals, on the other hand, brought in the changes too late – France not until 1789 – and Spain even later if at all.

7   The administration of income

Spending and the contractor state

The ordinary and extraordinary revenue of varied ilk we have been looking at in former chapters served to meet a specific need: growing war expenditure. This expenditure, as pointed out by Conway, Harding and Paul, had to be managed in such a way as to turn "financial strength into effective military and naval capacity" (Bowen et al. 2013: 249)[1]. In other words, the revenue, once raised, had to be spent efficiently by the government, in the right place and in the right time, to fulfil its duties and meet its goals. But could the public sector do this singlehandedly without turning to the private sector, the market? This is where the concept of contractor state comes in.

7.1 Contractor state: a precise concept

We understand this to be the activity whereby states had to call on the private sector, i.e., agents outside the government, for procuring goods and services to enable it to carry out its functions. In this sense the contractor state is the logical corollary of the fiscal state, since money was raised to meet a specific expenditure need. The expenditure modus operandi also had a feedback effect on revenue needs.

The opposite of the contractor state would not be a non-spending state, something that is impossible even to imagine, but a purely administrative state in which the public authority relied on itself to meet all its needs, with the whole caboodle being run, in the last instance, by paid public servants. But this would also seem an unlikely outcome. Taken to extremes, this purely administrative state would even have to make its own office furniture, for example, using paid functionaries. We know this extreme case never obtained in practice. Public authorities in fact bought many goods and services they needed on the market and liaised with the public at large through middlemen who were private contractors rather than public servants. This situation could be tackled from the by-now traditional concept of outsourcing, applied to the public sector, or the new and more significant concept of contestability (Sturgess 2015) but even though these analytical concepts are new the problems per se are not new in themselves but long-standing throughout history.

The concept is also bound up with other government activities such as tax farming versus direct administration, a dichotomy we have already looked at

(Chapter 4) or the "make or buy" dilemma. Applied to industry, this dilemma stoked up the eighteenth-century "Merchant Prince" debate, i.e., the controversy about whether the king, or the public authority on his behalf, should run his own factories. The general answer was no, although the overarching ideal of centralised control meant that in many places, including Great Britain, the state not only tried to dominate the work of state contractors (Conway 2006: 31) but even ended up running some industrial firms directly and also taking over some services geared towards military expenditure, especially naval expenditure (Knight 2014: 373, 378). In a broader sense the debate also raised the question of collaboration between the government and private individuals. Historians have since tended to come up with a positive answer to this: "shared mercantilism", they say, is the best bet, i.e., collaboration between the public and private sector towards the same mercantilist goals (Knight 2014: 23). There is no intrinsic incompatibility between wielding state power and contracting with private individuals, between state power and market friendliness (Conway 2006: 31; Parrot 2012: 308; Torres Sánchez 2013a: 178; Pérez Sarrión 2011).

Does the term "contractor state" denote a type of state? The answer is two-tier. If the question is put from a general perspective, in light of all we have just pointed out, then the answer would come out as no. All states depend more or less on the private sector and an open market, for many reasons. In this sense, when speaking of a state contracting someone for something we are talking of a commonplace, as pointed out by Knight and Wilcox (Bowen et al. 2013: 271) and the concept would be useful because all states in all ages have turned to the market, regardless of the degree and method of doing so.

That said, the concept of contractor state, expressed in these terms, is a very precise concept. Since only a few years ago historians have been applying the term to the aforesaid phenomenon of turning financial strength into military and naval capacity, or, what comes to the same thing, using financial power to procure armed-forces goods and services in general from private individuals. From this viewpoint the concept has been applied to the same states we have also been calling fiscal-military during the long eighteenth century. This is the sense, as might be expected, that it is being applied in this book. Thus viewed, all states can undoubtedly be considered to be contractor states, although each one chose different expenditure arrangements in dealing with the market and did so to varying degrees and within its own particular timeframe (Bowen et al. 2013: 243, 261).

Any external purchase could be taken as a case of contactor state but the term should strictly be reserved for important, state-typifying activities within its expenditure pattern. Moreover, the development of "contractor state" as a historiographical concept has been circumscribed exclusively to warfare-waging goods and services. This does not necessarily mean that other significant expenditure items could not be considered through the prism of a contractor state, such as civil and administrative expenditure. In general, however, studies to date have not taken it up for other expenditure, so we will restrict it too to military and naval expenditure for our purposes here, without claiming that the term is intrinsically exclusive.

From this restricted point of view, therefore, an attempt will be made to study how the contractor state mustered the men, equipment and supplies needed for warfare, with the support of private entrepreneurs and hence how the money raised from various revenue sources was spent thereon (Bowen et al. 2013: 240). It should not be forgotten here that the management of fiscal revenue also involved private agents, in some cases as tax farmers (especially in France and in Spain up to 1749), but also as financiers lending to the state, sometimes forming part of institutions like the Bank of England or privileged trading companies; this makes the borderline between the public and the private quite hazy. But there is a crucial difference between the management of tax revenue and the management of expenditure: in the former it was thought best to eschew private middlemen, whereas the latter continued to depend on private individuals. Quite another thing is at which particular administrative moment private individuals came into play, i.e., how much influence they came to exert on the administrative apparatus.

In any case, the state's relation with private markets and their agents was vital for expenditure management. Various authors have brought out the importance of connections between the state and private individuals and companies, and the emergence of a mutual and beneficial relation between the public and private, with models differing from country to country. Conway, Harding and Paul point to their development in Great Britain, above all from the moment when large navies and armies were set up in the last third of the seventeenth century (Bowen et al. 2013: 251). But the model had already appeared in various forms in the early modern era, such as in Imperial Spain or the seventeenth-century Low Countries (Thompson 1976; 't Hart 2014). In the case of Great Britain, Knight and Wilcox have stressed the advantages of this collaboration in the late eighteenth century: contractors could access markets that were almost off-limits for politicians; the contractors were also more *au fait* with market complexities and the necessary negotiating procedures, especially in the case of buying abroad. Their intervention offered the state financial advantages too, since it was contractors who initially defrayed the costs that the state would only have to foot much later. Finally, they expedited connections between state needs and the development of the country's economy in general and of industry in particular (Knight and Wilcox 2010: 10–11). If all these advantages were evident by 1800, it is also clear they might have obtained in earlier stages of the eighteenth century itself (Morris 2011).

The state authority's sphere of action in its own right thus had its limits and it had to fall back on contractors for many military and also civil services (Knight and Wilcox 2010: 210). In fact, the exact borderline between the government and private agents is difficult to trace. This is so because contractors often became functionaries and vice versa (Torres Sánchez 2013a: 189); the picture is muddied further by some officers of the armed forces who also acted as intermediaries with the *munitionnaires* or the relations of some *traitants* with victuallers, as occurred in France (Félix 2012: 103; Rowlands 2012: 83–84). There were also business and kinship relations uniting financiers with administrators: although each party carried out clearly differentiated functions there is an obvious confluence of interests. Lastly, there were some institutions that are difficult to classify as private or public, such as the privileged trading companies. The East India Company, in particular, ran a navy at the state's service and other companies in Spain and France also had close government ties. We can ask ourselves, following Conway, if these institutions were a branch of the state or private contractors (Conway 2006).

For the moment we will leave this question hanging. For now, we can agree with Knight and Wilcox that, regardless of all the questions still to be properly answered, the concept of the contractor state has by now been fairly well established (Bowen et al. 2013: 274). We can hence conclude that by the term "contractor state" we mean precisely the carrying out of necessary army and navy expenditure, including therein the state's way of managing this expenditure, always in relation to the private sector, even if this was done in various ways in time and space.

7.2 The contractor state and fiscal-military state

Historians have also pondered on the relationship between these two concepts that try to explain the early modern state from our days. What relation does the contractor state bear with the fiscal-military state? From a factual point of view, the two seem to be joined at the hip. Bowen has wondered whether they might be two sides of the same coin or whether there is some other relation. The two concepts, he suggests, would be joined together like "a Siamese twin" (Bowen et al. 2013: 241–42). This would seem to be clear. The same states that were looking for new present or future warfare-waging resources were at the same time spending money on this present war or preparing for the future one: then a state had to carry out the two activities at once.

From a purely conceptual point of view, we could speak of two phases: first, the raising of resources (fiscal-military); second, the spending of this money on the necessary wherewithal, with the support of the private sector (contractor). This approach is naturally theoretical and separates off the two concepts only to be able to study them more clearly. In actual practice, we insist, the two activities are mutually necessary and complementary; they are also carried out at the same time. Given that the money raised was the same money that was spent, their relation on a financial level is crystal clear.

The concept of fiscal-military state sets out to characterise a sort of state that, as we have already seen, refines, revamps and hones its various ways of obtaining new tax revenue to defray growing war costs. The term "fiscal-military state" would also denote a firm political will behind this endeavour and, ipso facto, a state in which the vast majority of its expenditure is accounted for by war. To some extent the term "fiscal-military state" is a way of conceptualising the state as a whole: its whole raison d'être is explained by the need of raising warfare resources and the ways it chooses to go about it. The term therefore aims to explain not only fiscal but also other political, economic and even cultural aspects, as we have already pointed out.

The contractor state of the long eighteenth century, on the other hand, is not strictly speaking a type of state; it would not seem to be a particular way of presenting or organising the state as a whole; neither does this concept embrace a total vision of what the state is or could be; it can certainly give no across-the-board explanation of the whole state. It is a question rather of an activity present in any state, albeit an essential part without which the state in question could hardly be understood. From the conceptual point of view, the contractor state represents the essential continuity of the fiscal-military state: first, raise and manage the revenue; then spend this money and manage the expenditure with the support of private individuals. The contractor state would be included within the fiscal-military state as a necessary corollary. Arguably, what descriptions of the fiscal-military state have lacked to date is precisely consideration of expenditure arrangements; in other words, what is missing from the picture is the contractor state.

It must also be said, however, that if the contractor state is a part of the fiscal-military state, it is a part in its own right. To say that money is spent is obvious; quite another thing is how this spending is managed. During the long eighteenth century, the contractor state meant first and foremost that military and naval expenditure, accounting for huge sums of money, took clear priority over any other part of state expenditure; this became increasingly clear as the century wore on. This expenditure, moreover, called for previous political decisions involving at least a three-way play between the government as manager, the private sector as expeditor and the armed forces themselves. All this had to be underpinned too by the real economy. First of all, the monetary and financial economy in terms of the means of payment employed. Then there was the productive economy, determining whether the necessary goods and services could be procured at home or whether they had to be imported. Other variables were their price, their quality, and their proximity at source to the place where they were to be used, etc. A fundamental aspect in all this is the means of transport, the problems they posed and the way these problems were tackled, especially when speaking of states that are imperial, drawing on their empires for supplies but also forced to defend huge global areas and keep up the supply lines. Finally, the contractor state brings us into contact with the markets and the people running them, the merchants, contractors, *munitionnaires*, *asentistas*, who all contract services with the state and are to a large extent the managers of economic life.

The contractor state concept has been applied to European states during the long eighteenth century and this is no mere coincidence. As we have seen, the idea of a fiscal-military state fits in particularly well with this historical period. Beforehand, during the middle ages, we would be hard put to identify a minimally centralised state. Afterwards, from the nineteenth century onwards, state powers in general soared, so even though fiscal-military relation continued to grow, it was no longer the hallmark feature as it might have been between 1650 and 1815. That said, if the contractor state is an essential part or necessary continuation of the fiscal-military state, it is only logical that the concept has been developed precisely for the historical moment in which the fiscal-military state existed in its purest and most all-embracing sense. In this sense today's historical investigation of the matter has largely arisen in response to the challenges posed by the study of army and navy financing, especially the need of studying expenditure and its processes, i.e., how states spent their money and how the economic-political systems responded and consequently, what impact this had upon military success (Harding and Solbes Ferri 2012: 10).

This is not to say that studies of state expenditure had not been carried out beforehand. But expenditure as a concept and in particular expenditure bound up with military provisioning, together with the concomitant participation of the private sector, has not exactly come in for a great deal of study hitherto; hence the importance of the contractor-state concept today. In any case centring the concept on the aforementioned period does not imply, at least on our part, any idea of exclusivity in terms of timeframe or geographical area: the concept and its possibilities could be fruitfully applied to any historical period and any state, on condition that this state is centralised enough for us to be able to speak cogently of a high-spending state, i.e., on the one hand, a central authority with the obligation of providing its armed forces with the necessary wherewithal and, on the other, armed forces that are also sufficiently big, permanent and largely dependent on this central authority.

In short, if the contractor-state prism cannot claim to visualise the whole state, application of this concept does nonetheless usher us into a host of economic, social and political factors that are essential for gaining a complete picture of the state and this outlook cannot feasibly be gained from any other methodological purchase. Analysing problems from the idea of the contractor state swivels attention to the moment of expenditure, with all concomitant factors of decision making, availability, priorities, management, private collaboration, etc.

7.3 Contractor state and mercantilism

The concept of the contractor state could clash with some classic mercantilist notions, especially two of them. First, the idea that a state is bound to supply itself with homegrown products, in other words, to be self-sufficient. Second, the other trademark mercantilist idea of the state's predominant role in public affairs, over and above the private sector. These two ideas certainly apply more to continental countries than Great Britain, but they are not totally foreign to the latter country either.

Self-sufficiency could be applied to some products that were easy to come by in each realm, such as uniforms or footwear, since every country had sufficiently developed textile and tanning industries for that purpose. But it was more difficult in other cases, particularly in the case of ship building, a key element of defence and of the contractor state. For example, it was not easy to get enough wood, except for a small number of ships. Some countries, especially Spain, built a large share of their ships in colonial shipyards (Havana, in particular, was the Spanish shipyard that built most ships in the eighteenth century); but in other cases this was impossible, or even if possible was simply not taken up. But the stark fact was that the national output of wood, for example, including any colonial sources, fell short of needs, or lacked the necessary quality, so it became necessary to import it. This product spawned a thriving trade, especially in the north of Spain

(Pourchasse 2006, 2013: 172) and also in the Mediterranean. Other necessary shipbuilding products had to be imported in an even higher proportion than wood, such as flax and hemp for sails and rigging; tar and pitch for hull coatings; iron and, above all, steel – also copper, especially when the copper sheathing of hulls became the norm.

All these products had to be bought abroad. This went for France too, where not even Colbert's avowed policy of keeping provisioning prices low made the country self-sufficient. As a result, as Félix and Pourchasse point out, this concept "was not always the expression of a mercantilist agenda"; rather was it France's mercantilist failings that caused its provisioning problems with all these products (Bowen et al. 2013: 264). The main problem of imports was the prices that had to be paid, especially when the markets were dominated by the Dutch and English, who both also had to turn abroad but secured better prices than France. Here Spain was at a disadvantage because it was further from the markets of northern Europe and had fewer outlets there: the whole procedure was more costly and, while the English managed to trim its provisioning prices as from about 1760, largely by improving transport arrangements (North 1965), the prices Spain had to pay continued to soar (Merino Navarro 1981a: 222).

Ships could also be bought abroad when necessary. Likewise, there was an international cannon market that all countries ended up turning to, sooner or later. Not even Spain managed to avoid it, despite the fact that self-sufficiency was vaunted there even more vehemently than elsewhere. It was even held up as the overriding ideal from the beginning of the century by such an influential thinker as Ustáriz. The truth was, however, that the country often had to fall back on foreign cannon purchases (González Enciso 2012d). Cannons were even bought from the enemy, an expedient that had begun from strict necessity in the seventeenth century (Alcalá-Zamora 1975).

As for the predominance of the public over the private sector, this also turned out to be impossible in all cases. Procurement management could be centralised – what was bought, who from and for how much – as in the case of the British Victualling Board, instead of entrusting this management entirely to the contractors as Spain did with the *asentistas*, but regardless of the management system, the private merchant still tended to rule the roost as the actual supplier. In this sense liberalism's criticism of mercantilism fails to take into account that mercantilism is also a form of collaboration between the state and its citizens (Minard 1998). Certainly the state sought to concentrate and control affairs, but the private individuals were also looking for good business opportunities and protection. In this context of mutual convenience-seeking it is hard to define exactly what freedom means; the private individuals, above all, showed that their own freedom, given market insecurity and the importance of state demand, called for a degree of protection and control. At the hub of it all stood quality: the merchant could not offer just any old product because the state demanded quality, especially in the case of ships and weapons. The merchants therefore had to accept government control in the form of standards, to the mutual benefit of everyone.

These standards were not always happily accepted. They were easier to take for large private manufacturers who ran their firms on capitalist principles, i.e., with centralised management and wage-earning workers and even a shareholding structure (Pritchard 2009: 167–68). The situation was harder to accept in the case of craftsman communities who all had their own methods, their own working ethos and also their pride in standing out from other producers (Alder 1997). This was the normal situation in the traditional guild-based system that still largely held sway (Epstein 2008: 78–79) especially for the supply of such products as small arms and clothing.

Be that as it may, the state, on the demand side, did not act so much as interventionist but rather as a fastidious client: this was the basis of all the quality standards. This occurred not only in France; it was also the common currency in Great Britain (Bowen et al. 2013: 251; Knight 2014: 370). Spain also went down this road, although, after 1760, Spain's governors concluded that to improve the quality of manufactured products it was not enough just to enforce standards and then let the private manufacturers work as they wished. A more centralised control was necessary in the case of strategic products, even involving direct state management (González Enciso 2013).

7.4 State, market and monopoly: how are supply procedures managed?

This last idea poses the central question of the contractor state: which supply system was best, private contractors or direct state management? This dilemma was by now an old chestnut (Buchet 1999: 29). In the last analysis it boiled down to a question of control and expenditure. If the government decided to turn to contractors, it was they who controlled the whole process and the state just sat back and paid the price they asked. This did not happen if the state ran things directly, though this in itself implied a managerial and organisation cost, overheads that the state had to take on. In any case the market always participated at one time or another; there were therefore always private individuals of some sort collaborating in the state's supply arrangements. For that reason, the real question, as Brandon has pointed out, should be "to what extent the state should manufacture or process its own supplies, and how far it should contract out for them" (Bowen et al. 2013: 272). In other words, the moot point is not why private individuals were turned to but how far and for which issues, under which particular contracting arrangements and with which particular contractors. Other salient factors are the way of harnessing opportunities, financing arrangements and any merchants' privileges. These and other similar questions of detail in themselves flesh out a concept of the contractor state.

The first of these questions we have already answered: need forced states to turn to private agents because, quite obviously, no state was capable of procuring on its own all the products or services needed. This leads us on to the second question of why the government needed these private agents and how far they were necessary. The answer can never be "for everything". There was indeed always some degree of private participation, but the real question is how much. In such a fundamental factor as the supply of victuals, all states relied heavily on private merchants. In Great Britain the Royal Navy's Victualling Board did so by means of an open market for any businessman. France chose a system of several *munitionnaires* and Spain a single *asentista*. These contractors were elected by restrictive auctions or even sometimes directly hand-picked by the state, albeit after perusing their bid, and then rewarding them with a general *asiento*. Regardless of the method chosen, states almost always turned to private merchants for supply of grains, forage for livestock, etc., i.e., foodstuffs in general. To a lesser but also significant extent they also did so for other products like wood, bitumen, tar or clothing, for example (Pourchasse 2012, 2013; Solbes Ferri 2012).

It is also important to note that the established purchasing method could be tweaked to suit changing needs. For example, what happened when the Victualling Board's supplies dried up or got to distant spots in a poor state? In the 1690s the English began to send storeships to colonies with supplies for the squadrons operating in its waters but the system took some time to get off the ground and even then tended to work sluggishly. In such circumstances there was no other choice but to buy in products from nearby ports (Rodger 2004: 304–05).

Turning to the army, we find similar problems. Supplying troops at home is pretty straightforward but when they were fighting in distant countries they had no choice but to seek out their own supplies, especially when they were fighting far from any coast, ruling out any sort of centralised organisation. This means that supplies organised by the regiment on the ground never disappeared completely. These supply problems sometimes also cropped up at home. The squadron formed in Ferrol in 1733, due to join up with the rest of the ships with which Spain would conquest Naples the following year, left the port well supplied by the general *asentista*. When it got to Cartagena some months later, however, some of the victuals were seen to be in a poor state, so a pro tem purchase had to be made from local markets. Similarly, the Spanish army that invaded Portugal in 1762 had also been well supplied at first, at least with grain. Nonetheless a need of other products soon made itself felt. Special purchase arrangements then had to be made, managed by Esquilache himself through a kind of an improvised "army commissariat" from which Esquilache coordinated the intendents of diverse regions of Spain to buy up the necessary products (especially vegetables and pulses) and get them to the army in Portugal (González Enciso 2006a: 172–74, 2014: 52). What this meant in both cases was that the supply arrangement actually used did not chime in 100 per cent with the established method, the state being forced to fall back on ad lib measures that were largely unforeseeable beforehand. In these cases, it was army or navy administrative powers themselves that had to deal with the problem without resorting to middlemen, even though their participation had initially been provided for.

Exceptions apart, however, the methods were also dictated by the product involved in each case. Bannerman makes a distinction between "non-military" and "military" products. Specific examples of the former he quotes are bread, forage firewood and horses. Of the latter he says nothing in particular. This distinction, so this writer argues, marries neatly with another distinction between products supplied mainly by merchants and those supplied by industrialists (Bannerman 2008: 3). This dichotomy, like any such classification, has its usefulness and its limitations. The first limitation is the difficulty of always making a neat division between the two types of supply. For example, are uniforms a military product or not? Then there is the production question. Uniforms once more crop up here and also small arms. It would seem that the latter could be classed as military material but muskets, pistols or swords, for example, were usually made by a scattered, guilds-based industry. The same goes for uniforms (Solbes Ferri 2012: 284–89). This meant that the supply arrangements were not in the hands of the manufacturers themselves, all of them small, but rather of merchants who coordinated and distributed the products from urban hubs (Parrot 2012: 212) as a sort of putting-out system. All these factors would seem to blur the simplistic though still useful dichotomy.

Apart from the supply of crop- and animal-farming products, merchant driven in all states, there are other products and services that the state could feasibly procure for itself. This involves a varied range of products taking in ships themselves, weapons, especially cannons, munitions, gunpowder or sails and rigging; also transport services. For all these products states tended to set up state factories; not in every case, certainly, but in many. Here is where the "Merchant Prince" concept comes into its own according to the mercantilist *dictum*. But merchant was a generic term at this time; it was really more a case of a manufacturing prince. If we go back to Bannerman's dichotomy we could say that the king was able to stand in for industrial manufacturers but not normally the merchants, except when the army lived off the land.

As for the transport of soldiers, horses, arms and provisions themselves, states widely used the method of hiring merchant ships, many enforced due to pressing need, paying the corresponding charter fee. Whenever possible, however, the state's own warships were used for transport arrangements of all types. States, for example Spain, also turned sometimes to official and regular arms-transporting contractors (González Enciso 2012b).

The states' choice of when to turn to private merchants would therefore seem to depend on the type of products involved, with a crucial distinction between products obtained on a scattered basis and those that could be manufactured in a single factory or only a few of them. In the first case any sort of control and concentration of the supply process would be difficult and laborious, due to the very nature of the product, its quantity, the diversity of origins (grain, wood or uniforms, for example). In this case there was therefore no choice but to rely heavily on private merchants. In the second case the production arrangements could be controlled better and direct state intervention could be efficient. Hence the creation of state shipyards and also the fact that many saw and took the chance to set up state factories for cannons, munitions, sails, rigging and even pulleys (Knight 2014: 376).

In such cases it would be more a question of "factory state" than a contractor state (González Enciso 2013), i.e., a state that made its own products in state-owned firms run by public officials. The idea of "factory state" therefore chimes

in with state companies, *reales fábricas* (royal factories) or *manufactures royales*
as applied to military industries. There were also some mixed forms in which state
firms and private activities intermingled on a fairly equal basis or collaborated
when strictly necessary. A particular example of this is state shipyards (Bowen
et al. 2013: 252, 263), which were run by the state but still depended on private
merchants for the supply of many products. Even the construction of warships
might be entrusted to private entrepreneurs, albeit within the king's shipyards.

7.5 From open market to monopoly

As we have already seen the crux of a contractor state is reliance on a more or less
open market. It was Great Britain that most eschewed state patronage and most
opened up the market (Bannerman 2008: 57). The other bookend case was Spain's
general *asentistas* of victuals or other products, who enjoyed a *de facto* monopoly
system that took in the armed forces as a whole. Exceptions were few and privileges were many (Torres Sánchez 2002a). France's model differs from Spain's.
The army *munitionnaires* were more numerous and were more closely related to
the state. On occasions they could be companies that might pool scores of financiers. In some periods, however, the important ones were few, usually spread around
to suit war scenarios and hence the particular location of the armies in each case
(Félix 2012).

These models did not take in all these countries' armed-forces supply systems.
As we have already seen there were many products, and the supply of each one
could be organised in a different way, also changing over time. In general, the
more trust a state placed in the market for its supplies, the more free and varied
the system would become, with more merchants coming forward. This meant
more opportunities for the mercantile community and a more direct relationship
with the real economy. In these cases, although the state did exert some pressure on its suppliers, it bought their products at more or less competitive market
prices; competitive at least for such merchants as could afford to enter into contracts of this type. In these cases, too, there is less overlapping of private contractors and state officials and therefore less of a clash of interests; this gave greater
leeway to both sides. This model evolved most in places with a very developed
mercantile economy. As Brandon has pointed out for the Low Countries, this
also opened up access to capital markets and meant that the state could adapt
its supply needs more fleet-footedly to the particular conditions of each sector
(Bowen et al. 2013: 248).

Conversely, the less a state relied on the open market, the less varied would
be the resulting contractor state. There would be fewer merchants participating in
it and fewer opportunities for the mercantile community. This outcome occurred
when monopolies and restrictive concessionary mechanisms were brought in
systematically, with decision making being hemmed in by state patronage and
prices being determined by political pressure rather than market forces. In these
cases too, there was a closer relationship between contractors and the state over
and beyond their economic business. Many of them doubled up as tax farmers or

held state positions, making the whole contracting process a more privileged and exclusive system.

The state-market relationship can be broken down into two different procurement systems: first, when purchases are made by merchants themselves, and second, directly by government officials (Tallett 1992: 204). Although all armies continued to some extent to live off the land and make purchases at the regimental level, the great bulk of provisions were supplied in all parts by private merchants. During the long eighteenth century there were many dry runs of a *régie* system for direct state purchase of army victuals. Spain tried it in 1730 and, somewhat differently, in 1753, but it never worked in either case. France tried it in 1741, also without success (Torres Sánchez 2002a: 492, Félix 2012: 107). Another attempt was made in France during the Revolution but the Empire turned back to supply by private merchants; witness the case of Ouvrard. Prussia's Frederick II tried a direct supply system too but this was then a small country in which some provinces had been devastated and a veritable colonisation plan had been set in motion (Corvisier and Coutau-Bégarie 1995: 232). None of these cases was a carbon copy of the British victualling model, except possibly the first years of its existence. By the eighteenth century, the agents of the Victualling Board were no longer buying directly; it only drew up contracts with the merchants; i.e., it centralised contracts but did not carry out the purchases itself. In the Spanish attempt, for example, the intendants liaised with local authorities to obtain the victuals in their local area. Here the merchant practically disappeared except for the very last instance.

If purchases were not made directly by the king's officials, then the moot point is who did? In the case of the Victualling Board for the British navy it was a competitive merchant freely contracting with a state agency; elsewhere it was a privilege-shrouded merchant with the exclusive market right to secure a contract for himself or his group. Both models are differentiated by how much the state went to market and how it went about it. The state's procurement activity might expedite or even boost competition; on the contrary, with the practice of shielded middlemen, it might confine and hobble competition. In the first case, the state agency, as a major purchaser with considerable economic clout, could afford to cherry pick the right merchants at the best prices. This was one of the salient features of the Victualling Board's management procedures, nurturing rather than curtailing a competitive market.

In the second case, on the other hand, a breach is opened up between the state's purchasing activity and the real economy. The whole procedure is now being driven not by market forces but by political interests, since the bargaining yardstick is no longer market prices but the weight of influence and privilege. This may be one of the main reasons why war in these counties did not redound to the benefit of all in business terms, only a privileged few, whereas the more market-friendly practices tended to benefit the whole economy. The nod we are making here to the idea of "a profitable war" does not aim to dig up the debate about the effects of war on the economy; we are referring here only to the possible effect on the economy of provisioning procedures once the war was already underway. Regardless of whether the military victualling demand was good or bad for farming output, which has sometimes been called into question (Tallett 1992: 220–21), the contracting systems unquestionably had some sort of effect.

In the cases in hand here it is quite obvious that the British system was the most market friendly, opening it up almost completely in some cases, although the British did also set up some state-run firms, especially for shipbuilding and arms production. In France and Spain, on the other hand, the preferred model was for the state to set up a political market for itself. In this set-up *asentistas* not only had to fight to win the always lucrative state contracts, not exempt of risk since the state was a poor payer (many contracts at low prices, payment arrears), but also had to double up as tax farmers or hold down posts in the government, often bought. In such cases the state was also more beholden to the particular interests of the financial elites. In these countries there was a long tradition of close interaction between finances and military supplies (Dessert 1984; Rowlands 2002; Potter 2003: 135); unlike in Great Britain, therefore, these interests tended to be tied in with the government sphere rather than the commercial world strictly speaking. In these countries there were also more state firms than on the other side of the channel though the same sectors were involved in both cases, shipbuilding and arms.

Privilege and state patronage existed everywhere, including Great Britain (Bannerman 2008: 42, 54); in Spain and France, however, patronage was a key feature, whereas in Great Britain it was seldom the only reason for awarding a contract. But it did exist. In any case patronage did not always spell inefficiency. A privilege-based choice did not necessarily mean the contractors were incompetent. All of them in general, regardless of the method used to select them, fulfilled their remit. "Patronage was tempered by the need to find capable men", sums up Bannerman (Bannerman 2008: 57), a pithy phrase that might be applied to all countries on either side of the channel. Although patronage certainly weighed more heavily as a contract-awarding factor on the continent than in Great Britain, this did not necessarily mean that the service rendered was poor and inefficient. Indeed, the state weighed up the bids on the table, which could come only from capable companies or people, barring one-off exceptions. The contractor, whoever he may be, had to look smart if he wished to hang onto the business. Competition existed too within patronage systems, even though the ground rules were different.

Supply deficiencies in Spain and France, in comparative terms with Great Britain, seemed to stem more from the whole administrative set-up and the chain of middlemen rather than contractors' failures or ineptitude. Great Britain's administrative procedures had been honed throughout much of the eighteenth century; this really became notable in the final decades of the century (Knight 2014). France's administrative organisation, on the contrary, was frequently stymied by the effects of venality and the low-efficiency post-owning system. It is possible, as we have already seen, that French sailors were worse fed than the British (Acerra and Zysberg 1997: 246, 251), but these authors claim that a large part of this difference stemmed from the organisation rather than the contract holder or the way he had come by it. Spain's administrative procedures did improve, especially after establishment of the single-contractor system for the major general *asientos*; this did work against market enhancement, however.

Patronage, therefore, is not necessarily the reason behind a poor service; services sometimes failed in Great Britain too. Where patronage's effects bit deepest was in the general economy because the privileged market operators were chasing the same products at unequal odds. A privileged contractor had a bigger leeway for playing with the prices of products and transport than an unshielded merchant playing by market rules. This warped market forces. Normal competition was replaced by unfair competition; unprivileged businessmen worked at a disadvantage and new merchants were kept out of the fold altogether.

7.6 The contractor state and army victualling

Army and navy victualling is the clearest example of the need to work with the market and the various ways of tackling this need, simply because victualling was any state's biggest item of warfare expenditure. It was "the great business of the time", or at least that is certainly what Spanish *asentistas* thought. In this section we will be looking at the organisational models for army provisioning, while the following chapter will look at the supply of some products for the navy.

The armed-forces victualling methods used in the different countries during the eighteenth century were based on the experience of the previous century, improving the systems where possible. The old victualling method at regimental and local level had pretty much given over in time to large-scale contracts with almost monopolistic characteristics (Parrot 2012: 206, 324). This change was long term but the model had become widespread by the second half of the seventeenth century, especially where systems had only been inchoate beforehand. In some places, as in the Spanish monarchy, there had been a more centralised model. The switching back to *asentistas* has been interpreted by Thompson as state weakness, showing up in administrative decentralisation, among other features (Thompson 1976). This may be true but only up to a point. If it could be applicable, to a certain point, to the Spain of Charles II, it is also true that centralising processes in fact abounded in many places in the second half of the seventeenth century (France, Austria, England) with a widespread recourse to private contractors (Tallett 1992: 201–03).

Private merchants loomed ever larger from then on, a reflection rather of increasing military needs than state weakness. The process would then continue in the eighteenth century within the overall provisioning picture. It soon became clear, however, that the participation of the private sector did not mean that the government could just sit back and let the merchants get on with it. Indeed, the government tended to exert a growing control, however this was done. Government money could be spent in different ways: it could be handed over to the current contractor; it could be awarded to army officials to buy victuals locally or even to be shared out among the soldiers for each to look out for himself. The latter was the worst option due to the ensuing chaos. In short, there was a variety of methods and each one had its own particular meaning and significance within the particular circumstances and the traditional way of doing things (Parrot 2012: 228).

Although local supplies were still necessary in many cases, especially when the army was operating far from supply bases and sure storage facilities (Tallet 1992: 19–21, 63–65), the tendency was to supply the army by means of major contracts, such as the *entreprises générales* in France, necessary above all for the larger-scale operations (Corvisier and Coutau-Bégarie 1995: 230–31). In other words, whenever necessary, the state relied increasingly on private experience in victual distribution logistics and economics, a situation that became increasingly common in the eighteenth century (Bannerman 2008: 1), taking in an ever large supply range within almost all European armies.

The participation of the private sector, therefore, did not rule out government control and management. Where was the line drawn between them? The aforementioned example of the British navy's Victualling Board serves as our guideline: a government body that centralised all contract arrangements and tailored them to needs. Market participation did not exclude government control, expressed through a competent body: on the one side, centralised control and supervision of contracts; on the other, a free market adapted to the terms and conditions laid down by state demand.

Great Britain's army supply arrangements, with no permanent control body, were not as centralised as its navy's. The reason for this would surely have been the dismantling of the army during peacetime, whereby no central body was thought necessary (Bannerman 2008: 8). "Non-military" supplies, specifically foodstuffs, depended on the Treasury, which formalised the contracts with the merchants participating in this business. The main remit of these merchants was then to supply the army when it was in camp or on campaign. They also saw to the supply of straw, forage and firewood in Great Britain (Morris 2011: 357). The growing presence of contractors, especially as from William III's reign, did not mean that royal commissioners were no longer necessary, since the supervision and control work was always carried out by government personnel. For a long time, however, it was not necessary to organise a permanent commissariat, not even on the occasion of the War of Succession of Spain. This meant that the provisioning work could not be carried out from Great Britain (Bannerman 2008: 11–12; Jones 1988), this situation lingering on even after the end of the war. During peacetime any centralisation was seen to be even less necessary and military needs did not receive much attention. Only in the middle of the century was the need felt to improve the organisation of large-scale provisioning, especially if it had to be done overseas.

When troops were sent overseas, the Victualling Board provided their food during the journey. In distant lands supply lines were stretched, so the contractors based in Great Britain often did not want to take on the responsibility. In such a case the corresponding troop officers, especially the quartermaster-general, would seek out their own supplies on the spot at regimental level; this expenditure was charged to the Treasury's extraordinary financing account. This whole process was controlled by ad hoc commissioners.

The system could be problematic when needs were great. The contractors could not always cope with these needs; in extreme cases they might even find it hard to drum up credit. From 1740 to 1748, therefore, the Victualling Board took on responsibility for victualling troops overseas (Morris 2011: 56–57). All this called for many new contracts, especially for the biggest garrisons. A ban went out on buying provisions already guaranteed by the contracts; this system won out by the middle of the century (Bannerman 2008: 25). Under the supervision of two controllers of the Army Account, the commissioners could enter into contracts, ensure that the supplies got to the troops and sign the accounts to acknowledge the debts thereby run up (Morris 2011: 357). For troops in Europe local merchants were often called on, foreigners from the British perspective. Many looked askance at this practice but it turned out to be efficient because these locals knew their patch and could speak with local suppliers in their own language. There were some exceptions, such as the Humes, father and son, who were able to act in Flanders and Germany precisely because they knew the language. Another of their advantages, as is only logical, was their experience and mercantile connections on the continent (Bannerman 2008: 26, 30).

The system, with a low organisational profile, worked well during the first half of the eighteenth century. Afterwards, as the number of soldiers posted overseas grew, the administrative organisation became more complicated. During the Seven Years' War, in particular, the number of commissioners had to be increased, working under the eye of a superintendent of extraordinary expenses. In practice what was created during the war was a new body, the Treasury Commissariat, which supervised troop provisioning procedures, with a special eye on the victualling. Food was obtained by different methods, by means of contractors and agents, from local residents and by government officials (Morris 2011: 360). In 1779 the responsibility for sending food to the army overseas was given back to the Navy Board and Victualling Board, but in 1793 the Army Commissariat was set up. This centralised army supply procedures from then on and ended the practice of setting up offices in the places were the troops were deployed (Morris 2011: 12, 74, 271; Knight 2014: 97, 155).

There were some differences between the contracts made for troops garrisoned overseas and those based in camps in Great Britain. In the first case, the initiative was taken by the government; it was government officials that contacted merchants asking for victualling bids. In the second case, the method used was to publish needs in newspaper adverts for the merchants to put in their own bids directly, similar to the system used in the Victualling Board (Bannerman 2008: 46,59). It could be argued that the modus operandi of approaching individual merchants to offer them a contract restricted competition, resembling more a relational contracting method (Bowen et al. 2013: 273). To some extent, this was true. Nonetheless, the contracts were fairly short term and the whole mercantile community, aware of their end date, was poised to step in and try to outbid current holders. At the end of the day, however, it was a method that favoured patronage and benefited the bigger merchants of London over any smaller candidates from the provinces (Bannerman 2008: 48).

As in the case of other public-private sector relations, the contractors supplying the army were often criticised for excessive profits, lack of control, patronage-based corruption and inefficiency, among other complaints (Bowen et al. 2013: 241–42, 252).

On quite a few occasions this flak was justified, but recent historical studies have shown that private contractors were strictly necessary. They were able to tap outlets that the government could not reach singlehandedly; they were also experts in their business and were keen to perform well if only to hang onto their contracts and keep raking in the profits. Private interest, in short, was not at loggerheads with public interest, and the system became increasingly efficient in terms of phasing in necessary improvements from both parties as need arose (Bannerman 2008: 38; Morris 2011: 12; Bowen et al. 2013: 242, 250).

In France the army provisioning system differed from the British system in various aspects. It was dominated by people with close government links or even holding a government post. It was these people who put themselves forward directly as contractors, *munitionnaires généraux*, or stood behind them. They formed large companies that specialised in providing given products and services, especially the troop's *pain de munition*. These companies often took on responsibility for specific geographical areas, since French armies usually fought in the country's border zones (Tallett 1992: 64; Bannerman 2008: 10; Bowen et al. 2013: 262).

The patronage system, bound up with venality and the king's need to negotiate political and military affairs with various groups of the social elite, went a long way back (Parrot 2012: 274). The eighteenth-century changes involved mainly who these people were and where they came from. During the War of the Spanish Succession, for example, the ministries of war and finances were staffed with people who had previously worked in extraordinary warfare expenditure and were still involved in army supply and payment tasks. When they were brought into the government, moreover, these contractors also brought with them their particular clique of hangers on, their *amis* (friends). All of them were clearly identified with the supply of the army's bread. Witness the Berthelot brothers, the Paris or Mauricet brothers, from the times of Chamillart and Desmaretz, whose families controlled several posts in the world of royal finances and sundry supplies, especially bread to the armies of Flanders and Italy (Rowlands 2012: 216–17, 222).

The presence of these people and their circles of influence tell us we are dealing here with a purely relational rather than transactional victualling contract awarding system (Bowen et al. 2013: 273). Any transactions would be carried out at other political and social levels rather than in an openly competitive market. This is not to say that any business profits did not sometimes get to other people. As Félix and Pourchasse have pointed out, widespread venality in military affairs also encouraged army officers to become military entrepreneurs (Parrot 2012: 275–77; Bowen et al. 2013: 260). To be able to carry out their business, moreover, *munitionnaires* had to subcontract out much of their work, bringing them into contact with other social and economic levels and other possible middlemen.

After the arrival of peace in 1713 the French supply system tended to shrink, as had also happened in Great Britain, limiting itself to meeting local needs. With the War of the Austrian Succession, calling once more for a big military effort from France on many fronts, the supply system had to be revamped. The previous small contractors no longer sufficed for the new needs. In 1741 a *régie* system was set up for the armies of Germany, soon being dropped on the grounds of inefficiency and expensiveness. The *régie* system was still kept on for the supply of forage and also served on a makeshift basis for some supplies that were considered to be too risky by most contractors (Félix 2012: 107).

In 1744 the *munitionnaires généreaux* system was brought back for all military expenditure, similar to that which had existed in the times of Louis XIV. The system limited government contacts to a dozen or so main intermediaries who enjoyed a *de facto* monopoly over a whole series of army services in the various theatres of operations. The *munitionnaires* naturally had to rely on a bevy of sub-contractors, both French and foreign. The business was more complicated when dealing with armies overseas. Cadet, for example, *munitionnaire* for Canada from 1755, had to juggle with purchases and shipments from Canada, France and the West Indies (Félix 2012: 107).

In no time at all major companies were re-established. The *munitionnaire* who actually came to the plate was in fact a representative of a major company that pooled many other merchants and financiers. The most famous company in the middle of the century was the company called *Munitionnaires généreaux de vivres de Flandres et d'Allemagne*, led by Jaques Marquet de Bourgade, one of France's main financiers, who also held high-up posts in the government. He was the son of a Bordeaux wheat merchant who had thrown his hat into the victualling ring in the difficult year of 1709. The whole company was a family firm dominated by the Marquet family, with other associates like Nesme and the Paris brothers, also running family businesses of similar characteristics. The Paris brothers, who built up a notable presence within the company, ended up marrying into the Bourgade family in the next generation (Félix 2012: 108–09). The company was especially active during the Seven Years' War to supply the armies of Flanders and Germany.

As occurred with other contractors, the members of this company were accused of creaming off excessive profits at the king's cost. The minister Duvernay and the contractors justified themselves by pointing out the essential profit-making nature of any private company; they also claimed that some leeway was needed to be able to cope with the business's problems without going bankrupt and thereby jeopardising the king's service. Within a monopoly system the contractor could no doubt afford to trim its margins, giving a better deal for the state, while also still making healthy profits. Duvernay, in any case, was not given to much discussion about prices; above all, the price had to ensure the contractor's desire to affront the high business risks and strain on credit, since the government was sure to pay up with some arrears. To this extent the contractor had to double up as a wheat-supplying merchant and money-lending financier (Félix 2012: 115–16). This double act made it very difficult for the government to do without them since their participation had been factored into the government's debt system. Changing the system would have meant coughing up many costly payments or, on the other hand, not paying anything at all, thereby ruining a large part of the finance world and part of the government itself.

The figures of a company like that of the Flanders and Germany victualling company are eye-catching. According to Félix, the company might have had up to 4,000 employees; during the Seven Years' War it turned over about 25 million livres a year and might chalk up a profit of 2.5 million. This 10 per cent profit rate was more or less in line with the going rate at the time for business in the king's service. The *munitionnaire* also had a chance to lever up its profit as high as 3 million depending on the price of wheat and transport hiring rates (Félix 2012: 121).

What comes across from all the examples studied is just how important it was for the king's service to be performed, no matter how. The overriding concerns were punctuality, quantity and quality rather than the actual way of going about it. The same went for Spain, even though the victualling and provisioning system was organised differently there. Under the Spanish system the state's victualling demand did not drive the development of a competitive market; to this extent the Spanish system resembled the French more than the British. Nonetheless, the Spanish case also differed from the French on two points: first, *asentistas* were much less closely linked in with the government machine. They collaborated with the government but did not usually hold government posts. There were some exceptions and the protégé-based system could certainly shroud many peccadillos, and it was not unheard-of for some *asentistas* to have family relations in the government, but this certainly did not occur with the same intensity as it did in France. The second point of difference was that Spain's *asentista-general* system represented a single business house that was not necessarily the head of a major general company.

During the first half of the century the same characters tended to double up as *asentistas* and tax farmers. The high risks posed by both businesses, above all due to government payment arrears, meant that strong financial backing was required to tide them over between payments, as we have just seen. In Spain this backing was sought in the tax farming business (González Enciso 2008b). Examples to hand suggest that the *asiento* came before the tax farming. This represented the culmination of a career that began in trade, building up enough importance to win an *asiento* and then ending up in the highest financial spheres with the tax farming contract. It has to be borne in mind here that in the first half of the century most of the characters were new to the business after the scythe wielded by the former crisis and also due to the changeover in social elites with the new dynasty. Especially important here was the ousting of foreign financiers and the new opportunities created with the War of Succession. The whole system was therefore created *ex novo* in line with the new circumstances.

During the War of Succession, the government awarded the troop victualling *asiento* to a whole string of financiers on a short-term basis of a few years each one. It was not a general *asiento*, taking in a single zone instead, albeit spacious like Castile or Andalusia, for example (Kamen 1974: 81–82). The main reason for changing the *asentista* was their business failure (Dedieu 2011). This helped to bring in new blood. Most of these newcomers no longer had anything to do with the former *asentistas* of the previous century like the Cortizo or Montesino clans, for example (Sanz Ayán 1988); the new niches were filled rather by financiers who had fledged and spread their wings in the 1690s (Valdeolmos, Rodríguez de los Ríos, López de Castro, José Aguerri), those of the Navarre group of Goyeneche and Soraburu, some Flemish businessmen (Flon, Hubrecht) and some Frenchmen linked to Orry (Duplessis, Sartine). These were not isolated groups; they formed companies involving an amalgam of people from different origins, who also competed against each other (Sanz Ayán 2002, 2011; Dedieu 2011).

The salient feature in this period is the variation in the main provisioning *asientos*, due to the aforesaid reason of business failure, a frequent event at this time. This reflects both the economic difficulties of the government and the weakness of the companies, despite always being backed up by other government perks like supplementary provisioning or tax-farming contracts.

Table 7.1 shows the succession and replacement sequence in the provisioning business. By "replacement" here we mean enforced substitution when the *asentista* was unable to continue with the contract, as occurred in 1704. The Marqués de Santiago stood down because the state failed to come up with the money. This ushered in a first attempt at direct administration under the eye of a state-organised and controlled company, along the lines of England's initial victualling system. Finally, there was a process of consolidation spurred by the growth of a powerful group capable of offering the states sufficient guarantees of regular supply, the group of Goyeneche and López Ortega, backed up by the powerful house of Valdeolmos.

Table 7.1 Succession and replacement in the grain provisioning business in Spain

1703	M. López de Castro		Andalusia, Old Castile, Extremadura, Galicia
1704	E. Rodríguez de los Ríos, Marqués de Santiago	His partners	Extremadura
		C. Aguerri, Marqués de Valdeolmos	Andalusia
		Marqués de Campoflorido	Galicia
		José de Soraburu	Navarra
		Esteban Moriones	Aragón
1708	Direct administration State-dependent company		
1710	Sartine, Leotardi		Aragón, Valencia, Catalonia
1712	Goyeneche, López Ortega, Herederos de Valdeolmos		Nearly all regions

Source: Kamen 1974: 81–82, Dedieu 2011, Aquerreta 2001a: 112–13.

This contract opened up a new supply stage with more stability and longer terms. The contract of Goyeneche, of his partners and then his heirs, was to last until 1719, in two phases. In the first stage, running up to 1717, they held a provisioning *asiento* for the armies of Aragon, Valencia, Catalonia, Extremadura and Castile, plus the *Guardias de infantería* (household guard) of the court; this made it a very sizeable contract, albeit not taking in the whole range of Spanish armies. In the second phase, the *asiento* run by Juan Francisco Goyeneche took on provisioning arrangements for all Spanish troops. It was shorter lived than the former contract, however, above all because the company, which would last for another few years, turned to more lucrative business, also with the state (Aquerreta 2001a: 116–17, 126).

After 1720 turmoil returned. Attempts were made to calm things down again by dealing with a single *asentista* in the person of Urbán Ruiz Velarde, in 1726–27. The conditions agreed upon therein served as a model for all subsequent contracts (Torres Sánchez 1997: 167). This development, however, was once more cut short, this time by the policies of Patiño who decided to bring in direct administration in 1730. The provision came under control of a general provisioning accounting office (*Contaduría*) which coordinated the work of the intendents in charge of buying provisions in their respective provinces and liaising with private authorities to ensure supply lines. The results were poor: worse management at a higher price, but the system was kept on until 1739. In this year it was scrapped due to the dual effects of the bankruptcy and war urgencies. In such circumstances the *asentista*'s creditworthiness was once again the crucial factor, above all if the new merchant offered to take on the *asiento* with an eye-catching price reduction (Torres Sánchez 2002a: 492–94, 2010: 251).

This was no easy task. After doubt-ridden years of partial *asientos* and fruitless negotiations with diverse financiers, the government awarded a new general victualling *asiento* in 1744 to Francisco Mendinueta, a well-known businessman who had already run previous *asientos* and tax-farming contracts (Aquerreta 2002a, 2002b: 88–89). Mendinueta won the *asiento* by lowering the asking price and also relaxing other terms, thereby vaunting his creditworthiness and dependability. In return he was given privileges that strengthened him against market vicissitudes (Torres Sánchez, 2002b: 120–23).

But the management of the *asiento* was complex. To start with, it had to be renewed each year. The *asentista* soon invoked difficulties in prices and transport arrangements, causing him to edge up his asking price in each successive renewal. This upwards trend was not allowed to drift on too long; the government finally bargained Mendinueta down again, producing new difficulties for both parties. The chosen solution was odd: a return to direct management under Mendinueta as director general of provisioning arrangements. The thinking behind this was clear enough; direct administration allowed the government to enforce its own conditions, including price cuts and more favourable advance-payment arrangements; on the other hand, the appointment of Mendinueta allowed the government to tap into his business expertise and relations, all conditions sine qua non of a successful provisioning arrangement. This compromise solution meant turning the *asentista* into a high-up government official. Peacetime favoured this expedient for a while but it still proved impossible in the end to keep prices steady and upfront money without a financial reserve, which the government did not seem to have. The solution lasted only two years, 1753 and 1754, after which there was no choice but to bow to Mendinueta's terms, once more acting as private *asentista* charging higher prices (Torres Sánchez 2002b: 125).

Mendinueta's new predominance did not last long. The juicier business encouraged more and more financiers to try to muscle in, muddying contract renewal negotiations. But the main threat came from the new minister, Esquilache, determined to cut down the cost for the government. His policies favoured the appearance of new candidates, forcing Mendinueta to lower his prices in his last *asiento*, which he would hold for only three years from 1760 to 1763. This was the beginning of the *asentista*'s end (Torres Sánchez 2002b: 130–33).

The following years showed that Esquilache's policy was risky. Cutting prices to the bone deprived *asentistas* of the profits needed to run a big business successfully. This came out clearly after 1764 when negotiations were held with the Dugues brothers (Zylberberg 1993: 167), who proved in the end to be unable to meet the state's demands, despite being backed by two mighty Madrid financiers, Partearroyo and Larralde. Once Esquilache had gone, the government had to fall back once more on a single, strong, privilege-shrouded group. This sidestepped provision risks and many transaction costs, even though the government, in return, had to pay higher prices. This marked the advent in the provisioning business of the *Cinco Gremios*, who, in 1768, pulled off a notably high provisioning price (Capella and Matilla Tascón 1957: 197; Torres Sánchez 2014: 275).

The problems encountered by the government from the fifties onwards in finding a trustworthy *asentista* were bound up with the disappearance of tax farming in 1749. As we have already pointed out, tax-farming was the main payoff, privileges apart, that allowed the *asentista* to offset any losses from excessively low bids or government payment arrears. Tax farming was also the necessary source of liquidity for the upfront payments needed under the victualling business. Once this crutch had been kicked away, *asentistas* had to look for other props. If Mendinueta survived during the fifties this was because he retained several *asientos* and business interests, including the Eugui munitions factory, the arms transport *asiento* and his share of the *Compañía de Buenos Aires* (Martínez del Cerro 2002: 135, González Enciso 2012b); a great help too were his kinship and financial relations with his Arizcun cousins, another important group that sometimes lent him money (Aquerreta 2002a: 95).

The *Cinco Gremios Mayores de Madrid* was also a major company who intended to cope with and profit from the victualling contract on the strength of their many business interests in Spain and its American colonies. It was also an important up-and-running bank, a fact that afforded it big reserves. The *Gremios* also retained a pair of tax farming contracts, as an exception to the general rule, i.e., the revenue of Madrid and the *excusado* church tax. Furthermore, the *Gremios* had wrested more privileges from the government than earlier *asentistas* in terms of higher government advance payments or the right to pass on to the government some provisioning costs such as the purchase of perishable products or transport rentals (Torres Sánchez 2014: 276–78).

During the seventies the *Gremios* not only managed to up the *asiento* period but were also able to buy in supplies at lower prices thanks to higher farming yields at that time. They also played the silver-exportation (*saca de la plata*) card for all they were worth, thereby gaining from the government perhaps the most important trade-off of all. At that time Europe needed more and more money for its burgeoning economic activity. The *Cinco Gremios* justified their silver-exportation need on the argument that they had to buy in provisions from abroad when too little was available at home, as was usually the case.

As it panned out, however, this apparently crucial provisioning *asiento* trade-off backfired on them. Other great financiers, equally interested in silver exportation, pricked up their ears. Simón de Aragorri and Cabarrús, for example, tried to stymy this new step forward by the powerful company and make with the victualling business themselves. It was Cabarrús who eventually pulled it off on the strength of his recently created *Banco de San Carlos*. His prominent position enabled him to win the *asiento* for the *Banco de San Carlos* in 1783 (Tedde de Lorca 1988: 160 ff.). Cabarrús's backlog of political and financial problems eventually caught up with him, however, and the *Gremios* won back the victualling *asiento* in 1790. Now the company enjoyed a theoretically more solid position than ever, but the cycle of war that began in 1793 was to spell ruin for the *Cinco Gremios Mayores*, too (Torres Sánchez 2014: 280–81).

Note

1   In 2013 Bowen published a contractor state "Forum" in the *International Journal of Maritime History*. The "Forum" contains an introduction by Bowen and several articles on specific countries written by one or several authors: The Dutch Republic, by Brandon; Britain, by Conway, Harding and Paul; Spain by González Enciso, Torres Sánchez and Solbes Ferri; France by Félix and Pourchasse and the Portuguese Empire by Moreira, Machado and Cordeiro. There is also a final "Response" by Knight and Wilcox. Although reference is made in the text to the corresponding authors, we will always cite this work as Bowen et al. 2013.

8 Shipbuilding, the navy and the contractor state

8.1 Victualling the navy

In England the Royal Navy Victualling Board was set up at the end of the seventeenth century. It took its first form in 1654 when Thomas Alderne, a former contractor, became a salaried official of the government. Upon his death in 1657, a Victualling Board was set up under the orders of the Admiralty. This was the first time any state had ever taken on direct responsibility for its navy victualling procedures (Buchet 1999: 29; Rodger 2004: 43). The Restoration at first brought about a return to the old system in which a syndicate of contractors took charge of victualling under the orders of a chief victualler contractor, who was the real boss. The first appointment fell to Gauden. The system's organisation was improved but it ran into economic problems due to the lack of a proper budget (Rodger 2004: 105).

The definitive system took shape between 1679 and 1683. On the first date the Admiralty, after changing the general victualler, created the post of Surveyor of Victuals to oversee the contractor and make sure he fulfilled his remit honourably. This was the first step towards strengthening of state control, which became definitive in 1683 when the post of Surveyor was scrapped and replaced by the Victualling Board, dependent on the Navy Board, comprising seven salaried commissioners. Basically it was a finer-honed version of the 1655 model. But the new Board soon ran into problems due both to inexperience and, above all, a lack of money (Buchet 1999: 30; Rodger 2004: 109). Even so, the organisation of 1683 "was to remain the permanent form of naval victualling for a Century and a half" (Rodger 2004: 109). This tended to consecrate what Buchet has called an original organisation, alloying the flexibility and firmness of two different systems: on the one hand, the private and competitive business world, capable of securing the best prices, and, on the other, state control and public service, which ensured proper control of the private agents and forestalled any abuse of power (Buchet 1999: 27).

It is worthy of note that the creation of the Victualling Board, which ensured greater state control in its financial and commercial relations with private agents, coincided in time with the disappearance of tax farming. As such it represents one more element of state centralisation during the final years of the Restoration regime, which ring-fenced the two spheres of responsibility and action more clearly: the public side, which controlled service efficiency but did not intervene directly in the market; and the private side, which traded in the market but did not, for its part, tamper with administrative matters. The difference from tax collection procedures is clear. In these the state dealt directly with the taxpayers through its organisations and fiscal rules. On the expenditure side, on the contrary, the state had no direct dealing with the final product but only with the merchant or manufacturer who acted as middleman between the government and the final recipient: the soldiers. The greater the leeway given to these middlemen, the less freedom granted to the market.

The Victualling Board handled the provisioning of state shipyards and granted the contracts for the primary produce; it packaged the produce and also ended up processing the food if need be (Knight 2014: 155). This could not be defined as an untrammelled free-market system. The supply side was controlled by government officials and the Board itself had a much higher demand capacity than any other purchaser, so its market clout was hefty. It was, however, the most open form possible of organising the general supply of products, especially after the 1701 instructions made it obligatory for the victualling tendering procedures to be public (Rodger 2004: 193). This meant any merchant could now realistically bid for these contracts. Quite another thing is whether they could handle the work, because this system helped the Board to drive down prices.

The Victualling Board went through a long period of evolution after its initial establishment. Experience had to be built up before the service could be significantly improved. Problems came thick and fast until 1715, especially a deficient budget. After this watershed year the organisation improved substantially and its economic capacity increased too (Buchet 1999: 33–34; Rodger 2004: 305). One of the main aspects of this ongoing improvement was better food quality, something the Board seems to have managed by about 1739. From 1740 storage procedures improved and the beer distilling capacity increased. As Rodger has pointed out, all this allowed the Board "to do nearly all of its own brewing, packing and milling, reducing dependency on contractors and giving higher quality at lower cost" (Rodger 2004: 306).

One of the biggest problems was the overseas storage problem. Allowing captains to supply their own ships would have opened up the door to fraud. The chosen solution, therefore, was to set up local victualling agencies or to arrange for the official victualler to accompany the corresponding squadron. Another possibility, in the case of an overseas navy station, was to turn to a local contractor for its supply, such as the firm Mason and Simpson in Jamaica, in the times of Vernon. That the problems were sizeable is clear. Apparently, even Vernon himself doubted whether the Board would be capable of supplying a fleet as big as the one they planned to bring together in the West Indies, i.e., "so far from home". Vernon indeed ran into problems, because Mason and Simpson were given short notice and were not able to muster all necessary supplies, but Vernon's possible rival, the French d'Antin, fared even worse, having to go back to France due to lack of supplies (Harding 1991: 88; Rodger 2004: 306).

Despite the problems with Mason and Simpson, the local-contractor option was still thought to be the best idea during the forties. During the Seven Years' War there was a land-bound official victualling agent only in Gibraltar and another onboard the West Indies squadron. The bulk of supplies, however, were rustled up by contractors, who found their wherewithal not in London, where the price would have been higher, but in the cheaper markets of New England and Ireland. By 1760 the Victualling Board had built up good levels of efficiency, raising quality standards and its capacity for taking on longer and more distant operations. Victualling 70,000–85,000 men in the Seven Years' war cost about the same as supplying the 40,000–50,000 in the War of the Spanish Succession, and the food quality was much better (Harding 1991: 52–60; Buchet 1999: 158–204; Rodger 2004: 306).

These improved procedures came good in the American War when the Board had to take on the supply of unprecedented forces across the Atlantic without being able at this time to tap into the markets of New England. Up to that time, the overseas victualling contractors had depended on the Treasury; from then on the Victualling Board took on direct responsibility for overseas victualling procedures. At the helm stood Atkinson, a major grain merchant who had hitherto been a private contractor. The result was a clear improvement in efficiency and economy (Rodger 2004: 377; Knight 2014: 39–40).

Organisation and economy are key factors to explain the success of the Victualling Board. Its employees "monitored prices in the food markets across the country" (Knight 2014: 112); this meant long working hours but the payoff was crucial bargaining power in contract negotiations. It would seem clear that whenever the Victualling Board was working well, which was almost always, especially in the second half of the century, this favoured British sea control. Timely and top-quality victualling was crucial for the extension of the Royal Navy's activities. This was especially decisive in the war against Napoleon, when the various squadrons had to operate simultaneously in several European theatres to offset Napoleon's continent-wide dominion. The Board also had to tackle the supply of ships spending a long time on the sea to effect blockades. This was not simple, even though the fleets were not far from Great Britain. It was necessary to set up a victualling convoy system. To provision troop-landing ships in more distant spots, the Board, showing a pragmatic flexibility, drew on local markets near the war theatre, like Malta or Turkey in the case of the 1801 expedition to Egypt, for example (Knight 2014: 155–56, 172).

In comparison with the growing efficiency of the English system, based on centralisation of free contracts with private agents, France's victualling system was much more questionable. On the one hand it could indeed be classed as a success, managing as it did to victual many large fleets without any significant complaints from the parties involved (Pritchard 2009: 180); on the downside, it was a corrupt and expensive system, which also lost efficiency as the century wore on (Rodger 2004: 307), just when the British system was improving most quickly. This sheds some light on the disparate feats of both navies in general terms, the gap growing particularly as from 1759.

The French navy's victualling also drew on private contractors. Unlike the British system, however, it was not a case of private merchants freely opting into a public bid invitation. The French system was based on a strong syndicate (*parti*) of monopoly-shielded merchants. It was a similar system in its way to the indirect tax farming *ferme*. The syndicate was represented by the victualler-general or *munitionnaire-général de la marine*. The system blended public and private means. Food was prepared in the state shipyards, in navy furnaces and stores. At the same time the victualler-general ran his own employees in the *arsenaux* (royal dockyards) and also onboard ships to prepare the sailors' food rations (Pritchard 2009: 179).

This system was a clear improvement on the first abuse-prone models in which captains took on responsibility for victualling their own ships. But the improvement was more in terms of organisation than food quality, which was apparently quite poor in general. Some technical explanations could be put forward for this inability to ensure food conservation with eighteenth-century resources (Baugh 1965: 422–24) but this seems to be partly belied by the apparent difference in quality between the meals of the British and French navies. The main reason for this may lie in the organisation, especially the long chain of middlemen in the French victualling system in comparison with the British, and also the time and distance between production sites and *arsenaux* stores in France. Daily organisational problems were also sparked off by the presence of the victualler-general's private employees in the *arsenaux* and on ships outside the jurisdiction and control of the navy (Pritchard 2009: 179).

In any case the system did work reasonably well. French merchants of the syndicate, for example, were capable of finding new markets when necessary, as in 1756 when the British government scrapped the ban on exporting Irish salted meat to Great Britain. Until that time France had had no problem with this product for its West Indies operations. Like the British it had skirted the ban on Irish salted meat by trading under false flags to forestall enemy reprisals (Rodger 2004: 307). When the ban was lifted in 1756, however, the whole Irish market swung to Great Britain, whereupon the French had to search out other markets (Pritchard 2009: 181–82).

These and other problems were easily surmounted by the victualler-general and his partners. What the syndicate could not solve, however, was the French government's financial straits. The Seven Years' War wreaked a system-buckling strain on French finances. Syndicate merchants were also loath to give the government any short-term loans as it fell further and further behind on its monthly payment commitments. In the end, if the French ships were poorly victualled during the English blockades in the three final years of the war, this was not so much due to the enemy ships as the government's own financial collapse.

Victualling procedures must have improved during the American War, judging from the navy reforms undertaken at the time and its feats during the war, barring the Battle of Saintes (Rodger 2004: 357; Acerra and Zysberg 1997: 73–75; Villiers 2013: 65–75). But the actual victualling system underwent no change at all and it would seem that by the time of this battle France's sailors were worse fed than Britain's (Acerra and Zysberg 1997: 246, 251). Improvements were patchy; the situation for the Indian Ocean territories actually worsened. Referring to the reasons for the withdrawal of Orves's squadron from India in 1781, Orain holds up the victualling problem as crucial. Mauritius, the French squadrons' revictualling point, suffered from a dearth of practically everything. Few provisions ever got there; the actual amounts were normally less than the invoiced amounts and much of it was in a bad state. The author's overall judgment is pretty negative: the *arsenaux* failed to withstand the war effort due to a lack of planning; the *munitionnaires* were not mindful of their responsibilities and administrators covered up for them. All this led to grave victualling defects, at least for the Indian Ocean (Orain 2014).

Spain's navy victualling system was even more constrained than France's. There was only one general victualling *asentista*. Although this single person would no doubt have had to contract out some services to other helpers in the various production sites, there is no record of them forming a syndicate or *parti*, as in France, or even that the general *asentista* had any sort of obligation towards them. All the responsibility, all the work and all the eventual profits fell on a single person, head of a family trading house in every case.

There are at least two reasons for this paring down of participants. Firstly, the state's desire to control things. It felt more comfortable with a single *asentista* than when working with several. Secondly, at the beginning of the eighteenth century, when the system was reorganised, the navy was very small and its needs could therefore be met by a single major merchant. This viewpoint, however, defendable at the start of the century, was adhered to too rigidly thereafter. The only exception was the galley squadron, which subsisted until the mid-century, also victualled by a single *asentista*, Pedro Astrearena, besides the general navy victualler. Neither was the general *asentista* responsible in general for colonial territories, which were victualled only at the point of departure, Cádiz. In the case of less perishable products attempts were at any rate made to ensure that the boarded foodstuff was enough for the round journey. As the century wore on, the local Hispano-American suppliers were boosted with the produce of the Thirteen Colonies, especially flour (Torres Sánchez 2010: 237). Taking on supplies in the Americas became particularly necessary when the ships had left Spain urgently with only makeshift supplies, as for example in 1740 (Baudot 2014: 105).

The single-victualler solution with a major merchant was therefore convenient for the government, as we have already seen, but exactly what did this convenience consist of? Probably the main reason was the complexity of the sailors' food rations, comprising a great variety of products, which moreover had to be properly prepared and packaged to keep for several months (Pérez Fernández-Turégano 2006: 107). As we have seen, Great Britain's choice was for the Victualling Board to perform all these tasks. This state office therefore took on all preparation tasks for the food bought from the contractors. This means the state that most vaunted the free-market option for obtaining its raw materials did tend thereafter to centralise the processing and packaging of the final foodstuff to be boarded.

In Spain, as in France, these processes depended too on the contractors and the state wished to receive the produce in a finished state ready for consumption. The organisational complexity of these operations called for a single hand on the rudder: Spain opted for the hand of a single *asentista*. On the ship the food was controlled both by an onboard victualling official called *maestre de raciones* and an onboard factor of the *asentista*, who looked out for conservation and consumption (Guzmán Raja 2006: 81). This complexity also favoured a certain inertia in these posts. In practice, when *asiento* renewal time came round, very few people came forward to replace the incumbent general *asentista*, probably because very few could match this *asentista*'s expertise built up during years of monopoly (Torres Sánchez 2010: 226).

The single-*asentista* policy for the navy was kicked off by Patiño, still superintendent general of the navy (Pulido Bueno 1998; Pérez Fernández-Turégano 2006). In 1719 he granted to Puche an across-the-board navy-victualling contract. Paradoxically, the same Patiño who would later be so keen to do away with tax farming procedures, now preferred one general navy victualling *asentista* and another one for the army, as we will see later. Puche's *asiento* was for three years. At the end of this term, in 1722, Norberto Arizcun, a prominent businessman linked to the mighty band of Navarre businessmen headed by Juan de Goyeneche, leaned on these business relations to undercut Puche and make with the *asiento* (Torres Sánchez 2010: 235).

Arizcun's *asiento* was also for three years. The new *asentista* would liaise only with the Navy Minister (*Secretario de Marina*) to establish annual needs. He would be shielded by a slew of privileges very similar to those of other *asentistas*. His particular perks included customs and local-tax exemptions (a total exemption kept up until 1767), the entitlement to sequestrate private means of transport and use state establishments for his activity, such as stores, furnaces and mills. He was asked to give preference to national products under an overarching mercantilist outlook. This was presumably possible for some time but we know that, at least in the second half of the century, the victualler had to buy in from abroad due to increasing needs and urgencies that sometimes proved too much for national production.

In 1725 Arizcun managed to renew his *asiento* for a five-year term and at a slightly lower price. Shortly afterwards he died and the *asiento* passed on to his nephew Miguel Arizcun. In 1730 Miguel had to stave off an attempt to bring navy victualling under direct state administration, as was done in this same year with army victualling. His best bargaining ploy was another price reduction, winning him another five-year term. In 1735 Arizcun managed to renew the *asiento* without another price reduction (Torres Sánchez 2010: 226, 243–45). The government now depended on the *asentista*, owing him over 17 million *reales* in the 1739 crisis (Ibáñez Molina 1986: 358). Upon Arizcun's death in 1741, the government, despite the wartime urgencies of that moment, waited for the company to choose a new manager. Finally, the post fell to Ambrosio del Garro, one of the company's directors and Arizcun's cousin. Garro had to overcome the opposition of the minister Campillo, who, like Patiño, would have preferred direct administration or an *asentista* creaming off less profit than the alleged earnings of the Arizcun family (Ibáñez Molina 1994: 58–59). But the government's debts with the company were huge. In his negotiations with the government Garro agreed to waive the customs-exemption privilege in return for setting off the value of these customs against the government's debt with the company. Garro got his way. Later, under Ensenada's watch, Garro managed to renew his *asiento* for a longer term and recoup the forfeited customs exemption. Key in these negotiations was another reduction in his asking price; even so, the supplier proved capable of coping with the continually increasing number of sailors and the growing complexity of the business (Torres Sánchez 2010: 250–54).

Worse problems were in the offing. Firstly, the scrapping of tax-farming arrangements. Like many other *asentistas* Garro had hitherto doubled up as tax farmer to be able to finance his raw material purchases and withstand the state's payment arrears. This second string to his bow was now removed. Secondly, Esquilache, arriving in Spain at the end of 1759, was to shake up the government's *asiento* policies. In the victualling arena Esquilache made Campillo's wish come true: if unable to bring in direct administration, he did manage to knock down the asking price considerably. In 1765, therefore, Simón de Aragorri, a prominent businessman with connections to the markets of northern Europe, undercut Garro and wrested the *asiento* from him. His idea was to offset the price reduction with a silver-exporting permit, which would undoubtedly stand him in good stead for his trading activities (Torres Sánchez 2010: 256–58).

But Aragorri proved unable to hold on for long. Three years later he negotiated an extension at a higher asking price, but he ended up dropping out of the contract. Enter the Arizcun company once more, in the person of Nicolás del Garro. Nicolás was the son of Ambrosio; he was also grandson of Miguel Arizcun since Ambrosio had married Arizcun's daughter. Nicolás del Garro thus came in for full inheritance of the house of Arizcun or Iturbieta[1]. The new *asiento* was signed in 1772, following the price-rising formula set by Aragorri's extension. In this case the hike was bigger, way above the price paid to the company in Ambrosio's last *asiento* up to 1765. The increase was reprised in the 1776 renewal. The new prices, at an all-time high, reflected not only the general inflation at the time but also the enlargement and greater complexity of the business itself, since the navy had continued to grow in size and the victuals demand with it. All these difficulties would then be further complicated when war broke out. Although *asiento* prices were held steady, the government had to support the *asentista* with advanced payments to finance the extraordinary victualling needs. But the produce supplied was worth more than the government's advanced payment, so its debt with Garro continued to rise, reaching 43.6 million *reales* by the end of the war.

The sheer size of this debt tended to lock the government into the *asiento* as the only way of paying it off. But the government's debt-payment policy changed at the end of the war. Under the influence of Cabarrús the newly created *Banco de San Carlos* ended up with the business, holding it under a monopoly regime with similar privileges to those enjoyed so long by Arizcun's company (Torres Sánchez 2010: 260–61).

Army victualling procedures in all countries followed a similar pattern to the one already seen with the navy. In all cases it was also a separate service run by different persons and organisations, albeit at times with overlapping tasks. Army provisioning procedures were simpler in terms of the products involved, almost always limited to grain and fodder; other foodstuffs were obtained by the armies themselves at regiment level and they also lived off the land. On the other hand, army suppliers had to deliver their products in very varied spots, always changing, whereas navy supply sites were fixed, usually the dockyards/*arsenales*/*arsenaux* themselves.

8.2 The contractor state and shipbuilding: the British experience

One of the stiffest challenges facing the contractor state was the construction and maintenance of many warships, some of them mighty vessels. The construction of a warship, especially a 70-gun ship of the line, (the usual gunpower by the second half of the eighteenth century) was one of the most complex and capital-intensive ventures of the time. To be truly efficient the process called for centralised production, which in turn entailed the organisation of a complex network of supply lines taking in a varied range of products, many of them far not only from the actual production site but even the country itself.

Shipyards in Spain were broken down into *astillero* (shipyard) and *arsenal* (fully-fledged state-run shipyard for naval warships and armaments), loosely comparable to the British distinction between merchant yard and royal dockyard or the French *chantier*/*arsenal* distinction. The traditional warship-building site had always been the *astillero*, an unenclosed shipbuilding site with provisional, wooden slipways. Many of these *astilleros* were never enlarged or increased in capacity. In time they were ousted by the much more complex *arsenal*. Although there was the classic precedent of the *Arsenale di Venezia* (Concina 1987), this larger-scale industrial concept of the shipyard was developed in seventeenth-century western Europe. They were fixed, spacious, enclosed sites set up on a permanent basis, favouring better organisation (Concina 1987: 12–13). *Arsenales* included the *astillero* as an essential component, knitted into the rest of the shipbuilding facilities. But a great variety of ship-maintenance work was also carried out in the *arsenal*, calling for a whole set of buildings, machines, stores, factories, etc. A specific feature of the *arsenal* was the dry dock for the perfection of ship- and hull-repair work. The two main reasons for the advent of these great shipbuilding and maintenance centres were the new navies' dual need to build more and better ships, on the one hand, and ensure their quick and efficient maintenance once built. The *arsenal*/dockyard, much more than the simple *astillero*/*chantier*/merchant yard, is the key element of a large and efficient war navy.

Astilleros might be publicly or privately owned and geared towards the construction of any type of craft; *arsenales*, almost by definition, were a government affair, "property of the king with facilities both for the maintenance and construction of warships" (McDougall 1982: 7). Furthermore, any of the *astillero* activities, including at times the construction of warships themselves, could be carried out by contractors, albeit under set standards and the control of the king's officials. The abovementioned scheme could be applied to any country; the difference resides in the moment the larger-scale royal dockyards began to be developed and organised in each country. England and France were running royal dockyards by the last third of the seventeenth century, the English ones being better equipped than the French (Rodger 2004: 301). Spain's *arsenales* were late on the scene; the country had been running good *astilleros* for some time but *arsenal* construction did not get underway until the War of Succession and they took some time to complete.

The development of the dockyard over the merchant yard, including shipbuilding, did not completely eliminate the latter. From the contractor-state point of view, in any case, it is interesting to note the degree of participation of private constructors in shipbuilding in general. In Great Britain, for example, private manufacturers, who worked in merchant yards, had been important beforehand (Rodger 2004: 188) and continued to exist during the whole period under study here; not only that, but when needs grew during war years, private shipbuilding grew in line. Without the efficiency of private shipbuilding the British navy's development might have been balked (Acerra and Zysberg 1997: 30). Merchant yards depended on an entrepreneur or company, which entered into a contract with the government for the construction of a given number of ships. They were numerous, smaller than royal dockyards and suffered from no important management problems (Rodger 2004: 298). Throughout the eighteenth century they were normally contracted for construction of small craft and even for smaller ships of the line. From 1763 this included 74-gun ships. For these ships the merchants were given a construction deadline of up to three years, with shorter terms for smaller ships. The government phased in payments on agreed instalments from the signing of the contract to the launching of the vessel (Morris 2011: 133–34). The development of the British royal dockyards, moreover, was partly spurred by the strategic change brought about by the growing importance of the Atlantic, as also occurred in France and Spain. The oldest ones, Woolwich, Chatham, Deptford and Sheerness, all lying on the Thames estuary to fend off the Dutch threat, were then joined by Portsmouth and Plymouth in the final years of the seventeenth century, once the Dutch threat had waned and the Atlantic theatre waxed, calling for a more westerly thrust (Acerra and Zysberg 1997: 29, 31).

Private shipbuilding posed the problem of quality. By the sixties, therefore, the merchant yards had been whittled down to the Thames and Medway rivers, a demarcated zone where it was easier for the royal officials to keep track of habitual entrepreneurs (such as Barnard, Dudman, Randall, Brent and Wells, working in the River Thames). But the navy's growth needs then tended to swell this geographical area, multiplying the number of private entrepreneurs. Merchant yards then grew up in the coastal zones of southern England, Devon and Cornwall, with prominent builders such as B. Tanner and R. Davy (Knight 2014: 365). The growth of private shipbuilders is clear: from 1688 to 1755, only 29 per cent of Royal Navy warships were of private construction; from 1756 to 1815 this proportion rose to 52 per cent (Morris 2011: 135). Over a shorter timeframe we find that the proportion grew most at the beginning of the nineteenth century, when merchant yards were more active than ever: from 1803 to 1815 they built 433 out of a total of 515 warships (Knight 2014: 359).

The qualms about the quality of contractor-built ships and some concomitant doubts about the uprightness of the entrepreneurs, remained throughout the whole period. But the private builders offered the government many advantages. One was the price. Private builders were cheaper, although this could work against the quality of the final product (Rodger 2004: 301). There were other advantages: the state's expenditure was put back in time; it saved the need of increasing the infrastructure of the royal dockyards and fewer workers were needed; dockyards were also spared a work overload (Wilkinson 2004: 101). But in any case, although doubts did remain about private shipbuilders, they had to be resorted to in many cases, especially when war was waging. As from 1804 it was increasingly argued that quantity and construction speed outweighed quality, even at the expense of a shorter life for the ships, simply on the grounds that so many ships were needed, especially frigates and smaller craft like brig-sloops and gun-brigs (Knight 2014: 361, 366).

Although private shipbuilders became more dependable and capable of building bigger vessels, the merchant yards could not cope with the construction of bigger ships (over 90 guns), so this was still reserved for the royal dockyards. The royal dockyard's increased ship-maintenance load during war years, especially the Napoleonic wars, also has to be factored into the picture, since this cramped their construction capacity. The upshot was that merchant yards built nearly five times more vessels than royal dockyards between 1803 and 1815, whereas the dockyards accounted for one-third of the tonnage (Knight 2014: 24, 367).

Quite apart from shipbuilding, dockyards proved to be essential for keeping the navy on a continual war footing. This called for a permanent supply of all necessary wherewithal: wood, iron, flax and hemp for sales and rigging, pulley blocks, pitch, tar, etc.; plus gunpowder arms and munition. If we then factor in the need of storing not only these products but also the foodstuffs supplied by the Victualling Board (Knight and Wilcox 2010), we find that the royal dockyards were not only a complex working environment but also a world of manufacture and storage, although the latter could be spread out along different spots of the British coast (Morris 2011: 144). The logistical and organisational problems were not only domestic. They extended near and far to other storage spots within Great Britain and to distant parts of Europe and the colonies where some of the necessary products came from.

The products were supplied by two methods: by contracts with merchants or by agents working on commission. The Navy Board drew up annual contracts for most of the dockyard's important consumables, especially imported products like wood, masts, pitch, tar and hemp (Morris 2011: 172). The private merchants involved were pretty constant from one contract to another, to be able to tap into their knowledge of the internal mechanisms of the mercantile and financial world. This expertise was essential for trading in difficult environments and coming up with huge amounts of this material at affordable prices. Procedures were honed throughout the century and great care was taken to keep the markets competitive. This system of "standing contractors" responded well to the fluctuating demand but it was not necessarily the cheapest option (Rodger 2004: 301). But the government no doubt found it convenient and reassuring to work with known merchants. Agents on commission, on the other hand, were normally turned to whenever market conditions prevented standing contractors from mustering sufficient supplies.

All these contracts could either be centralised in the Navy Board or set up by commissioners in the dockyards themselves. In either case the whole process was overseen by state organisations, from the merchant bid right through to the signing of the contract (Morris 2011: 172; Knight 2014: 23). They had to keep track of price fluctuations to discern the best time and terms to reach the definitive agreement. From then on, however, the task was taken on by the merchants themselves, who had to abide by the terms agreed and deliver the material on time.

Governments and merchants worked in tandem in many fields other than economic transactions (Bowen et al. 2013: 252). Their joint work was especially important when vital products only obtainable abroad proved hard to come by, such as hardwoods, mast timber and hemp from the Baltic in general and Russia in particular. In this case, not only did the merchants need to be trusted but their trade defended (Davey 2011). In other cases, it was the merchants' expertise and knowledge that bailed out the government. This occurred with the adoption of copper sheathing for hulls. The process had begun in 1778. It meant ships could sail more quickly but it did lead to electrolysis problems, which ended up rusting the bolts[2]. Enter Thomas Williams, the government's main contractor and an important industrialist known as the "Copper King". He developed a copper alloy to make the bolts just as tough as the previous metal bolts but less prone to react with the copper sheathing (Knight 2014: 35–36).

Another example of public-private collaboration came with the importation of products such as iron. It was the Navy Board that took on responsibility for iron imports, especially from Sweden but also from Spain (García Fernández 2006: 218, 313) and Russia. The iron was then handed over to private contractors to make the necessary parts for the ships and sell them under contract to the dockyards (Rodger 2004: 302).

Not everyone was in favour of this recourse to private contractors, especially because of the widespread cases of corruption and abuses (Bowen et al. 2013: 250) or simply the poorly run dockyards. This was not a new problem and could at times be recurrent (McDougall 1982: 52). The Admiralty had sometimes been prompted to take drastic measures like cuts and sackings to lower costs or to try and improve the organisation; this had a knock-on effect on contractors, with varied results (Rodger 2004: 300). At some moments corruption had gone just too far. This was certainly the view of Addington when he entered the government in 1801. Accusations of corruption against the former navy administration led to a suspension of all wood-purchase and shipbuilding contracts in merchant yards and a policy of saving and dismissals in the dockyards, creating a climate of doom and gloom (Rodger 2004: 478; Knight 2014: 215). In this particular case the peace ushered in by the Treaty of Amiens meant that the stymying of the country's shipbuilding did not have grave consequences. Nonetheless, the perception of contractors was to change. When war broke out anew, the only way of putting more ships on the sea was to turn back to private contractors. In 1804 many more contractors were therefore brought into the fold (Knight 2014: 223).

This joint working with private contractors by no means meant that the government or many critics were unaware of the importance of exerting much tighter government control over such a vital task as shipbuilding and maintenance. The contractors certainly played a crucial role from the supply point of view but not across the board. In fact, in many cases the government sought to wield direct control over supply or production procedures. The very management of dockyards as purely state enterprises was an explicit example of this trend, but there are many other cases of specific activities. Ongoing attempts to improve dockyard infrastructure were stepped up in the eighties with new wharfs and buildings (McDougall 1982: 121). Particularly important here was the refitting of dry docks, especially Plymouth's, so that ships of bigger draught could use them at any moment. If the dry dock was not very deep, the bigger ships could enter them only during the highest tides. These came round only every 15 days, so the obligatory downtime led to many maintenance delays, which could be crucial during any conflict (Knight 2014: 33–34).

In other cases, private participation was reduced or eliminated. A case in point is mooring ropes, hawsers and cables. For some time, these had been made in the dockyards, but in the eighties the need was felt to build a rope-house where the work could be concentrated. A new rope-house was built in Chatham, capable of turning out cables up to 900 feet long, the necessary length for anchoring a ship of the line. None of this ousted private supply lines completely, especially when needs grew in the nineties (Morris 2011: 181; Knight 2014: 33). Another example is pulley blocks. Marc Isambard Brunel, a French émigré in the nineties, had designed a new machine for making them. He offered it to the contractor working for the navy, a member of the Taylor family who had been working for the navy since 1759, who scorned Brunel's offer.

Walter Taylor had by then designed his own machine: it made smaller pulley blocks than former versions, with less friction, enabling ships to be sailed with a smaller crew, among other advantages. All this made British ships much more manoeuvrable, at least until the end of the century, when France implemented the system on its own ships (Rodger 2004: 302). Small wonder that the Taylors should look down on Brunel's invention. The Frenchman offered it directly to the Admiralty, which ordered 1,000 to be fitted in Portsmouth on a trial basis. Brunel's machine was found to work more quickly and to be more resistant, being made of iron. The project then took on so quickly that the former contractor was discharged. To increase production, however, an agreement had to be reached with a manufacturer to make more of Brunel's machines. These machines were then coupled up with steam engines. Portsmouth's output then became so big that it outstripped the capacity of any private manufacturer (Knight 2014: 376–78).

Metal processing factories were also set up in the dockyards, so the supply of copper sheets and bolts could be withdrawn from contractors. These measures were taken under the eye of the inspector general of naval works, Samuel Bentham, who firmly believed that dockyards could be so developed as to totally do away with private contractors. Paring dockyards' relations with the commercial world to the bone, with an equal and offsetting investment from the state, might be possible in times of peace. But war called for immediate growth fuelled by greater collaboration. Private participation, therefore, at its various levels, was still one of the keys to the success of the British navy, even though direct state presence was still advocated by many.

8.3 The strategic worries of France

Development of the French naval dockyards (*arsenaux*) was hemmed in both by strategic constraints and the characteristics of the coastline; not all sites were suitable for harbouring big ships. Toulon was kept on in the Mediterranean, on the strength of its good characteristics; on the Atlantic coastline, on the other hand, Brest had to be reinforced with Rochefort. Later on Lorient was also brought on stream when the *Compagnie des Indes* disappeared. The dockyards were backed up by other sites where smaller ships were made and provisioning bases like the Isle of Indret. This gave rise to a *bi-pôle* supply system: on the one hand, zones for storage and the manufacture of some products and, on the other, shipbuilding sites that served as backup to a naval dockyard (Acerra and Zysberg 1997: 25–27).

The king's *arsenaux* in France controlled the bulk of the shipbuilding activity, with very little leeway, apparently, for private participation. Private yards (*chantiers*) did not have the capacity for building ships of the line, barring the yard of the *Compagnie des Indes*, insofar as it could be classed as private (Rodger 2004: 301). Private contractors, moreover, participated only in the construction of smaller craft and frigates. They did so, above all, after the Seven Years' War, using private *chantiers*, sometimes requisitioned, in commercial ports like Bayonne, Bordeaux, Nantes and other smaller ones, sometimes privateering bases, such as St. Malo (Acerra and Zysberg 1997: 27–28; Cailleton 1999). Only on isolated occasions, such as during the American War, did private manufacture, albeit still small, add up to much.

As for the supply of raw materials, the most important were wood, iron and hemp. The navy consumed huge amounts of all of them, plus many more products, but this threesome accounted for 80 to 90 per cent of the total value, excluding cannons and victuals (Pritchard 2009: 160). From the years of Louis XIV and up to c. 1725, the method *à l'éconmie* held sway, especially in the crucial supply of wood. This involved direct participation by navy services, which procured the products, first reserving them with a preferential purchase right, and then transporting them to the dockyard. As from 1725, due to budget shortfalls and manufacturing cutbacks, the government turned increasingly to the system *à l'entreprise*, whereby the procurement of supplies and their transport to the dockyard was contracted with an entrepreneur (Pritchard 2009: 161; Plouviez 2014: 79–83).

When shipbuilding practices were overhauled as from 1748, the contractor option was increased and the contract-award system was also changed. Since the seventeenth century the normal bid-invitation procedure had been used, now to be replaced in practice by private contracting. The bid invitations had in any case been much less open than in Great Britain, due mainly to defective publicity procedures so few could get their bids in on time. Personal contracting was logically much more restrictive still.

The method certainly had some flaws: it encouraged favouritism, curbed competition and gave the entrepreneur widely criticised advantages (Pritchard 2009: 165). But personal contracts did not necessarily mean the chosen entrepreneur was unskilled or incompetent. The state in fact insisted on appropriate skill and quality levels on pain of rejecting the merchandise; this was just as big a goad as competition might have been. Competition, in any case, did lie in wait behind, with rivals queuing up for the government to change its contractor, quite a common occurrence by all accounts. For the state it was the quickest, most flexible method, offering security when the right person was found but allowing for rejection in the event of a poor service because the contracts were drawn up in light of the state's real needs. Moreover, if this method strayed from the provisions laid down in the Ordinance of 1689, this was because said ordinance catered for a supply of regional scope. The different market conditions in the eighteenth century called for a much wider trawl, not even limited to France but also international, so the ordinance was a yoke that had to be shrugged off (Plouviez 2014: 85–87).

At moments of particular urgency or scarcity, especially in the thirties and sixties, the private contracting policy followed the formula of *marchés généraux* (entrusting the bulk of supply to major companies) (Acerra and Zysberg 1997: 114). Contracts of this type were drawn up with a single entrepreneur for a relatively long term, up to six years, for different materials, to be delivered in various *arsenaux* at once (especially Brest and Rochefort, which were usually lumped together). In the last third of the century, on the other hand, the trend to was draw up simpler, shorter-term contracts (Plouviez 2014: 89), without backing down on the preference for major merchants.

The contractor was chosen after negotiations between the entrepreneur and representatives of the dockyard or ministry, depending on the former's location. The main eligibility criterion was wealth, i.e., the entrepreneur's capacity to shoulder contract risks. Other important factors were uprightness and a good reputation, so the pertinent enquiries were made to that effect. On some occasions small entrepreneurs were also chosen if considered dependable for the particular contract in question (Plouviez 2014: 114–17). For purchases abroad the navy relied on large international companies, often British; this was the case of wood purchases, especially for masts, in the British-dominated Baltic (Pourchasse 2012, 2013: 182–83). In the Mediterranean, on the other hand, France was able to get by with diplomatic arrangements more than elsewhere (Pourchasse 2012: 259; Plouviez 2014: 119).

In general, the French navy dealt with two types of entrepreneurs, the big and the small. The smaller ones were often merchants trading close to the *arsenaux* – such as nearby woodland owners, sailcloth factories, ironworks – with whom it was easy to make arrangements for top-up or emergency supplies. The bigger contracts, however, were negotiated with major entrepreneurs capable of dealing with the *marchés généraux*, involving huge amounts of material. The small entrepreneurs entered into short-term contracts of one or two years, with a rapid turnover, normally because they could not cope with the state's payment arrears and irregularities (Pritchard 2009: 162). The major entrepreneurs' contracts were for much bigger amounts and longer terms, at times up to seven years. They were therefore able to hang on longer, though many did also go to the wall after two or three decades of contracts, again due to fitful payments (Plouviez 2014: 120–23, 137).

The *marchés généraux* were a big opportunity for major entrepreneurs, some of whom prospered under navy contracts, although these same contracts often spelled ruin for others. The most characteristic example is the Babaud de la Chaussade family, especially Jean and Pierre, French merchants trading initially in wood and then in iron. Its members held a continual string of contracts from 1728 to 1760. In the end Pierre was ruined by the demands of the navy ministry; among other things payment arrears prevented him from keeping up the network of companies that had grown up under the aegis of the many contracts (Pritchard 2009: 168–70; Plouviez 2014: 120, 146, 211). Other suppliers of iron, big or small, such as Claude Leblanc or Pierre Aguillon, suffered a similar fate.

In 1746 a royal sailcloth factory was set up in Darentel near Brest, run first by Vallet de la Touche and then by J.-F. Le Boucher. The latter turned out to be a fraudster. The failure of the Darentel factory together with increasing needs forced the state to fall back more on private manufacturers, like the Deshayes family in the forties and fifties and, later on, merchants and financiers like Dufour or Bomburg (Pritchard 2009: 173; Plouviez 2014: 145–46, 268). But the *arsenaux* did not give up on their idea of running their own sailcloth factories, sometimes managed by the government and sometimes by private merchants. Other important factories were also set up in the *arsenaux*, especially rope factories like the most famous one of Rochefort, *La Corderie*, built in 1667 (Woronoff 1998: 155; Plouviez 2014: 290).

8.4 New arrangements for supplying the Spanish navy

In Spain several *astilleros* were up and running in about 1700. At home these included Guarnizo and Santoña in Santander; San Sebastián and Pasajes in Guipúzcoa, and San Feliú de Guixols in Barcelona, where Alberoni prepared the ships for his revisionist policy of the Treaty of Utrecht (Pulido Bueno 1998: 134), or Barcelona itself for Mediterranean galleys. Overseas in the colonies there were other *astilleros* of diverse importance, almost all of them short-lived and low key. The only one of any consideration was the Havana shipyard (Serrano Álvarez 2008). Havana accounted for much of the shipbuilding activity, largely on the strength of the good quality of American wood. Unlike other countries Spain preferred to harness this wood *in situ* and ship to Cuba the rest of the necessary wherewithal. It was the only other country besides Portugal that built some of its ships in the Americas (Merino Navarro 1981a: 185).

The Spanish navy was down on its uppers at the beginning of the eighteenth century, but after 1713 shipbuilding was reactivated by harnessing existing facilities, especially the Cantabrian yards (Merino Navarro 1986: 87, 95–97; Valdez-Bubnov 2011: 127). It was during the eighteenth century that shipbuilding switched from the *astilleros* to the new *arsenales*, the former then gradually petering out. The first sign of change came in 1717 when a start was made on La Carraca, the future *arsenal* of Cádiz (Quintero González 2000: 61–64); in any case the changeover to *arsenales* was a slow process.

In 1726 the Maritime Departments were set up: Ferrol, Cádiz and Cartagena. Each would run its own *arsenal*, with its corresponding *astillero*. Nonetheless, although the Departments' administrative work did get underway fairly quickly, the construction of the new *arsenales* dragged on for some time: they were not fully up and running until 1750. Meanwhile, work was also underway in existing *astilleros*: until 1726 activity was concentrated in Guarnizo and the burgeoning yard of Havana. Guarnizo, had grown to have four slipways by the middle of the century, becoming Cantabria's most important *astillero* (Castanedo Galán 1993: 53–61) and the most active in Spain by about 1730. Guarnizo and Havana between them accounted for the bulk of the ships made in the first half of the century. Before 1750 the *astilleros* of the new *arsenales*, La Carraca (Cádiz) and Ferrol, built only one ship. After 1750, by contrast, with the *arsenales* now fully operational, their activity was much brisker. Ferrol replaced Guarnizo, barring one-off exceptions; fewer ships were built in Cartagena and even fewer in Cádiz. Their main functions were storage and squadron maintenance; activity grew, however, in Havana, which became Spain's most prolific shipbuilding *arsenal* in the eighteenth century.

8.4.1 Private asentistas and king's dockyards in Spain and overseas

In Spain, unlike in France, there was significant private participation in shipbuilding, even though the activity occurred in the king's dockyard. *Asentistas* represented a deep-seated, long-standing option in Spain (Goodman 2001: 180; Valdez-Bubnov 2011: 15, 92). Work under *asientos* continued in the Cantabrian *astilleros*, and *asientos* were also maintained for the ships built in the Mediterranean for Alberoni's expeditions in 1717–18 (Valdez-Bubnov 2011: 164). Under the *asiento* system the king provided the shipyard facilities and slipways together with the constructor, who then took charge of construction under established rules and standards. The *asentista* saw to the procurement of all materials and manual labour, hired the skilled labour and managed the whole construction procedure (Merino Navarro 1981a: 344).

Patiño stood out against the *asiento* system, and the new *arsenales* were designed in nearly all aspects to favour direct administration but this took some time to be brought in. Guarnizo soldiered on with the *asiento* system, defended by

Gaztañeta, at least until the advent of Campillo as superintendent in the twenties (Valdez-Bubnov 2011: 202, 217, 227).

The *asiento* system hung on doggedly. In Ferrol an *asentista*-control system was set up in an *asiento* signed in 1737. This *asiento* reflected the increasing hold of the Navy Minister over the *asentista* (Valdez-Bubnov 2011: 259). The direct administration system would then be developed in Ferrol, an *arsenal* designed to replace Guarnizo. Ensenada, however, revived this *astillero* and turned anew to private constructors. Witness the *asientos* of Fernández de Isla in the fifties. Isla was already a known wood *asentista* when he took charge of several ships of the line in 1752 (Maiso González 1990: 235, 314).

The ships in Fernández de Isla's *asiento* were built under the English method, so some adaptations had to be made to the old *astillero*, largely inactive in previous years. Guarnizo would see another change, too. In 1765 the constructor Gautier brought in the French method, so some tweaks had to be made to the ships still being built under the *asiento* signed with Zubiría in 1763. Activity dragged on until 1769, when the last ship built there in the eighteenth century was launched (Mercapide 1981: 75, 80). Afterwards Gautier was able to enforce the French system, not only in technical aspects but also administrative aspects, i.e., direct administration. Under this method the *asentista* bought the materials but then handed them over to the *arsenal*, whereupon the navy authority took on all arrangements, shipbuilding included.

Havana kept on the *asiento* system for longer, albeit in an idiosyncratic manner, for the constructors were functionaries and *asentistas* at the same time. The activity of this yard, starting out as an *astillero* and then turned into an *arsenal*, began to grow at least from 1710 (Serrano Álvarez 2008: 47). Up to 1750 there was certainly no consensus about the fittingness of promoting Havana; there were also management problems due to rivalry between three would-be constructors and wrangles between them and the political authorities. Despite these difficulties, construction did continue, money permitting, on a needs-be basis. Patiño's watch saw the triumph of Juan de Acosta, a wealthy local who doubled up as constructor and *asentista*. Acosta followed the rules of Gaztañeta, albeit with some licence.

Ensenada also plumped for Havana as from 1741. But the times of Acosta had gone and the new-era *asiento* fell to the recently created *Compañía de La Habana*. This company took on the whole *astillero* management, making it Spain's most prolific shipyard in the forties (Serrano Álvarez 2008: 85–87). The *astillero* also had a heavy workload of repair and general maintenance of the Caribbean squadrons; this involved a hefty expenditure, which was probably not properly calculated beforehand. The company was also affected by the aftermath of the 1739 bankruptcy and the crippling expense of the wars against England and Italy. The crown fell behind on its payments to the company and it ended up dropping out of the *asiento*, which came to an end in 1750 (Gárate Ojanguren 1993: 65; Serrano Álvarez 2008: 94).

In the sixties, with the *arsenales* now up and running and the French system established, the direct-administration shipbuilding system was enforced. But there were still some exceptions, not only the aforementioned *asientos* still underway in Guarnizo, which would be the last ones there, but also the *asientos* with various Italian shipbuilding contractors in Cartagena (Valdez-Bubnov 2011: 310, 317). Little by little Gautier's system won out in the *arsenales* at home during the seventies and also during the American War. It was not brought in without some discussion, however; nor without a shower of new *asiento* bids, all rejected. The same method would be continued by Gautier's successor, Romero Fernández de Landa (Valdez-Bubnov 2011: 344–47).

Direct administration took in a wide range of fields and implied the predominance of the General Navy Corps (*Cuerpo General de la Marina*) (Merino Navarro 1981a: 45), whereby only the procurement of supplies was entrusted to private *asentistas*, but this labour was reduced to a mere appendage of the shipbuilding process. In other words, private initiative came under the yoke of a militarised state bureaucracy, albeit efficient in general, at least until the end of the century (Merino Navarro 1981a: 46; Valdez-Bubnov 2011: 346). Supplies of the basic materials also tended to be centralised. Until then each particular product had been dealt with by *asentistas* specialising in each type of material. As from 1784, however, many of these products (Baltic wood, iron and nails, victuals) were awarded to a single, big *asentista*, the *Banco de San Carlos*.

This represented a switch to the model of choosing one major company to replace a clutch of smaller *asentistas*. In some ways it resembles the *marchés généraux* system in France, whereby a few big entrepreneurs or companies were favoured and promoted. It also follows in the line of the general victualling procedure we have already seen, under which the Spanish state tried to pare down the number of *asentistas* it had to deal with, ensuring at the same time that it was doing business with a strong, dependable contractor. It turned out to be wrong on this score. The *Banco de San Carlos* ran into unforeseen problems, so these same *asientos* passed on in 1788 to the *Cinco Gremios Mayores* de Madrid, considered to be a more reliable option among other reasons because it was a mercantile company rather than a bank (Valdez-Bubnov 2011: 361, 413; Torres Sánchez 2014: 280).

Even though the direct-administration shipbuilding system had won the day, the jury was still out on its appropriateness during the eighties. There seemed to be a consensus that it was dearer than an *asiento*-based arrangement. But two factors overrode this consideration. Firstly, at some moments it proved difficult to find private entrepreneurs ready to come forward for the construction of a ship of the line, probably because previous policies had ousted private initiative from this business. Secondly, the navy authority valued other aspects more highly than price. Private agents might have been a cheaper option but many pundits considered that quality suffered as a result and it also hindered the state's desire of wielding some control over the whole shipbuilding process. Spain too staged the same quantity-quality debate we have already seen in Great Britain, boiling down in the end to an *asiento*-administration dilemma. This debate, raging fiercely since the sixties, did not end until 1792, when the Navy Minister plumped definitively for direct administration. This meant an official rubber stamping of the method that had been in operation in general for some time and would now be maintained throughout the whole nineties (Valdez-Bubnov 2011: 364, 420–22).

In Havana, in any case, the lack of money left no other option than to give greater rein to private entrepreneurs. It was the private agents who financed ship construction, so the whole system to some extent depended on them. There was even the odd private shipbuilding *asiento* and other proposals from private agents for the same purpose. Nonetheless, direct control and militarisation won out in the end in Havana too, where the *asiento* system also came in for a fair amount of flak (Valdez-Bubnov 2011: 372, 382, 420).

8.4.2 Between asiento and administration in key naval supplies

As regards naval supplies, there was the same *asiento*-administration debate. In nearly all cases we find the same desire of centralisation clashing with various difficulties, such as the price or the scattered supply lines. What tended to carry the day in the end was the particular shibboleth of the minister in post at the time. The general picture, however, was an acceptance of *asientos* in the first half of the century, albeit on the understanding that the *asentistas'* price should be bargained down as low as possible (Uztáriz 1968: 220–21). Patiño was against the *asiento* in general, but his *arsenal* system was dragging its feet. Ensenada, for his part, preferred *asentistas*. This minister, who has gone down in history as a Francophile, here showed himself to be more in tune with the British: ousting private agents from the tax-farming arrangements but keeping them in the *asientos* in the case of the navy. In the second half of the century, on the other hand, following Esquilache's lead and the more pro-French bent of Charles III, direct administration was brought in wherever possible.

Pragmatism still ruled however, whenever supplies were urgently needed. Take wood, for example. Like France Spain had enough wood at home and in the Americas to make imports only a one-off recourse here and there (Merino Navarro 1981a: 186). Felling operations seem to have been organised directly by navy officials, both in Spain and in the Americas. At times, however, there was no other option than to call in private agents when urgencies overwhelmed the state's supply capacities or for carrying out special programmes. Since the start of the century there had been a system of navy commissioners such as Jacinto Navarrete in Santander, who organised the felling arrangements and chose the best storage sites. As regards contracts with private agents, one of the most interesting was the aforementioned Isla, a major Cantabrian businessman, who not only felled timber in Santander but also imported it from the Baltic through the offices of his partner Gil de Meester (Merino Navarro 1981a: 193–94).

Although in general felling operations were organised by navy officials, the state still had to fall back on private merchants – lumberjack companies – to carry them out, also to mend paths, to provide overland transport and, on occasions, sea transport to the established destination. Ships were hired for this purpose, such as the bustling traffic between Santander and Ferrol, for example, or *asientos* were entered into, like the one with the Meester family, who took on the transport of wood from Catalonia and the East Coast to Cartagena *arsenal* (Merino Navarro 1981a: 212).

The purchase system seemed to depend on the particular site in each case. In Cantabria in the north and Sierra de Segura in the south official commissions were the chosen system, whereas in Navarre, in 1766, wood purchases were awarded to *Compañía de Caracas* in a 15-year *asiento* up to 1782. The destination was Ferrol. The amount involved was not large, but it came out cheap and proved convenient for the navy, allowing it to dip into reserves to meet its needs just when wood was running short elsewhere (Merino Navarro 1981a: 216–19, 228; Gárate Ojanguren 1990: 542–44). The scarcity of nearby timber meant it had to be felled further and further away, increasing the cost. This prompted the government to exploit the wood resources of Asturias from the sixties onwards, or, later, inland woodland from Soria or Burgos, in all cases under *asientos* (Merino Navarro 1981a: 235, 250–53).

Overseas wood was normally procured from foreign *asentistas*, but not always; some Spanish *asentistas* were used too. From the mid-century Baltic planking timber for all *arsenales* was commissioned from merchants like Gil de Meester, the Soto family from Cádiz or Retortillo, a well-known Madrid financier. Sundry *asentistas* also bought Italian wood (Merino Navarro 1981a: 215, 221). Masts too, barring a few exceptions, arrived by *asiento*. Some were procured from within Spain but most were bought from northern Europe by mediation of the Dutch market: the Meesters, Soto, Retortillo, Chone or Maracci are names that often feature in the *asientos* of the second half of the century until 1782. Attempts were then made to procure supplies from Russia by direct administration (Merino Navarro 1981a: 262).

Pitch is another good example of the navy's supply problems and the solutions involving private businessmen. From the end of the seventeenth century pitch had been obtained by *asiento*, such as the contract signed with D. Vanheden in 1697, which would then pass on in 1703 to Juan de Goyeneche, who then held it at least up to 1723 (Aquerreta 2001a: 102–04). This pitch came at a very high price from the Catalonian Pyrenees, Spain's main production site. In the thirties the navy spread its net further to take in France and northern Europe, obtaining it at lower prices, as shown by the 12-year *asiento* signed in 1742 with Catalan *asentistas*. Meanwhile, in 1750, the intendent of Cádiz, Gerbaut, managed to buy in Swedish pitch, also at low prices. A new *asiento* in 1757, with Santibáñez of Cádiz, was signed at an even lower price (Merino Navarro 1981a: 282–83).

Asentistas turned above all to foreign pitch, especially from northern Europe, via French ports like Bayonne, but they were also asked to continue buying it from Tortosa, Spain's main production site. The product had to be delivered to all the *arsenales*. The main problem was to ensure supply; the next concern was the price paid and lastly came the desire for a home supply. But the navy's dependence on *asentistas* made it feel awkward so it decided to set up its own pitch factory. The first project got underway in 1758 in Castril, in the Sierra de Segura within the province of Granada. The success of the project prompted the navy to extend the direct production system. In 1770 the navy took over management of the Tortosa factory. In 1773, however, supplies run short, so the Ferrol *arsenal* was allowed to enter into a private *asiento* with Felipe Chone. Ferrol turned out to be a decisive *arsenal* because pitch was also sent from there to Havana (Merino Navarro 1981a: 284).

After the war with Great Britain and the consequent price rise (Hamilton 1988: 195–96), the navy decided to increase its pitch factories. The chosen site now was Quintanar de la Sierra in the province of Burgos, where a start was made on making furnaces in 1786. The project was a resounding success, so much so that there was even overproduction by the end of the year and the navy had to sell some off to private parties. But this was exceptional. It was difficult to find workers for the furnaces of Quitanar, so the factory fell into decline. Oddly enough, the selfsame thing happened in Tortosa: local people preferred to work in agriculture, even though they were offered incentives in the form of privileges. This situation, moreover, coincided with the shipbuilding crisis of the nineties, so the pitch factories were no longer as necessary as before. The low-key demand could now be met by a private *asiento* signed in 1805 (Merino Navarro 1981a: 285–86).

We know something more about the problems posed by the supply of hemp. This was another essential product, used for making sailcloth and even more so, apparently, for rigging, both the manufacture and maintenance thereof (Merino Navarro 1981a: 269). Apart from gauging how abundant the raw material was (Uztáriz 1968: 216), we are also interested here in the Spanish navy's supply policy for this product. During the first half of the century *asentistas* held sway, buying most of the supply in Spain. The *asientos* followed quickly on from each other, often overlapping in time, simply because the procurement was carried out separately by each *arsenal* (Díaz Ordóñez 2009: 25). Each *arsenal* therefore had its own supply zone: Cádiz tapped into the hemp of Granada; Cartagena drew on Valencia, Catalonia and Italy. Ferrol posed the biggest problems due to its distance from the production sites. Unsuccessful attempts were made to grow hemp as a crop in Galicia. Ferrol then turned to Aragón and Navarre and was also the *arsenal* drawing most heavily on Baltic sources (Merino Navarro 1981a: 273), a longstanding tradition (Sanz Ayán 1992).

Just as motley as the supply area was the origin of the *asentistas*: Flemish merchants trading in Spain since the end of the seventeenth century, like A. Roo and B. Kiel (Enciso Recio 1963), tax farmers and financiers, like J. de Goyeneche and company, foreigners like the Englishman Burnaby, or Barcelona's cordage guilds, very actively engaged in fitting out the ships of the Mediterranean campaign in the twenties and thirties (Díaz Ordóñez 2009: 195). The contracts signed with these *asentistas* are similar, and none of them, least of all the last in the series, managed to guarantee the navy a sure and affordable supply. This seems to have been achieved at last in the *asiento* signed with the Basoras in 1733. Coming from Barcelona's cordage guild, these people had held contracts before and played an essential part in a moment of pressing need at the start of the Italian campaigns and the corresponding preparation of squadrons in several Spanish ports (González Enciso 2014).

The Basora contracts, which would continue until 1740, fell foul in the end of the mercantilist zeitgeist of the time. The state, intervening in the market in its own benefit, had tended to give its *asentistas* more privileges (Torres Sánchez 2002a).

At first it had privileged the Basoras over and above the former guilds, but then it turned to privileged companies. The method is well known. While the state tried to drive down the suppliers' asking price, it also shielded the current *asentista* with a growing slew of privileges. From 1738 to 1749 both the *Compañía Guipuzcoana de Caracas* and the *Compañía de La Habana*, which were already running other crown businesses, took on the supply of the navy's rigging and sailcloth. The main goad was Havana's growing rigging need, calling for an *asentista* capable of drumming up supplies in European Markets. The rest of these companies' crown business, especially of the *Compañía Guipuzcoana*, suggested they would be a good option for increasing Cuban supply and making it more responsive to demand (Díaz Ordóñez 2009: 375). The *Compañía de La Habana* also took on procurement and transportation of the goods needed in Cuba when the company took over management of the Havana *arsenal* (Díaz Ordóñez 2009: 408).

As all the above shows the navy never turned its back on private *asentistas*, even striving to make them more solvent and efficient, with a greater mercantile and financial capacity and bolstered by connections abroad. Along the same lines it was also making an effort to modernise the supply of rigging, albeit without breaking the mould of mercantilist ideas and privileges. Results, however, still fell short of requirements and the navy had to take other measures, especially in times of war, to boost the supply of rigging in the Americas. To do so it turned back to private, one-off contracts, sometimes with foreign merchants to obtain the product in French ports where the hemp continued to arrive from the north via Holland (Díaz Ordóñez 2009: 410–19). At times navy officials in the Americas bought it directly in markets of the North American colonies, after failure of attempts to grow the crop in the Spanish colonies (Serrera Contreras 1974; Merino Navarro 1981a: 275).

During the War of Jenkin's Ear, the navy looked for a powerful and specialist group to boost its supply. It ended up finding one in 1741 in the *Compañía del Asiento de Jarcias*, a group of Barcelona merchants and industrialists who pulled off a juicy *asiento*. The group's trading capacity was huge. It had correspondents in Spain and abroad; it could muster the raw materials, rigging and pitch (the two usually went together) or even make its own rigging in factories it ran in Barcelona, Cartagena and Cádiz; it also had fingers in other pies such as masts and spars, shipbuilding and maritime insurance (Díaz Ordóñez 2009: 434). By the end of the *asiento* term, the group was ready to form a great privilege-shrouded company, the *Real Compañía de Comercio de Barcelona*, set up in 1756 for trade with the Americas (Oliva Melgar 1987).

Up to 1750, therefore, there were two phases. One we might dub inheritance of the modus operandi of the seventeenth century; another, kicking off in the forties, especially after the Navy Ordinances of 1748, represented an attempt to rationalise many aspects of the navy, *asientos* included, fleshing out a model in which crown interests were more clearly defined (Merino Navarro 1981a: 19; Díaz Ordóñez 2009: 619). But the mercantilist mindset of the time pleaded more state control over such an important material as hemp; this therefore ushered in a third phase in which, without eschewing *asientos* completely, for they were still necessary, an attempt was made to pass on to direct supply lines by setting up a royal rigging and sailcloth factory.

This phase also involved the participation of some private parties, i.e. rigging and sailcloth manufacturers trading in concentrated, partially mechanised firms according to an industrial model that was spreading around Spain, especially in the last third of the eighteenth century (González Enciso 1980: 155). Cases in point in the hemp sector were the factories of Cervera del Río Alhama (Soria), of Estepa (Seville) or of Gómez Moreno in Granada. But it was above all the navy that struck down this path with the aim even of ousting private traders by setting up its own factories in the *arsenales*, beginning with Cartagena. After 1749, with Ensenada's wholehearted support, the *arsenal* made significant headway: a wharf, stores, workshops, cordage factory, artillery depot and the *astillero* integrated into the whole set (Merino Navarro 1984: 25–26). But the work was slowed up by terrain difficulties, water infiltration and other snags (Pérez-Crespo 1992: 48–51). In Cádiz the rigging factories were set up in Puente de Zuazo and Puerto Real but an important cordage factory was set up within the *arsenal*. The factory had originally been called for by Gerbaut in 1758 but work did not actually begin until 1775 due to lack of money, finishing two years later in 1777 (Quintero González 2003). After this the *arsenal* was deemed to be complete.

In Ferrol ropes, cables and hawsers were bought from the private factories of Sada, with the navy keeping a close eye on quality. In 1763, due to fears of an English attack, manufacture was temporarily moved inside the *arsenal*. In subsequent years, in any case, the preference switched back to *asientos*, and the construction of a special building was de trop. In some ways Ferrol was ahead of its time, insofar as it did not set up a cordage factory like the others. Not long afterwards, in 1803, a report from the navy ministry mooted scrapping of the rigging and cordage factories in the *arsenales*, "in the sure conviction that it should never fall to Your Majesty to be a manufacturer or craftsman" (Merino Navarro 1981a: 277). Quite clearly another change was in the air.

In all likelihood this conclusion had been drawn due to the failure of the former system. The change to navy factory supply, in the opinion of those in charge, called for a control over national hemp harvests. The factories could not prosper without buying up hemp in bulk at a good price. According to the pundits of the time, this in turn would be impossible without control over the farmers and an exclusive purchasing policy. The navy deployed a contingent of commissioners throughout the cultivation zone but it ran into considerable difficulties and resistance from farmers loath to sell off their whole output at bargain prices (Merino Navarro 1975). They also wanted payment in cash since they were all small farmers with no easy access to urban financial markets. Neither was the quality of all buyable hemp guaranteed. The whole system of direct purchase from the farmers by commissioners turned out to be a pipe dream due to the failure to take proper account of market conditions (Torres Sánchez 2012b: 328–31).

The upshot of all this was an incapacity of harnessing the national production of hemp properly, and a consequent need of buying it in from abroad, in particular the Baltic. Needs were still soaring so attempts were made to bring in a merchant capable of mustering large amounts. The choice fell on Felipe Chone, already known to the navy from other *asientos*. In 1767 he was given an important hemp *asiento* (Torres Sánchez 2012b: 334).

According to the habitual practice at this time, the government, well aware of the *asentista*'s crucial role, tended to bolster him with important tax privileges. From 1774, in light of the likelihood of increasing needs in a sabre-rattling atmosphere, the business was strengthened by bringing in Miguel Soto, Conde de Clonard, a Cádiz merchant who also had important mercantile relations with the navy. Both merchants were given economic aid to ensure they could meet their remit; in these years they therefore enjoyed a *de facto* monopoly over Baltic supplies. Nonetheless, the difficulties stoked up by the war, including British control of the Baltic market (Pourchasse 2012), caused the *asentistas* to drop out of the business in 1780. The government's solution to this problem was to try to set up direct diplomatic contacts with Baltic merchants like Pedro Normande of St. Petersburg, to procure the yearned-for hemp. (Torres Sánchez 2012b: 339–40, 341–42). Once more, the government showed a pragmatic turn of mind when looking for solutions. Indeed, their actual practices flouted their own mercantilist tenets, because hemp continued to be bought mainly in the Baltic rather than Spain.

Notes

1 This business house also went by the name of Iturbieta, since the founder, Norberto Arizcun, had been granted the title of Marqués de Iturbieta shortly before dying in 1741, the title then passing on to his heirs.
2 The iron of the bolts reacted with the copper in a saline environment and ended up rusting away.

9 Arms provisioning and the contractor state

Getting the ships on the sea was not the end of the story; the men had to be able to fight as well. The contractor state had to handle the provision of arms, munitions and gunpowder. This was a varied clutch of products involving very different production systems, meaning that the procurement processes were different, too. A common denominator in all these products, however, is that they all had to be fabricated, so a distinction has to be made between the manufacturer, supplier and purchaser. The purchaser was always the state; this stands to reason, but the supplier and manufacturer might well be different; and the state itself could become a manufacturer, too.

9.1 The king's powder

Take the case of gunpowder. In Great Britain, for example, although it was normally made in private factories, the government did buy its own gunpowder factory in 1759 in Faversham (West 1991: 149–66, 197). The Board of Ordnance's only responsibility was to lay down the quality standards for the gunpowder received (Morris 2011: 194); this meant rejecting some batches as substandard but the same went for Faversham gunpowder before the state takeover. This rejection problem was perhaps the reason for the opinion held by some in the eighties that the factory should be sold off, on the grounds that privately procured gunpowder was higher quality. This measure was not taken in the end because experiments made in the Royal Laboratory managed to improve the quality of British gunpowder; in 1789, moreover, the state bought the private factory of Waltham Abbey (Knight 2014: 44–45). The Royal Laboratory, set up in Woolwich, continued to quality-check all gunpowder and also experimented with quality innovations at the end of the century (Morris 2011: 217; Knight 2014: 371).

In Spain the king also set up government-run gunpowder factories, as had been habitual since the sixteenth century (Jiménez Estrella 2010); nonetheless, *asiento*-based supply with private parties always loomed large in the general picture, since royal production was meagre. In the eighteenth century business was usually done with a single *asentista*. There are records, for example, of the *asientos* of Miguel Aldecoa, one in force in 1719 and another agreed in 1727. Under the first, the *asentista* undertook to deliver 11,000 *quintales* of gunpowder a year.

This amount must have fallen short of real needs because he was asked for an additional 4,000 *quintales* in this same year of 1719[1]. The contract ran into supply difficulties because there were constant complaints of shortfalls, not only in times of peace or pre-war sabre-rattling, as in 1735 (Villar Ortiz 1988: 57), but also during open war as in 1740. In the forties there were also other problems, such as the high risk of transporting gunpowder in war conditions or, above all, economic difficulties that led to payment arrears by the state[2].

The Spanish monarchy also made gunpowder in New Spain, an activity set up back in the sixteenth century. The gunpowder produced, however, was not always of good quality; this problem came to a head in 1752[3]. The manufacture and provision of gunpowder in New Spain was, at the same time, a farmed-out tax and supply contract. The tax was levied on private consumption, a market cornered by the state (*estanco*) since gunpowder could be bought only from the *asentista*. The *asentista* paid a sum for the farmed out tax and delivered the contracted amount of gunpowder for state supply. Attempts were made from the mid-century onwards to bring both legs of this arrangement into direct administration but it was not until Gálvez at last enforced direct administration in 1767 that *asientos* fell out the picture (Villar Ortiz 1988: 59–69).

This was the response to a real problem: i.e. the low ratio of king's gunpowder in the total supply. Back home in Spain itself much the same occurred; in 1760, for example, only 23 per cent of saltpetre was made in the king's factory, the remaining 77 per cent being produced in private factories (García Torralba 2010: 572–73). The change to direct administration in New Spain, however, did not solve the problems. Witness the fact that in 1781 massive private purchases had to be made to offset the fall in official output (Núñez Torrado 2002). This occurred at the same time as significant contracts with strong *asentistas* were being entered into in Spain, such as Cabarrús and Lalanne in 1779 or Gil de Meester in 1776 and in 1780 (Torres Sánchez 2000). The king's gunpowder was still largely a matter of *asentistas*.

The same happened with other products made in scattered workshops, such as the uniforms of the armed forces in Spain. These uniforms were made in various textile factories spread out among Spain's traditional textile production zones; the state itself, however, did business with a single *asentista*, an entrepreneur-financier who coordinated the supply lines (Solbes Ferri 2012, 2013). Here there were no royal factories. The system was kept up throughout the whole century even though several ministers mooted a change to direct administration. This was attempted at some moments, unsuccessfully, as with the case of victualling arrangements.

9.2 Small arms: the kingdom of craftsmen

Turning our attention to weapons, we find that another group of products that remained in the hands of *asentistas* was small firearms, pistols and muskets. The supply arrangements here were very similar across the board in all countries, based on low-tech, craftsmen-based manufacture. No significant changes were brought in until the nineties, with the American and Austrian models (Black 1994: 53–54;

Knight 2014: 47). In Great Britain the king did come to organise his own factories in this sector, albeit tardily. Meanwhile the Board of Ordnance kept a close eye on arms manufacture as from 1715 (Bowen 1998: 66).

In general, small arms were made piecemeal (barrels, locks, knapping, for example) in separate workshops where each craftsman specialised in each part. Even the assembly itself could be done by different people, some to fit the butt, others for the final finish. All these tasks were still being done by hand in the eighteenth century. It was the rich, market-savvy merchant-manufacturers who coordinated the contracts with the government. These merchants also participated in some parts of the manufacturing process, especially the final assembly; they also ran testing workshops to make sure the arms worked properly before marketing them (Glover 1963: 47–48).

This system, by its own nature, limited output. Indeed, the only way of upping production was to increase the number of workers; Great Britain, nonetheless, produced huge amounts of small arms and greatly boosted its industry. Oddly enough this growth was driven not only by national demand but also from abroad; this proved to be a great help for the craftsmen involved. In other types of supply the British Treasury was usually punctual with its payment obligations; the small arms merchants, on the contrary, kept up a continual wail of complaints throughout the nineties about arrears and defaults, many of the craftsmen eventually being forced to the wall.

The solution was to increase production to supply the armed forces of other countries too. In some cases, this raised no problem. Portugal or Spain, for example, were allies during the revolutionary wars. But a curious case cropped up in 1792 when war with Austria broke out, whereupon France ordered arms from Birmingham manufacturers. When Great Britain joined the war the weapons already manufactured could no longer be delivered. The Board of Ordnance did not want to take them on because they had been made to suit French specifications and hence were no good for the British army. In the end the manufacturers did manage to sell their arms to the Treasury for some special expeditions (Glover 1963: 48).

The combination of administrative disorderliness and the need of increasing output prompted the state to get more involved in the manufacture of small arms. In the first years of the nineteenth century "state and contractor combined to speed up production". Among other measures, in 1804 an office of the Ordnance Board was set up in Birmingham, the area where most contracts were signed, to carry out tests there and correct any manufacturing defects *in situ*. Afterwards the Ordnance would expand its factories at least for the final assembly of arms, though it still depended on contractors for the rest (Knight 2014: 24, 372).

In France the Saint-Etienne factory was the country's biggest musket producer. There weapons were made both for the king and for private parties. The king's weapons had to be quality-tested but those made for the civil market escaped this obligation. As in other sites the "factory" here was a clutch of handcraft-based workshops coordinated by merchant-entrepreneurs. It was the merchants who procured the state's supply. The introduction in 1778 of a new musket model and the attempt to bring in tighter technical supervision of the manufacturing process, including centralisation of production according to the guidelines laid down by the artillery inspector Gribeauval (McLennan 2003), showed in this case the limitations of the contractor state (Alder 1997: 277–78).

In theory the new type of musket was to be the lever whereby royal inspectors would improve the production process but the opposition of craftsman and merchants scuppered this intent in practice. Most refused to work under the new specifications; by the eighties output had fallen so alarmingly low that the state mooted bringing the manufacture *en régie*. This change was not in fact made and military output continued to fall, although production carried on for the civil market (Maguin 1990). In 1792, when war with Austria broke out, the Saint-Etienne manufacturers, with all their output now going to the civil market, refused to work for the state under the old prices (Alder 1999: 164). This would undoubtedly have been the main reason why the French government had to buy muskets in Birmingham, as we have just seen. In the end, France opted in 1793 for state control of arms manufacture (Knight 2014: 25). In this case the failure of the contractor state stemmed from a top-down decision to change the technological models, which neither merchants nor craftsmen accepted.

In Spain too light arms were made by the artisans of the pistol- and rifle-manufacturing guilds. Over and above the personnel of each master stood the guild, which had to pull all the strings to meet government needs. This task was taken on by the merchant-manufacturers, who effectively became *asentistas* at the state's service. Their manufacturing procedures were concentrated in the western valleys of Guipuzkoa (Éibar, Vergara, Placencia); in Biscay (Larrañaga 1981; Suárez Menéndez 1995: 219); and also in some zones of Catalonia, such as Ripoll, Manresa, Igualada; or in Barcelona itself (Martí 2004). This sector worked with the advantage of being able also to sell goods to the general public, such as hunting arms, or to the nobility. In theory, therefore, it was not completely dependent on state demand though the state did at times try to enforce exclusivity. Its establishment, moreover, was not so heavily dependent on natural circumstances. During Philip V's reign a concentrated factory was set up in Silillos, Madrid. It came on stream in about 1720 but was closed down only a few years later due to excessive costs. It had another fleeting period of existence from 1769 to 1773, with greater dependence on court administration (Suárez Menéndez 1995: 222; Ocete Rubio 2008: 20)[4].

In Guipuzkoa diverse light-arms manufacturing sites, organised on a guilds basis, had been up and running since the sixteenth century. The work, however, had to be controlled and this need gave rise in 1576 to the king-appointed official called *veedor* (royal inspector), who monitored the output and quality of all the workshops as well as retail arrangements to ensure that none of the output was sold off to private parties until such time as the state had been properly supplied (Calvo Poyato 1989: 54–55). These tasks were carried out from the Royal House of Placencia, which functioned as administrative centre. The whole privilege-shrouded ensemble went under the name of Royal Factories. With time, administrative control became tighter, and the sector also lost its retail freedom, with sales for some time being restricted to the army. Manufacturers ran into problems due to late payments and even short payments; nonetheless output continued to grow until the middle of the century, falling away thereafter (Carrión 2000). Since the seventeenth century four main guilds had been working in Placencia: *cañonistas* (barrel makers), *chisperos* (specialists in firing mechanisms), *aparejeros* (finishers) and *cajeros* (assemblers); these were basically the same in the eighteenth century.

After the War of Succession broke out, measures were taken to stoke up production. This involved increasing state control by setting up the post of *superintendente general* in 1705 (Calvo Poyato 1989: 58) to replace the previous *veedor*. Rigid state control of production then slackened again in 1721, when the *asiento* system was re-established. In that year a contract was signed with one Martín de Isasi-Isasmendi. The *asentista* had to negotiate with each one of the guilds the terms and prices for arms manufacturing and assembly operations. Examining masters had the remit of checking that the delivered arms and parts met specifications. The stipulated number of rifles a year was 12,000, although in 1728, for example, the *asentista* was asked to deliver 18,000 muskets with bayonets[5].

One of the new features of the revived *asiento* system was the renewed permission for the manufacturers to make arms too for the civil market, on condition that there were no outstanding commitments with the king. This licence, however, proved to be counterproductive; the quality of the arms delivered to the king fell and sometimes delivery commitments were not met. All this also produced clashes between the *asentista* and guilds. The *asentista* was accused of putting his own interests above the king's and of whittling down the number of artisans working for the crown.

To solve these problems, the crown turned to the *Real Compañía Guipuzcoana de Caracas* in 1735. This company owed money to the king, so the idea was to offset the Plasencia arms *asiento* against this debt. Thereafter, the *asiento* would be financed against the navigation rights accrued by the company (Gárate Ojanguren 1990: 344–45). This made it possible to pay the arms manufacturers, whereupon output grew, without the manufacturers having to forfeit the civil market. By 1747, when relations between the company and the factory were broken off, a total of 18,000 muskets a year were being turned out. An attempt to bring the company back under direct administration (understanding this to be control of collective output) did not prosper; in 1753 the *Guipuzcoana* recovered the *asiento*, holding onto it thereafter until its transformation into the *Compañía de Filipinas* in 1785 (Díaz Trechuelo 1965). The new company also took on the light-arms *asiento* until the Basque factories were destroyed during the War of the Convention, whereupon production switched to Asturias. During most of the eighteenth century, therefore, the state drew on *asentistas*, either individual merchants like Isasi-Isasmendi or a privileged, share-based company.

9.3 Iron ordnance: the kingdom of gunfounders

The star turn of naval armaments at this time was the iron cannon. This was a crucial aspect, since firepower, growing significantly from the seventeenth to eighteenth century, was likely to be decisive in any battle. The Spanish squadron of Dunkirk, which sailed across to defend the coasts of Spain in 1609, had 12 ships with a total of 195 cannons, averaging out as four- to six-pounders. This firepower was tantamount to a single, 100-gun, three-decker ship-of-the-line of the late eighteenth century and the projectiles were smaller (Alcalá-Zamora 2004: 62). The 1609 cannons, moreover, were almost all bronze whereas eighteenth-century cannons were all iron. This represented a sea change in less than two centuries. The three main changes were, firstly, the definitive adoption of iron cannons, secondly larger calibres and thirdly a higher number of guns of greater variety judiciously distributed around the ships. All this called for a notable technical and economic effort from the states to bring their ships into line with the new strategic needs.

The production of cast-iron cannons was honed in the sixteenth century, especially in England, and they were widespread in the seventeenth century (Cipolla 1965: 36). By the end of that century they had been taken up by all European navies, bronze cannons being phased out according to the production capacity of each country and the quality of its iron. Holland and Sweden were the frontrunners (Cipolla 1965: 66); Spain was a bit late on the uptake. In 1637 one of the chiefs of the aforementioned Dunkirk squadron proposed increasing the squadron's size, arguing that it should have at least 50 per cent of cast-iron cannons to bring it up to Holland's ratio (Cipolla 1965: 66; Goodman 2001: 208–10; Alcalá-Zamora 2004: 34); defeat in the Battle of the Downs in 1639 and the weakness of the monarchy in the times of Charles II slowed down the overhaul in the second half of the seventeenth century; nonetheless some headway was made, judging from the maintenance of cast-iron production, albeit at a lower level, in Liérganes (Goodman 2001: 213–14; Alcalá-Zamora 1975, 2004: 104–08). During the eighteenth century cast-iron cannons were universal in all navies, Spain included. Bronze cannons were still being used in the army.

The aspect of interest to us here from the contractor-state point of view is the supply method, i.e., whether the state bought or made its own cannons and the ensuing problems in both cases. It is striking to find that all countries decided to make their own bronze cannons (Bowen 1998: 66; Étienne-Magnien 1991: 91–92; Segovia Barrientos 2008: 59–83; Aguilar Escobar 2010) and buy the iron ones from private manufacturers. In England the state bought its cast-iron cannons from the Wealden manufacturers, which had dominated the market since the sixteenth century. Although cannons were made in other areas, most came from the Weald, where the industry had depended on state patronage since at least the wars with Holland. Activity picked up anew after 1689 and then things held steady in the area until the Seven Years' War. After this war the area's importance declined, but until that time the state had continually contracted with the ironmaster of Wealden, who always offered the best prices at that time (Tomlinson 1976: 385–87).

It was a scattered industry highly dependent on subcontracting, making it difficult to find out who the actual hands-on smelters were in each case. We know who signed the contract – smelters, but also merchants and financiers. From 1700 to 1770, 17 of the 26 smelters who received payments from the Ordnance Board were definitely working in the Weald. Five of them accounted for over 50 per cent of the area's output in value terms (Tomlinson 1976: 398). In the Seven Years' War, 90 per cent of the Ordnance Board's payments still went to the Weald (Morris 2011: 184).

The Wealden area had also grown up on the strength of its proximity to the centres of supply, the royal dockyards, but the raw material market was by no means so handy. As navy needs grew, and therewith cannon orders (more, bigger cannons at a higher price per ton), manufacturers from other areas got in on the act, levering their lower production costs due to cheaper raw materials or transport. This allowed them to undercut Wealden's asking price. The main competition came from the Carron company, set up in 1759 in Falkirk, and able as from 1764 to offer much cheaper cannons (Tomlinson 1976: 387, 399). At this time the gun-founding industry also took off in the Midlands and in Wales (Morris 2011: 184).

But it was not only the price. Wealden's output per furnace was low and undependable: it varied greatly due to irregular water currents. There were also doubts about quality, since the methods had not changed since the sixteenth century, and there were other technical and supply problems. All this prevented it from matching Carron's offer in 1764. Wealden's output therefore started to fall away. But neither was Carron completely dependable. In 1771 the company's reputation suffered; quality shortfalls stemming from capitalisation problems led to an unacceptable rate of test-piece failures (Bryer 2006: 711). In 1773 the Ordnance Board not only cancelled contract renewal but also ordered all Carron cannons to be removed from the ships where they had been fitted. After that there would be no more long-cannon contracts with Carron until 1795 (Tomlinson 1976: 388; Morris 2011: 206).

Meanwhile, the company had to switch to other products. To restore its prestige after 1773, a renewed Carron Company made initial experiments with smaller calibres; then, in 1778, it began to produce its carronades, mounting them on its own transport ships and then on some privateers. In 1779 they were tried out in Woolwich. The navy started to use them in 1780, still of small calibre, but they were not taken up for all ships until one or two years later (Morris 2011: 207–08, 212–13).

Carron's failure with the long cannons favoured a revival of Wealden's output in 1773–75, so the outbreak of the American War of Independence gave its industry a new shot in the arm; nonetheless, the new quality demands ruined the activity. In 1775 the Ordnance Board decreed that only solid-cast, bored cannons would be accepted henceforth. This technique had been fairly well honed with bronze cannons but took some time to be adapted to cast-iron cannons, and in the seventies it was still pretty callow in Great Britain (Jackson and Beer 1973; Bret 2009: 55–56). Apart from solidity, a big advantage of the solid-casting and subsequent boring technique was improved accuracy. Its implementation, however, called for a hefty outlay, which the over-complacent Wealden contractors had blithely neglected to do. The new decree therefore spelt doom for Wealden's activity (Tomlinson 1976: 388; Morris 2011: 185, 187).

The new technology, on the other hand, meant that many companies with a cheaper supply of iron, coal and water or transport could now afford to undertake the technical improvements and come to the plate for the Ordnance Board. Indeed, the number of contractors grew as from 1780, riding the increased naval demand fuelled by the American War. Once this war was over, Carron Co. again became the main supplier of the navy's guns together with the Walker family of Rotherham. The two of them together provided the lion's share of the thousands of tons supplied from the late eighties onwards (Knight 2014: 47, 370). In the 1790s, although some deals were closed in London, the biggest orders still went to contractors trading near raw-material sources and far from London; transport posed no problem since it could be done by water, cheapening costs (Morris 2011: 189–90).

A corollary of the increasing number of contractors was a higher rate of test-piece failures, rising from 12.5 per cent in 1780 to 25.6 per cent by 1795. From the late eighties, Blomefield, artillery inspector, stiffened up the tests, thereby improving quality but also cutting down the pool of manufacturers who came up to scratch. He also experimented with a new design that began to be distributed in 1790. By 1796 the failure rate with the new design had fallen to 16 per cent, plunging to 5.6 per cent by 1797. The manufacturers brought in innovations and improvements to try to win new contracts. The larger-scale contracts called for by the revolutionary wars served as a goad to innovation and modernisation of production processes (Morris 2011: 204–05, Knight 2014: 46–47).

In France, Colbert kick-started naval renewal. There too iron cannons were made by private manufacturers; the state's first tactic was to support the host of foundries scattered around the whole of France and then it started to favour big companies capable of boosting industrial output (Léon 1970: 221, 223) such as the Landouillettes of Logivière and their Rancogne and Planchemenier factories. State support came in the form not only of its orders but also the concession of diverse privileges in the supply of iron and also for the workers. Colbert's efforts took some time to bear fruit but by about 1680 the factories set up in Périgord and Angoumois gave satisfactory results and were able to supply the western *arsenaux*. Elsewhere, on the other hand, success was more chequered and Toulon had supply problems. The situation would not improve much in the years following Colbert. Only the foundry of Saint-Gervais in Grenoble worked well until the beginning of the eighteenth century (Cipolla 1965: 69–71; Plouviez 2014: 323).

The post-1715 fall in output meant that for a good part of the first half of the eighteenth century there was a dominant contractor for iron cannons, Mlle. de Logivière, whose family played a key role from 1684 to 1732. In turn the Grenoble firm was bought by the state and leased to various entrepreneurs but its output was smaller (Plouviez 2014: 317, 322, 326). The lacklustre rate of orders up to the middle of the century discouraged investment, causing many potential suppliers to drop out of the race and the temporary decline of many previously thriving foundries such as those of Ans and that of Plassac (Pritchard 2009: 145).

Navy-revival measures were taken as from 1748 and several manufacturers were contracted, but needs were great and money was short. This chronic lack of money was in fact the French navy's major eighteenth-century headache (Legohérel 1965: 184), impinging heavily on artillery needs as in Spain. At the start of the fifties, cannons were bought abroad and contracts were signed with several manufacturers, including Montalembert and Reix des Fosses[6], in the conviction that the state would not be capable of setting up its own factory (Pritchard 2009: 143–48). Due to panicky, last-minute contracting procedures, the manufacturers did not always come up to scratch; neither was the natural quality of the iron used always good (Woronoff 1998: 126). An important entrepreneur at this time was Bertin, *contrôleur des finances* in 1759 and then minister, owner of workshops in Ans and Chignac that were vital for the casting of the larger guns (Plouviez 2014: 317).

The entrepreneurs ran into other problems, since the privileges granted often clashed with other vested interests of the time. Iron-transport privileges, for example, or worker tax-exemptions were not always respected in fact, and the roads running from the factories to navigable rivers were not repaired. There were also problems with the woodland conservation authorities, whose trees was needed for furnace firewood, and the local authorities worried about the local population's firewood supply (Woronoff 1998: 113–14; Plouviez 2014: 315). Inland local authorities did not seem to be too concerned about the navy cannon-makers' needs, among other reasons because the workers' corvée-exemption privilege caused many former farmers to leave the land. Oddly enough, however, neither were the country workers too keen to enter the foundries, fearing they would be working only for the private interest of the manufacturers (Pritchard 2009: 156–57).

Another problem was the patchwork nature of the iron industry. There was no unified iron market in France; work was done mainly to meet local needs; this meant there were no great quality stipulations and neither was the industry required to be very fleet-footed in adapting to changing demand. The owners' attitude, moreover, was often not conducive to productiveness. Many nobles with a significant mining property (Woronoff 1998: 128–29) worried only about raking in more profit rather than improving their facilities and equipment. Other proprietors, like the Dalliez family, founders of iron-producing companies in Nivernais and Dauphiné, were also functionaries at the same time (Léon 1970: 222) so their interests were not solely focused on the iron side of their business activities. This negative view of noble proprietors has been partly rethought since on the grounds that they did in fact have to compete with each other and some of them, like Montalembert, came in for flak that proved to be ill-founded (Plouviez 2014: 345). Some noble proprietors, moreover, hired out their holdings to financiers, members of the Parisian business nobility, who were well versed in running them (Plouviez 2014: 318). In any case the system was nowhere near flexible enough to meet quality- or quantity-driven surges in state demand, as occurred for example in the mid-eighteenth century (Pritchard 2009: 158).

Although problems like the high rejection rate and dearth of possible manufacturers lingered on after the War of the Austrian Succession, this very war served as a goad to the necessary technological innovation. This came from the hand of J. Maritz II (Minost 2005), who brought in his horizontal boring machines as from 1753, first in companies of the contracted *asentistas* and afterwards while at the helm of the Ruelle factory, requisitioned by the state in 1755 when Machault replaced Montalembert as manager due to the debts run up by the latter. The navy also expanded its contracts to new entrepreneurs around Périgord and Angoumois, who were to work under the eye of Maritz, who introduced the solid-casting, horizontal-boring system (Bret 2009: 56; Pritchard 2009: 152–53); this represented an early success in the adaptation of this technique to cast iron.

The state now seemed to control a significant share of the production, dominating entrepreneurs who had not always proved to be trustworthy in the past while they also improved the quality of the parts, right on the brink of the Seven Years' War. Although output grew, needs still ran ahead. In 1756 Machault was forced to enter into contracts with new entrepreneurs. The urgency of the needs led to a certain disorderliness. For example, only the weight of the required metal was specified, so entrepreneurs exploited this loophole to offer cannons of a calibre that was not always necessary. The new minister, Moras, would regulate purchases to achieve greater efficiency, redounding in an improvement in procurement procedures and quality standards. In 1760 many boring machines were installed, about 25 in all. Even so, quality improvements were slow and still fell well short of need (Pritchard 2009: 155; Plouviez 2014: 346–47).

After the war, orders slackened but did not dry up completely as in previous post-war periods. This meant the foundries could be kept on, although the state tended to pare down the number of companies to a trustworthy few, in terms of both financial solvency and quality standards. This chosen few included, above all, Ruelle, Indret, Le Creusot and Cosne-Guérigny. By about 1770, however, the cannon-casting factories had fallen into a slough of despond and would not buck up until well into the decade, in response to the American War. The key feature then was foresight: greater state involvement leading to bigger investments, technical improvements and state ownership of some firms. This also spurred private initiative, drawn in by soaring orders: from 1776 to 1782, for example, France built 76 ships (ships-of-the-line and frigates). If we prolong the period up to 1792 we then find a century-high shipbuilding rate for France (Acerra 1993; Plouviez 2014: 351, 361–62).

The period shows two phases. From 1776 to 1781 the state splashed out heavily to improve the casting technique in several foundries. This was under the watch of Sartine, considered to be a high-spending minister. Companies like Ruelle, Forge Neuve and Indret were founded or upgraded. All of them came under state ownership and management at one time or another but were soon seen to work better under private management, whereupon the state limited its involvement to conceding privileges and entering into *asientos* with the new managers. As from 1782, however, the state's investments ceased. Significant outlays were made only in restoring the ancient foundries of Chaussade, which remained as a state company, *en régie*, but this was an exception to the rule. In general, the state was rethinking its budgetary capacities, opting clearly for private ownership and management, although there was some state participation in newly created companies like Le Creusot (Plouviez 2014: 367–69).

A special case here was Indret, a company created by the state in 1777. Formerly a storage site and nexus between the hinterland and the Atlantic *arsenaux*, Indret would become a metallurgical centre when Sartine decided to set up there some barrel boring workshops and shortly afterwards a reverberatory furnace, the first in France. To do so he summoned one of the two Wilkinson brothers, William (Harris 1998: 250). The Englishman would be technical director for some time, but in 1781 the company was leased to an artillery official and private entrepreneur, Ignacio Wendel, head of a powerful financial company. The Indret factory would end up installing a steam-powered boring machine in 1785 (Bret 2009: 57–61).

Wendel's success was largely due to his capital-raising capacity thanks to his good relations with high-ups among the government, with even the king himself becoming a shareholder (Plouviez 2014: 318). Indret, at first, drew on the output of the associated foundries. When these passed into private hands he then obtained his supplies from the new company of Le Creusot, created by Wendel himself and other financial groups. Le Creusot had also been driven by the state but had only a small input of state capital and was always run as a private firm. It had four blast furnaces and was the first French foundry to run on coke (Léon 1970: 224; Corvol 1999: 109).

The Indret-Le Creusot ensemble became the hub of French smelting at the end of the eighteenth century, ousting from first place Ruelle-Forge Neuve (Plouviez 2014: 370–71). But this ensemble took some time to build up a big enough output and Indret always suffered from quality problems. To this extent it fell short for some time of its managers' hopes. In 1790, for example, it was commissioned to bore and delivery 600 cannons from a stock of parts from both Le Creusot and England. The parts from Le Creusot were substandard and hard to work with. The English parts were not only higher quality but also cheaper. The failure could not be blamed so much on Indret as Creusot, but at the end of the day it was a failure of the whole ensemble (Bret 2009: 65). Furthermore, if Le Creusot began solely as a cast-iron production site for Indret, later on it would produce its own cannons, but its first navy-cannon contract was not signed until 1792. Its output was important only as from 1796.

In comparison with Great Britain, France did not enjoy the same quality of iron; neither did it have the economic base to drive the development of the iron industry more vigorously. The casting and steam-power techniques were imported from Great Britain. The state did not always organise its orders well and failed to come up with enough capital at crucial moments. Although private entrepreneurs pitched in, they suffered from the fickleness of military demand (Chaline 2004: 290) and managed to hang on only because their companies were varied and their diversified activity allowed them to trade in the civil market whenever state orders or payments dried up. In any case, in 1789 only five entrepreneurs had cannon-supply contracts signed with the navy.

In the end it is surprising, given the number of companies participating at one time or another in the manufacturing process and the size of the French navy, that France's total eighteenth century iron-cannon output was about 21,000 of all calibres. This figure is similar to Spain's, with an estimated output of 20,000 cannons from a single factory, and its navy was smaller than France's (Alcalá-Zamora

2004: 268; Plouviez 2014: 488). Calculation problems apart, the similarity of the figures suggests a low French output during a good deal of the century and perhaps an inefficient casting technique. This inefficiency would be reflected in a high rate of rejection by navy officials on some occasions (Plouviez 2014: 344), alternating with other times of recognised quality. Moreover, if private agents coughed up the money, French technological renewal was driven by the state's initial investments, bailing out the quality of the output in the last quarter of the century.

9.4 Military entrepreneurs in Spain's cast-iron cannon factories

In Spain there had been a long tradition of cast-bronze and wrought-iron cannons dating right back to the fifteenth century (Vega Viguera 1992), but cast-iron production did not start until 1622. There would be only one factory from then on, until 1834 (Alcalá-Zamora 2004). The reason for Spain's comparative backwardness (Cipolla 1965: 33) could be that fact that its war theatres at that time were abroad and the government therefore drew on the foundries of the Low Countries or northern Italy. It was not until peace was achieved at the start of the seventeenth century and military activity ceased in the Low Countries that thought could be given to the setting up of iron-cannon factories in Spain.

Different management attempts finally gelled in 1622, when the state accepted the proposal of J. Corte from Liege, known in Spain as Curcio, to set himself up in Spain. Crucially, Curcio would input the technical expertise and know-how of the Liege entrepreneurs. Under his scheme an *asentista*-based model of cannon manufacture was set up. The entrepreneur at the head of the business could now be classed as capitalist, i.e. a person with capital who was familiar with the techniques involved in the business but acted above all as entrepreneur and financier (Vázquez de Prada 1994: 476). These businessmen also had connections with politics and some of them, like Curcio himself, held government posts. On this basis, the model established in Liérganes in the seventeenth century was that of a free manufacturing firm whose owners – entrepreneurs – hoped to sign an exclusive contract with the government to sell their products. It was really a *de facto* monopoly regime (González Enciso 2000).

Juan Curcio's business started slowly and finally failed, because the state in those years had little money, having suffered a bankruptcy episode in 1627. But the activity itself was underway, even if the undertaking changed hands. In 1630 Jorge de Bande was able to sign an *asiento* for making 200 artillery pieces, small as yet, and then rode the post-1633 boom, when Liérganes's own output grew and was swelled further by the annexation of La Cavada. Bande showed himself to be a great entrepreneur, endowed with initiative, managerial skills and negotiating capacity with the government (Alcalá-Zamora 2004: 94).

The subsequent *asentistas* had similar experiences to Curcio and Bande, i.e., a stop-go system swinging wildly from a situation of low state demand, little help and low prices when the government was short of cash to a contrasting rush of orders, flood of help and higher prices when needs were pressing or when there was any continual production and armaments policy. The fickleness of state needs, or of its spending power, determined the price the state was ready to pay for its artillery supplies. The situation would change after 1715 under the ownership of Nicolás Xavier de Olivares, heir of previous owners, albeit a minor at the time, when state demands surged anew. A particularly good time was the 1726–37 period, with a navy boom driven by Patiño and also an increase of the price paid by the government in the *asientos*. Olivares thus produced a similar situation to de Bande's a century earlier as the government once more decided to invest more in its *asentistas* to their mutual benefit. Nicolás Xavier died in 1737, succeeded by his son Joaquín, who would then run the factory during the central decades of the century (Alcalá-Zamora 2004: 106, 110).

Family relationships played a key role in the hands-on of factory ownership. At first ownership of the Liérganes factory passed from one partner to another; later, however, family inheritance and agreements held sway as the Olivares inherited the business from earlier *asentistas* on the strength of inter-family marriages. From 1738 onwards Joaquín de Olivares ran the companies successfully. He chalked up three contracts with the state and always met deadlines comfortably. Well set up in the court, he received in 1742 the title of Marqués de Villacastel and important privileges in 1754–55[7]. This official recognition was reward not only for his business acumen but his canny sense of give-and-take, knowing when to accept a reduction in prices or an increase in output. In the end, however, his swathe of privileges turned out to be a millstone around his neck and brought his business down.

The main source of friction was the problems created by management of woodlands, as had occurred earlier (Maiso González 1990: 147, 320), bringing local authorities and the population into confrontation. In the case of Liérganes, the government was already seeking to nationalise the firm by 1759 and local opposition was used as an important argument to back up the decisions finally taken by Charles III. Villacastel died in 1759, leaving an ample fortune and a buoyant production but a host of problems too, including lawsuits that his heirs were unable or unwilling to tackle in defence of their ownership. Thus, from 1650 to 1760, there was a continual line of an industrial family firm, sometimes with other participants, who ran their factory on the strength of *asientos* with the government and grew rich on this manufacturing business.

Cannons needed munitions. The cannon factories also made the corresponding cannonballs, two-headed bullets (angels) and other projectiles, but there are few records of exclusively projectile-making companies. Spain's case was idiosyncratic, with several factories and a much more diversified supply range. The first factory was set up in 1689 in Eugui (Navarre) by transforming for this purpose an ancient royal ironworks that has previously made helmets and armour during the sixteenth century. This would then produce all types of cannon-, mortar- and handgun-projectiles like grenades, bombs and the like, all going under the umbrella term of "munitions". Later on another two iron companies appeared in Navarre, contracting with the king for the manufacture of all these products: Asura in 1723 and Iturbieta in 1726. Both were short lived, the former lasting until 1739 and the latter until 1737 (González Enciso 2010: 198–208).

The Eugui factory lasted longer, hanging on until 1794. By then three other munitions factories had cropped up: San Sebastián de la Muga in Gerona, Jimena de la Frontera in Cádiz, and Orbaiceta in Navarre, which came on stream in 1768, 1778 and 1784, respectively (Alcalá-Zamora 1999: 360). All three were fleeting, not making it to the end of the century. In 1794 two other companies appeared: Sargadelos in Lugo and Trubia in Asturias. In all cases these firms made cast-iron products with blast furnaces.

The possibilities of this business sector were hemmed in by several constraining factors. First of all, there was the rigidity of the natural resources, the iron ore, and the need of abundant woodland and water. As areas of easier access were used up, other more logistically difficult sites had to be roped in. Then there was the hefty capital outlay needed to set up the blast furnaces. Furthermore, any would-be entrepreneurs were forced to eschew both the private market and the export market, so the sector's viability depended on a clear commitment from the state, the only customer. All these factors hobbled the entrepreneurial development of these activities.

The Eugui factory is the other significant metallurgic firm. Like Liérganes it was born in the seventeenth century on the initiative of an entrepreneur, José de Aldaz, later Marqués de Monte Real. Aldaz based his possibilities on the munitions-supplying *asientos* signed with the government. Son of a merchant and a merchant himself, he realised that investing in a munitions factory could be an interesting business project. The opportunity came with the stepping up of the war effort against Louis XIV, whereupon munitions supplies were found to be wanting. The cannon output of Liérganes had to be increased but there was no time or spare capacity for munitions production; they would have to be looked for elsewhere. This represented a fine profit-making opportunity for an entrepreneur ready to invest in a factory in return for a government agreement.

The Eugui factory, state owned, had existed for some time. It was in fact Spain's oldest iron-making firm, having functioned as a royal armoury since 1534 making mainly helmets and armour (Rabanal Yus 1987: 32). By 1689 the factory had been abandoned due both to the relative obsolescence of its output and the government's financial straits. Aldaz proposed buying the factory from the king and turning it into a modern munitions-producing ironworks. The opportunity of relaunching Eugui came with the war, but the moot point is why the state decided to do so under an *asiento* with a private merchant. In all likelihood a government in such financial straits could not have found any other way of financing the venture than a well-heeled merchant ready to invest in a munitions factory.

Aldaz showed that this activity could be big business. In 1702 he enlarged his firm and boosted its output; in Eugi, in fact, Spain's second blast furnaces were set up after those of Liérganes and La Cavada (Alcalá-Zamora 1999: 357). The factory became in the end Aldaz's biggest business line (Andueza Unanua 2007: 104). But this very success attracted the interest of a rival merchant group run by one Loperena, whose company obtained from the king both the ownership and the *asiento* in 1719. Aldaz had some problems with government authorities. There was a marked contrast between the behaviour of the *asentista*, who met all his deadlines, and the government's payment arrears and enforced price reductions in each contract renewal. Aldaz's problems worsened when he was sued by the local authority of Eugui for his use of the local woodland, losing his *asiento* and company in the ensuing litigation. Loperena exploited the entrepreneur's discomfiture, winning out in 1719 by promising that his company would respect local woodland interests (González Enciso 2010: 168–69, 181).

Loperena y Compañía was basically a group of related merchants who decided to invest in a manufacturing company. It also ran into problems. Some came from Aldaz himself, who lodged a claim against Loperena. As a result of this claim, ownership of the factory reverted to his widow in 1730; nonetheless the king reserved the right to keep Loperena on as *asentista*, though from then on he had to pay a rental to the factory owner, the Marquesa Viuda de Monte Real (Andueza Unanua 2007: 106–08). Litigation, however, was not Loperena's only problem. The war of 1719 ravaged the area and destroyed part of the factory; he also had to stomach continual government-enforced price reductions; finally, he also had to cope with competition from the rival factories of Asura and Iturbieta, robbing Loperena of his *de facto* munitions monopoly.

The advent of this competition was a new demonstration of the importance of politics and court influence. Loperena had previously benefited from this influence in 1719 but later on Arizcun and Mendinueta, related to Aldaz, gained the upper hand. In about 1725, in a moment of peace, there had already been a shutdown in Eugui, the government then dithering over which side to take in the dispute. The competition set up their factories in 1727, with rumours of war rumbling in the background. It was just at this time that Patiño was most vigorously driving navy renewal and it was probably the increasing needs deriving therefrom that bailed out Loperena for a time. He kept the *asiento*, with Asura and Iturbieta lurking in the wings as complementary figures, But the victory was pyrrhic. Loperena limped to the end of his *asiento* and never renewed it[8].

The die was now cast and in 1735 the signature on the Eugui *asiento* was Francisco Mendinueta's. There are striking coincidences here between the start of Loperena's problems and the setting up shop of Asura and Iturbieta, and also between Loperena's demise, Mendinueta's triumph in Eugui and the disappearance of the latter's other two companies with Arizcun. It is quite clear that Mendinueta, with Arizcun's help, was pulling strings to carry out a pincer movement against Loperena as rival manufacturer and courtier. Not only did he obtain *asientos* for his two small companies, chipping away at Loperena's empire, but then managed to oust him from the Eugui *asiento*. Once Mendinueta had won the Eugui contract, the Asura and Iturbieta factories were no longer of interest to anyone and ground to a halt.

Mendinueta decided to concentrate his manufacturing business in Eugui because he had more chances there of improving quality and boosting output than at Asura or Iturbieta. The latter two factories, moreover, suffered from transport problems, since their only viable outlet was northwards through Guipúzcoa to the Cantabrian sea. Indeed its output was sent to a store in Rentería, Guipúzcoa, before being shipped out from Pasajes, as provided for in the *asiento* of 1723[9]. This constraint remained in force years later but it was awkward because Cantabrian outlets were tricky during war years. A good idea of the size of this problem can be gained from the fact that even though the Asura agreement was renewed in 1728, there were still munitions in store in Rentería as late as the forties[10].

The Cantabrian outlet, in any case, flouted the standard practice of encouraging the Ebro River route to the south of Navarre, both for Eugui's output and shipments of Pyrenean wood. Not only did this policy favour this important river route; it also fed into the squadron-formation supply needs in the Mediterranean, one of Spain's overriding concerns from 1715 to 1745 (González Enciso 2012b). This was yet another reason working against the Asura factory, whose transport problems were reckoned to be unviable as early as the thirties.

Mendinueta was another type of *asentista*. He was not himself a manufacturer or even a merchant; rather, he was a businessman, financier and *asentista*. Although the son of a merchant, his move to the court confirmed his connections with the Navarre clique of rent farmers and *asentistas* and also the milieu of Juan de Goyeneche, to whom he was related, giving him a shoo-in to many important *asientos*. His manufacturing vein came from his relations with the Arizcun family, who had also invested in the iron-production business (Aquerreta 2000: 659, 2002). Arizcun's support was reckoned to have been the lever winning Mendinueta four important *asientos* at the start of his career: firstly, that of Asura, as from 1723, with Arizcun; then, apparently single-handedly now, those of Iturbieta in 1726, Eugui in 1735 and, finally the munitions- and arms-transporting-*asiento* of 1737 (Aquerreta 2002a: 88–89). Thus, although Mendinueta figures as an *asentista*-cum-manufacturer in Eugui, his *asentista* facet chimes in rather with that of major businessman running various *asientos*. He was in fact the great *asentista* of his time.

In the Eugui *asiento* of 1735, Mendinueta managed to up the price paid by the state, agreeing on the prices of 1717, much higher than those paid to Loperena[11]. This was the honeymoon period. Afterwards Mendinueta encountered the same problems as former *asentistas* in terms of the state's erratic policy, trimming the price paid at each contract renewal, as well as payment arrears or supererogatory orders to meet pressing needs, which were once more poorly paid. Mendinueta's Eugui *asientos*, which lasted until 1765, were a mixed bag of success and problems as military needs waxed and waned according to the imminence of war. The two first *asientos*, those of 1735 and 1745, were signed during moments of war but lasted into periods of peace during which the state often fell down on its contractual commitments. The last *asiento*, signed in 1755, worked well for a time but then fell off a cliff-edge (González Enciso 2010: 188).

The personages involved in the iron munitions and cannons factories represent two different models of *asentistas*. Liérganes had a family line running through it, growing rich as the factory prospered; in Eugui, on the other hand, we see a sundry clutch of *asentistas* whose wealth came from different sources in each case. Fast forward almost half a century to 1794 and we find another type again.

The Pyrenean factories now destroyed, the state looked westwards and entered into new contracts with private Galician *asentistas* like Antonio Raimundo Ibáñez, who would bring in the first blast furnace of Sargadelos to work for the army supply. He was a private merchant who signed a munition-supply *asiento* with the state, but his backstory was different again from the examples we have just seen above. Ibáñez came to the iron-making industry after a long career as one of the most important wholesalers of Galicia. In 1787 Ibáñez turned his sights to industry, plumping first of all for linen before he cottoned on to the navy's soaring demand for iron products and switched his attention to ironworks. In 1788, in an increasingly favourable juncture, Ibáñez moved into the manufacture of iron fittings for the navy. As well as other business with his partners, Ibáñez, with the cooperation of José de Andrés García, set up an ironworks and smelting furnace in Sargadelos in 1791. Three years later, the blast furnace's production switched from its initial target output of Bordeaux-type cooking cauldrons to munitions for the army. Although the *asiento* was not signed until 1796, Sargadelos had been producing munitions for the army since 1794 when the Pyrenean factories were destroyed (Carmona Badía 2012: 69–90).

9.5 From purchaser state to manufacturer state: nationalisation of the arms factories in the seventies

Until 1759 the cast-iron arms sector was exclusively a question of a contractor state, i.e. a state buying the products it needed from a privilege-shielded *asentista*. In the manufacture of bronze cannons, however, the owner of the factories was always the state, even though the actual smelter did business in his own right as an *asentista*. The situation changed radically during Charles III's reign. The new monarch, worried by growing British power in the Seven Years' War, with particularly eye-catching and crushing British victories in the very year he came to the throne, 1759 (McLynn 2004), decided to drop the previous peacekeeping policy (Téllez Alarcia 2012: 95, 106). This called for a much tighter control over strategic companies to achieve a substantial increase in arms output, both in quantity and quality. This effort went hand in hand with a policy of increasing state control over financial and taxation resources (Torres Sánchez 2012a). From the sixties onwards, therefore, there was a clear nationalisation drive in the sector (González Enciso 2013). It is well worthwhile recording the milestone events.

In the case of Liérganes, the monarch seems to have had clear ideas in mind even before coming to Spain. Then things happened quickly: in 1760, technical intervention; in 1763, direct state management; and, in 1769, full expropriation. Government managers found it fairly straightforward to steer the situation towards their own interests since the Marqués de Villacastel had won himself many enemies by now. The privilege-renewing decree in fact argued that these privileges balked competition and hence worked against the public good. The monarch therefore found himself bound to revoke them afterwards. This competition-cramping argument is ironic and somewhat two-faced since it was used in fact to bring in a state ownership regime that quashed all competition completely. This suggests that the real thinking behind the move was that it was the state rather than competition that was conducive to the public good (Alcalá-Zamora 2004: 114; Maiso González 1990: 152).

But what really concerns us now, in any case, is not so much the political leanings as the fact that the state decided to switch from purchaser to maker, doing so explicitly. In the case of this particular factory this policy ran counter to a tradition of almost 150 years. The decision was positive insofar as the quality of Liérganes's output had been falling; neither had any technological advances been brought in. Under state ownership this necessary renewal might now prove possible. In fact, it failed. Liérganes was unable to bring in solid casting so in the end there was no technological renewal. The negative knock-on effect was twofold. The entrepreneurial sector suffered from the loss of a real business opportunity; the state suffered from spending more without anything to show for it.

In 1766 it was Eugui's turn to be nationalised. In this case the government waited for Mendinueta's last *asiento* to run its term, at the end of 1765. But by the last months of the year a committee had been set up to go to Eugui and report on the company's situation and the measures to be taken; at the start of 1766 the factory was bought from the heirs of Monte Real[12]. After years of inactivity the company had fallen into a poor state and the committee missed no chance to point this out, arguing that the state would have to take over a company that had been poorly run for selfish gain. In Eugui too technological backwardness seems to have been one of the arguments brandished to justify nationalisation but the decision was apparently a foregone conclusion in any case. Nationalisation increased output temporarily but this soon dropped away. The unit cost, moreover, was much higher than the price previously paid to the *asentista* (González Enciso 2012c: 435). This also represented a missed chance of obtaining the same results by spending less and stimulating private business.

The state-ownership model was enforced in the creation of new munitions factories. In 1768 construction began under the aegis of the war ministry of a factory in San Sebastián de la Muga, Gerona, driven not only by the need for more munitions but hopes of top quality ore. The factory would fold in 1794. The programme continued undaunted in the seventies with the establishment of the factory of Ximena de la Frontera, Cádiz, to make cannonballs for the Americas, although it did not actually begin production until 1780 (Alcalá-Zamora 1999: 250–54, 366–67). In 1784 work began on the munitions factory of Orbaiceta, Navarre, due to the danger of Eugui running out of fuel as nearby woodland was used up. As from 1788, almost certainly because of the closure of Ximena, Orbaiceta would be enlarged to take on America's supply too (Gómez Campelo 1991: 316–17; Alcalá-Zamora 1999: 260).

From 1760, in short, we see a triumph in this sector of the old mercantilist "Merchant Prince" ideal, i.e., the king as owner of the firm and manufacturer. This same drive had been felt in France but budget shortfalls there limited state action to the promotion of technological renewal, after which the state bowed out. In Spain, on the other hand, even though the main remit of technological renewal was flunked, the state retained factory ownership on ostensible grounds of strategic convenience.

The destruction of the Pyrenean factories in 1794 forced a switch of the activity to Trubia in Asturias, also a state-owned firm, where experiments were made with modern casting techniques, unsuccessfully, up to 1808 (Adaro Ruiz-Falcó 1986). Meanwhile, the state had to buy in munitions from Sargadelos, a private company that worked normally until 1808. By the end of the century, therefore, given the disappearance of all army munition supply firms, nationalised back in the times of Charles III, a private merchant once more stepped into the breech and supplied the state with munitions while doing fine business himself. During these years Raimundo Ibáñez, like all the former *asentistas*, was above all a manufacturing *asentista*, owner of his own firm and linked to the state through a munitions supply *asiento*.

9.6 The limitations of the model

Leaving aside the private demand for light arms, the common denominator of the whole military armaments sector is the narrowness of the market. The demand, depending exclusively on state needs, was fickle and urgency-driven. The state did not earmark a fixed sum for arms supplies but responded on a seat-of-the-pants basis to the needs of each moment. When war had broken out and for as long as it lasted, the arms demand was brisk, then disappearing with peace. Throughout the whole of the eighteenth century there was a continual stream of complaints from politicians and the military about military supply shortfalls: ships and forts without guns, lack of projectiles or gunpowder, garrisons with few soldiers using a small number of personal arms. Frantic attempts were made to solve these shortages only as war loomed up. But there was often a time lag between the effort and the actual supply, since none of these products could be conjured out of thin air. What happened in these cases is the government would renege on the main tenets of mercantilism, turning to the overseas market.

Buying arms in from abroad was certainly not unheard of before; neither was it exclusive to Spain. Despite the much-vaunted mercantilist pipedreams of the time, all countries turned to foreign markets for many of their supplies, as we have repeatedly seen. In the case of Spanish arms things came to a head during the War of Succession at the end of the seventeenth century when the arms industry was at a low ebb due to the former crisis (Kamen 1974). After this war foreign purchases fell but by no means went away completely. Iron cannons were ordered from abroad on no fewer than 12 occasions from 1718 to 1778, adding up to a total of 8,385 guns of different calibres. For various reasons only 5,089 useful guns were actually bought in the end, but this is still a considerable number, representing as it does 26.36 per cent of the total output of Liérganes (González Enciso 2012d: 149). It was not only cannons that were bought. There were also some purchases of projectiles. Another problem that cropped up at diverse moments of the century was the quality of Spanish bombs; as a result bombs were bought from France at least from 1732 to 1736, and afterwards from 1766 at least until 1770, judging from the *asiento* with the Frenchman Conte de Rostaing[13].

The purchases reflect an inherent contradiction: the Spanish state did not always promote the private manufacturer as much as it should have done; then, when needs were pressing, it was forced to buy in from abroad. The state-supplying entrepreneur, moreover, was painted into a corner. When orders fell there was no inland private market for its now unwanted products; neither was there any outlet abroad as the entrepreneur could not export its products. The only solution was to sidestep the problem beforehand by building up a diversified portfolio of products and thus reduce the dependence on the state's military demand. This meant the entrepreneur needed to strike the right balance to ensure that the amount of its productive capacity given over to cannons and munitions did not stymy its other business outlets.

But both aspects – diversification of products and balancing out of investments – worked against a good service to the state, which would in truth call for a greater input of resources. This situation posed a dilemma not only for the *asentistas* but also for the government when choosing its suppliers. If the *asentista*, keen to secure the contract, threw itself into the business unreservedly, it then became over-dependent on the vagaries of state demand. The government, for its part, needed a solvent, trustworthy merchant capable of withstanding temporary order droughts as well as the state's habitual payment arrears. This gave rise to a mutual spiral of dependence that was by no means exclusive to Spain. In France contractors might also become "prisoners of the navy" (Pritchard 2009: 169). A Spanish instance is the Olivares family's string of iron-cannon *asientos*, possible due only to the privileges received, in all likelihood the only way of withstanding the economic problems deriving from cost increases (for example the rising prices of fuel and raw material). Mendinueta in 1735 also achieved in Eugui a situation that others had been unable to match. Oddly enough, in any case, the government did not always treat these vital *asentistas* well; witness Mendinueta's forerunners in Eugui or the Olivares family as from 1759.

A second problem deriving from the exclusivity terms enforced on these firms was falling product quality, due to both complacency and the manufacturer's reluctance to pour in too much money. In 1760, only a few months after Charles III's advent to the throne, and amidst another episode of military emergencies, a quality problem raised its head in Liérganes, with Eugui catching the virus soon after. It would seem that after more than 12 years of peace the technology had become obsolete. This supposition would seem to be borne out by two bad experiences at that time. One of these was the 1760 quality test conducted on La Cavada's cannons, with a rejection rate of over 11 per cent (Helguera Quijada 2012: 158). This ratio was regarded as eminently improvable and the government insisted on the need of reforming the production system. The second bad experience, apparently of a lesser calibre, was the opinion voiced by a high-up among the French military that the Eugui bombs used in the armed intervention in Portugal in 1762 were of poor quality. These declarations and opinions would undoubtedly have been tinged with political and ideological prejudices but they do in any case show the quality problems that did exist in Spain's military iron industry of the time.

The most cursory comparison with the technology used elsewhere shows that Spain's technology had indeed fallen behind the times. Since the forties, when so many cannons, projectiles and bombs had proven their mettle, technological progress had ground to a halt. Why was this? It is by no means easy to come up with an answer, but from the entrepreneur's side it is fairly clear that one of the reasons lay in the reluctance to experiment with new technologies, largely because of the cost. Revealing here is the comment made by Alcalá-Zamora about Jorge de Bande, second *asentista* of Liérganes from 1629 to 1649, who not only made a fortune but also managed to set up several successful factories, always with generous state subsidies. Alcalá-Zamora wondered aloud whether Bande would have been able to develop his factories so enthusiastically without his high profit rate (Alcalá-Zamora 2004: 104). The opposite picture was the dominant one in the eighteenth century.

It cannot be said that *asentistas* were not interested in quality. The state always quality-tested the products received and sent out periodical instructions about the techniques to be used. Most factories also employed technical inspectors and official manufacturing managers to watch out for these matters. Lack of quality meant client rejection of the product, which would be sent back to the manufacturer without payment. The lack of technological improvements, therefore, was not due to lack of interest or watchfulness but rather commercial insecurity: the entrepreneurs could not afford to splash out too much on improvements without a sure market to work with. Both in France and Spain, therefore, the state had to step in to renew technological processes, with patchy results.

The idiosyncrasy of the Spanish case, however, is that the state was ready to make this effort only if it owned and ran the factories. Charles III's nationalisation drive stemmed not only from the desire to improve quality but also from an ideological prejudice that was apparently not so strong in France, where the state also got involved but without claiming ownership. In the last quarter of the century, moreover, France was able to put together strong entrepreneurial consortia – which have even come to be called "cartels" (Léon 1970: 262) – made up by several entrepreneurs who could all afford big investments. In Spain this possibility did not exist. In the end the state had to invest in state companies more money than it had previously paid to the former *asentistas* without necessarily obtaining more products or achieving better results.

Notes

1 Archivo General de Simancas, Guerra Moderna, suplemento, 8, and Secretaría de Hacienda, 21.1.
2 Archivo General de Simancas, Secretaría de Guerra, 951,5810; Secretaría de Marina, 660, 661.
3 Archivo General de Simancas, Secretaría de Marina, 662.
4 There is some documentation in Archivo General de Simancas, Secretaría de Guerra, 506.
5 Archivo General de Simancas, Secretaría de Hacienda, 21.1.

6 Reix des Fosses is the name used by Pritchard while Plouviez refers to same as Dereix Desfossés.

7 Archivo General de Simancas, Secretaría de Guerra, 7904.

8 The final settlement was not signed until 1749, showing the problems they found in clearing up the accounts. Archivo General de Simancas, Secretaría de Guerra, 439.

9 Archivo General de Navarra, AF, caja 1, carpeta 6.

10 Archivo General de Simancas, Secretaría de Marina, 660.

11 Archivo General de Navarra, AF, caja 1, carpeta 8; Archivo General de Simancas, Secretaría de Marina, 660

12 Archivo General de Simancas, Secretaría de Hacienda, 804,1.

13 Archivo General de Simancas, Secretaría de Guerra, 950. AGS, Dirección General del Tesoro, Inventario 25, leg. 17.

Conclusions

These conclusions will be fairly brief, largely because we have already drawn many interim conclusions at various points of this book. But there always remains something to say, even at the risk of a certain repetition.

The long eighteenth century was a pivotal moment in the international balance of powers. 1713 saw the first signs of England's rise and France's decline, with Spain, though still a considerable power in its own right, lagging well behind these two powers. In any case this changing of the guard did not become complete until nearly a century later in 1815. Even though Great Britain took the forefront, it still had to grow into its new worldwide role. British defeat at the Battle of Cartagena de Indias in 1741 was a clear sign that the country was not yet ready for more power than it wielded at that moment. This would come in time. It seems to have learned the lesson from this setback in 1763 when it traded back Havana and Manila for Florida, lying adjacent to its own colonial territory. For the time being Great Britain attacked Spain's empire only through trade.

It was precisely in trade where Britain's advantage and the weakness of its rivals most showed. Great Britain played with two fundamental arms: firstly, a free-trade system for the British within its own colonial sphere and, secondly, expansion of its trading range. In the first case it held a clear advantage over Spain, which enforced until 1778 a state monopoly with overruled and controlled private shipping rights to the Spanish Americas. Spanish merchants had to ship their goods in the fleets setting out from Cadiz, only twice a year in theory and sometimes even less in practice. This rigidity, among other drawbacks, tended to foster contraband and fraud of different kinds and represented a loss for Spain, both actual and potential. As regards France, Great Britain could exploit the sheer breadth of its markets. Although French colonial trade had grown a lot during the eighteenth century, the 1763 defeat deprived France of the French Americas and its colonies in India. It was in the extension of its markets where Great Britain found the lever for racking up its trade and thus generating more tax revenue.

Flexibility and consumer demand were, as we have seen, the mainstays of Britain's taxation system. Flexibility because it was underpinned by a clutch of taxes – especially excise – that grew along with the expanding tax base. Consumer demand, for its part, was fuelled by the sharp growth in colonial trade and re-exportation to Europe, another of its trump cards that depended in turn on control of the Mediterranean markets. If Great Britain, as we have already seen, was capable of withstanding a huge and growing public debt, this was because it could also increase its tax base to finance this debt. Another important factor is that the British government never ever fell down on its payment commitments, thus helping to build up a sense of confidence in public-debt investments.

Great Britain's advantage over France and Spain, and over any other country of the eighteenth century, was hence based on its ability to run up a huge debt without investors ever doubting that the debt would be punctually paid back, meaning that more and more were willing to come to the plate. French debt, on the contrary, was more tightly tied in with political-administrative interests. Anyone unshackled by these interests was also free to ditch public-debt investments whenever the outlook was bleak. This meant that French debt was a much less dependable system, both for investors and the state itself, which could not extend it with such ease. It did so, but with dire consequences. In Spain, for its part, the structural difficulty of paying off the debt without a corresponding revenue increase made the government fight shy of debt by and large, trusting rather in the periodical arrival of precious metals from the Americas to bridge the gap. This system, although it worked on a makeshift basis up to the nineties, was incapable of driving economic growth.

In any case the problem resided not so much in the system, which was certainly hemmed in by limits, both in Spain and France, but the way it was handled. The French system had its drawbacks but it would have worked better if managed with more prudence and foresight. Pundits point to the fact that France's public-finance system was riddled and hidebound by chronic venality. Spain's government procedures, at least in theory, were freer but also conservative. The government was loath to change anything and trusted in the ongoing validity of the traditional system and its monopoly revenue. France sparked off its own failure by forcing the situation. Spain produced deadlock by failing to make more changes in time.

Could Spain in fact have pulled off these changes? This is the moot point for scholars of eighteenth-century Spain. In theory the answer is yes. Spain's eighteenth-century tax and commercial reforms could have been brought in earlier; they had certainly been mooted by many for quite some time. If this had been done they would have swelled the tax base, allowing for higher expenditure and a securer public-debt system.

But the answer could also be no. If we bear in mind the political situation at each particular moment, we find that advocates of these reforms either had insufficient clout to enforce them or drew back for fear of potential enemies. Both the financial crisis of 1739 and the 1766 revolt against Esquilache, plus the fallout of both, show the difficulties lurking behind these reforms and hence the limited possibilities of state structures and of their capacity to exercise international power. Spain, in brief, had failed to pave the way for these reforms by earlier political and social change. So the burning question remains unanswered, though at least we now have more information to go on.

We can in any case make two pertinent observations here. Firstly, Spain's resources were much thinner on the ground than in France or Great Britain: a smaller population, less fertile land and a scattered territory that made communications difficult. It is often claimed that Spain was resource-rich due to the king's treasure trove of precious metals but the truth is that it was much less of a money earner than other monarch's public-debt systems. Spain's precious metals paid off the state's deficits, acting to that extent as a debt system, but Spain's deficits corresponded to much lower expenditure rates than Great Britain's or France's. Spain did indeed survive, thanks to the bailout of precious metals but this in no way guaranteed its erstwhile dominion. The times of the *Siglo de Oro* had gone. Back then precious metal from the Americas had outstripped the revenue possibilities of other countries. By the eighteenth century this was no longer the case; it is true that the amount of metal flooding in increased but no less true is that the tax revenue of Spain's enemies had increased much more.

With so few resources to work with, it was logical for the Spanish state to try to keep its *asentistas* sweet. Strapped for cash, however, it would also want to pay as little as possible and reinforce control. Spain's mercantile weakness meant it produced few solvent financiers capable of creating a healthy climate of competition within the state's supply business. France's administration was somewhat disorderly but at least the French financiers, operating in a land of fertile soil and large population, had enough resources to be able to offer the state good deals. The state itself, moreover, could afford to pay handsomely thanks to its bountiful tax revenue.

In 1700 the British state was not as powerful as the French but it made up for this with an orderly administration that was gradually able to bring its contractors under a tighter rein. Great Britain's thriving trading and financial activity also meant the pool of would-be contractors was large. This allowed the government to play them off against each other, bargaining down the asking price and racking up its quality requirements.

From the mid-seventeenth century onwards, therefore, Great Britain boasted an organised and centralised administration; at the start of the eighteenth century it brought in a significant change in its taxation structure, underpinned by a single umbrella tax that could grow as the real economy blossomed. This tax and its mercantile capacity facilitated not only the creation of the Bank of England but also the setting up of the public-debt system. Its blessed administration enabled it to control its armed-forces supply system by encouraging competition among would-be suppliers in an open market within a thriving business environment. No other European country managed all these things at the same time, conjoining state power with market capacity. In other countries the weaker state was unable to exert such a favourable influence on the development of markets, as in the case of Spain, or the markets ruled the roost at the state's cost, partly due to the vested mercantile interests within the administration itself, as in France. Only Great Britain managed to keep the two spheres apart to the mutual benefit of both.

It is clear by now that we need to ditch forthwith the myth of Great Britain as a "small" state. The parliamentary system did not produce a small state; quite on the contrary, it nurtured a "big" and strong state, i.e., centralised and with the power to exploit its resources to the full. In absolutist countries, on the other hand, the lack of any representative institutions meant that the power struggles had no ground rules to match Britain's parliamentary procedures. The upshot was that these struggles led to an untidy and sluggish political system, limiting the states' ability to exploit its resources as it might have liked. Great Britain's political and economic fleet-footedness in its war preparations was its hallmark feature in this century, giving it the upper hand over its rivals. This speed was based on the country's confidence in its institutions and resources.

As we can see there are many diverse factors behind Britain's final triumph over its rivals and its ability to develop a more centralised and successful state than the rest. These factors did not come into being all at once; nor are they a consequence of the transformations of 1689; rather were they also developed in competition with external rivals. While Great Britain came onto the world stage with a new-broom mentality of sweeping out the old and bringing in a better organisation, hoping thereby to build a hitherto unknown level of world power, France and Spain rested on their laurels, making do with all their old, fault-ridden, creaky structures that trundled on by inertia and changed agonisingly slowly. In France the inherited structures were just too vast to be changed overnight; in Spain the inherited structures were too frail to be dealt with robustly. Meanwhile, Great Britain edged further ahead with each step down its new path, although it was certainly no cakewalk and it did not come into its full power until the very end of the century.

Bibliography

Aalbers, J., 1977, "Holland's Financial Problems (1713–1733) and the Wars against Louis XIV", in A. C. Duke, A. C. and C. A. Tamse (eds.), *Britain and the Netherlands, War and Society: Papers Delivered to the Sixth Anglo Dutch Historical Conference*, The Hague, VI, 79–93.

Acerra, M., 1993, *Rochefort et la construction navale française, 1661–1815*, Paris, Librairie de l'Inde.

Acerra, M. and Zysberg, A., 1997, *L'Essor des marines de guerre européennes, 1680–1790*, Paris, SEDES.

Adaro Ruiz-Falcó, L., 1986, *Los comienzos de las fábricas de municiones gruesas de Trubia y de armas de Oviedo: 1792–1799*, Oviedo, Imprenta La Cruz.

Aguilar Escobar, A., 2010, *Cañones de bronce para el Ejército. Historia de la Real Fundición de Sevilla en el siglo XVIII*. Madrid, Ministerio de Defensa.

Albareda, J., (ed.), 2015, *El declive de la Monarquía y del imperio español. Los tratados de Utrecht (1713–1714)*, Barcelona, Crítica.

Alcalá-Zamora, J., 1975, *España, Flandes y el Mar del Norte (1618–1639): la última ofensiva europea de los Austrias madrileños*, Barcelona, Planeta.

Alcalá-Zamora, J., 1999, *Altos hornos y poder naval en la España de la Edad Moderna*, Madrid, Real Academia de la Historia.

Alcalá-Zamora, J., 2004, *Liérganes y La Cavada. Historia de los primeros altos hornos españoles (1622–1834)*, Santander, Estudio.

Alder, K., 1997, "Innovation and Amnesia: Engineering Rationality and the Fate of Interchangeable Parts Manufacturing in France", *Technology and Culture*, 38, 2, 273–311.

Alder, K., 1999, *Engineering the French Revolution: Arms and Enlightenment in France, 1763–1815*, Princeton, Princeton University Press.

Allen, R. C., 2009, *The British Industrial Revolution in Global Perspective*, Cambridge, Cambridge University Press.

Andrés-Gallego, J., 2003, *El motín de Esquilache, América y Europa*, Madrid, C. S. I. C. and Fundación Mapfre.

Andrés Ucendo, J. I. and Lanza García, J. R., 2008, "Estructura y evolución de los ingresos de la Real Hacienda de Castilla en el siglo XVII", *Studia Historica. Historia Moderna*, 30, 147–90.

Andueza Unanua, P., 2007, "De padre cerero a hijo marqués: José de Aldaz y Aguirre, marqués de Monte Real", in A. González Enciso (ed.), *Navarros en la Monarquía española en el siglo XVIII*, EUNSA, Pamplona, 89–122.

Andújar Castillo, F., 2014, "Más continuidad que cambio: la venalidad de los empleos en España en el siglo XVIII", in A. Morales Moya (ed.), *1714. Cataluña en la España del siglo XVIII*, Madrid, Cátedra, 185–206.

Angulo Teja, C., 2002, *La Hacienda española en el siglo XVIII. Las rentas provinciales*, Madrid, Centro de Estudios Políticos y Constitucionales.

Aquerreta, S., 2000, "La casa de Arizcun, 1725–1742: Las estrategias financieras de un hombre de negocios en el Madrid de la Ilustración", in J. A. Ferrer-Benimeli (dir.), *El conde de Aranda y su tiempo*, Zaragoza, Institución Fernando el Católico, 659–78.

Aquerreta, S., 2001a, *Negocios y finanzas en el siglo XVIII: la familia Goyeneche*, Pamplona, EUNSA.

Aquerreta, S., 2001b, "Reforma fiscal y continuidad en el sistema de arrendamientos: la renta de lanas en el reinado de Felipe V", in A. González Enciso (ed.), *El negocio de la lana en España (1650–1830)*, Pamplona, EUNSA, 109–34.

Aquerreta, S., 2002a, "<De su cuenta y riesgo y por vía de asiento>. Trayectoria y negocios de Francisco Mendinueta (1744–1763)", in S. Aquerreta (coord.), *Francisco Mendinueta: finanzas y mecenazgo en la España del siglo XVIII*, Pamplona, EUNSA, 77–100.

Aquerreta, S. (coord.), 2002b, *Francisco Mendinueta: finanzas y mecenazgo en la España del siglo XVIII*, Pamplona, EUNSA.

Artola, M., 1982, *La Hacienda del Antiguo Régimen*, Madrid, Alianza.

Bannerman, G. E., 2008, *Merchants and the Military in Eighteenth-Century Britain*, London, Pickering and Chato.

Barbier, J. A., 1980, "Towards a New Chronology for Bourbon Colonialism: The 'Depositaría de Indias' of Cádiz, 1722–1789", *Ibero-Amerikanisches Archiv*, 6, 4, 341–42.

Barbier, J. A., 1984, "Indies Revenues and Naval Spending: The Cost of Colonialism for the Spanish Bourbons, 1763–1805", *Jahsbuch für Geschichte von Staat, Wirtschaft und Gesellschaft Lateinamerikas*, 21, 169–88.

Barbier, J. A. and and Klein, H. S., 1985, "Las prioridades de un monarca ilustrado: el gasto público bajo el reinado de Carlos III", *Revista de Historia Económica*, 3, 473–95.

Barrio Gozalo, M., 1988, "Introducción, transcripción y notas", in G. Anes (ed.), *Cartas [de Carlos III] a Tanucci*, Madrid, BBV, 1–33.

Barrio Gozalo, M., 2010, *El clero en la España Moderna*, Córdoba, C. S. I. C. and Caja Sur.

Baudot Monroy, M., 2012, *La defensa del Imperio. Julián de Arriaga en la Armada (1700–1754)*, Madrid, Ministerio de Defensa.

Baudot Monroy, M., 2014, "Armar en tiempos de Guerra. La movilización naval para la defensa colonial en 1739–1740", in M. Baudot Monroy (ed.), Madrid, Polifemo, 85–116.

Baugh, D. A., 1965, *British Naval Administration in the Age of Walpole*, Princeton, Princeton University Press.

Bayard, F., Félix, J. and Hamon, P., 2000, *Dictionnaire des surintendants et des contrôleurs généraux des finances*, Paris, Comité pour l'Histoire Économique et Financière de la France.

Beckett, J. V., 1985, "Land Tax or Excise: The Levying of Taxation in Seventeenth- and Eighteenth-Century England", *English Historical Review*, 100, 285–308.

Beloff, M., 1966, *The Age of Absolutism, 1660–1815*, New York, Harper Torchbooks.

Bernardo Ares, J. M. de, 2008, *Luis XIV rey de España. De los imperios plurinacionales a los estados unitarios (1665–1714)*, Madrid, Iustel.

Bethencourt Massieu, A. de, 1998, *Relaciones de España bajo Felipe V. Del tratado de Sevilla a la guerra con Inglaterra*, Madrid, Fundación Española de Historia Moderna.

Black, J., 1989, "Introduction", in J. Black and P. L. Woodfine (eds.), *The British Navy and the Use of Naval Power in the Eighteenth Century*, Atlantic Highlands, Humanities Press International, 1–31.

Black, J., 1991, *A Military Revolution? Military Change and European Society, 1550–1800*, London, Macmillan.

Black, J., 1994, *European Warfare, 1660–1815*, London, UCL Press.

Black, J. and Woodfine, P. L. (eds.), 1989, *The British Navy and the Use of Naval Power in the Eighteenth Century*, Atlanctic Highlands, Humanities Press International.

Bonney, R. (ed.), 1995a, *Economic Systems and State Finance*, Oxford, Clarendon Press.

Bonney, R., 1995b, "Revenues" in R. Bonney (ed.), *Economic Systems and State Finance*, Clarendon Press, 423–506.

Bonney, R., 1999a, "France, 1494–1815", in R. Bonney (ed.), *The Rise of the Fiscal State in Europe, c. 1200–1815*, Oxford, Oxford University Press, 123–76.

Bonney, R., (ed.), 1999b, *The Rise of the Fiscal State in Europe, c. 1200–1815*, Oxford, Oxford University Press.

Bonney, R., 2004, "Towards the Comparative Fiscal History of Britain and France During the 'Long' Eighteenth Century", in L. Prados de la Escosura (ed.), *Exceptionalism and Industrialisation. Britain and Its European Rivals, 1688–1815*, Cambridge, Cambridge University Press, 191–215.

Bordo, D. and White, E., 1991, "A Tale of Two Currencies: British and French Finance During the Napoleonic Wars", *The Journal of Economic History*, 51, 2, 303–16.

Bosher, J. F., 1970, *French Finances, 1770–1795: From Business to Bureaucracy*, Cambridge, Cambridge University Press.

Bowen, H. V., 1998, *War and British Society, 1688–1815*, Cambridge University Press, Cambridge.

Bowen, H. V. and González Enciso, A., 2006, *Mobilising Resources for War: Britain and Spain at Work During the Early Modern Period*, Pamplona, EUNSA.

Bowen, H. V. et al., 2013, "Forum: The Contractor State, c. 1650–1815", *International Journal of Maritime History*, XXV, 1, 239–74.

Braddick, M., 2000, *State Formation in Early Modern England c. 1550–1700*, Cambridge, Cambridge University Press.

Brading, D. A., 1971, *Miners and Merchants in Bourbon Mexico, 1763–1810*, Cambridge, Cambridge University Press.

Branda, P., 2005a, "La guerre a-t-elle payé la guerre ?", in T. Lenz (ed.), *Napoléon et l'Europe: regards sur une politique*, Paris, Fayard, 250–71.

Branda, P., 2005b, "Les finances et le budget de la France napoléonienne: la guerre a-t-elle payé la guerre ?", *Revue du souvenir napoléonien*, 457, 25–34.

Braudel, F., 1958, "La longue durée", *Annales. Économies, Sociétés, Civilisations*, 13, 4, 725–53.

Braudel, F., 1985, *La dinámica del capitalismo*, Madrid, Alianza.

Braudel, F. and Labrousse, E. (dirs.), 1970, *Histoire économique et sociale de la France*, T. II, Paris, PUF.

Bret, P., 2009, "La fonderie de canons d'Indret. De quelques modes de circulation technique à la fin du XVIII siècle", *Quaderns d'Història de l'Enginyeria*, X, 53–66.

Brewer, J., 1989, *The Sinews of Power. War, Money and the English State, 1688–1783*, London, Unwin Hyman.

Bruguière, M., 1991, "Les receveurs généraux sous Louis XVI: fossils ou précurseurs", in M. Bruguière, *Pour une renaissance de l'histoire financière, XVIIIe–XIXe siècles*, Paris, Comité pour l'Histoire Économique et Financière de la France, 457–97.

Bryer, R., 2006, "Capitalist Accountability and the British Industrial Revolution: The Carron Company, 1759–circa. 1850", *Accounting, Organizations and Society*, 31, 687–734.

Buchet, C., 1999, *Marine, économie et société. Un exemple d'interaction: l'avitaillement de la Royal Navy durant la guerre de sept ans*, Paris, Honoré Champion.

Buist, M. G., 1974, *At Spes non Fracta. Hope &Co. 1770–1815*, The Hague, Martinus Nijhoff.

Cailleton, B., 1999, *La construction navale civile dans l'amirauté de Nantes au XVIIIe siècle: Nantes, Basse-Indre, Indret, Paimboeuf. Infrastructures, hommes, fonctionnement*, Hérault, Cholet.

Calvo Poyato, J., 1989, "La industria militar española durante la Guerra de Sucesión", *Revista de Historia Militar*, 66, 51–71.

Canales, E., 2008, *La Europa napoleónica, 1792–1815*, Madrid, Cátedra.

Canga Argüelles, J., 1968 [1833], *Diccionario de Hacienda*, Madrid, Instituto de Estudios Fiscales.

Capella, M. and Matilla Tascón, A., 1957, *Los Cinco Gremios Mayores de Madrid. Estudio crítico-histórico*, Madrid, Imprenta Sáez.

Carande, R., 2004, *Carlos V y sus banqueros*, Barcelona, Crítica.

Carlos Morales, J. C. de, 1996, *El Consejo de Hacienda de Castilla, 1523–1602. Patronazgo y clientelismo en el gobierno de las finanzas reales durante el siglo XVI*, Valladolid, Junta de Castilla y León.

Carmona Badía, X., 2012, "Antonio Raimundo Ibáñez, un empresario en el filo de dos épocas", in J. Ocampo Suárez-Valdés (ed.), *Empresas y empresarios en el norte de España (siglo XVIII)*, Oviedo, Trea, 69–90.

Carrera Pujal, J., 1945, *Historia de la economía española*, Barcelona, Bosch.

Carrión, I., 2000, "Sixteenth and Seventeenth Century Arms Production in Gipuzkoa", in *Proceedings of the XXth International Congress of History of Science* (Liége 20–26 July 1997), vol. VII, Technology and Engineering, Brepols, Turnhout.

Castanedo Galán, J. M., 1993, *Guarnizo, un astillero de la Corona*, Madrid, Editorial Naval.

Castro, C. de, 2004, *A la sombra de Felipe V. José de Grimaldo, ministro responsable (1703–1726)*, Madrid, Marcial Pons.

Chaline, O., 2004, *La France au XVIIIe siècle*, Paris, Belin.

Chaline, O., Bonnichon, P. and Vergennes, C. -P. de (dirs.), 2013, *Les Marines de la Guerre d'Indépendance Américaine (1763–1783). I- L'instrument naval*, Paris, PUPS.

Chamley, C., 2011, "Interest Reductions in the Politco-Financial Nexus of Eighteenth Century England", *The Journal of Economic History*, 71, 3, 555–89.

Cheung, H. and Mui, L. H., 1975, "Trends in Eighteenth-Century Smuggling Reconsidered", *Economic History Review*, XVIII, 28–43.

Cipolla, C., 1965, *Guns, Sails and Empires*, Minerva Press.

Clay, C., 1978, *Public Finance and Private Wealth: The Career of Sir Stephen Fox, 1627–1716*, Oxford, Clarendon Press.

Clément, P., 1861, *Lettres et mémoires de Colbert*, Paris, Imprimerie Impériale.

Cobban, A, 1969, *The Eighteenth Century*, New York, McGraw-Hill.

Concina, E., a cura di, 1987, *Arsenali e città nell'Occidente europeo*, Roma, La Nuova Italia Scientifica.

Conway, S., 2006, *War, State and Society in Mid-Eighteenth Century Britain and Ireland*, Oxford, Oxford University Press.

Conway, S., 2007, "Checking and Controlling British Military Expenditure, 1739–1783", in R. Torres Sánchez (ed.), *War, State and Development. Fiscal-Military States in the Eighteenth Century*, Pamplona, EUNSA, 45–68.

Conway, S. and Torres Sánchez, R. (eds.), 2011, *The Spending of States. Military Expenditure During the Long Eighteenth Century*, Saarbrücken, VDM.

Corvisier, A. and Coutau-Bégarie, H., 1995, *La Guerre. Essais historiques*, Paris, Perrin.

Corvol, A., 1999, *Forêt et Marine*, Paris, L'Harmattan.

Croce, B., 1938, *La storia come pensiero e come azione*, Bari, Laterza.

Crouzet, F., 1966, "Angleterre et France au XVIIIe siècle. Essai d'analyse comparé de deux croissances économiques", *Annales, E. S. C.*, XXI, 254–91.

Crouzet, F., 1993, *La Grande inflation. La monnaie en France de Louis XVI à Napoléon*, Paris, Fayard.

Cuenca Esteban, J., 2009, "Was Spain a Viable Fiscal-Military State on the Eve of the French Wars?", in *Post-Conference for the XVth World Economic History Congress*, Greenwich.

Daniel. J. -M., 2012, *8 Leçons d'Histoire économique*, Paris, Odile and Jacob.

Daunton, M., 2001, *Trusting Leviathan. The Politics of Taxation in Britain 1799–1914*, Cambridge, Cambridge University Press.

Davey, J., 2011, "Securing the Sinews of Power: British Intervention in the Baltic 1780–1815", *International History Review*, 33, 2, 161–84.

Davies, B., 2012, *Warfare in Eastern Europe, 1500–1800*, Leiden, Brill.

Davies, R., 1954, "English Foreign Trade, 1660–1700", *Economic History Review*, 7, 150–66.

Davies, R., 1962, "English Foreign Trade, 1700–1774", *Economic History Review*, 15, 285–303.

De Vries, J., 2009, *La revolución industriosa: consumo y economía doméstica desde 1650 hasta el presente*, Barcelona, Crítica.

Deane, P. and Cole, W. A., 1963, *British Economic Growth, 1688–1959*, Cambridge, Cambridge University Press.

Decker, M., 1756 [1744], *An Essay on the Causes of the Decline of the Foreign Trade*, Edinburgh.

Dedieu, J. -P., 2011, "Les groupes financiers et industriels au service du roi. Espagne fin XVIIe–début XVIIIe siècle", in A. Dubet and J. -P. Luis (dirs.), *Les financiers et la construction de l'État. France, Espagne (XVIIe–XIXe siècle)*, Rennes, Presses Universitaires de Rennes, 87–104.

Delgado Barrado, J. M., 2007, *Aquiles y Teseos. Bosquejos del reformismo borbónico (1701–1759)*, Granada, Universidad de Granada and Universidad de Jaén.

Delgado Barrado, J. M., 2015, "En torno a Utrecht y Aquisgrán: el pensamiento político-económico español sobre asiento de negros y navío de permiso (1701–1750)", *Anuario de Estudios Americanos*, 72, 1, 57–96.

Delgado Ribas, J. M., 2007, *Dinámicas imperiales (1650–1796). España, América y Europa en el cambio institucional del sistema colonial español*, Barcelona, Bellaterra.

Dent, J., 1973, *Crisis in Finance: Crown, Financiers and Society in Seventeenth Century France*, New York, St. Martin's Press.

Dessert, D., 1984, *Argent, pouvoir et société au Grand Siècle*, Paris, Fayard.

Deyon, P., 1969, *Le mercantilisme*, Paris, Flammarion.

Díaz Ordóñez, M., 2009, *Amarrados al negocio. Reformismo borbónico y suministro de jarcia para la Armada Real (1675–1751)*, Madrid, Ministerio de Defensa.

Díaz Trechuelo, L., 1965, *La Real Compañía de Filipinas*, Sevilla, Escuela de Estudios Hispano-Americanos.

Dickson, P. G. M., 1967, *The Financial Revolution in England. A Study in the Development of Public Credit, 1688–1756*, London, Macmillan.

Doyle, W., 1981, *The Old European Order, 1660–1800*, Oxford, Oxford University Press.

Doyle, W., 1996, *Venality: The Sale of Offices in Eighteenth-Century France*, Oxford, Clarendon.

Dubet, A., 2008, *Un estadista francés en la España de los Borbones. Juan Orry y las primeras reformas de Felipe V (1701–1706)*, Madrid, Biblioteca Nueva.

Dubet, A., 2012, "Comprender las reformas de la hacienda a principios del siglo XVIII. La buena administración según el marqués de Campoflorido", *Revista HMiC: Història moderna i contemporània*, X, 20–52. URL: http://webs2002.uab.es/hmic/2012/HMIC2012.pdf.

Dubet, A., 2013, "La *Nueva Planta* et la réforme du contrôle des comptes en Espagne", in Y. Levant, H. Zimnovitch and R. Sandu (eds.), *Mélages offrerts à Yannick Lemarchand*, Paris, L'Harmattan/Presses Universitaires de Sceaux, 25–49.

Dubet, A., 2015a, "El gobierno de la Real Hacienda de Felipe V y la actividad de los <interesados>, según Alejandro de Vega", *Tiempos Modernos*, 30, 2015/1. URL: www .tiemposmodernos.org.

Dubet, A., 2015b, *La Hacienda Real de la Nueva Planta (1713–1726), entre fraude y buen gobierno. El caso Verdes Montenegro*, Madrid and México, Fondo de Cultura Económica.

Dubet, A. and Luis, J. -P. (dirs.), 2011, *Les financiers et la construction de l'État. France, Espagne (XVII–XIX siècle)*, Rennes, Presses Universitaires de Rennes.

Duffy, M., 1980, *The Military Revolution*, Exeter, University of Exeter.

Dunning, C., 2014, "Were Muscovy and Castile the First Fiscal-Millitary States?", *Questio Rossica*, 1, 191–97.

Dunning, C. and Smith, N. S., 2006, "Moving Beyond Absolutism: Was Early Modern Russia a Fiscal-Military State?", *Russian History*, 33, 1, 19–43.

Durand, Y., 1971, *Les Fermiers généraux au XVIIIe siècle*, Paris, Presses Universitaires de France.

Durand, Y., 1976, *Finance et mécénat. Les fermiers généraux au XVIIIe siècle*, Paris, Hachette.

Elliott, J. H., 1969, "Revolution and Continuity in Early Modern Europe", *Past and Present*, 42, 35–56.

Elliott, J. H., 1990, *El Conde-Duque de Olivares*, Barcelona, Crítica.

Elliott, J. H., 2006, *Empires of the Atlantic World: Britain and Spain in America, 1492–1830*, New Haven, Yale University Press.

Elliott, J. H. and de la Peña, J. F., 1981, *Memoriales y cartas del Conde-Duque de Olivares*, Madrid, Alfaguara.

Enciso Recio, L. M., 1963, *Los establecimientos industriales españoles en el siglo XVIII. La mantelería de La Coruña*, Madrid, Rialp.

Epstein, R. S, 2008, "Craft Guilds, Apprenticeship, and Technological Change in Pre-industrial Europe", in S. R. Epstein and M. Prak (eds.) *Guilds, Innovation and the European Economy, 1400–1800*, Cambridge, Cambridge University Press, 52–80.

Ertman, T., 1994, "The *Sinews of Power* and European State-Building theory", in L. Stone (ed.), *An Imperial State at War: Britain from 1688 to 1815*, London, Routledge, 33–51.

Ertman, T., 1997, *Birth of the Leviathan: Building States and Regimes in Medieval and Early Modern Europe*, Cambridge, Cambridge University Press.

Ertman, T., 1999, "Explaining Variations in Early Modern State Structures: The Cases of England and the German Territorial States", in J. Brewer and E. Hellmuth (eds.), *Rethinking Leviathan*, Oxford, Oxford University Press, 23–52.

Escobedo Romero, R., 2000, "El contrabando y la crisis del Antiguo Régimen en Navarra (1778–1808)", *Príncipe de Viana*, 221, 695–730.

Escobedo Romero, R., 2007, *El tabaco del rey. La organización de un monopolio fiscal durante el Antiguo Régimen*, Pamplona, EUNSA.

Étienne-Magnien, A., 1991, "Une fonderie de canons au XVII siècle: les frères Keller à Douai (1669–1696)", *Bibliothèque de l'école de chartes*, 149, livraison 1, 91–105.

Félix, J., 1994, "Les dettes de l'État à la mort de Louis XIV", *Études et Documents*, IV, 603–608.

Félix, J., 1999, *Finances et politique au siècle des Lumières. Le ministère L'Averdy, 1763–1768*, Paris, Comité pour l'Histoire Économique et Financière de la France.

Félix, J., 2005, "The Financial Origins of the French Revolution", in P. Campbell (ed.), *The Origins of the French Revolution*, Basingstoke, Palgrave, 48–55.

Félix, J., 2006, *Louis XVI et Marie-Antoinette. Un couple en politique*, Paris, Payot.

Félix, J., 2011, "Modèles, traditions, innovations. Le Peletier des Forts et la renaissance de la finance sous le règne de Louis XV", in A. Dubet and J. -P. Luis (dirs.), *Les financiers et la construction de l'État. France, Espagne (XVII–XIX siècle)*, Presses Universitaires de Rennes, Rennes, 2011, pp. 125–54.

Félix, J., 2012, "Victualling Louis XV's Armies. The Munitionnaire des Vivres de Flandres et d'Allemagne and the Military Supply System", in R. Harding and S. Solbes Ferri (eds.), *The Contractor State and Its Implications, 1659–1815*, Las Palmas de Gran Canaria, Universidad de Las Palmas, 103–30.

Félix, J., 2015, "La monarquía francesa y los financieros en el Antiguo Régimen. El ejemplo de los *traitants* durante la Guerra de los Nueve Años, 1689–1697", *Tiempos Modernos*, 30 (2015/1). URL: www.tiemposmodernos.org/tm3/index.php/tm/index.

Félix, J. and Tallett, F., 2009, "The French Experience, 1661–1815", in C. Storrs (ed.), *The Fiscal-Military State in Eighteenth-Century Europe: Essays in Honour of P. G. M. Dickson*, Farnham, Ashgate, 147–66.

Fernández Albaladejo, P., 1977, "El decreto de suspensión de pagos de 1739: análisis e implicaciones", *Moneda y Crédito*, 142, 51–81.

Fernández Armesto, F. 1999, "Visiones del fin del siglo XVII en España", in R. Carr, *Visiones de fin de siglo*, Madrid, Taurus, 65–92.

Fernández de Pinedo, N., 2009, "Jenkins' Ear and Tax Collection in Spain in the 18th Century", in *XVth International Economic History Congress*, Utrecht.

Fisher, J., 1985, *Commercial Relations between Spain and Spanish America in the Era of Free Trade, 1778–1796*, Liverpool, TBC.

Floridablanca, conde de J., 1982 [1787], "Instrucción reservada", in J. Ruiz Alemán (ed.), *Escritos políticos: la Instrucción y el Menorial*, Murcia, Academia Alfonso X el Sabio.

Fritschy, W., 't Hart, M. C. and Horlings, E., 2012, "Long-term Trends in the Fiscal History of the Netherlands, 1515–1913", in B. Yun Casalilla and P. K. O'Brien with F. Comín Comín (eds.), *The Rise of Fiscal States: A Global History, 1500–1914*, Cambridge, Cambridge University Press, 39–66.

Fugier, A., 1930, *Napoléon et l'Espagne, 1799–1808*, Paris, Félix Alcan.

Gárate Ojanguren, M., 1990, *La Real Compañía Guipuzcoana de Caracas*. San Sebastián, Caja de Ahorros Municipal de San Sebastián.

Gárate Ojanguren, M., 1993, *Comercio ultramarino e Ilustración. La real Compañía de La Habana*, San Sebastián, Departamento de Cultura del Gobierno Vasco.

García-Baquero González, A., 1972, *Comercio colonial y guerras revolucionarias*, Sevilla, Escuela de Estudios Hispano-Americanos.

García-Baquero González, A., 1976, *Cádiz y el Atlántico (1717–1778): El comercio colonial español bajo el monopolio gaditano*, 2 vols., Sevilla, Escuela de Estudios Hispano-Americanos.

García-Baquero González, A., 2003, *El comercio colonial en la época del absolutismo ilustrado. Problemas y debates*, Universidad de Granada, Granada.

García Fernández, M. N., 2006, *Comerciando con el enemigo: El tráfico mercantil anglo-español en el siglo XVIII (1700–1765)*, Madrid, Consejo Superior de Investigaciones Científicas.

García Fuentes, L., 1982, *El comercio español con América, 1650–1700*, Sevilla, Diputación Provincial.

García Torralba, E., 2010, *La artillería naval española en el siglo XVIII*, Madrid, Ministerio de Defensa.

García Zúñiga, M., 1993, "Haciendas forales y reformas borbónicas. Navarra 1700–1808", *Revista de Historia Económica*, 2, 307–34.

Gat, A., 2006, *War in Human Civilization*, Oxford, Oxford University Press.

Gelabert, J., 1997, *La bolsa del rey: rey, reino y fisco en Castilla: (1598–1648)*, Barcelona, Crítica.

Gelabert, J., 1999, "Castile, 1504–1808", in R. Bonney (ed.), *The Rise of the Fiscal State in Europe c. 1200–1815*, Oxford, Oxford University Press, 201–42.

Glover, R., 1963, *Peninsular Preparation: The Reform of the British Army, 1795–1809*, Cambridge, Cambridge University Press.

Gómez Campelo, R., 1991, "El envío de municiones navarras a América. Las fábricas de Eugui y Orbaiceta", *Príncipe de Viana*. Anejo 13, LIII, 311–19.

González Enciso, A., 1979, *España y USA en el siglo XVIII. Crecimiento industrial comparado y relaciones comerciales*, Valladolid, Universidad de Valladolid.

González Enciso, A., 1980, *Estado e industria en el siglo XVIII: la fábrica de Guadalajara*, Madrid, Fundación Universitaria Española.

González Enciso, A., 2000, "La promoción industrial en la España Moderna: intervención pública e iniciativa privada", in L. A. Ribot García and L. de Rosa (dirs.), *Industria y Época Moderna*, Madrid, Actas, 15–46.

González Enciso, A., 2006a, "Spain's Mobilisation of Resources for the War with Portugal in 1762", in H. V. Bowen and A. González Enciso (eds.), *Mobilising Resources for War: Britain and Spain at Work During the Early Modern Period*, Pamplona, EUNSA, 159–90.

González Enciso, A., 2006b, "Tabaco y hacienda, 1670–1840", in L. Alonso, L. Gálvez Muñoz and S. de Luxán (eds.), *Tabaco e historia económica*, Madrid, Fundación Altadis, 43–69.

González Enciso, A., 2007, "A Moderate and Rational Absolutism. Spanish Fiscal Policy in the First Half of the Eighteenth Century", in R. Torres Sánchez, (ed.), *War, State and Development: Fiscal-Military States in the Eighteenth Century*, Pamplona, EUNSA, 109–32.

González Enciso, A., 2008a, "La reforma de las alcabalas por Lerena en 1785", in R. Franch and R. Benítez (eds.), *Estudios de Historia Moderna en homenaje a la profesora Emilia Salvador Esteban*, Valencia, Universidat de València, vol. I, 249–68.

González Enciso, A., 2008b, "Les finances royales et les hommes d'affaires au XVIIIème siècle", in A. Dubet (coord.), *Les finances royales dans la monarchie espagnole (XVIè–XVIIIè siècles)*, Rennes, Presses Universitaires de Rennes, 227–44.

González Enciso, A., 2009a, "Guerra y economía en la Ilustración. España como Estado fiscal militar en el siglo XVIII", in J. Astigarraga, M. V. López Cordón and J. M. Urkia (eds.), *Ilustración, ilustraciones*, Donostia-San Sebastián, Sociedad Estatal de Conmemoraciones Culturales, vol. II, 511–30.

González Enciso, A., 2009b, "La Hacienda Real y la Hacienda castellana en el siglo XVIII" in L. A. Ribot García (dir.), *Las finanzas estatales en España e Italia en la Época Moderna*, Madrid, Actas, 209–37.

González Enciso, A., 2010, "Empresarios navarros en la industria de municiones para la artillería", in R. Torres Sánchez (ed.), *Volver a la <hora navarra>. La contribución navarra a la construcción de la Monarquía española en el siglo XVIII*, Pamplona, EUNSA, 159–212.

González Enciso, A., 2012a, *Philip V: Economic and Social Reform in Spain. Transforming Spain in the First Half of the Eighteenth Century*, Saarbrücken, Lambert Academic Publishing.

González Enciso, A., 2012b, "La renovación del asiento de transporte de municiones y armas en 1793 y el protagonismo de una familia navarra", *Memoria y Civilización*, 15, 51–69.

Gonzalez Enciso, A., 2012c, "Estado militar y empresarios de industrias militares", in A. González Enciso (ed.), *Un Estado militar: España, 1650–1820*, Madrid, Actas, 423–47.

González Enciso, A., 2012d, "Buying Cannons Outside: When, Why, How Many? The Supplying of Foreign Iron Cannons for the Spanish Navy in the Eighteenth Century", in R. Harding and S. Solbes Ferri (coords.), *The Contractor State and Its Implications, 1659–1815*, Las Palmas de Gran Canaria, Universidad de Las Palmas, 135–58.

González Enciso, A., 2013, "Del *contractor state* al Estado fabricante. El cambio de propiedad en la fábrica de municiones de Eugui en 1766", *Revista de Historia de la Economía y de la Empresa*, VII, 475–76.

González Enciso, A., 2014, "La escuadra de Ferrol, 1733", in M. Baudot Monroy (ed.), *El Estado en guerra. Expediciones navales españolas en el siglo XVIII*, Madrid, Polifemo, 23–59.

González Enciso, A., 2015, "La supresión de los arrendamientos de impuestos en la España del siglo XVIII", *Tiempos Modernos*, 30, 2015/1. URL: www.tiemposmodernos.org.

Goodman, D., 2001, *El poderío naval español. Historia de la armada española del siglo XVII*, Barcelona Península.

Green, J. P. and Morgan, P. D. (eds.), 2009, *Atlantic History. A Critical Appraisal*, Oxford, University Press.

Guenée, B., 1973, *Occidente durante los siglos XIV y XV: los Estados*, Barcelona, Labor.

Guzmán Raja, I., 2006, "Normativa contable en la Armada española durante el período 1700–1850: especial referencia a la administración de provisiones", *De Computis. Revista Española de la Contabilidad*, 5, 65–142.

Hales, J., 1893 [1581], *A Discourse of the Common Weal of this Realm of England*, edited by E. Lamond, Cambridge.

Hamilton, E. J., 1946, "The First Twenty Years of the Bank of Spain", *Journal of Political Economy*, LIV, I, 17–37; II, 116–40.

Hamilton, E. J., 1988, *Guerra y precios en España, 1651–1800*, Madrid, Alianza.

Harding, R., 1991, *Amphibious Warfare in the Eighteenth Century: The British Expedition to the West Indies, 1740–1742*, Woodbridge, The Boydell Press.

Harding, R. and Solbes Ferri, S. (eds.), 2012, *The Contractor State and Its Implications, 1659–1815*, Las Palmas, Universidad de Las Palmas de Gran Canaria.

Hargreaves, E. L., 1930, *The National Debt*, London, Edward Arnold.

Harris, J. -R., 1998, *Industrial Espionage and Technology Transfer. Britain and France in the Eighteenth Century*, Ashgate, Aldershot.

Harsin, P., 1970, "La finance et l'État jusqu'au System de Law", in F. Braudel and E. Labrousse (dirs.), *Histoire économique et sociale de la France*, T. II, Paris, PUF, 267–321.

Hartmann, P. C., 1979, *Das steuersystem der Europäischen staaten am ende des ancien regime*, München, Artemis Verlag.

Hatton, R. (ed.), 1976, *Louis XIV and Absolutism*, London, Macmillan Press.

Hazard, P., 1968, *La Crise de la conscience européenne: 1680–1715*, Paris, Fayard.

Helguera Quijada, J., 2012, "De La Cavada a Trubia. Intervencionismo estatal y cambio tecnológico en las fundiciones de artillería del norte de España (1760–1800)", in J. Ocampo Suárez-Valdés (ed.), *Empresa y empresarios en el norte de España (Siglo XVIII)*, Oviedo, Trea, 153–82.

Henshall, N., 1992, *The Myth of Absolutism: Change and Continuity in Early Modern European Monarchy*, London, Longman.

Herr, R., 1971, "Hacia el derrumbe del Antiguo Régimen: crisis fiscal y desamortización bajo Carlos IV", *Moneda y Crédito*, 18, 37–100.

Hoffman, P. T., Postel-Vinay, G. and Rosenthal, J. -L., 1995, "Redistribution and Long Term Private Debt in Paris, 1660–1726", *Journal of Economic History*, 55, 2, 256–84.

Hoffman, P. T., Postel-Vinay, G. and Rosenthal, J. -L., 2000, *Priceless Markets: The Political Economy of Credit in Paris, 1660–1870*, Chicago, University of Chicago Press.

Hoppit, J., 1990, review of *The Sinews of Power*, *The Historical Journal*, 33, 1, 248–49.

Horn, D. B., 1967, *Great Britain and Europe in the Eighteenth Century*, London, Clarendon Press.

Ibáñez Molina, M., 1986, *Rentas provinciales, administración real y recaudadores en el reinado de Felipe V (1700–1739)*, Doctoral Dissertation, Universidad de Granada, microfiche edition.

Ibáñez Molina, M., 1994, "D. José del Campillo ante los problemas fiscales a principios de 1741", *Cuadernos de Investigación Histórica*, 15, 47–68.

Iturrioz Magaña, A., 1987, *Estudio del subsidio y excusado (1561–1808). Contribuciones económicas de la Diócesis de Calahorra y La Calzada a la Real Hacienda*, Logroño, Instituto de Estudios Riojanos.

Jackson, M. H. and Beer, C. de, 1973, *Eighteenth Century Gunfounding*, Surrey, David and Charles.

Jiménez Estrella, A., 2010, "Asentistas militares y fraude en torno al abastecimiento de pólvora en el reino de Granada (siglo XVI)", *Investigaciones Históricas*, 30, 11–30.

Jones, D. W., 1988, *War and Economy in the Age of William III and Malborough*, Oxford, Basil Blackwell.

Jurado Sánchez, J., 2006, *El gasto de la Hacienda española durante el siglo XVIII. Cuantía y estructura de los pagos del estado (1703–1800)*, Madrid, Instituto de Estudios Fiscales.

Kamen, H., 1974, *La guerra de Sucesión en España, 1700–1715*, Barcelona, Grijalbo.

Kamen, H., 1980, *Spain in the Later Seventeenth Century, 1665–1700*. London, Longman.

Kennedy, P., 1989, *Auge y caída de las grandes potencias*, Madrid, Plaza y Janés.

Kindleberger, C. P., 1984, *A Financial History of Western Europe*, London, George Allen & Unwin.

Knight, R., 2014, *Britain Against Napoleon: The Organization of Victory, 1793, 1815*, London, Penguin.

Knight, R. and Wilcox, M., 2010, *Sustaining the Fleet, 1793–1815: War, the British Navy and the Contractor State*, Woodbridge, The Boydell Press.

Krieger, L., 1970, *Kings and Philosophers, 1689–1789*, New York, Norton.

Kuethe, A., 1999, "El fin del monopolio: los Borbones y el Consulado andaluz", in E. Vila Vilar and A. J. Kuethe (eds.), *Relaciones de poder y comercio colonial: nuevas perspectivas*, Sevilla, Escuela de Estudios Hispano-americanos.

Kwass, M., 1999, "A Welfare State for the Privileged? Direct Taxation and the Changing Face of Absolutism from Louis XIV to the French Revolution", in W. M. Ormrod, R. Bonney, and M. Bonney (eds.), *Crises, Revolutions and Self-Sustained Growth: Essays in European Fiscal History*, Stamford, Paul Watkins Publishing, 344–76.

Ladero Quesada, M. A., 1973, *La Hacienda Real de Castilla en el siglo XV*, La Laguna, Universidad de La Laguna.

Ladero Quesada, M. A., 1981, "Ingreso, gasto y política fiscal de la Corona de Castilla. Desde Alfonso X a Enrique III (1252–1406)", *Hacienda Pública Española*, 69, 25–55.

Larrañaga, R., 1981, *Síntesis Histórica de la Armería Vasca*. San Sebastián, Caja de Ahorros Provincial de Guipúzcoa.

Le Goff, T., 1999, "How to Finance an Eighteenth-Century War", in W. M. Ormrod, R. Bonney, and M. Bonney (eds.), *Crises, Revolutions and Self-Sustained Growth: Essays in European Fiscal History*, Stamford, Paul Watkins Publishing, 377–413.

Legay, M. -L., 2011, *La Banqueroute de l'Etat royal. La gestion des finances publiques de Colbert à la Révolution française*, Paris, EHESS.

Legay, M. -L., Félix, J. and White, E., 2009, "Retour sur les origines financiers de la Révolution française", *Annales Historiques de la Révolution Française*, 356, 183–201.

Legohérel, H., 1965, *Les Trésoriers généraux de la Marine (1517–1788)*, Paris, Editions Cujas.

Léon, P., 1970, "L'Élan industriel et commercial", in F. Braudel and E. Labrousse (dirs.), *Histoire économique et sociale de la France*, T. II, Paris, PUF, 499–528.

Levy, J., 1983, *War in the Modern Great Power System, 1495–1975*, Lexington, University Press of Kentucky.

Livi-Bacci, M., 1999, *Historia de la población europea*, Barcelona, Crítica.

Luckett, T. M., 1996, "Crises financières en la France du XVIIIe siècle", *Revue d'Histoire Moderne et Contemporaine*, 43, 2, 266–93.

Luxán Meléndez, S. de, Gárate Ojanguren, M. and Rodríguez Gordillo, J. M., 2012, *Cuba-Canarias-Sevilla. El estanco español del tabaco y las Antillas (1717–1817)*, Las Palmas de Gran Canaria, Cabildo de Gran Canaria.

Luxán Meléndez, S. de, (dir.), 2014, *Política y hacienda del tabaco en los imperios ibéricos (siglos XVII–XIX)*, Madrid, Centro de Estudios Políticos y Constitucionales.

Lynn, John A., 1999, *The Wars of Louis XIV, 1667–1714*, London, Longman.

Maguin, P., 1990, *Les armes de Saint-Etienne*, Maguin, Saint-Etienne.

Maiso González, J., 1990, *La difícil modernización de Cantabria en el siglo XVIII*, Santander, Ayuntamiento de Santander.

Malamud, C., 1986, *Cádiz y Saint Malo en el comercio colonial peruano (1698–1725)*, Cádiz, Diputación Provincial.

Marcos Martín, A, 2001, "España y Flandes, 1618–1648: la financiación de la guerra", in J. Alcalá-Zamora and E. Belenguer (coords.), *Calderón de la Barca y la España del Barroco*, Madrid, Centro de Estudios Políticos y Constitucionales, vol. II, 15–39.

Marcos Martín, A., 2006, "Deuda pública, fiscalidad y arbitrios en la Corona de Castilla en los siglos XVI y XVII", in C. Sanz Ayán (ed.), *Banca, crédito y capital. La Monarquía hispánica y los antiguos Países Bajos (1505–1700)*, Madrid, Fundación Carlos de Amberes, 345–77.

Marichal, C., 2007, *Bankruptcy of Empire. Mexican Silver and the Wars between Spain, Britain and France, 1760–1810*, Cambridge, Cambridge University Press.

Marina Barba, J., 1993, "La contribución extraordinaria del diez por ciento de las rentas de 1741", *Chronica Nova*, 21, 279–355.

Marion, M., 1979 [1923], *Dictionnaire des institutions de la France aux XVIIe et XVIIIe siècles*, Paris, Éditions A. and J. Picard.

Martí, R., 2004, *Cataluña armería de los Borbones. Las armas y los armeros de Ripoll, Barcelona, Manresa, Igualada...de 1714 a 1794*, Barcelona, Salvatella.

Martínez del Cerro, V., 2002, "Francisco Mendinueta y la trata de negros en América (1753–1765)", in S. Aquerreta (coord.), *Francisco Mendinueta: Finanzas y mecenazgo en la España del siglo XVIII*, Pamplona, EUNSA.

Martínez Ruiz, E. (dir.), 2007, *Diccionario de Historia Moderna de España. II. La Administración*, Madrid, Istmo.

Mathias, P. and O'Brien, P., 1976, "Taxation in Britain and France, 1715–1810. A Comparison of the Social and Economic Incidence of Taxes Collected for the Central Governments", *The Journal of European Economic History*, 5, 601–50.

Matilla Tascón, A., 1980, *Las rentas vitalicias: inventario*, Madrid, Ministerio de Cultura.

Matthews, G. T., 1958, *The Royal General Farms in Eighteenth-Century France*, Nueva York, Columbia University Press.

McDougall, Ph., 1982, *Royal Dockyards*, London, David and Charles.

McKay, D. and Scott, H. M., 1983, *The Rise of the Great Powers, 1648–1815*, London, Routledge.

McLennan, K., 2003, "Liechtenstein and Gribeauval: 'Artillery Revolution' in Political and Cultural Context", *War in History*, 10, 3, 249–64.

Mclynn, F., 2004, *1759: The Year Britain Became Master of the World*, New York, Atlantic Monthly Press.

Mendels, F., 1972, "Proto-industrialization: The First Phase of the Industrialization Process", *Journal of Economic History*, XXXII, 241–61.

Mercapide, N., 1981, *Guarnizo y su Real Astillero*, Santander, Institución Cultural de Cantabria.

Merino Navarro, J. P., 1975, "Cultivos industriales: el cáñamo en España, 1750–1800", *Hispania*, 131, 567–84.

Merino Navarro, J. P., 1981a, *La armada española en el siglo XVIII*, Madrid, Fundación Universitaria Española.

Merino Navarro, J. P., 1981b, *Hacienda y Marina en Francia. Siglo XVIII*, Madrid, Juan March.

Merino Navarro, J. P., 1984, "L'Arsenal de Carthagène au XVIIIème siècle", *Neptunia*, 155, 21–32.

Merino Navarro, J. P., 1986, "La Armada en el siglo XVIII", in M. Hernández Sánchez-Barba and M. Alonso Baquer (dirs.), *Historia social de las fuerzas armadas españolas*, Madrid, Alhambra, 85–149.

Merino Navarro, J. P., 1987, *Las cuentas de la Administración Central española, 1750–1820*, Madrid, Instituto de Estudios Fiscales.

Merino Navarro, J. P., 1989, "L'affaire des piastres et la crise de 1805", *Comité pour l'Histoire Économique et Financière de la France. Études et Documents*, I, Paris, 121–26.

Merino Navarro, J. P., 2014, *La Hacienda de Carlos IV*, Madrid, Rh+ ediciones.

Meyer, J., 1983, *Le poids de l'Etat*, Paris, Presses Universitaires de France.

Minard, P., 1998, *La Fortune du colbertisme. État et industrie dans la France des Lumières*, Paris, Fayard.

Minost, L., 2005, "Jean II Maritz (1711–1790) et la fabrication des canons au XVIIIe siècle", *CERMA. Cahiers d'études et de recherches du musée de l'Armée*, hors série, 2, 47, 94–157.

Mitchell, B. R. and Deane, P., 1962, *Abstract of British Historical Statistics*, Cambridge, Cambridge University Press.

Moral Ruiz, J. del, 1990, "Estudio preliminar", in P. López de Lerena (ed.), *Memoria sobre las rentas públicas y balanza comercial de España (1789–1790)*, Madrid, Instituto de Estudios Fiscales.

Morineau, M., 1980, "Budgets de l'État et gestion des finances royales en France au dix-huitième siècle", *Revue Historique*, 536, 289–336.

Morineau, M., 1985, *Incroyables gazettes et fabuleux métaux*, Paris, Editions de la Maison des Sciences de l'Homme.

Morris, R., 2011, *The Foundations of British Maritime Ascendancy: Resources, Logistics and the State, 1755–1815*, Cambridge, Cambridge University Press.

Moya Torres y Velasco, F. M. de, 1992 [1730], *Manifiesto universal de los males envejecidos que España padece*, edited by A. Domínguez Ortiz, Madrid, Instituto de Cooperación Iberoamericana.

Muret, P., 1937, *La prépondérance anglaise, 1715–1763*, Paris, Alcan.

Naef, W., 1973, *La idea del estado en la Edad Moderna*, Madrid, Aguilar.

Neal, L., 1990, *The Rise of Financial Capitalism: International Capital Markets in the Age of Reason*, Cambridge, Cambridge University Press.

Neal, L. (ed.), 1994, *War Finance*, vol. II, Aldershot, Edward Elgar.

Neal, L., 2015, *A Concise History of International Finance: From Babylon to Bernanke*, Cambridge, Cambridge University Press.

North, D., 1965, "The Role of Transportation in the Economic Development of North America", in *Les Grandes voies maritimes dans le monde, XVe–XIXe siècles*, Paris, S.E.V.P.E.N.

North, D. and Weingast, B., 1989, "Constitutions and Commitment: The Evolution of Institutional Governing Public Choice in Seventeenth-Century England", *The Journal of Economic History*, XLIX, 4, 803–32.

Núñez Torrado, M., 2002, "Estudios de costes en la renta de la pólvora de Nueva España ante la implantación de un nuevo sistema de gestión (1766–1785)", *Revista Española de Financiación y Contabilidad*, 111, 47–74.

O'Brien, P., 1988, "The Political Economy of British Taxation, 1660–1815", *The Economic History Review*, XLI, 1, 1–32.

O'Brien, P., 1991, *Power with Profit: The Estate and the Economy, 1688–1815*, Inaugural Lecture, University of London.

O'Brien, P., 2002, "Finance and Taxation", in H. T. Dickinson (ed.), *The Blackwell Companion to 18th Century History*, London, Blackwell.

O'Brien, P., 2006a, "The Formation of a Mercantilist State and the Economic Growth of the United Kingdom 1453–1815", United Nations University Research paper, 2006/75.

O'Brien, P., 2006b, "Foreword", in H. V. Bowen and A. González Enciso (eds.), *Mobilising Resources for War: Britain and Spain at Work During the Early Modern Period*, Pamplona, EUNSA, 9–12.

O'Brien, P., 2008, "The Management of the Public Debt in England, 1756–1815", in F. Piola Caselli (ed.), *Government and the Financial Markets*, London, Pickering and Chato.

O'Brien, P., 2009, "The Triumph and Denouement of the British Fiscal State: Taxation for the Wars Against Revolutionary and Napoleonic France, 1793–1815", in C. Storrs (ed.), *The Fiscal-Military State in Eighteenth-Century Europe: Essays in Honour of P. G. M. Dickson*, Farnham, Ashgate, 167–200.

O'Brien, P., 2014, "War and Long Term Economic Growth", Keynote *NIAS Pre-conference: "The Economic Impact of War 1648–1815"*, Wassenaar.

O'Brien, P. and Duran, X., 2010, "Total Factor Productivity for the Royal Navy from Victory at Texal (1653) to Triumph at Trafalgar (1805)", *Working Papers*, 134/10, London School of Economics.

O'Brien, P. and Hunt, P. A., 1999, "England, 1485–1815", in R. Bonney (ed.), *The Rise of the Fiscal State in Europe c. 1200–1815*, Oxford, Oxford University Press, 53–100.

O'Gorman, F., 1997, *The Long Eighteenth Century. British Political and Social History, 1688–1832*, London, Hodder Arnold.

Ocete Rubio, R., 2008, *Catálogo de armas*, Sevilla, Junta de Andalucía.

Ogilvie, S. C., 1996, *European protoindustrialization*, Cambridge, Cambridge University Press.

Oliva Melgar, J. M., 1987, *Cataluña y el comercio privilegiado con América en el siglo XVIII: la Real Compañía de Comercio de Barcelona a Indias*, Barcelona, Publications de la Universitat de Barcelona.

Orain, A., 2014, "Les contraintes d'approvisionnement pendant la guerre d'Indépendance américaine: une étude de cas dans l'océan Indien", in D. Plouviez (dir.), *Défense et colonies dans le monde atlantique, XVe–XIXe siècle*, Rennes, Presses Universitaires de Rennes, 231–48.

Pagden, A., 1995, *Lords of All the World: Ideologies of Empire in Spain, Britain and France, 1500–1800*, New Haven, Yale University Press.

Palacio Atard, V., 1987, *España en el siglo XVII: derrota, agotamiento, decadencia*. Madrid, Rialp.

Parker, G., 1988, *The Military Revolution*, Cambridge, Cambridge University Press.

Parrot, D., 2012, *The Business of War. Military Enterprise and Military Revolution in Early Modern Europe*, Cambridge, Cambridge University Press.

Pérez Fernández-Turégano, C., 2006, *Patiño y las reformas de la administración en el reinado de Felipe V*, Madrid, Ministerio de Defensa.

Pérez-Mallaína Bueno, P. E., 1982, *Política naval española en el Atlántico, 1700–1715*, Sevilla, Escuela de Estudios Hispano-Americanos.

Pérez Sarrión, G., 1984, *Agua, agricultura y sociedad en el siglo XVIII. El Canal Imperial de Aragón, 1766–1808*, Zaragoza, Institución Fernando el Católico.

Pérez Sarrión, G. (ed.), 2011, *Más Estado y más mercado. Absolutismo y economía en la España del siglo XVIII*, Madrid, Sílex.

Pérez Sarrión, G., 2012, *La Península comercial. Mercado, redes sociales y Estado en España en el siglo XVIII*, Madrid, Marcial Pons.

Pérez-Crespo Muñoz, M. T., 1992, *El arsenal de Cartagena en el siglo XVIII*, Madrid, Editorial Naval.

Pieper, R., 1992, *La Real Hacienda bajo Fernando VI y Carlos III (1753–1788). Repercusiones económicas y sociales*, Madrid, Instituto de Estudios Fiscales.

Pieper, R., 2012, "Financing an Empire: The Austrian Composite Monarchy, 1650–1848", in B. Yun Casalilla, P. O'Brien with F. Comín Comín (eds.), *The Rise of Fiscal States: A Global History 1500–1914*, Cambridge, Cambridge University Press, 164–90.

Pincus, S. and Robinson, J., 2013, *Wars and State Making Reconsidered: The Rise of the Interventionist State*, URL: www.law.nyu.edu/sites/default/files/upload_documents/Wars and State-Making Reconsidered.

Plouviez, D., 2014, *La Marine française et ses réseaux économiques au XVIIIe siècle*, Paris, Les Indes savantes.

Potter, M., 2003, *Corps and Clienteles: Public Finance and Political Change in France, 1688–1715*, Aldershot, Ashgate.

Pourchasse, P., 2006, *Le Commerce du Nord: La France et le commerce de l'Europe septentrionale au XVIIIe siècle*, Rennes, Presses Universitaires de Rennes.

Pourchasse, P., 2012, "Buying Supplies from Your Enemy or How the French Navy Stocked up with Products from the North in the Eighteenth Century", in R. Harding and S. Solbes Ferri (eds.), *The Contractor State and Its Implications, 1659–1815*, Las Palmas de Gran Canaria, Universidad de Las Palmas, 253–72.

Pourchasse, P., 2013, "Les munitions navales du Nord: produits et circuits d'approvisionnement", in O. Chaline, P. Bonnichon, and C. -P. de Vergennes (dirs.), 2013, *Les Marines de la Guerre d'Indépendance Américaine (1763–1783). I- L'instrument naval*, Paris, PUPS, 171–86.

Prados de la Escosura, L. (ed.), 2004, *Exceptionalism and Industrialisation: Britain and its European Rivals, 1688–1815*, Cambridge, Cambridge University Press.

Pritchard, J., 2009, *Louis XV's Navy 1748–1762*, Montreal and Kingston, McGill-Queen's University Press.

Pulido Bueno, I., 1998, *José Patiño. El inicio del gobierno político-económico ilustrado en España*, Huelva.

Quintero González, J., 2000, *El arsenal de La Carraca (1717–1736)*, Madrid, Ministerio de Defensa.

Quintero González, J., 2003, *Jarcias y lonas. La renovación de la Armada en la bahía de Cádiz, 1717–1777*, Jerez de la Frontera.

Rabanal Yus, A., 1987, *Las Reales Fábricas de Eugui y Orbaiceta*, Pamplona, Institución Príncipe de Viana.

Reinhard, W., 1996, "Élites du pouvoir, serviteurs de l'État, classes dirigeants et croissance du pouvoir d'État", in W. Reinhard (dir.), *Les élites du pouvoir et la construction de l'État en Europe*, Paris, P. U. F., 1–24.

Ribot García, L. A., 1993, "La España de Carlos II" in P. Molas (coord.), *La transición del siglo XVII al XVIII. Entre la decadencia y la reconstrucción*, t. XXVIII, *Historia de España fundada por Menéndez Pidal*, Madrid, Espasa, 61–203.

Ribot García, L. A., 2002, *La monarquía de España y la guerra de Mesina (1674–1678)*, Madrid, Actas.

Ribot García, L. A., 2010, *Orígenes políticos del testamento de Carlos II. La gestión del cambio dinástico en España*, Madrid, Real Academia de la Historia.

Riley, J. C., 1980, *International Government Finance and the Amsterdam Capital Market, 1740–1815*, Cambridge, Cambridge University Press.

Riley, J. C., 1986, *The Seven Years' War and the Old Regime in France: The Economic and Financial Toll*, Princeton, Princeton University Press.

Riley, J. C., 1987, "French Finances, 1727–1768", *The Journal of Modern History*, 59, 2, 209–43.

Ringrose, D. R., 1983, *Madrid and the Spanish Economy 1560–1850*, Berkeley, University of California Press.

Roberts, M., 1967 [1955], "The Military Revolution, 1560–1660", in M. Roberts, *Essays in Swedish History*, London, 195–225.

Rodger, N. A. M., 2004, *The Command of the Ocean*, New York, Norton.

Rodríguez Casado, V., 1980, *Orígenes del capitalismo y del socialismo contemporáneo*, Madrid, Espasa Calpe.

Rodríguez Garraza, R., 1974, *Tensiones de Navarra con la administración central (1778–1808)*, Pamplona, Institución Príncipe de Viana.

Rodríguez Garraza, R., 2003, "El tratamiento de la libertad de comercio y las aduanas en Navarra (1717–1841)", *Notitia vasconiae. Revista de Derecho Histórico de Vasconia*, 2, 129–90.

Rodríguez Gordillo, J. M., 1984, *Un archivo para la historia del tabaco*, Madrid, Tabacalera.

Rodríguez Gordillo, J. M., 2000, "Las estadísticas de la Renta del Tabaco en el siglo XVIII: nuevas aportaciones", in S. de Luxán Meléndez, S. Solbes Ferri and J. J. Laforet (eds.), *El mercado de tabaco en España durante el siglo XVIII. Fiscalidad y consumo*, Las Palmas de Gran Canaria, Universidad de Las Palmas, 53–104.

Rodríguez Gordillo, J. M., 2002, *La creación del estanco del tabaco en España*, Madrid, Fundación Altadis.

Rodríguez Gordillo, J. M., 2005, *Historia de la Real Fábrica de Tabacos de Sevilla*, Sevilla, Focus Abengoa.

Rodríguez Gordillo, J. M., 2006, "La Renta del Tabaco: un complejo camino hacia la administración directa en el siglo XVIII", in L. Alonso, L. Gálvez Muñoz and S. de Luxán (eds.), *Tabaco e historia económica*, Madrid, Fundación Altadis, 71–92.

Rodríguez Gordillo, J. M. and Gárate Ojanguren, M. (eds.), 2007, *El monopolio español de tabacos en el siglo XVIII. Consumos y valores: una perspectiva regional*, Madrid, Fundación Altadis.

Rodríguez-Villasante, J. A., 1984, *Historia y tipología arquitectónica de las defensas de Galicia*, A Coruña, Ediciós do Castro.

Rogers, C. (ed.), 1995, *The Military Revolution Debate*, Westview, Boulder, CO.

Rowlands, G., 2002, *The Dynastic State and the Army under Louis XIV: Royal Service and Private Interest*, Cambridge, Cambridge University Press.

Rowlands, G., 2012, *The Financial Decline of a Great Power. War, Influence, and Money in Louis XIV's France*, Oxford, Oxford University Press.

Sánchez Belén, J. A., 1996, *La política fiscal de Castilla durante el reinado de Carlos II*, Madrid, Siglo XXI.

Sánchez Belén, J. A., 2002, "La Hacienda Real de Carlos II", in *Actas de la Juntas del Reino de Galicia*, vol. XI, A Coruña, Xunta de Galicia.

Sanz Ayán, C., 1988, *Los banqueros de Carlos II*, Valladolid, Universidad de Valladolid.

Sanz Ayán, C., 1992, "Negociadores y capitales holandeses en los sistemas de abastecimiento de pertrechos navales de la Monarquía Hispánica durante el siglo XVII", *Hispania*, 182, 915–45.

Sanz Ayán, C., 2002, "Financieros de Felipe V en la Guerra de Sucesión. Huberto Hubrecht", in A. Crespo Solana and M. Herrero Sánchez (eds.), *España y las 17 Provincias de los Países Bajos. Una revisión historiográfica (XVI–XVIII)*, Córdoba, Universidad de Córdoba, vol. II, 565–81.

Sanz Ayán, C., 2006, "Administration and Resources for the Mainland War in the First Phases of the War of the Spanish Succession", in H. Bowen and A. González Enciso, *Mobilising Resources for War: Britain and Spain at Work During the Early Modern Period*, Pamplona, EUNSA, 135–58.

Sanz Ayán, C., 2011, "Négoce, culture et sens de l'opportunité dans la construction d'un lignage. Le premier marquis de Santiago pendant la Guerre de Succession", in A. Dubet and J. -P. Luis (dirs.), *Les financiers et la construction de l'État. France, Espagne (XVII–XIX siècle)*, Rennes, Presses Universitaires de Rennes, 105–24.

Sargent, T. and Velde, F., 1995, "Macroeconomics Features of the French Revolution", *Journal of Political Economy*, 103, 474–518.

Schroeder, P. W., 1994, *The Transformation of European Politics, 1763–1848*, Oxford, Clarendon Press.

Scott, H. M., 2006, *The Birth of a Great Power System, 1740–1815*, London, Longman.

Segovia Barrientos, F., 2008, *Las Reials Drassanes de Barcelona entre 1700 y 1936. Astillero, cuartel, parque y maestranza de artillería, Real Fundición de bronce y fuerte*, Barcelona, Museu Marítim de Barcelona & Angle Editorial.

Serrano Álvarez, J. M., 2008, *El astillero de La Habana y la construcción naval, 1700–1750*, Madrid, Ministerio de Defensa.

Serrera Contreras, R. M., 1974, *Lino y cáñamo en Nueva España*, Sevilla, Escuela de Estudios Hispano-Americanos.

Smith, W. D., 1984, "The Function of Commercial Centres in the Modernization of European Capitalism: Amsterdam as an Information Exchange in the Seventeenth Century", *The Journal of Economic History*, XLIV, 4, 985–1006.

Solbes Ferri, S., 2012, "Contracting and Accounting: Spanish Army Expenditure in Wardrobe and the General Treasury Accounts in Eighteenth Century", in R. Harding and S. Solbes Ferri (eds.), *The Contractor State and Its Implications, 1659–1815*, Las Palmas de Gran Canaria, Universidad de Las Palmas, 273–94.

Solbes Ferri, S., 2013, "Campillo y Ensenada. El suministro de vestuario para el ejército durante las campañas de Italia (1741–1748)", *Studia Historica, Historia Moderna*, 35, 201–34.

Solbes Ferri, S., 2016, "Privilegios territoriales en la España borbónica del siglo XVIII: reforma o consolidación", *Mélanges de la Casa de Velázquez*, 46, 1, 117–26.

Stasavage, D., 2003, *Public Debt and the Birth of the Democratic State: France and Great Britain, 1688–1789*, Cambridge, Cambridge University Press.

Stein, S. J. and Stein, B. H., 2000, *Silver, Trade, and War: Spain and America in the Making of Early Modern Europe*, Baltimore, Johns Hopkins University Press.

Stein, S. J. and Stein, B. H., 2005, *El apogeo del Imperio. España y Nueva España en la era de Carlos III, 1759–1789*, Barcelona, Crítica.

Stone, L. (ed.), 1994, *An Imperial State at War. Britain from 1689 to 1815*, London and New York, Routledge.

Storrs, Ch. (ed.), 2009, *The Fiscal-Military State in Eighteenth Century Europe*, Ashgate, Farnham.

Storrs, Ch., 2013, *La resistencia de la Monarquía Hispánica, 1665–1700*, Madrid, Actas.

Sturgess, G. L., 2015, *Contestability in Public Services: An Alternative to Outsourcing*, The Australia and New Zealand School of Government, Research Monograph, April.

Suárez Menéndez, R., 1995, "La industria militar española anterior a 1808", *Militaria. Revista de Cultura Militar*, 7, 207–26.

Sussman, N. and Yafeh, Y., 2006, "Institutional Reforms, Financial Development, and Sovereign Debt: Britain 1690–1790", *The Journal of Economic History*, LXVI, 906–35.

Swann, J., 2003, *Provincial Power and Absolute Monarchy. The Estates General of Burgundy, 1661–1790*, Cambridge, Cambridge University Press.

't Hart, M. C. (ed.), 1997, *A Financial History of the Netherlands*, Cambridge, Cambridge University Press.

't Hart, M. C., 1999, "The United Provinces, 1759–1806" in R. Bonney (ed.), *The Rise of the Fiscal State in Europe, c. 1200–1815*, Oxford, Oxford University Press, 309–26.

't Hart, M. C., 2014, *The Dutch Wars of Independence: Warfare and Commerce in the Netherlands, 1570–1680*, London, Routledge.

Tallett, F., 1992, *War and Society in Early-Modern Europe, 1495–1715*, London, Routledge.

Tedde de Lorca, P., 1987, "Los negocios de Cabarrús con la Real Hacienda (1780–1783)", *Revista de Historia Económica*, 5, 527–51.

Tedde de Lorca, P., 1988, *El Banco de San Carlos (1782–1829)*, Madrid, Alianza.

Téllez Alarcia, D., 2012, *El ministerio Wall. La <España discreta> del <ministro olvidado>*, Madrid, Marcial Pons.

Thompson, I. A. A., 1976, *War and Government in Habsburg Spain, 1560–1620*, London, The Athlone Press.

Tilly, Ch. (ed.), 1975, *The Formation of National States in Western Europe*, Princeton, Princeton University Press.

Toboso Sánchez, P., 1987, *La deuda pública castellana durante el Antiguo Régimen (juros) y su liquidación en el siglo XIX*, Madrid, Instituto de Estudios Fiscales.

Tomlinson, H. C., 1976, "Wealden Gunfounding: An Analysis of Its Demise in the Eighteenth Century", *The Economic History Review*, 29, 3, 383–400.

Torres Sánchez, R., 1997, "Servir al rey más una comisión. El fortalecimiento de los asentistas en la corona española durante la segunda mitad del siglo XVIII", in P. Fernández Albaladejo (ed.), *Monarquía, Imperio y Pueblos en la España Moderna*, Alicante, Fundación de Historia Moderna, 149–67.

Torres Sánchez, R., 2000, "Producir o comprar. La demanda de la Corona española de productos industriales en el siglo XVIII", in L. A. Ribot García and L. de Rosa (dirs.), *Industria y Época Moderna*, Madrid, Actas/Istituto Italiano per gli Studi Filosofici, 95–131.

Torres Sánchez, R., 2002a, "Cuando las reglas del juego cambian. Mercados y privilegio en el abastecimiento del ejército español en el siglo XVIII", *Revista de Historia Moderna. Anales de la Universidad de Alicante*, 20, 487–511.

Torres Sánchez, R., 2002b, "El gran negocio de la época, la provisión de víveres al ejército por Francisco Mendinueta (1744–1763)", in S. Aquerreta (coord.), *Francisco Mendinueta: finanzas y mecenazgo en la España del siglo XVIII*, Pamplona, EUNSA, 101–34.

Torres Sánchez, R., 2006, "Public Finances and Tobacco in Spain for the American War of Independence", in H. V. Bowen and A. González Enciso (eds.), *Mobilising Resources for War: Britain and Spain at Work During the Early Modern Period*, Pamplona, EUNSA, 191–224.

Torres Sánchez, R. (ed.), 2007, *War, State and Development. Fiscal-Military States in the Eighteenth Century*, Pamplona, EUNSA.

Torres Sánchez, R., 2008, "Incertidumbre y arbitrariedad. La política de deuda pública de los Borbones en el siglo XVIII", *Estudis. Revista de Historia Moderna*, 34, 263–82.

Torres Sánchez, R., 2010, "Los navarros en la provisión de víveres a la Armada española durante el siglo XVIII", in R. Torres Sánchez (ed.), *Volver a la <hora Navarra>. La contribución Navarra a la construcción de la Monarquía española en el siglo XVIII*, Pamplona, EUNSA, 213–63.

Torres Sánchez, R., 2012a, *La llave de todos los tesoros. La Tesorería General de Carlos III*, Madrid, Sílex.

Torres Sánchez, R., 2012b, "Contractor State and Mercantilism. The Spanish-Navy Hemp, Rigging and Sailcloth Supply Policy in the Second Half of the Eighteenth Century", in R. Harding and S. Solbes Ferri (eds.), *The Contractor State and Its Implications, 1659–1815*, Las Palmas de Gran Canaria, Universidad de Las Palmas, 317–44.

Torres Sánchez, R., 2013a, *El precio de la guerra. El estado fiscal-militar de Carlos III (1779–1783)*, Madrid, Marcial Pons.

Torres Sánchez, R., 2013b, "Administración o asiento. La política estatal de suministros militares en la Monarquía española del siglo XVIII", *Studia Historica. Historia Moderna*, 35, 159–99.

Torres Sánchez, R., 2014, "In the Shadow of Power: Monopolist Entrepreneurs, the State and Spanish Military Victualling in the Eighteenth Century", in J. Fynn-Paul (ed.), *War, Entrepreneurs, and the State in Europe and the Mediterranean, 1300–1800*, Leiden, Brill, 260–83.

Torres Sánchez, R., 2015a, *Constructing a Fiscal-Military State in Eighteenth Century Spain*, Basingstoke, Palgrave.

Torres Sánchez, R., 2015b, "El gasto público en la España del siglo XVIII", in E. Sánchez Santiró (coord.), *El gasto público en los imperios ibéricos, siglo XVIII*, México, Instituto de Investigaciones José María Luis Mora, 23–72.

Tourón Yebra, M., 1995, *La Guerra de Sucesión en Galicia (1702–1712)*, Lugo, Diputación de Lugo.

Ulloa, M., 1977, *La Hacienda Real de Castilla en el reinado de Felipe II*, Madrid, Fundación Universitaria Española.

Uztáriz, G. de, 1968 [1742], *Theorica y practica de comercio y de marina*, edited by G. Franco, Madrid, Aguilar.

Valdez-Bubnov, I., 2011, *Poder naval y modernización del Estado: política de construcción naval española (siglos XVI–XVIII)*, México, Universidad Autónoma de México.

Vázquez de Prada, V., 1969, "Los vales reales en el mercado de Barcelona (1780–1800)", *Anuario de Historia Económica y Social*, 2, 2, 423–69.

Vázquez de Prada, V., 1994, "Los hombres de negocios de Burgos (s. XIV–XVI), ejemplo de mentalidad emprendedora", in P. Klep and E. Van Cauwenberghe (eds.), *Entrepreneurship and the Transformation of the Economy (10th–20th Centuries): Essays in Honour of Herman Van der Wee*, Leuven, Leuven University Press.

Vega Viguera, E. de la, 1992, *Sevilla y la Real Fundición de Cañones*. Seville, Guadalquivir.

Velde, F. R. and Weir, D. R., 1992, "The Financial Market and Government Debt Policy in France, 1746–1793", *The Journal of Economic History*, LII, 1, 1–40.

Vilar, P., 1972, *Oro y moneda en la historia, 1450–1920*, Barcelona, Ariel.

Villar Ortiz, C., 1988, *La renta de la pólvora en Nueva España (1569–1767)*, Sevilla, Escuela de Estudios Hispano-Americanos.

Villiers, P., 2013, "Sartine et la préparation de la flotte de guerre française, 1775–1778: reformes ou constructions neuves?", in O. Chaline, P. Bonnichon and C. -P. de Vergennes (dirs.), *Les Marines de la Guerre d'Indépendance Américaine (1763–1783). I- L'instrument naval*, Paris, PUPS, 65–77.

Viner, J., 1965 [1937], *Studies in the Theory of International Trade*, New York, Harper and Brothers.

Vries, P., 2012, "Public Finance in China and Great Britain in the Long Eighteenth Century", *Working Papers*, 167/12, London School of Economics.

West, J., 1991, *Gunpower, Government and War in the Mid-Eighteenth Century*, London, Royal Historical Society.

White, E., 1989, "Was There a Solution to the Ancient Regime's Financial Dilemma?, *The Journal of Economic History*, XLIX, 3, 545–68.

White, E., 1995, "The French Revolution and the Politics of Government Finance, 1770–1815", *The Journal of Economic History*, LV, 2, 227–55.

Wilkinson, C., 2004, *The British Navy and the State in the Eighteenth Century*, Woodbridge, The Boydell Press.

Williamson, J. G., 1984, "Why Was British Growth So Slow During the Industrial Revolution?", *The Journal of Economic History*, XLIV, 3, 687–712.

Wilson, C. H., 1939, "The Economic Decline of the Netherlands", *Economic History Review*, IX, 2, 111–13.

Wilson, C. H., 1965, *England's Apprenticeship, 1603–1763*, London, Longman.

Wilson, C. H., 1966, *Anglo-Dutch Commerce and Finance in the Eighteenth Century*, Cambridge, Cambridge University Press.

Wilson, C. H. and Parker, G., 1977, *An Introduction to the Sources of European Economic History, 1500–1800*, New York, Cornell University Press.

Wilson, P. H., 2000, *Absolutism in Central Europe*, London, Routledge.

Woodfine, P. L., 1988, "Ideas of Naval Power and the Conflict with Spain, 1737–1742", in J. Black and P. Woodfine (eds.), *The British Navy and the Use of Naval Power in the Eighteenth Century*, Humanities Press International, Atlantic Highlands, NJ, 71–86.

Woronoff, D., 1998, *Histoire de l'industrie en France du XVIe siècle à nos jours*, Paris, Editions du Seuil.

Yun Casalilla, B., 1999, "Del centro a la periferia: la economía española bajo Carlos II", *Studia Historica. Historia Moderna*, 20, 45–76.

Yun Casalilla, B., 2004, *Marte contra Minerva. El precio del Imperio español, c. 1450–1600*, Barcelona, Crítica.

Zafra Oteiza, J., 1991, *Fiscalidad y Antiguo Régimen. Las rentas provinciales de Granada (1746–1780)*, Madrid, Instituto de Estudios Fiscales.

Zylberberg, M., 1993, *Une si douce domination. Les milieux d'affaires français et l'Espagne vers 1780–1808*, Paris, Comité pour l'Histoire Économique et Financière de la France.

Index